Programming PLUG AND PLAY

James Kelsey

SAMS PUBLISHING
201 West 103rd Street
Indianapolis, Indiana 46290

FIRST EDITION

International Standard Book Number: 0-672-30703-0

Library of Congress Catalog Card Number: 94-74884

98 97 96 95 4 3 2 1

Interpretation of the printing code: the rightmost double-digit number is the year of the book's printing; the rightmost single-digit, the number of the book's printing. For example, a printing code of 95-1 shows that the first printing of the book occurred in 1995.

Composed in AGaramond and MCPdigital by Macmillan Computer Publishing

Printed in the United States of America

Trademarks

Publisher
Richard K. Swadley

Acquisitions Manager
Greg Wiegand

Managing Editor
Cindy Morrow

Acquisitions Editor
Grace Buechlein

Development Editor
Kelly Murdock

Software Development Specialist
Tim Wilson

Production Editor
Jill D. Bond

Editorial Coordinator
Bill Whitmer

Editorial Assistants
Carol Ackerman
Sharon Cox
Lynette Quinn

Technical Reviewer
John Tibbits

Marketing Manager
Gregg Bushyeager

Assistant Marketing Manager
Michelle Milner
Cover Designer
Jay Corpus

Book Designer
Alyssa Yesh

Director of Production and Manufacturing
Jeff Valler

Imprint Manager
Kelly Dobbs

Team Supervisor
Katy Bodenmiller

Manufacturing Coordinator
Paul Gilchrist

Production Analysts
Angela Bannan
Dennis Clay Hager
Bobbi Satterfield

Graphics Image Specialists
Teresa Forrester
Clint Lahnen
Tim Montgomery
Dennis Sheehan
Greg Simsic
Susan VandeWalle
Jeff Yesh

Page Layout
Mary Ann Cosby
Terrie Deemer
Aleata Howard
Ayanna Lacey
Shawn MacDonald
Susan Van Ness
Michelle Worthington

Proofreading
Georgiana Briggs
Michael Brumitt
Donna Harbin
Donna Martin
Brian-Kent Proffitt
Erich Richter
SA Springer

Indexers
Jeanne Clark
Tina Trettin

Overview

Contents

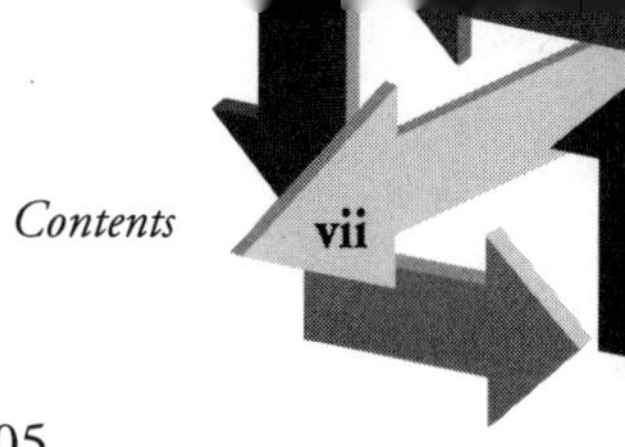

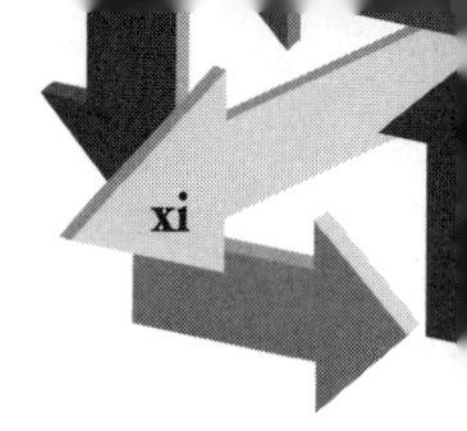

Acknowledgments

Special thanks to Robert Angelo and his cadre, Cathy (I *am* the BIOS guy) Kristofferson, the brothers Rallis, Mike Michaud, Tim Hennessey, Mike and Doug in Redmond, John Tibbets, Rich Crowe, Anatoly Podpaly, Grace Buechlein, and the support staff at Sams, without whom this book might have been published, but not in this century. Special, special thanks to my wife Shari for having assumed the role of the first Plug and Play widow, and for taking the opportunity to learn the Plug and Play technology, whether she wanted to or not.

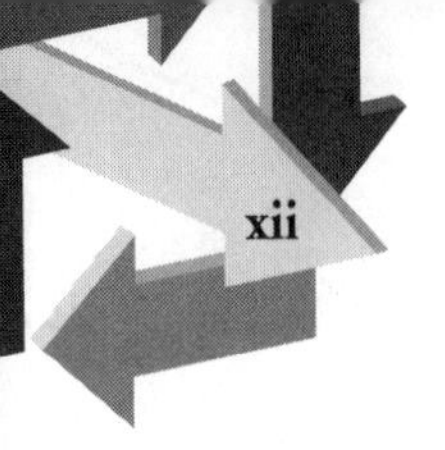

About the Author

Jim Kelsey is the manager of platform development at SystemSoft Corporation. He has developed PC software in a wide variety of areas including Windows 3.1 applications, GPIB control software, data acquisition device drivers and libraries, system BIOS, and Plug and Play BIOS. Jim currently resides in Hopkinton, MA.

Conventions Used in This Book

The following typographic conventions are used in this book:

- Code lines, commands, statements, variables, and any text you see on-screen appears in a `computer` typeface.
- Command output and anything you type appears in a **`bold computer`** typeface.
- Placeholders in syntax descriptions appear in an *`italic computer`* typeface. Replace the placeholder with the actual filename, parameter, or the element it represents.
- *Italics* highlight technical terms when they first appear in the text, and sometimes are used to emphasize important points.

NOTE

The programming information in this book is based on information for developing applications for Windows 95 made public by Microsoft as of September 9, 1994. Because this information was made public before the final release of the product, there may be changes to some of the programming interfaces by the time the product finally is released. We encourage you to check the updated development information that should be part of your development system for resolving issues that might arise.

The end-user information in this book is based on information on Windows 95 made public by Microsoft as of September 9, 1994. Because this information was made public before the release of the product, we encourage you to visit your local bookstore at that time for updated books on Windows 95.

If you have a modem or access to the Internet, you can always get up-to-the-minute information on Windows 95 direct from Microsoft on WinNews:

On CompuServe, type `GO WINNEWS`

On the Internet, type

`ftp://ftp.microsoft.com/PerOpSys/Win_News/Chicago`

`http://www.microsoft.com`

On AOL, type

`keyword WINNEWS`

On Prodigy, type

`jumpword WINNEWS`

On Genie, type

`WINNEWS file area on Windows RTC`

You also can subscribe to Microsoft's WinNews electronic newsletter by sending Internet e-mail to `news@microsoft.nwnet.com` and putting the words **SUBSCRIBE WINNEWS** in the text of the e-mail.

1

The Plug and Play Mission

Personal computer buyers simply want what the industry promises them—powerful, affordable systems that they can upgrade to take advantage of emerging operating systems and technologies such as multimedia and CD-ROM. Too often, what users end up with are systems that work well when first taken out of the shipping container, but later are difficult, or even impossible to reconfigure or upgrade. Systems that are difficult to configure frustrate end users, cause vendor technical support costs to skyrocket, and in the long run, tarnish the reputation of the PC itself.

The objective of Plug and Play is to defuse both ends of the system configuration time bomb by making personal computers easier to configure and in turn, easier and less expensive to support.

According to Microsoft, the role of the Plug and Play system is "...to allow the computer's BIOS, hardware components, and operating system software to automatically install, configure, and use any combination of cards, devices and configuration environments...."

The Need for Plug and Play

The early PC flourished because it was one of the first systems to introduce an *open architecture* bus. Its ISA (Industry Standard Architecture) bus was well documented, simple for designers to understand and use, and offered relatively good performance for the time.

The Dawn of the PC

A great number of those who dared to add plug-in peripherals to early PC systems were engineers who didn't seem to mind having to set jumpers and switches to select DMA channels, IRQ channels, and so on.

Most of the remaining personal computer users dealt only with machines configured as word processors in an office environment. If their machine ever needed upgrading, a service engineer suddenly would show up, disassemble the system, and spend a couple of hours tinkering with adapters and cables until the system functioned properly once again.

The remaining few users that attempted upgrades were neither engineers, nor did they have access to a service engineer. After tinkering with their own systems, many users in this group either gave up, bought a different type of machine, or suffered in quiet desperation, but for the most part, life in the world of PC's was good...

The Middle Ages

...until systems became affordable enough for users to buy them and bring them home by the millions. Pretty soon, sound cards, multimedia kits, CD-ROM upgrade kits, scanners, and all sorts of other peripherals became both available and affordable, and people started bringing home upgrade kits and plugging in upgrade boards and peripherals. That's when the trouble started.

The trouble started because home users want to own personal computers in the same fashion that they own stereos, VCRs, televisions, and a host of other complicated electronic appliances. When a consumer buys a stereo, the stereo industry doesn't expect him or her to open the stereo chassis and adjust potentiometers to change the volume output. If this were true, then stereo sales would plummet. In the same fashion, the personal computer industry can't risk its future, expecting home users to learn how to tweak IRQ channels, I/O ranges, and DMA channels to properly configure something as commonplace as a SCSI CD-ROM upgrade kit.

The Renaissance

Rather than painting a picture of doom for the PC, this book examines the burgeoning industry shift toward self-configuring Plug and Play systems. If the user *plugs* in a sound card, and the sound card *plays* music, then life will be good again in the world of PC's—in fact, it will be great.

Despite the age of the PC architecture, there recently has been a great influx of new technologies designed to increase the functionality and performance of the personal computer. Examples of newer technologies include such things as PCI (Peripheral Component Interconnect) adapters, credit card sized PCMCIA (PC Card) adapters, and Plug and Play ISA adapters. Each of these three types of devices is uniquely identifiable and configurable purely through software control.

HISTORICAL TIDBIT

Interestingly enough, only Plug and Play ISA devices were designed exclusively for Plug and Play. PCI and PCMCIA cards were designed specifically to function in both PC and non-PC systems.

NOTE

A system's *resources* consist of its DMA channels, IRQ channels, I/O ranges, and address ranges.

Why Current Systems (Sometimes) Can't Configure

The majority of system configuration problems occur either because of resource conflicts or incorrect resource assignments. *Resource conflicts* occur when two or more devices have been assigned a single, non-shareable system resource such as a range of I/O addresses. Incorrect *resource assignments* exist when an application or operating system's understanding of the resource usage of a device does not match the device's electrical configuration, whether that configuration was achieved through on-card jumpers, switches or software control.

Device Resource Conflicts

Devices whose resources are configurable only through jumpers or switches, or via a proprietary software programming sequence, are considered to be *static*, or *legacy devices*. If two legacy devices have been configured to use the same resource, a resource conflict exists between the two devices. In the event of an I/O range conflict, at least one of the devices experiencing the conflict will behave erratically, and the system probably will hang due to invalid data or electrical glitching on the system bus.

When a system fails due to a resource conflict, the user may find it difficult or even impossible to open the system and examine the configuration of devices that reside in its internal slots. Or, if the user opens the system, he or she is not going to know what to look for and will try to fix the machine using the only means left—trial and error. At this point, one of two things happens—either man conquers machine, or man returns unit to local computer store for a full refund.

Incorrect Device Resource Assignments

When users install multimedia upgrade kits, sound cards, and many other common add-in peripherals, the installation program adds a device driver program to the system's CONFIG.SYS file. Additionally, it's quite common for the CONFIG.SYS device driver

statement to include command line options specifying an IRQ channel, DMA channel, and I/O range for the upgrade adapter.

Problems with this type of upgrade device occur if the user accepts the default device driver values and accidentally changes the adapter's jumper settings, or vice versa. In some cases, the device driver will verify during its load sequence that the adapter settings match the device driver setting and warn the user of any mismatches. In many cases, however, the device fails because its device driver is monitoring for activity on the wrong IRQ channel, trying to transfer data on the wrong DMA channel, or is using some other user-specified configuration setting that does not apply to the physical device hardware.

As is the case with resource conflicts, in order to fix this problem, the user must check every jumper or switch setting for every device in the system. Even then, he or she may not know to check the CONFIG.SYS file, or that a CONFIG.SYS file even exists.

What's Being Done to Fix the Configuration Problem

The Plug and Play effort is a concerted, industry-wide attempt to tackle the problem of system configuration by defining new hardware, firmware, operating systems, and applications that share a common format for device identifiers and resource assignment data structures.

During its load sequence, the Plug and Play operating system, such as Windows 95, exhaustively catalogs the type and configuration of the system's hardware by invoking functions in the Plug and Play BIOS, if one exists. Even in a system that lacks a Plug and Play BIOS, Windows 95 snoops around looking for hardware that its built-in enumerator modules recognize.

In either case, the Plug and Play OS provides runtime resource *arbitrators* and *configurators* that balance and reassign resources amongst dynamically configurable devices, such as PCMCIA cards and notebook docking stations.

Device Identifiers

Device identifiers simply are strings that uniquely identify the properties of a particular system device. Despite their simplicity, device identifiers perform the crucial function of enabling the operating system to determine the number and capabilities of each device installed in the system.

In a Plug and Play system, each device and bus is described by some type of device identifier. For example, systemboard-resident devices and buses are described by 7-byte `EISA ID` strings that, when compressed, occupy 32 bits and are appropriately called *32-bit EISA format* identifiers. The Plug and Play BIOS helps the operating system identify systemboard devices by including an `EISA ID` in each systemboard *device node.* If a device node contains the seven-character device identifier `PNP0800`, its contents apply to a 100 percent PC/AT compatible, systemboard-resident speaker.

The format for individual device identifiers varies according to the bus for which the device is intended. The following table lists each type of device that might appear in a Plug and Play system, and the type of device identifier that applies to that device.

Table 1.1. The format of device identifiers according to device bus type.

Device Type	*Format of Device Identifier*
Legacy ISA	32-bit EISA format
Plug and Play ISA	32-bit EISA format
Systemboard	32-bit EISA format
EISA	32-bit EISA format
MicroChannel	16-bit IBM-supplied vendor adapter identifier
VL (Video Local) Bus	32-bit EISA format
PCMCIA	PC Card Standard device identifier "tuples"
PCI	16-bit device ID, 16-bit vendor ID, 8-bit revision ID

A description of the 32-bit EISA ID format appears in Chapter 2. In addition to the previously listed device ID types, PCI and systemboard devices report a three-byte *class code*, as defined in the *PCI Local Bus Specification.* A complete list of device identifiers and device class codes appears in Appendix A.

Software Configurable Device Resources

System vendors rapidly are switching to devices whose configurations are more easily verified and changed. Devices such as PCI, Plug and Play ISA, and PCMCIA adapters, that contain unique device identifiers, and whose resource configurations can be read and changed via software control, are considered to be Plug and Play devices. Their appearance in mainstream systems represents a significant industry trend toward configuration management.

The OS Registry and Hardware Tree

The Plug and Play operating system combines the capability to identify devices and configure their resource needs into a powerful, runtime device configuration database called the *hardware tree*. The operating system, or *registry*, which is a similar database, creates and maintains disk-based records describing each device that has ever been introduced to the system, as well as a group of records pertaining to standard PC/AT devices and popular add-in adapters. Together, the registry and runtime hardware tree enable the operating system to quickly correlate physical devices with disk-based device drivers, applications, and so on.

The Plug and Play operating system's registry records contain device identifiers and a list of device drivers used by each device. In most cases, the registry can provide the operating system the information it needs to automatically locate and load device drivers, thereby lessening the chance for human error. After a device driver is loaded, the operating system's enumerator adds to the runtime hardware tree a device node pertaining to that driver's device.

Plug and Play BIOS Reports Systemboard Device Nodes

The Plug and Play BIOS contains a series of device node records that represent the resource usage of devices on the systemboard. This device node mechanism relieves the long-standing problem of applications having to guess the number and type of peripherals resident on the systemboard.

During the system boot sequence, the OS BIOS enumerator reads a series of device nodes from the Plug and Play BIOS. The enumerator expands the BIOS-supplied device nodes into the OS device node format and adds these nodes to its runtime hardware tree.

BIOS Functions Report Legacy Device Resource Usage

Most legacy devices, such as older ISA and EISA devices, cannot be easily identified by the Plug and Play, or any other operating system. The Plug and Play BIOS provides functions that enable the operating system to read and write the resource usage of legacy devices to and from system non-volatile storage. The format in which the BIOS stores legacy device resource usage is implementation-specific.

In order to enable users and system integrators to enter those resources being consumed by legacy devices, the Plug and Play operating system provides a legacy device configuration program.

What Makes a System Plug and Play?

As a technology, Plug and Play has matured rapidly—first with specifications detailing PCMCIA adapters, and later with definitions for the Plug and Play BIOS, Plug and Play ISA devices, PCI devices, and other Plug and Play-compliant devices. What the Plug and Play initiative has lacked is a comprehensive operating system solution to manage each of the individual Plug and Play devices in a thorough, cohesive fashion. Plug and Play hardware devices have been, and remain, an integral part of the Plug and Play solution, but by themselves do not have "what it takes" to make a Plug and Play system.

The following sections outline both the hardware (such as PCI adapters and Plug and Play BIOS) and software Plug and Play components (such as the Windows 95 operating system) that together comprise a complete Plug and Play system.

Plug and Play Operating System Solutions

Plug and Play operating systems are the keystone to the Plug and Play effort. Currently, two operating system level Plug and Play solutions exist—the Intel DOS/Win 3.1 Plug and Play software suite, and the soon-to-be released Microsoft Windows 95 operating system. While the Windows 95 operating system is a more complete implementation, its release has been delayed due in part to the immense complexity of applying Plug and Play to a vast variety of notebook systems, desktop systems, and everything in between.

The Intel DOS/Win 3.1 Plug and Play solution is the first of its kind. Its DOS-based Configuration Manager driver and ISA Configuration Utility (ICU) provide a framework in which developers introduce many aspects of Plug and Play to DOS and Windows-based systems equipped with early versions of the Plug and Play BIOS.

Although comprehensive, the Intel solution falls short of implementing true Plug and Play because it operates in an environment shared by legacy, or non-Plug and Play-aware device drivers, operating system components, and applications.

Microsoft's Windows 95 is a true Plug and Play operating system that cures the shortcomings of the Intel solution by removing DOS and its non-Plug and Play aspects from the system. Additionally, Microsoft explicitly defines the Plug and Play technology via its Hardware Compatibility Test suite and Windows 95 logo certification program.

NOTE

For a list of Windows 95 system design requirements, consult Microsoft's *Hardware Design Guide for Microsoft Windows 95*, available from Microsoft Press.

The Plug and Play BIOS

At a minimum, compliant Plug and Play systems contain a system BIOS that adheres to the Plug and Play BIOS specification, revisions 1.0a and higher. The *Plug and Play BIOS* configures dynamically configurable devices (DCDs) and records those resources assigned to static, or legacy devices. Additionally, the Plug and Play BIOS may provide a variety of other services, including support for operating system messages, docking station information, APM (Advanced Power Management) device identification, Plug and Play ISA device isolation, and locked resource configurations.

Dynamically Configurable Devices

The Plug and Play BIOS is only a cornerstone in the process of building a Plug and Play system. The next level of flexibility is achieved by introducing *dynamically configurable devices* (*DCDs*) into the system. DCDs, such as Plug and Play ISA and PCI devices, contain special hardware that allows system level firmware or software to allocate, deallocate, and reassign device resources during the system's POST (Power On Self Test) or at runtime.

By themselves, DCDs only introduce the hardware necessary for runtime device reconfiguration; the task of managing dynamic devices falls into the hands of the operating system. In order to take advantage of the flexibility of DCDs, the operating system must provide a resident, runtime Configuration Manager to synchronize device configuration information among applications, device drivers, and the devices themselves.

In order to accomplish the daunting task of profiling and configuring a Plug and Play system, the Configuration Manager invokes various operating system components, including enumerators, that locate and identify DCDs; resource arbitrators whose complex algorithms balance the available pool of resources among the system's devices; and configurators that perform the hardware level reconfiguration of the system's installed devices.

Reconfigurable Systemboard Peripheral Devices

For the purpose of cost reduction, many system vendors install directly on the systemboard SCSI, multimedia, or super I/O style devices. Typical super I/O controllers provide serial port, parallel port, game port, IDE controller, and floppy drive controller logic in a single chip package. A fully configured super I/O controller consumes as many as five IRQs, five I/O ranges, and one DMA channel, regardless of whether the attachable peripherals actually are installed.

In the past, systemboard peripherals have been configurable only through the system setup utility, or by changing switches and jumpers located on the systemboard. In order to reconfigure these devices, the user historically has had to run a system setup utility and reboot, or alternatively power off the system, reconfigure jumper, and switch settings according to diagrams and directions included in thc system's literature kit.

This reconfiguration process is time consuming and unnecessarily complex. Many newer Plug and Play systems offer soft-settable systemboard peripherals whose resources the Plug and Play operating system can reconfigure at runtime by invoking the Plug and Play BIOS `GetNode` and `SetNode` functions. Resources freed from systemboard peripherals instantly become available to hot-inserted devices, such as docking stations, Plug and Play ISA adapters, and PCMCIA cards.

Plug and Play Aware Device Drivers

DCDs are of little use to the operating system or its applications, unless their associated device drivers can detect the device's current resource assignments and configuration, including answers to simple device driver configuration questions such as "Is the device currently installed?" or "Is the device currently enabled?"

Plug and Play device drivers must adhere to the following general rules:

- A Plug and Play device driver must be dynamically loadable and unloadable.
- Plug and Play device drivers must register as clients of the operating system Configuration Manager.
- During its Configuration Manager Client Registration process, the Plug and Play device driver supplies the Configuration Manager with the address of a messaging call-back function.

- Plug and Play device drivers retrieve configuration information pertaining to their device(s) from the operating system Configuration Manager.
- Plug and Play device drivers respond to all operating system call-back messages pertaining to their supported device or devices.

In order to support Plug and Play device drivers, the operating system provides two important interfaces—the Configuration Management Layer and the device driver call-back function.

The Device Configuration Management Layer

Plug and Play device drivers never query resource or configuration information directly from a device. Instead, they use the operating system-supplied configuration management functions.

NOTE

Currently, many Plug and Play device drivers operate in an environment in which Plug and Play configuration management support may be present. Some device drivers currently shipping DOS/Win 3.1 systems, for example, are configured with Intel Configuration Manager driver, while others are not. In this case, the device driver must be capable of directly communicating with and configuring its Plug and Play ISA, PCI, or other device if CM support functions are not available.

The services provided by the Configuration Manager vary with the specific implementation. For example, the Intel DOS/Win 3.1 Configuration Manager provides, in addition to configuration management functions, a group of configuration access functions that enable device drivers to directly read and write registers within Plug and Play devices.

Configuration access functions are unavailable in the Windows 95 Configuration Manager. Instead, Windows 95 provides a registration mechanism that requires client drivers to supply the Configuration Manager with a call-back function to process runtime messages pertaining to their device or devices. The client driver call-back mechanism is unavailable in the Intel CM driver.

NOTE

Within systems that support the Intel DOS/Win 3.1 Configuration Manager, configuration management functions are supplied by the linkable library DOSCM.LIB (DOS applications and device drivers) and the dynamically linkable library WINCM.DLL (Windows applications and device drivers).

Within the Windows 95 environment, the majority of device drivers communicate with the Configuration Manager via the `VxD` call mechanism; however, the exact call mechanism implemented by a device driver depends on the driver's location in the Windows 95 driver layer.

The Device Driver Call-Back Function

The Plug and Play operating system may at any time enable, disable, or change the resource allocation strategy of a DCD. In order for the device driver to continue to function properly, it must be made aware of the operating system's changes to its device.

For this reason, Plug and Play operating systems such as Windows 95 require that device drivers register as a Configuration Manager client during their load sequence. As part of their client registration sequence, Plug and Play device drivers provide the operating system with the address of a *call-back function*.

At runtime, if the operating system reconfigures, enables, or disables a particular device, it notifies the device's driver software by invoking the driver's call-back function with some type of configuration change message. As one of its call arguments, the operating system passes the handle of the device node. Upon entry to its call-back function, the device driver verifies that the device node handle pertains to its own device. If this is not the case, the call-back function returns the message `CR_DEFAULT` to signal to the operating system that it performed no action during the call-back sequence.

If Windows 95 chooses to disable an unused Plug and Play ISA sound card, for example, it invokes the sound card's device driver with a `CONFIG_STOP` message to tell the device driver to cease processing and stop issuing Configuration Manager calls. Figure 1.1 displays the operating system Configuration Manager issuing the `CONFIG_STOP` message to the sound card device driver.

The call-back function mechanism is not available in the Intel DOS/Win 3.1 Plug and Play solution, but is recommended for future Plug and Play operating systems.

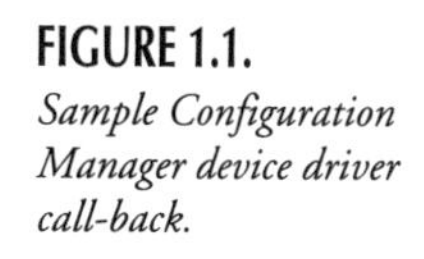

FIGURE 1.1.
Sample Configuration Manager device driver call-back.

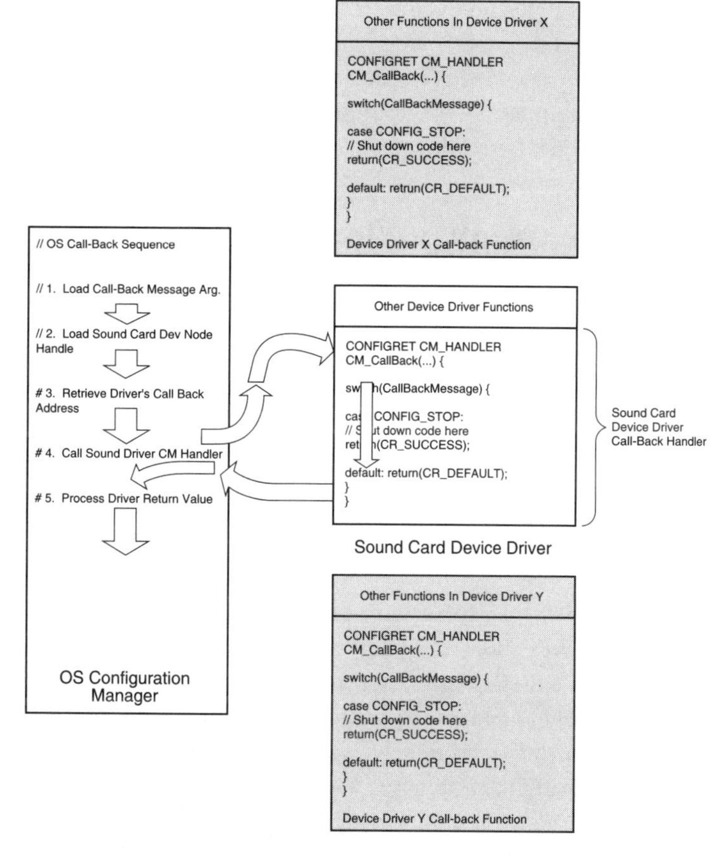

Plug and Play-Aware Applications

Plug and Play-aware applications detect the presence of operating system Configuration Manager and configuration access layers and perform all device configuration operations through one of these two interfaces.

In the Windows 95 environment, applications can bypass the task of identifying and locating configuration management support because the entire operating system is functioning in a Plug and Play context.

In the Intel DOS/Win 3.1 environment, however, configuration management and configuration access functions are available only if the Intel CM device driver DWCFGMG.SYS has been successfully loaded in the system's CONFIG.SYS file. In order to assist Plug and Play-aware DOS/Win 3.1 applications, the Intel CM provides the function `CM_GetVersion`, which returns the value `00H` if CM services are unavailable.

Designers of Plug and Play-aware DOS/Win 3.1 applications should design their products to function properly whether or not the Intel CM driver has been loaded. If a Plug and Play ISA device driver detects that the CM driver and its configuration management API are missing, for example, rather than simply aborting, it locates and configures its own device by directly accessing the device's on-board registers.

Hot-Swappable Devices

Runtime, or *hot-swappable* devices, such as PCMCIA adapters (PC Cards), present at the same time the most flexibility and the greatest challenge to the Plug and Play system because their requests for resources are not only diverse, but also occur asynchronously to the operating system's normal execution.

From the standpoint of usefulness, PC Cards allow users to hot-swap devices ranging in functionality from Static RAM (SRAM) -based drives to modems, LAN adapters, and rotating fixed disks. One particular vendor has even introduced a Global Positioning System that plugs into any of the system's PCMCIA slots.

PC Cards, however, suffer from the fact that the PCMCIA subsystem most often deals with a "leftover" pool of resources, notably those resources that have not already been allocated to systemboard devices and plug-in adapters. The Plug and Play operating system greatly enhances the viability of PC Cards by being able to recover system resources from other unused DCDs and configurable systemboard devices at runtime, and reallocating these newly freed resources to hot-inserted PC Cards.

The following two sections detail various problems that the Plug and Play operating system overcomes during the hot insertion and removal of a PC Card.

PC Card Insertion

When a PC Card is inserted, the PCMCIA Card Services layer within the operating system takes a snapshot of the available resources in the system and matches the list of available resources with those resources that the PC Card is capable of using. Because the insertion of a PC Card occurs in an asynchronous fashion, the operating system's enumerators, arbitrators, and configurators must be available at any time.

PC Card Insertion Example

The issues involved in supporting PC Cards and other hot-swappable devices, such as docking stations, reach far beyond the comparatively simple process of locating and assigning resources to a device. Consider, for example, that the user inserts a PC Card LAN adapter that requires an IRQ channel currently being used by another device. At this point, the operating system has three choices for dealing with the LAN adapter.

- Locate another IRQ channel that the LAN adapter is capable of using
- Deallocate an IRQ from another dynamically configurable device and assign the newly available IRQ to the LAN adapter
- Reject the LAN adapter

Obviously, rejecting the LAN adapter is the least favorable option. In order to ensure that the LAN adapter receives a usable, conflict-free resource configuration, the operating system enumerator and arbitrator will exhaustively re-evaluate the current resource assignments in the system, possibly disabling unused devices in order to configure the newly inserted PC Card, and will only as a last resort reject the card due to a lack of resources.

PC Card Removal

The removal of a PC Card requires that the PCMCIA Card Services layer identify and deallocate those resources that the removed PC Card has been using and notify the Configuration Manager of the newly freed resources. Currently, the PCMCIA architecture provides no mechanism for physically locking PC Cards in their sockets. As a result, the removal of these devices occurs in a completely asynchronous fashion. The PCMCIA Card Services layer and its associated client drivers must be able to not only detect the asynchronous removal of PC Cards, but also coordinate resource deallocation during the Card Services card status change event handler, which is invoked via a hardware interrupt during each PC Card insertion or removal.

Importantly, Card Services' card status change event handler enables the PCMCIA subsystem to return resources belonging to removed PC Cards to the Configuration Manager's runtime resource pool. Resources that have been returned to the Configuration Manager become available to other, dynamically configurable system peripherals, including other PC Cards.

Self-Identifying Peripherals

Like PCMCIA, Plug and Play ISA, and PCI devices, certain other PC/AT peripherals provide software-accessible identification and device configuration information.

ATA Devices (CD-ROM, IDE Drives)

The SFF (Small Form Factor) Committee AT Attachment document defines a `100H` byte configuration drive capabilities header that ATA-compatible devices return in response to an ATA `Inquiry` command. System firmware and device drivers write certain locations in the device header to configure such parameters as device timing, logical device geometry, and multi-sector read/write operations.

Although the ATA device capabilities header does not provide for IDE device resource configuration, it does allow the operating system to verify the presence and capabilities of any installed IDE devices, such as fixed disks and CD-ROM drives. For example, the fixed disk enumerator in many operating systems issues the ATA `Identify` command to the standard primary (`1FxH`) and secondary (`17xH`) IDE controller task registers in order to verify that the system BIOS' fixed disk reporting mechanism matches the system's installed equipment.

Pointing Devices/Serial Devices

According to the *Plug and Play External COM Device Specification*, all serial devices connected to the system's COM ports must return an 18-entry device identification string upon being plugged in or enabled.

The serial device identification contains such information as the device's EISA product ID and device class, thereby enabling the Plug and Play operating system to choose the appropriate driver for the device. The format of the serial device identification string, and the method required to transmit the string appear in the Plug and Play External COM Device Specification.

NOTE

The Plug and Play External COM Specification (in addition to many other Plug and Play specifications) is available on the CompuServe Plug and Play forum. You can access this forum by logging into CompuServe and typing `GO PLUGPLAY`.

Docking Stations

A *docking station* (sometimes called a *convenience base*) provides a bay into which the user can insert a notebook system in order to introduce additional peripherals to the notebook system, or change default peripherals. For example, the user might travel with a notebook system, and then insert it into its docking station to create a desktop system at the office. Upon docking, his or her notebook switches from its internal display to a larger, external VGA monitor, and replaces the notebook's internal trackball and keyboard with larger, external devices attached to the docking station.

With the support of Plug and Play, docking station-capable systems can quickly and safely switch between the portable and desktop environment. The following sections briefly describe the docking station model. Chapter 7 revisits the docking station technology with technical descriptions of docking station hardware, event handling, Plug and Play BIOS support functions and multi-station capable portable systems.

The OS Device Node Hardware Tree

The Windows 95 Plug and Play operating system maintains a RAM-resident *device hardware tree* whose device node records contain a device identifier and resource configuration information for each installed bus and device. Importantly, the operating system's components have access to hardware tree information at runtime, thereby enabling applications access to the most current system configuration.

During the system boot process, the Plug and Play BIOS provides the operating system with device identifiers for each of the systemboard primary, or *root* buses. The operating system's *bus enumerators* create a device node for each systemboard device and root bus. The enumerators then scan each root bus for additional devices and secondary, or *child* buses, creating additional device nodes for each device and child bus in the system.

When the OS' enumerators are finished building the system hardware tree, control of the hardware tree passes to the OS *Configuration Manager*, whose primary function is to manage the hardware tree contents at runtime. The Configuration Manager invokes enumerators, configurators, and resource arbitrators at runtime if new devices or buses are introduced to, or removed from the system. If the user *docks* a notebook system into its *convenience base*, for example, the Configuration Manager invokes a docking station enumerator to update the contents of the hardware tree to include those devices located in the convenience base.

If resource conflicts exist between the notebook's devices and those in the docking station, the Configuration Manager invokes its resource arbitrator. After the arbitrator completes its task of resource balancing, the Configuration Manager invokes OS configurators to assign resources to, and configure devices in both the docking station and notebook unit, if necessary.

Figure 1.2 shows the OS runtime Configuration Manager subsystem.

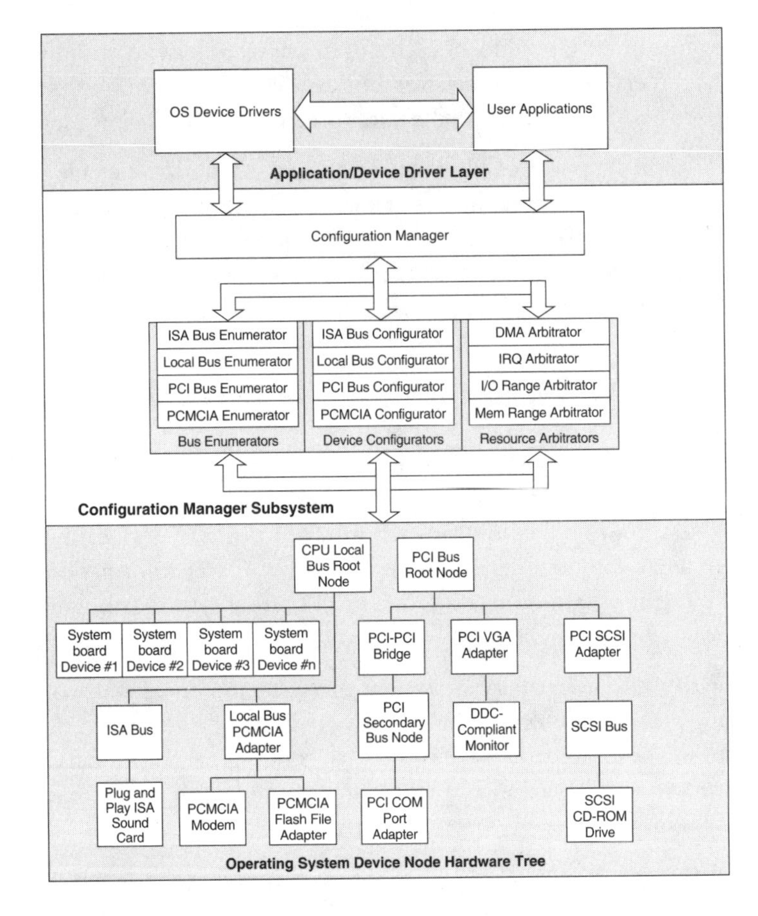

FIGURE 1.2.
The Plug and Play operating system runtime Configuration Manager subsystem.

The Purpose of Programming for Plug and Play

Programming for Plug and Play presents the techniques involved in programming configurable devices in such a way that engineers can apply the concept of Plug and Play at a system, as well as a register or device level.

Similarly, great pains have been taken to discuss and present the vast number of industry specifications in a single publication. The intent is to save the reader time needlessly lost in locating and cross referencing industry documentation.

For example, Plug and Play ISA devices and systemboard devices have two things in common—they share a common resource descriptor format, and the Plug and Play BIOS provides a function that returns the total number and `READ_DATA` address of the system's Plug and Play ISA adapters.

And yet, the reader can understand neither type of device without first having read and understood both the Plug and Play ISA and Plug and Play BIOS specifications. Whenever the source of documentation is not intuitively obvious, this book alerts the reader.

Lastly, in cases where Plug and Play information appears in long lists, as is common with computer specifications containing large amounts of tabular information or exhaustive lists of function descriptions, the reader is referred either to an appendix, or to the appropriate industry specification, document, or association from which the information can be obtained.

Related Documents and Industry Groups

Several PC industry leaders have been involved in documenting and defining the various technologies involved in the Plug and Play mission, while other independent committees, special interest groups (SIGs) and associations have recently appeared for the sole purpose of generating consensus and ensuring future compatibility between vendors of Plug and Play systems, firmware, adapters, software applications, and hardware.

Following is a list of available Plug and Play-related documents and industry groups.

References

Adaptec Inc., AT&T Global Information Solutions, Digital Equipment Corporation, Future Domain Corporation, Maxtor Corporation, and Microsoft Corporation, *Plug and Play SCSI Specification*, version 1.0, March 30, 1994

Compaq Computer Corporation, Intel Corporation, and Phoenix Technologies, Ltd., *Extended System Configuration Data Specification*, version 1.03, December 12, 1994

Compaq Computer Corporation, Intel Corporation, and Phoenix Technologies, Ltd., *Plug and Play BIOS Specification*, version 1.0a, May 5, 1994

Intel Corporation, *External Plug and Play Interfaces Specification for MS-DOS and Windows Runtime Configuration Services*, version 1.0, April 15, 1994

Intel Corporation, *Plug and Play BIOS Extensions Design Guide*, revision 1.2, May 1994

Intel Corporation, *Installation Software for Plug and Play Cards*, revision 1.0, July 18, 1994

Intel Corporation and Microsoft Corporation, *Plug and Play ISA Specification*, version 1.0a with clarifications, August 9, 1994

Intel Corporation, *Plug and Play Architecture for the MS-DOS and Windows 3.1 Operating Systems*, revision 1.0, June 21, 1994

Microsoft Corporation, white paper entitled "Plug and Play BIOS Functionality" and Windows "Chicago"

Microsoft Corporation, *Plug and Play Device Driver Interface for Microsoft Windows 3.1 and MS-DOS*, version 1.0d, August 31, 1994

Microsoft Corporation, *Microsoft Windows and the Plug and Play Framework Architecture*, March 1994

Microsoft Corporation, *Plug and Play Parallel Port Devices*, version 1.0, February 11, 1994

Microsoft Press, *Hardware Design Guide for Microsoft Windows 95*, ISBN 1-55615-642-1, copyright 1994, Microsoft Corporation

PCI Special Interest Group, *PCI Local Bus Specification*, revision 2.1

PCI Special Interest Group, *PCI BIOS Specification*, revision 2.1, April 26, 1994

PCMCIA Committee, *PCMCIA PC Card Standard*, revision 2.0

PCMCIA Committee, *PCMCIA Card Services Specification*, revision 2.1

PCMCIA Committee, *PCMCIA Socket Services Specification*, revision 2.0

Industry Groups, Associations, and Documentation Providers

The sources listed here provide information regarding individual technologies that participate in Plug and Play systems.

PC/AT Architecture

EISA Vendor ID's, *EISA Specification*

BCPR Services
P.O. Box 11137
Spring, TX 77391-1137

Peripheral Component Interconnect (PCI)

PCI Local Bus Specification, PCI BIOS Specification

PCI Special Interest Group
P.O. Box 14070
Portland, OR 97214

Telephone (800)433-5177 (U.S.)

(503)797-4297 (International)

(503)234-6762 (Fax)

PCMCIA

PCMCIA PC Card Standard

PCMCIA Card Services Specification

PCMCIA Socket Services Specification

Personal Computer Memory Card International Association
1030 East Duane Avenue, Suite G
Sunnyvale, CA 94086

Plug and Play

The following sources provide information targeted specifically at the Plug and Play technology as a whole.

CompuServe PLUGPLAY Forum

ESCD Specification

Plug and Play BIOS Specification

Advanced Power Management BIOS Interface Specification

Plug and Play ISA Specification

Plug and Play Parallel Port Device Specification

Plug and Play External COM Port Specification

CompuServe users type **GO PLUGPLAY** to join this forum.

Plug and Play Association

The Plug and Play Association
P.O. Box 14070
Portland OR, 97214-9499

Telephone (800)433-3695

Fax (503)234-6762

Microsoft Compatibility Labs

Plug and Play hardware, software compatibility testing and information

Microsoft Corporation
One Microsoft Way
Redmond, WA 98052-6399

Telephone (206)635-4949

Fax (206)936-7329

Internet `mclinfo@microsoft.com`

CompuServe ID `72350,2636`

2

The Plug and Play Architecture

The first chapter explains that programming Plug and Play is a system-wide technology most effectively implemented when both the software and hardware play along. While the battle for system resources between competing adapters in a PC will never end, the Plug and Play technology at least makes the system a level playing field. Now that you understand that Plug and Play involves the entire system, take a look at PCI, PCMCIA, Plug and Play ISA, and systemboard devices to get a better idea which devices are being plugged in and how to play with them.

Despite the introduction of new buses, chipsets, and adapters, today's PC systems still are primarily based on the PC/AT architecture that was unleashed on the programming public in 1984. That architecture provides a limited amount of resources—16 interrupt levels, 8 DMA channels, 16-bit, addressable I/O space, and 384K of expansion ROM address space—and for reasons too numerous to mention, it has changed little in its 10-year life.

To compound the problem of limited resource availability, the PC/AT architecture upon which Plug and Play systems are based is one steeped in history, and not all of the resources listed here are available to emerging technologies—many of them having been spoken for by systemboard devices, firmware, and standard peripherals.

The task of the Plug and Play system at its lowest levels is to abstract software from the confusing PC/AT architecture and report, in a uniform manner, resource usage to layers at the operating-system or application level.

For example, all systems (Plug and Play or otherwise) are equipped with resource-hungry, embedded systemboard devices, such as the DMA controller and keyboard controller. Although you cannot remove or configure embedded devices, you can be sure of the resources they use.

The system BIOS has an intimate knowledge of which embedded devices have been installed on the systemboard, and it actually contains descriptor tables that describe the resources assigned to the embedded devices. For each embedded device, the system BIOS stores a resource descriptor in the form of a device node, as the Plug and Play BIOS specification requires.

Device nodes are a fundamental building block within a Plug and Play system, and many of this book's Plug and Play discussions are based on device nodes and their contents.

The Plug and Play operating system enumerates systemboard devices by calling Plug and Play BIOS functions to retrieve all system device nodes. The operating system enumerator then parses each device node's resource allocation description block to determine which resources the device consumes (see Figure 2.1). At the end of Chapter 3 is a C program that correctly parses a system's device nodes and prints their contents.

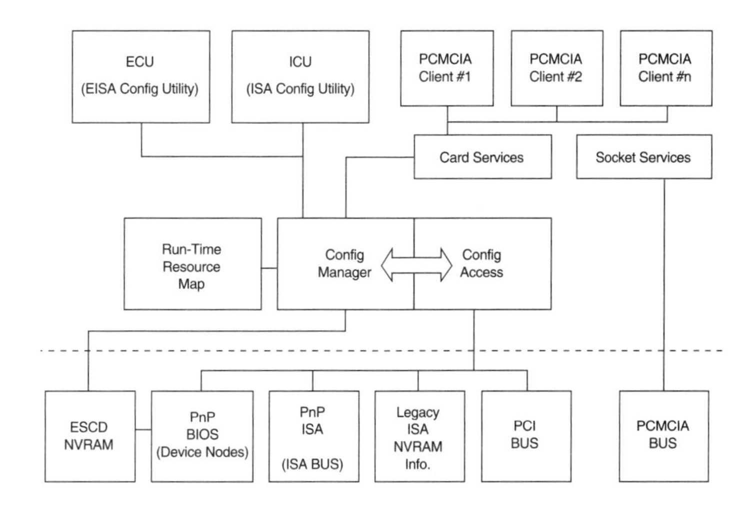

FIGURE 2.1.
Plug and Play system framework.

As this book progresses, you will discover that the Plug and Play operating system enumerates non-systemboard device resources using structures that are similar in format to the device node, or it may introduce new and completely different structures for enumerating devices for which the device node format is inadequate. First, however, make sure you build a good foundation of understanding at the node level.

The Total Plug and Play System

From the application layer downward, Plug and Play programming consists of many hardware and software relationships, which, when working in concert, make up the Plug and Play system. Even as the Plug and Play devices at the register level are discussed, you need to remember to work with these devices and the buses on which they reside as part of that larger system. Now that you have been introduced to many of the devices involved in Plug and Play programming, let's return to and expand upon the total system concept introduced in the opening chapter of the book.

It will help you to have a firm understanding of the definitions given here before continuing on. These terms will continue to reappear throughout the rest of the book as we build an understanding of the Plug and Play system one piece at a time.

Arbitration, Resource—Also called resource balancing, this is the process of allocating system resources in such a way that no active resource conflicts exist.

Configuration—In a Plug and Play system, configuration is the process of allocating resources to a device and then leaving this device in a known state. A configurator allocates resources to devices and peripherals based on information provided to it by device enumerators and resource arbitrators.

Device—A device is a chipset, adapter, peripheral, or other physical system component that either uses system resources or provides functionality to the Plug and Play system.

Enumeration—In a Plug and Play system, enumeration is the process of determining and cataloging current and possible resource allocations for devices and peripherals. An enumerator gathers and catalogs the number and type of resources allocated to devices installed in the system.

ESCD (Extended System Configuration Data)—Based in the Plug and Play BIOS's non-volatile storage, the ESCD is a set of records that describes both physical and logical device resource allocation. ESCD records are created by BIOS, and created, maintained, and deleted by an OS-based configuration utility and the Plug and Play BIOS may be able to interpret their contents. The Plug and Play BIOS that supports ESCD acts as a vehicle for assisting the operating system to read and write slot records to and from system NVRAM. Additionally, the BIOS may convert CMOS into ESCD records.

Function— A function is a stand-alone, resource-consuming hardware entity within a device, such as a sound chip on a multimedia adapter that also contains a SCSI controller. A device contains one or more functions, each of which the Plug and Play operating system enumerates and configures separately.

IPL (Initial Program Load)— The Initial Program Load occurs when the system BIOS transfers control to the operating system. An IPL device is a device capable of booting the system. An IPL manager is a firmware or operating system level application that enumerates all system IPL devices, and selects a single IPL device to begin the system boot process.

Legacy (as in legacy ISA, or legacy system)—The term legacy describes a system, device, or piece of software that either pre-dates Plug and Play or does not conform to Plug and Play standards. The DOS operating system, for example, is a legacy operating system.

NVRAM (Non-volatile RAM)—NVRAM describes storage media implemented in the form of SRAM, CMOS, FLASH ROM, or some other type of RAM whose contents remain intact when the system is powered off.

NVS (Non-volatile Storage)—An information storage media, such as NVRAM or a disk file, whose contents remain intact when power is removed from the system.

Plug and Play System—The Plug and Play system allows the computer's BIOS, hardware components, and operating system software to automatically install, configure, and use any combination of cards, devices, and configuration environments.

Resource—A resource is any of the system's IRQ channels, DMA channels, I/O ports or addressable memory ranges

Layers of the Plug and Play System

From a programmer's perspective, Plug and Play systems are made up of three different layers: hardware, software, and a third layer that is called middleware. The middleware group is used to categorize system and adapter firmware, as well as Plug and Play code modules whose physical location is implementation-dependent. The IPL (Initial Program Load) or boot device manager, for example, belongs in the middleware layer because it may either reside in firmware or in the operating system's early boot loader.

The Plug and Play Software Layer

A system's Plug and Play *software layer* consists of the following:

- A Plug and Play operating system
- Plug and Play-aware applications
- OS level device drivers
- Hardware profiler
- Device registry
- Configuration Manager, which contains the following:
    - Device configurators
    - Device enumerators
    - Resource Arbitrators

Like the overall Plug and Play system, the Plug and Play software layer introduces several new concepts and terms, some of which are the following:

Configuration Manager— The Configuration Manager is a resident module within the operating system whose job it is to provide runtime Plug and Play support to the operating system, OS applications and drivers, and system firmware. The Configuration Manager has two primary functions. First, it provides a uniform, high-level interface by which applications can communicate device resource configuration information. Second, the Configuration Manager is the operating system's central coordinator of any transactions between OS enumerators, configurators, and profilers, thereby insuring that the system's resources are allocated and reported in a conflict-free fashion.

`Devnode` *Tree*— The `devnode` tree is a runtime, hierarchical list of all hardware currently present in the system. The format of a `devnode` tree entry is a superset of the system BIOS device node. In addition to the information contained in a system BIOS device node, OS device nodes allow the specification of device-specific enumerators and child nodes. The `devnode` tree is hierarchical in that the Configuration Manager sorts devices according to the bus on which they reside. For example, configuration information pertaining to SCSI devices is stored in a different branch from that belonging to the system's PCI devices.

Profile—A profile is a structure that outlines the fundamental hardware characteristics of the target system. During each system boot, the operating system invokes its hardware profiler and is returned the system's profile. Later in the boot sequence, the OS Configuration Manager will refer to the profile to determine which buses, devices, and peripherals it must enumerate and configure.

Registry— The Registry is a disk-resident database that contains information for all devices ever installed in the system. When users install a new device in the system, the operating system "registers" the device, along with information such as the name of an .INF file that aids in configuring the device. The purpose of the registry is to accelerate the system enumeration process by providing a centralized, non-volatile record of all system devices. Windows 95 includes other information in its registry, such as device-specific configurations, the last known working system configuration, and information pertaining to non-Plug and Play adapters that the system was able to detect during the boot sequence.

The Plug and Play software layer takes control from the system BIOS at boot time. From this point forward, the Plug and Play software layer may invoke functions within the system BIOS or Plug and Play BIOS; however, the reverse is never true.

NOTE

The system BIOS never assumes that there is a Plug and Play operating system on the selected IPL device. It may, however, provide Plug and Play support modules, such as a firmware-based IPL selector, to detect and choose an IPL device from among those installed in the system. Similarly, the Plug and Play operating system never assumes that the underlying physical system is Plug and Play-compliant, it will invoke and use Plug and Play BIOS functions if it detects them.

Early in the IPL sequence, the operating system invokes its hardware profiler, which builds a hardware profile, or description, of the target system's basic architecture. The Configuration Manager uses this profile to enumerate all devices, peripherals, and buses.

The operating system's Configuration Manager begins to execute shortly after the target machine's hardware profile has been created. Based on the profile's contents, the

Configuration Manager decides which buses and system devices to enumerate. If the system is equipped with both a PCI and ISA bus, for example, the Configuration Manager needs to enumerate systemboard device nodes, legacy adapter information, Plug and Play ISA adapters, and PCI adapters.

The Configuration Manager's enumeration consists of two parts. First, the Configuration Manager evaluates all statically-allocated resource information. It gets this static information from the Plug and Play BIOS system device nodes, legacy ISA node, and ESCD database, if one exists. The process is as follows:

1. The Configuration Manager receives the system profile from the hardware profiler.
2. The Configuration Manager begins to build the operating system `Devnode` tree, first by retrieving systemboard device nodes and converting them to the OS form of device node.

   If the systemboard does not support the optional ESCD extensions, then the Configuration Manager instead retrieves legacy device information via Plug and Play BIOS function `0AH`, `Get Legacy ISA Information` and appends this information to the device node tree.

NOTE

ESCD consists of static resource allocation records whose format differs greatly from that of the Plug and Play BIOS legacy ISA information. ESCD-equipped systems must, however, support the basic Plug and Play BIOS functions in order to be compliant. Interestingly enough, the Plug and Play BIOS' legacy ISA resource information is a subset of the information that ESCD systems maintain in their extended NVRAM resource database. For the purpose of simplicity, the Plug and Play BIOS typically supports either ESCD or legacy ISA functions, but not both. Otherwise, the Plug and Play BIOS would have to translate between two different resource information formats.

If functions `0ah` or `0AH` return any error code of `USE_ESCD`, then the OS enumerator must maintain all static information through the ESCD BIOS functions.

After the Configuration Manager has evaluated the machine's systemboard device nodes, ESCD data, and Plug and Play BIOS legacy ISA information, it has a clear picture of all statically-allocated system resources. The Configuration Manager's next task is to enumerate and configure the resource needs of the system's dynamic, or Plug and Play devices. Today's dynamic devices include those that conform to the PCI or Plug and Play ISA hardware specifications.

The Configuration Manager shifts gears to deal with Plug and Play devices. During the Plug and Play phase of system enumeration, the Configuration Manager must act not only as an enumerator, but also as an arbitrator and configurator.

These terms may sound like a mouthful of technology, but the concepts involved are not so difficult. After having enumerated the devices whose resources cannot be reconfigured, the Configuration Manager now is faced with assigning leftover resources to dynamic adapters. It does this by determining the possible configuration for each Plug and Play device, arbitrating resources from the overall system profile, and finally configuring each device. Plug and Play adapters that have been assigned resources and configured are added to the `devnode` tree, and the device enumeration process is complete...

...or almost complete. Why is it that PCMCIA adapters have not yet appeared in the system's configuration process? PCMCIA devices are, in fact, Plug and Play-compliant, yet their capability to be inserted and removed at runtime forces the operating system to use a different mechanism for enumerating and configuring this type of device.

The reasoning for not enumerating PCMCIA card resources during the boot process is simple. If your system enumerated PCMCIA adapters at boot time, you could initially detect a PCMCIA card present, such as during execution of the OS hardware profiler, and assign it resources. Shortly thereafter, before the operating system had a chance to load the Configuration Manager, the user might innocently remove the adapter from its socket. Because the Configuration Manager depends on hardware profile information, it would assign resources to a card that no longer exists in the system. Not only would this be a waste of resources, it also would result in the operating system's profile being incorrect.

Instead, PCMCIA devices make use of the Configuration Manager's CM function interface that allows applications to access system resource information at runtime, once the initial enumeration/configuration process is complete. When the user inserts or removes a PCMCIA device, the PCMCIA controller generates a card status change signal. The operating system's Card Services module detects this signal and interrogates the controller to determine whether the event involved a card insertion or removal.

In the case of a card insertion, Card Services calls first to interrogate the resource needs of the newly inserted card, and then calls Configuration Manager to determine which resources remain in the system. If a suitable set of resources exists, then Card Services configures the card and issues a second call to the Configuration Manager to indicate which resources have been allocated to the PCMCIA card. Otherwise, Card Services rejects the card and notifies the user that the card cannot be configured. After a successful card insertion, the Configuration Manager adds the resources allocated to the card to the system `devnode` tree and system execution resumes.

When the user removes a PCMCIA card from the system, the PCMCIA controller notifies Card Services of a card removal event. Card services then notifies the Configuration Manager that this card's resources are now available to other devices in the system. At this point, the Configuration Manager removes the PCMCIA adapter from the system's devnode tree.

The Plug and Play Hardware Layer

A Plug and Play system's *hardware layer* consists of the following:

- Plug and Play BIOS (with optional ESCD extensions)
- Plug and Play-compliant devices (such as Plug and Play ISA, PCI, and PCMCIA)
- Noncompliant devices (such as legacy ISA, EISA, and MCA)
- System firmware
    - PCI BIOS
    - System BIOS
    - Power management firmware
    - VGA, or other video controller firmware
- Dock/undock indicator hardware (dockable notebook systems only)
- NVRAM, or some other type of non-volatile storage

Plug and Play systems operate in legacy mode during early portions of the BIOS POST, or Power On Self Tests. As with legacy systems, the Plug and Play system's BIOS configures DRAM, cache, timing, and other parameters within the systems chipset, and performs diagnostics on the system's DMA controller, interrupt controller, keyboard controller, and other peripherals.

What sets a Plug and Play system apart from its legacy counterparts is the presence of a Plug and Play BIOS. The Plug and Play BIOS is the fundamental hardware building block in a Plug and Play system. In addition to providing the system with functions for enumerating systemboard device resource usage, the Plug and Play BIOS manages docking station insertions and removals, maintains a special device node of legacy ISA resource usage, and configures PCI and Plug and Play ISA boot devices. Also, the Plug and Play BIOS might support extended functions to report an APM 1.1 (Advanced Power Management) device and support the ESCD extensions; however, these functions are not required for Plug and Play BIOS compatibility.

Different Ideas on Device Configuration

At this point, you might be wondering which Plug and Play devices the Plug and Play BIOS configures. This is a valid question, as it is not specifically addressed in any of the current Plug and Play specifications.

At a minimum, the Plug and Play BIOS must configure all devices that are capable of participating in the boot sequence. This makes sense considering that it is perfectly valid for the user to want to boot from any bootable device, whether or not that device is Plug and Play-compliant.

Any devices not specifically required for boot, such as sound cards, modems, and so on, may be configured (assigned resources), but must be left disabled once the boot process is launched. The assumption here is that the Plug and Play operating system is fully capable of enumerating, configuring, and enabling non-bootable Plug and Play devices during the IPL process. If the system has no underlying Plug and Play support, you assume that the device drivers that accompany Plug and Play adapters also are capable of enumerating, configuring, and enabling their particular device, although without the surety of resource conflict resolution that the Plug and Play operating system provides.

The presence of ESCD support in a Plug and Play BIOS markedly affects the degree to which the Plug and Play BIOS configures Plug and Play devices during POST. The Plug and Play BIOS in an ESCD-equipped system works in close conjunction with the ESCD database the operating system maintains in the system's NVRAM. Bear in mind, however, that the primary purpose of the ESCD is to allow the operating system to designate specific, or "locked," configurations for individual Plug and Play adapters.

Consider a system that contains devices ABC and XYZ. Although device XYZ is capable of using any available IRQ, device ABC can only use IRQ 10. After having enumerated each device in the system, the Plug and Play operating system discovers that it must assign IRQ 11 to device XYZ in order to guarantee that IRQ 10 remains free for device ABC. In order to guarantee that both devices function properly, the Plug and Play operating system writes "locked configuration" records to the system's ESCD database. One record stipulates that device XYZ always receives IRQ 11; the other specifies that device ABC receives IRQ 10, the only IRQ that the device is capable of using. During POST, the Plug and Play BIOS will reference the ESCD, and upon encountering devices ABC and XYZ, both on the bus and in ESCD storage, will assign these devices' IRQs based on the locked configuration records that the operating system stored in the ESCD.

In systems that are not equipped with ESCD, the Plug and Play BIOS approaches each boot sequence as an entirely new resource allocation scenario, and assigns resources to Plug and Play devices as it encounters them. If the Plug and Play BIOS detects a conflict between the resources that a device requires and those still available, it may reinitiate its resource balancing algorithm and attempt to resolve the conflict, or it simply may continue and reject the adapter for which no resources were available.

So which type of system is superior? Well, both are because they add Plug and Play capabilities to the system. And each has its own shortcomings.

The ESCD-equipped system works correctly until the user adds an adapter whose possible resource configurations conflict with those already locked down for installed devices, or the system simply runs out of resources for any additional devices. When this occurs, the user must keep booting, running a device configuration utility and rebooting, and so on until such time that the operating system can devise a resource allocation scheme by which all adapters are guaranteed the resources they need, or the OS determines that it is not possible to properly assign resources to all devices within the system. The latter situation is aggravated by the fact that many Plug and Play adapters can be configured to use only one of three or four IRQs, or one of two DMA channels.

The non-ESCD system faces similar challenges in that the system simply may run out of resources as the Plug and Play BIOS tries to configure Plug and Play adapters. The advantage of the non-ESCD system is that the exhaustion of resources becomes apparent immediately during POST, and no time-consuming configuration process is needed to determine whether a particular adapter cannot be configured for lack of resources.

The best solution for maximizing the capabilities of both the ESCD and non-ESCD Plug and Play BIOS is rooted in the Plug and Play adapter designs. Ideally, all Plug and Play ISA, PCI, and systemboard devices should be configurable to the widest variety of IRQs, DMA channels, I/O ranges, and memory ranges. When this is true, the system rejects adapters only when every possible resource has been used.

Unless you're dealing with devices at the BIOS level, the preceding concerns may be beyond the scope of your project. You may, however, encounter a situation in which the Plug and Play system has booted and the device you want to use is disabled or has been assigned no resources. This is a good time to start looking back at the BIOS.

The Plug and Play Middleware Layer

This section closes with a quick discussion of the Plug and Play middleware layer. This section is designed to fill in some gaps regarding the location and role of certain software modules in the Plug and Play system.

It is clear that modules such as the system BIOS, VGA BIOS, and Plug and Play BIOS reside closer to hardware because they are almost exclusively located in ROM, or Read-Only Memory space, while the operating system, its Configuration Manager, and device drivers are purely software, executing only at the point in which the system BIOS has transferred execution from ROM to the IPL device.

Somewhere in between lies a narrow, yet important, region called *middleware.* There are two modules that belong to the middle-ware family—namely the IPL manager and PCMCIA Socket Services. The intent of this discussion is not to solve the issues that arise from middleware applications, but rather to make you aware of this class of software and maybe get your creative juices plugging and playing.

IPL Manager

Where should the IPL device manager reside? The *IPL manager* provides users with the option to select the system's boot device from among all those installed. It must be aware of and be able to select any boot device within the system.

You cannot assume that the IPL manager resides on a fixed disk because it couldn't have been loaded unless the user already selected a boot device.

If the IPL manager resides in firmware, however, it cannot select a boot device that has not yet been configured. Consider an ESCD-equipped system that has not yet balanced resources to the point in which the desired IPL device has been assigned the resources it needs to boot. The Plug and Play BIOS will detect that this device suffers from a resource conflict and will ignore it during the boot-device selection process.

So, has it been proven that the implementation of an IPL manager is fruitless? Not by any means. IPL managers simply demand an understanding of the issues on the part of the person who is configuring the system. In fact, Plug and Play systems that incorporate legacy boot devices, such as MCA or EISA drive controllers, may require several reboot sequences before enough resource balancing has occurred to allow these controllers the IRQs or I/O ranges they need to get going.

Socket Services

As mentioned previously, Socket Services are the primary communication channel between PCMCIA adapters and PCMCIA client applications. Socket Services provides a variety of functions by which Card Services and other PCMCIA client applications can interrogate and configure a system's PCMCIA controller without needing to understand the underlying specifics of the system's hardware. The fact that Socket Services don't depend on any operating system features enables it to reside either in ROM or in driver form within the operating system.

Often, it is advantageous that PCMCIA Socket Services reside in ROM rather than in OS-loadable driver form. To appreciate this, consider a notebook system that, for reasons of portability, has no floppy diskette. This type of notebook must have a mechanism by which the user can boot from an operating system other than the one resident on the system's hard disk. This is accomplished by locating Socket Services in firmware and equipping the system with a small Socket Services client that can recognize and kick start certain bootable PCMCIA adapters to boot the machine.

PC/AT Hardware Review

As Plug and Play developers, our chief concern is to correctly report, enumerate, and configure system resources. Before continuing, we should define exactly what those resources are. The best way to do this is by using the PC/AT architecture as a model.

This does not imply that all Plug and Play systems are based on the PC/AT, nor does it imply by any means that the PC/AT is a Plug and Play machine. It is safe to assume, however, that the majority of Plug and Play systems, notebooks, and desktop systems start with a resource pool similar to that of the original AT system. For those who want a fuller understanding of Plug and Play system hardware compatibility, Microsoft supplies the *PC '95 Hardware Design Guide*, available from the Microsoft press.

The resources in a Plug and Play system consist of IRQ channels, DMA channels, and I/O and memory ranges. The following section briefly reviews each type of resource and its allocation scheme in the AT-class machine.

IRQ (Interrupt ReQuest) Channels

The PC/AT system has two Intel 8259-compatible *programmable interrupt controllers* (or PICs), each capable of supporting eight separate interrupt request signals. IRQs `0-7` are assigned to the primary PIC and IRQs `8-15` are assigned to the secondary `8259`, which was added when designers realized that the XT's eight interrupt channels were inadequate to satisfy the multitude of add-on adapters that were beginning to appear in the market.

IRQs signal asynchronous hardware events to the system. The original PC/AT, in its barest form, allocates IRQs as shown in Table 2.1.

Table 2.1. Allocation of IRQs in the original PC/AT.

PIC	*IRQ*	*Device*
Primary	`0`	System Timer Tick (8254 Channel 0)
Primary	`1`	System Keyboard Controller (8042)
Primary	`2`	Secondary PIC Cascade/Shareable
Primary	`6`	Floppy Disk Controller
Secondary	`8`	RTC Periodic Alarm
Secondary	`14`	IDE Disk Controller

Out of a possible 16 IRQ channels, almost half already have been spoken for by system devices. The number of IRQ channels available to add-on peripherals becomes even more sparse when you start to add communications ports. Each serial or parallel port consumes an additional IRQ. The typical AT clone, which comes standard with two serial devices and one parallel port, has only seven IRQs left for users. Throw in an optional secondary parallel port and PS/2 pointing device support, and you're left with just four IRQs.

NOTE

Although, technically IRQ 2 is available to plug-in adapters, many adapter vendors are hesitant to use IRQ 2 because of compatibility inconsistencies in older system BIOSes.

By the time users upgrade their system with an IRQ-hungry multimedia kit, they have something like a one-in-three chance of picking an unused interrupt channel, if you take into account the fact that these adapters cannot be configured to use IRQs 0-2, 6, 8 and 9. Table 2.2 depicts the IRQ usage for the majority of desktop systems shipped today.

Table 2.2. The IRQ usage for the majority of desktops shipped today.

PIC	*IRQ*	*Device*
Primary	0	System Timer Tick (8254 Channel 0)
Primary	1	System Keyboard Controller (8042)
Primary	2	Secondary PIC Cascade/Shareable
Primary	3	COM 2 Serial Port Device
Primary	4	COM 1 Serial Port Device
Primary	5	LPT 1 Parallel Port Device
Primary	6	Floppy Disk Controller
Primary	7	LPT 2 Parallel Port Device
Secondary	8	RTC Periodic Alarm
Secondary	9	Unassigned
Secondary	10	Unassigned
Secondary	11	Unassigned
Secondary	12	PS/2 Mouse
Secondary	13	Unassigned
Secondary	14	Fixed Disk Controller
Secondary	15	Unassigned

In a true Plug and Play system, the Plug and Play BIOS reports IRQ usage by delivering resource-reporting device nodes to the operating system enumerator software. Any IRQs not reported as having been allocated are available to the operating system, its associated device drivers, and applications. Chapter 3 discusses methods for calling the Plug and Play BIOS to retrieve device nodes that contain this valuable IRQ allocation information.

System I/O Range Resources

An *I/O range* is a group of addresses to which a device responds during an Input or Output CPU cycle. This type of CPU cycle is generated when the processor executes an `IN` or `OUT` type instruction. During an I/O cycle, the CPU simultaneously asserts a 16-bit I/O address and either the `IORD#` (I/O Read) or `IOW#` (I/O Write) signal.

I/O addresses consist of either 8 or 16 significant bits, depending on the CPU instruction used to perform the operation. If the CPU executes an 8-bit I/O instruction, the upper 8 address bits are asserted as zeroes, in order to form a full 16-bit address.

The Plug and Play system's I/O range spans a full 64KB address locations, some of which belong to PC/AT style system devices. Most PC/AT devices occupy I/O ranges located in the `0-3FFH` range; however, it is not uncommon to find such things as PCI host controllers statically mapped to I/O locations in the `400H–0FFFFH` range.

Table 2.3 outlines those I/O ranges used both by standard PC/AT systemboard devices and many common add-in peripherals. This table is meant to be only a guideline. The actual I/O ranges consumed by static devices within a Plug and Play system are contained in a ROM-based table within the Plug and Play BIOS and are entirely system specific.

Table 2.3. The I/O ranges used by both standard PC/AT systemboard devices and many common add-in peripherals.

I/O Range	*Device*
00H–1FH	DMA Controller 0 (Address, Status, Count Registers)
20H–3FH	Primary PIC (8259 Programmable Interrupt Controller)
40H–5FH	System Interval Timer (8254)
60H–6FH	System Keyboard Controller
70H–71H	System Real Time Clock/CMOS I/O Ports
80H–9FH	Primary DMA Controller (Page Registers)
A0H–BFH	Secondary PIC (8259 Programmable Interrupt Controller)

continues

Table 2.3. continued

I/O Range	*Device*
C0H–DFH	DMA Controller 1 (Address, Status, and Count Registers)
E0H–EFH	Reserved
F0H–FFH	Math Coprocessor Registers
100H–16FH	Reserved/Unused
170H–177H	Secondary Fixed Disk Controller
178H–1EFH	Reserved/Unused
1F0H–1F7H	Primary Fixed Disk Controller
1F8H–1FFH	Reserved/Unused
200H–20FH	Game Port Control Registers
210H–277H	Reserved/Unused
278H–27FH	Parallel Port 3 Control, Status, and Data Registers
280H–2F7H	Reserved/Unused
2F8H–2FFH	Serial Port 2 Control, Status, and Data Registers
300H–36FH	Unused, Available To Add-In Adapters
370H-377H	Secondary Floppy Controller Control, Status, Data Registers
378H–37FH	Parallel Port 2 Control, Status, Data Registers
380H–3AFH	Unused, Available To Add-In Adapters
3B0H–3BAH	Miscellaneous MDA/EGA/VGA Registers
3BCH–3BFH	Parallel Port 1 Control, Status, and Data Registers
3C0H–3DFH	VGA Controller Registers
3E0H–3EFH	Unused, available to add-in adapters
3F0H–3F7H	Primary Floppy Controller Control, Data, and Status Registers
3F8H–3FFH	Serial Port 1 Control, Data, and Status Registers
400H–FFFFH	Unused, available to add-in adapters, system chipset
CFB–CFF	PCI host controller (PCI machines only)

As is the case with all Plug and Play resources, you need enumeration software that interrogates the Plug and Play BIOS device nodes in order to learn the allocation strategy for a particular system. An example enumerator appears in Chapter 3.

In the world of Plug and Play, we are not so much concerned with the historical I/O resource consumption of a PC/AT as with the resources reported by Plug and Play configuration management software. In the case of static motherboard devices, it is the task

of the Plug and Play BIOS to accurately deliver to the operating system level enumerator a device node that identifies exactly what devices are present and what resources that device consumes.

In a system that has no second or third parallel port, for example, the operating system enumerator would discover that all I/O ports within the ranges 378H-37FH and 3BCH-3BFH are not currently assigned. Potentially, the OS enumerator could assign these unused I/O ports to any Plug and Play device whose dynamic configurations fit within these ranges.

DMA Channel Usage

The *DMA*, or *Direct Memory Access* controller, provides four channels by which the system can read and write system memory, independent of any foreground processing. PC/AT compatible systems have two DMA controllers. The primary controller, which handles DMA levels zero through three, performs only byte-wide transfers. The secondary DMA controller, which handles DMA levels four through seven, performs only word sized transfers. As a result, DMA channels 0-3 can transfer a maximum of 64KB in a single operation, while channels 4-7 can transfer as much as 128KB at once.

The original PC/AT reserves DMA channel 0 for refreshing DRAM, channel 2 for the floppy disk controller, and channel 4 for cascading DMA request (DREQ) signals from the secondary controller to the primary.

Additionally, some systems are equipped with IDE drives that transfer data to and from system memory via yet another DMA channel. The Plug and Play BIOS reports DMA channel usage to the operating system via DMA descriptors, which is discussed in Chapter 3. In the meantime, refer to Table 2.4, which outlines DMA channel usage in an off-the-shelf PC/AT system.

Table 2.4. The DMA channel usage in an off-the-shelf PC/AT system.

DMA Channel	*Device*
0	PC/AT DRAM Refresh
1	Unused/Available To Add-In Adapters
2	Floppy Diskette Controller
3	Unused/Available To Add-In Adapters
4	Cascade Channel From Secondary DMA Controller
5	Unused/Available To Add-In Adapters
6	Unused/Available To Add-In Adapters
7	Unused/Available To Add-In Adapters

It seems simple enough to keep track of eight DMA channels, three of which usually are reserved for system devices. The situation becomes more complex when you consider devices that use DMA channels may be installed in the system. Both the floppy controller and DMA-driven IDE controller fall into this category.

Systems equipped with a dedicated, on-board floppy controller present no problem because there is no mechanism by which the DMA controller can be physically removed from the system. In this case, the system's Plug and Play BIOS contains a device node that simply reports that the DMA channel is non-dynamic, and has been assigned to the floppy controller.

Systems whose floppy controllers are removable present more of a problem to the Plug and Play solution because the Plug and Play BIOS cannot determine reliably the presence of the device. Therefore, the presence of the floppy controller must be recorded in the system's non-volatile storage via a Plug and Play BIOS `SetNode` function call. Remember that in the case of a removable, non-configurable device, such as a plug-in floppy controller that uses an IRQ, two I/O ranges, and a DMA channel, the Plug and Play BIOS merely acts as a holding tank for the device's resource information. The BIOS maintains the floppy controller's resource information as part of its non-volatile storage, which it reports during calls to `GetStaticResInfo`, or `ReadESCDInfo` if the function is supported.

Memory-Range Resources

The fourth and final type of system resource is the *memory range.* This nomenclature is somewhat misleading because the devices you are most concerned with in the Plug and Play arena are most often those that are ROM-based and contain no memory.

Be that as it may, the Plug and Play system must accurately identify those physical address ranges that have been consumed by DRAM, system firmware, expansion adapter firmware, and memory mapped devices. The accurate identification of memory ranges is crucial in order to resolve potential contentions between installed devices and software applications. For example, the operating system's EMS (Expanded Memory) driver, which pages extended DRAM in and out of virtual windows within the 384KB reserved area, must coexist with PCMCIA host bus adapters whose on-board address decoders operate in the same area.

Memory ranges are perhaps the most limited and widely desired resource within the system. The original PC/AT's memory range architecture, which has remained virtually unchanged since the design's inception, provides only 384KB of address space for system firmware, expansion ROM's, video ROM. Figure 2.2 displays the overall system map, including the hotly contested 384K reserved region that resides between `A0000H` and `FFFFFH` physical.

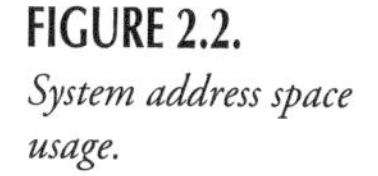

FIGURE 2.2.
System address space usage.

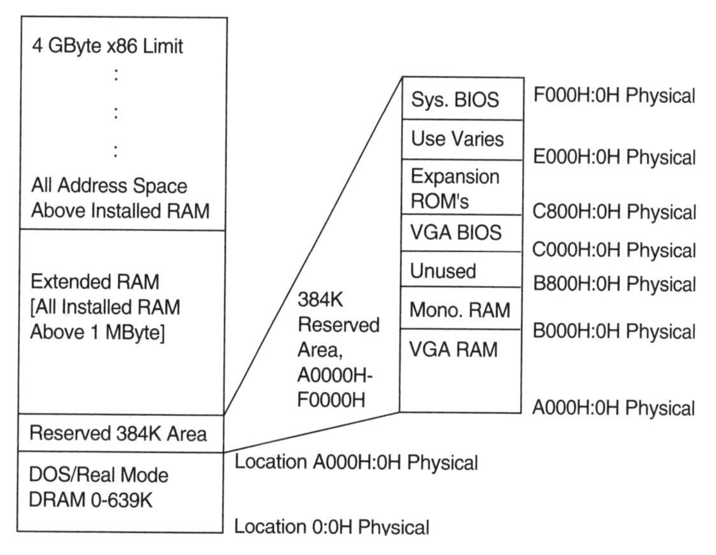

The process of enumerating system firmware and expansion adapters is the most difficult aspect of cataloging memory range usage. System DRAM, on the other hand, is the most straightforward consumer of addressable memory space. The system DRAM consumes all memory range space other than the 384K range between `0A0000H` and `F0000H` and that address space above installed memory.

The Plug and Play BIOS provides device nodes describing any memory ranges consumed by the system BIOS, on-board VGA BIOS, or any other non-dynamic, on-board firmware.

At the discretion of the operating system designer, Plug and Play memory enumerators can seek and size system DRAM using methods other than enumerating Plug and Play BIOS device nodes.

First, the memory resource enumerator can invoke software INT `15H` function `88H`, which returns the number of kilobytes of installed extended DRAM in the `AX` register. Because the `AX` register is only 16-bits wide, this limits INT `15H`'s memory reporting capability to 65535M, or 64MB of extended memory. Obviously, this method is of limited use in systems that contain more than 64MB of extended DRAM.

Secondly, some system BIOSes support the extended Microsoft INT `15H` function `E820H` (INT `15H`, `AX` equals `E820H`). This interrupt function returns the total amount of installed DRAM, a detailed map of address ranges, and the type of device to which the BIOS has allocated these ranges. This interrupt, although not supported by all system BIOS implementations, is gaining popularity and should be used if present.

Some authors of operating systems and enumerators, distrustful of the system BIOS' INT 15H function, turn to snooping out installed DRAM by executing sophisticated RAM detection algorithms. These algorithms write known patterns to location 0 of each physical 64KB segment of DRAM. If the algorithm reads back the pattern written, it assumes that this segment of RAM exists and increments the amount of total RAM installed by 64KB.

The Resourceful Plug and Play Device

Plug and Play devices earn their name by being able to dynamically occupy those resource holes left vacant by the basic system. In a complete Plug and Play system, the Plug and Play BIOS and operating system configures any Plug and Play adapters in such a way that their resource usage conflicts with neither that of the systemboard devices, nor any other adapters in the system. The family of Plug and Play devices that we are considering consists of the following:

- PCMCIA 2.*x* and higher compliant devices
- PCI 2.*x* and higher compliant devices
- Plug and Play ISA 1.*x* and higher compliant devices
- Plug and Play BIOS 1.0a and higher compliant system BIOS.

The Resourceful Plug and Play BIOS

At a minimum, the Plug and Play system is equipped with a Plug and Play BIOS. The Plug and Play BIOS maintains and reports resource usage for both systemboard devices and non-Plug and Play, or *legacy* ISA adapters via device node records. The Plug and Play BIOS also is responsible for selecting and launching IPL (Initial Program Load) devices from a pool of detected PCI, PCMCIA, or ISA devices.

Function of the Plug and Play BIOS

From the perspective of Plug and Play programmers, we regard the Plug and Play BIOS in two fashions. First, it is an adjunct to the standard PC/AT system BIOS in that it participates in the POST, or power-on sequence, of standard PC/AT device configuration, test, and initialization. In fact, the Plug and Play BIOS specification requires that the presence of a Plug and Play BIOS should in no way alter the system's PC/AT compatibility. During the boot sequence, the Plug and Play BIOS applies information supplied to it by the operating system during the previous runtime session in order to configure and initialize system devices.

Secondly, the Plug and Play BIOS provides a runtime operating system interface by which device driver software can interrogate or specify the allocation of resources to system devices. As part of its boot-time system enumeration process, the operating system issues repeated Plug and Play BIOS `GetNode` calls until it has retrieved all Plug and Play BIOS device nodes and thereby exhausted the BIOS' knowledge of system resource usage. The Plug and Play BIOS function interface is explained in Chapter 3.

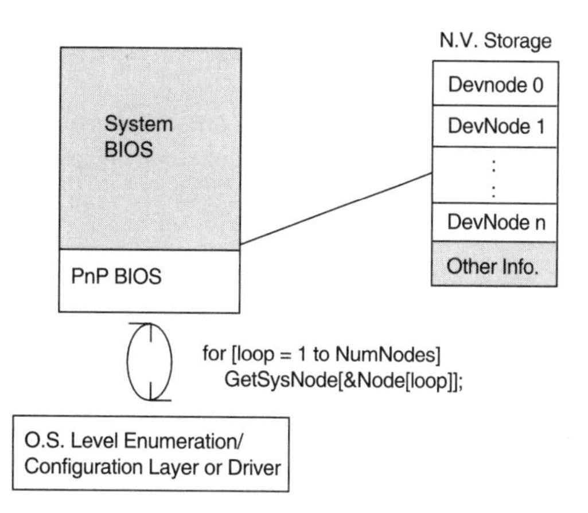

FIGURE 2.3.
Enumerating Plug and Play BIOS device nodes.

Internally, the Plug and Play BIOS contains simple enumeration and configuration functions that are capable of communicating with the PCI, Plug and Play ISA, and, in some cases, the PCMCIA bus. Because Plug and Play adapters store their particular configuration during a given runtime session, the Plug and Play BIOS need not maintain a record of the resources assigned to these devices. If the Plug and Play BIOS needs to determine which resources it has allocated to Plug and Play devices, it simply re-enumerates them and reconstructs the total system resource picture.

As an alternative to repeatedly enumerating system devices, many Plug and Play systems implement the ESCD (Extended System Configuration Data) interface, described in Chapter 7.

The ESCD interface serves two primary functions. First, it maintains the current allocation strategy for all statically assigned (such as legacy ISA, EISA, MCA, and systemboard) system resources in NVRAM. This increases the complexity of the system's firmware, yet simplifies the BIOS' or enumerator's task of getting a total system resource picture at any given time. Secondly, the ESCD mechanism allows operating system level configuration software to assign *locked configurations*, whereby the ESCD database specifies resource configurations for both static and Plug and Play adapters installed in the system.

At the discretion of the Plug and Play BIOS author, the BIOS may perform its own resource conflict resolution (that is, two or more devices requesting the same resource), or it may operate in tandem with the optional ESCD interface.

Because of code-size constraints, the Plug and Play BIOS leaves the chore of sophisticated resource conflict resolution to operating system enumerators that execute during the IPL sequence. Operating system level enumerators deal not only with devices reported by the Plug and Play BIOS, but also with those introduced at runtime, such as notebook docking stations and PCMCIA cards.

So, although the Plug and Play BIOS might resolve boot-time resource conflicts on its own, this task is much better served by the Plug and Play operating system, which is not limited by code size or the number of buses with which it is able to communicate.

Enumerating the Plug and Play BIOS

When we talk about enumerating the Plug and Play BIOS, we are concerned with retrieving all device resource allocation information about which the BIOS has knowledge. A standard Plug and Play BIOS maintains a pool of device nodes that specifies those resources belonging to systemboard devices and legacy ISA devices. If the system is equipped with optional ESCD extensions, its Plug and Play BIOS maintains an additional, NVRAM-based resource allocation database that might contain fixed resource configurations for Plug and Play devices.

As Plug and Play programmers, we treat the Plug and Play BIOS as follows: First, you locate the ROM-based Plug and Play BIOS signature header and validate its contents via a `checksum` byte located within the header structure. From this structure, you then retrieve either the real or protected mode address of the Plug and Play BIOS function interface entry point.

Next, you ask the Plug and Play BIOS for `NumNodes`, the number of device nodes present, and the size of the largest device node. Our enumerator uses this information to dynamically allocate the correct size buffer to receive the Plug and Play BIOS' information. Finally, you invoke the Plug and Play BIOS `GetNode` function `NumNodes` times, store the information into your newly allocated node buffer, and iteratively parse the nodes' contents.

In an ESCD-equipped system, the Plug and Play BIOS enumerates device resource allocation by directly accessing the Extended System Configuration Data block that resides in system NVRAM. The ESCD database consists of a group of logical slots whose resource information is maintained by an operating system level configuration utility.

The Resourceful PCI BIOS

Some Plug and Play systems are equipped with a high speed *PCI* (Peripheral Component Interconnect) bus that by specification supports devices whose resources are dynamically configurable. Sandwiched between the PCI bus and any system configuration software is the simple, yet robust PCI BIOS interface. Like the operating system, both the Plug and Play BIOS and system BIOS need to configure or enumerate PCI bus devices during the boot process. They do this by issuing calls to the PCI BIOS, which knows how to talk to PCI bus controller chipsets at the register level.

Devices that reside on the PCI bus adhere to a variety of electrical and mechanical requirements that are beyond the scope of this book, but are well detailed in the *PCI 2.x Specification* document, which is available in book form from the PCI SIG (Special Interest Group) (PCI Special Interest Group, Mail Stop JF2-51, 5200 N.E. Elam Young Parkway, Hillsboro, OR 97124-6497). The PCI BIOS, on the other hand, is of direct importance to you as a Plug and Play programmer, and is documented separately in the *PCI BIOS Specification*, also available through the PCI SIG.

Function of the PCI BIOS

The primary responsibility of the PCI BIOS is to provide programmers with a function interface that abstracts the nature of the underlying bus controller hardware, which differs from system to system. Unlike with the ISA bus, the PCI bus uses one of two mechanisms for reading and writing configuration registers and only the system's PCI BIOS knows which mechanism to use and which PCI registers to access.

In addition to converting the caller's parameters to the correct mechanism during a bus I/O operation, the PCI BIOS also provides a uniform interface for both real and protected mode applications. You later learn in more detail about the PCI BIOS interface, but first read about how devices appear on the bus.

PCI devices reside in logical slots on the PCI bus. Each logical PCI slot consists of a `100H` register configuration space. PCI-compliant adapters are responsible for responding to I/O reads and writes to each register in its own `100H` location slot. According to the PCI specification, the first `40H` registers within a particular PCI slot must adhere to the format presented in Table 2.4.

Table 2.4. The format for the 40H standard registers at the start of a logical PCI slot.

Offset	*Value*
x00H	Vendor ID
x02H	Device ID
x04H	Command
x06H	Status
x08H	Revision ID
x09H	Device Programming Interface
x0AH	Device Subclass Type
x0BH	Device Base Class Type
x0CH	Cache Line Size
x0DH	Latency Timer
x0EH	Header Type
x0FH	BIST (Built In Self-Test)
10H–27H	(Base Address Registers)
28H–2FH	Reserved
30H–33H	Expansion ROM Base Address
34H–3BH	Reserved
3CH	Maximum Latency
3DH	Minimum Grant
3EH	Interrupt Pin
3FH	Interrupt Line

A device known as the PCI bridge or host controller controls all I/O cycles that occur between the system CPU and the physical PCI bus. As mentioned previously, PCI bus controllers differ greatly between manufacturers, and as a Plug and Play programmer, you have no knowledge of how to communicate directly with devices in any PCI slot. You should rely on the fact that the PCI BIOS works correctly and avoid trying to deal with systems at the chipset level.

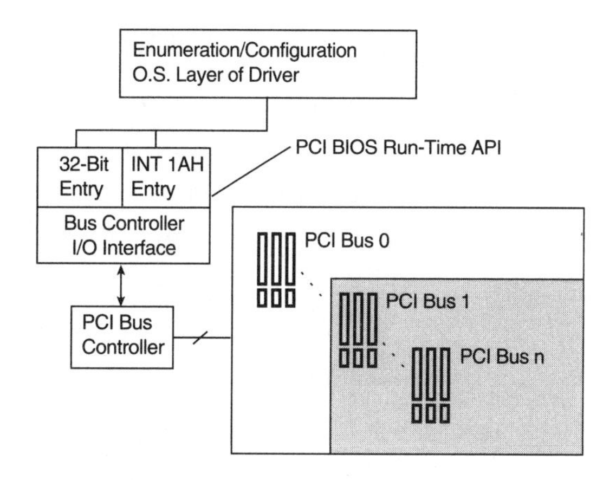

FIGURE 2.4.
Enumerating the PCI bus.

Enumerating the PCI Bus

Unlike the ISA bus, the PCI bus is hierarchical in nature, which simply means that the PCI system can contain multiple PCI buses, each stemming from the system's root PCI bus. In order to correctly enumerate the PCI bus, you first must determine whether a PCI BIOS is present within the system. Fortunately, the PCI BIOS provides a mechanism for detecting not only that the BIOS is present, but also how many buses are present in the system.

Detecting the presence of a PCI BIOS within a system is simplified by the PCI BIOS, which provides both an INT `1AH` and a 32-bit service entry point for callers searching for such support.

The simplest way to detect a PCI BIOS is by issuing software INT `1AH` with the following parameters:

```
AH = B1H
AL = 01H
```

Upon exit, the registers contain the following values:

`EDX = 'PCI '` or `50434920H` if a PCI BIOS is present

`AH` if `AH = 0` and `EDX = 'PCI '`, a PCI BIOS is present

If `AH = 0` and `EDX <> 'PCI '`, a PCI BIOS is not present

If AH <> 0, a PCI BIOS is not present, !0 equals PCI BIOS not present

Register	Bits	Value
AL	Bit [0]	= 1 if configuration mechanism #1 is supported
		= 0 if configuration mechanism #1 is not supported
	Bit [1]	= 1 if configuration mechanism #2 is supported
		= 0 if configuration mechanism #2 is not supported
	Bits [3:2]	= 0
	Bit [4]	= 1 if special cycles are supported by mechanism #1
		= 0 if special cycles are not supported by mechanism #1
	Bit [5]	= 1 if special cycles are supported by mechanism #2
		= 0 if special cycles are not supported by mechanism #2
	Bits [7:6]	= 0
BH		= major revision level of the PCI BIOS interface in BCD
BL		= minor revision level of the PCI BIOS interface in BCD
CL		= number of the last PCI bus in the system (0-based)
Carry flag		= 1 if no PCI BIOS is present
		= 0 if a PCI BIOS is present

Applications searching for a PCI BIOS must examine the CF (carry flag) bit, AX register, and EDX register in order to correctly determine whether a PCI BIOS is present in the system.

Alternatively, if your Plug and Play system supports the PCI bus, it supports system 32-bit services, which provide applications the capability to invoke system firmware from the flat-mode protected mode environment. The presence of 32-bit services does not guarantee that a PCI BIOS exists in the system because the PCI BIOS is not the only interface to use this special calling mechanism. Therefore, it's more straightforward to first search for the PCI BIOS using INT 1AH, although both methods produce the same effect.

To find your system's PCI BIOS via the 32-bit services mechanism, you first must determine whether your system supports these services. This is done by searching for the ASCII string _32_ on any 16-bit boundary within the range E0000H–F0000H physical. Once your application has located this string, it must validate the accompanying structure by performing a byte checksum of all 16 bytes within the paragraph where the _32_ identifier has been found.

Only after you locate and validate the 32-bit services directory can you issue calls to the 32-bit physical address that resides at location 4 within the services' directory. Your application issues the PCI BIOS presence detection call using the same parameters as the equivalent INT 1AH function shown previously. The 32-bit services directory is outlined in Table 2.5.

Table 2.5. 32-bit services directory.

Offset	*Description*	*Size*
00H	Signature string in ASCII (_32_) Bytes as they appear in memory: Offset 00H:_ Offset 01H:3 Offset 02H:2 Offset 03H:_	4 bytes
04H	32-bit physical entry point for the system 32-bit services	4 bytes
08H	Revision level for the 32-bit services	1 byte
09H	Length of this structure in paragraph (16-byte) units	1 byte
0AH	checksum byte for this entire structure	1 byte
0BH	Reserved, each byte must be zero	5 bytes

Once you determine that a PCI BIOS exists in the target machine, you are free to issue any other PCI BIOS function call either via the INT 1AH or 32-bit services entry points.

The process of enumerating all resources used by PCI devices involves scanning iteratively all installed buses (using the last bus number returned by the PCI presence system service) and all slots on each of the system's PCI buses. Later in this book, you will see an example that performs this function.

The Resourceful Plug and Play ISA Device

The Plug and Play ISA device is a new variation of standard ISA adapters that is capable of having its resources configured while residing on a standard ISA bus. Both the form factor and pinout of Plug and Play ISA adapters are identical to their non-Plug and Play ancestors, the legacy adapters which gain their configuration from switches and jumper straps.

Despite its aging interface and (by modern standards) mediocre performance, the ISA bus has survived because its simplicity and capability to adequately service slower peripherals, such as communication ports and sound boards. The introduction of the Plug and Play ISA technology enables adapter manufacturers to carry forth into the era of Plug and Play existing ISA designs without the additional worries of new mechanical form factors and markedly different electrical characteristics.

Of course, the additional hardware needed to retrofit an existing design to meet the Plug and Play ISA specification introduces extra logic (approximately 4,000 gates) and cost to the adapter; therefore, adapter vendors must decide whether the marketability of a Plug and Play ISA adapter outweighs its additional design and cost requirements. In any case, it's clear that the ISA adapter has yet to see its last day in the spotlight.

Function of the Plug and Play ISA Device

As is the case with other types of Plug and Play devices, there must be a configurator utility in the system capable of identifying, enumerating, and configuring Plug and Play ISA adapters. In a compliant Plug and Play system, the configurator can reside within the Plug and Play BIOS, the operating system enumeration layer, or in both places. Because Plug and Play ISA devices can be configured at any time, the operating system can modify any resources allocated to Plug and Play ISA devices by the Plug and Play BIOS.

At power-on time, both the Plug and Play ISA-specific logic and device-specific logic on each Plug and Play ISA device in the system are inactive, awaiting isolation and configuration by a Plug and Play ISA device enumerator in the BIOS or operating system. One important exception to this rule concerns bootable Plug and Play ISA devices. These devices (that is, disk controllers and bootable network cards) power on in a fully configured state because the software required to reconfigure them may only reside at the operating system level, and cannot execute until the system has booted. The exception, which allows bootable Plug and Play ISA devices to power on in a fully configured state, ensures that these devices will operate properly in non-Plug and Play systems, or systems that support Plug and Play ISA adapters only at the operating-system level.

Plug and Play ISA adapters are designed to respond to three new registers, the `ADDRESS`, `WRITE_DATA`, and `READ_DATA` registers. Both the Plug and Play BIOS and operating system enumeration/configuration utilities communicate with the Plug and Play ISA's Plug and Play interface through these three registers. These auto-configuration ports are described in Table 2.6.

Table 2.6. The Plug and Play ISA bus auto-configuration ports.

Register	*Description*
`ADDRESS`	I/O location `279H` (Parallel port status register), write-only
`WRITE_DATA`	I/O location `A79H` (`ADDRESS + 800H`), write-only
`READ_DATA`	I/O location is relocatable within the range `203H-3FFH` (read-only)

A Plug and Play ISA device powers on in an inactive state called *Wait For Key* state. In Wait For Key state, the device is waiting for system software to issue the initiation key sequence to the `ADDRESS` and `WRITE_DATA` configuration ports. During the system's POST, or Power On Self Test sequence, the system BIOS' Plug and Play ISA configurator generates the initiation key sequence in order to place all Plug and Play ISA adapters into Isolation state.

When an adapter first enters Isolation state, its CSN (Card Select Number) is zero. After an adapter is in Isolation state, it cannot progress to any further states until the configurator has assigned it a unique CSN.

The configurator isolates a Plug and Play ISA adapter by reading and validating the adapter's 72-bit Serial Identification Header, which contains a 32-bit Vendor ID, a unique 32-bit serial number, and an 8-bit `checksum`. The Plug and Play ISA protocol is designed in such a way that if there are multiple Plug and Play ISA adapters in a system, they will gradually *drop out* of the isolation sequence until just one adapter remains. When the configurator has successfully isolated a Plug and Play ISA adapter, it assigns to that adapter a CSN and continues the isolation sequence until no more adapters respond to the isolation sequence. After an adapter has been assigned a CSN, it no longer participates in the isolation sequence.

Directly after having been assigned a CSN during the configurator's isolation sequence, the Plug and Play ISA adapter enters *Config state*, during which the configurator can read and write the adapter's resource information. The configurator may choose to configure the adapter at this time, or it may transfer the adapter to Sleep state, in which case it can isolate all system Plug and Play ISA adapters before trying to assign resources for them.

Adapters that have been assigned CSN numbers now are free to transition between the Sleep, Isolation, and Config states. Once initially isolated, Plug and Play ISA adapters spend most of their time in Sleep state. In this state, they perform their intended tasks on the ISA bus until such time that a configurator issues them a `Wake` command. Figure 2.5 outlines the various states transitions that Plug and Play ISA adapters can perform.

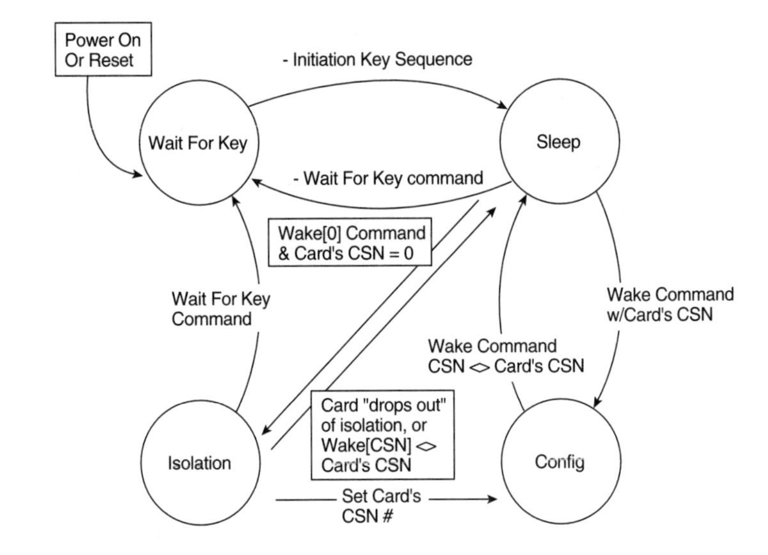

FIGURE 2.5.
Plug and Play ISA device states.

Enumerating The Plug and Play ISA Adapter

Plug and Play devices that have been configured and enabled by the Plug and Play BIOS or some other enumeration/configuration utility operate as standard ISA devices. The system configurator can, however, isolate and configure these adapters at any time. You discover later that the process of configuring a Plug and Play ISA adapter at runtime involves close coordination between the configurator and any device drivers associated with that adapter.

First, look about the somewhat simpler task of enumerating the Plug and Play ISA bus. Each Plug and Play ISA adapter contains resource descriptors that describe the adapter's current and possible resource configurations. In order to read this information, you first must get the adapter into Config state. There are two methods for getting a Plug and Play ISA adapter into Config state. First, the adapter automatically enters Config state when you assign it a logical CSN (Card Select Number) during the isolation sequence. Secondly, you can force the card to enter Config state by issuing a `Wake` command with that card's particular CSN.

The second method, by which you use the `Wake` command to begin configuring a Plug and Play ISA adapter, is the preferable method. The first method suggests that you still are in the middle of isolating adapters and don't have a total picture of which system resources have been allocated to the system's Plug and Play ISA adapters as a group.

In Chapter 4, you look in depth at the structure of a Plug and Play ISA adapter's on-board configuration space. For now, examine the overall strategy that an operating system could use to enumerate and configure the system's Plug and Play ISA adapters:

- Enumerate all other Plug and Play devices in the system in order to learn the current allocation of system resources to non-Plug and Play ISA devices
- Issue the initiation key sequence to put all Plug and Play ISA cards into Sleep state
- Isolate all Plug and Play ISA adapters one at a time, assigning each adapter a CSN. When assigned a CSN, adapters enter Config state
- Interrogate current and possible resource assignments from each Plug and Play ISA adapter and store these in a table (Adapters must be in Config state)
- Devise a conflict-free resource mapping strategy for each Plug and Play ISA adapter, reconfiguring Plug and Play devices on other buses if necessary
- Reprogram each Plug and Play ISA adapter's configuration space to its new resource allocation
- Issue a `Wake` command with `CSN = 0` to release all adapters to Sleep state

The Resourceful PCMCIA Bus

The last, but certainly not least, member in the family of Plug and Play adapters is the *PCMCIA device.* PCMCIA devices adhere to the PCMCIA (Personal Computer Memory Card International Association) architecture, which was originally proposed as a means of introducing small form-factor extended RAM to systems such as notebooks and embedded PC's. Recently, this technology has exploded with such popularity that it now includes ranging in functionality and complexity from the simplest SRAM cards to complete data acquisition and control, or even multimedia cards.

PCMCIA devices present entirely new challenges for Plug and Play programmers because they are hot-pluggable. While the user gains the luxury of being able to insert or remove PCMCIA devices at any time, the operating system is saddled with the task of managing resources in a runtime environment.

The Plug and Play operating system interacts with PCMCIA devices via the Card Services layer, which in turn invokes a variety of controller-specific functions within the Socket Services layer. Typically, Plug and Play Card Services exist in the form of an operating system level device driver or enumerator/configurator module, whereas Socket Services exist either as a device driver or system firmware-based module. Figure 2.6 shows these layers in a more easily understood, graphic form.

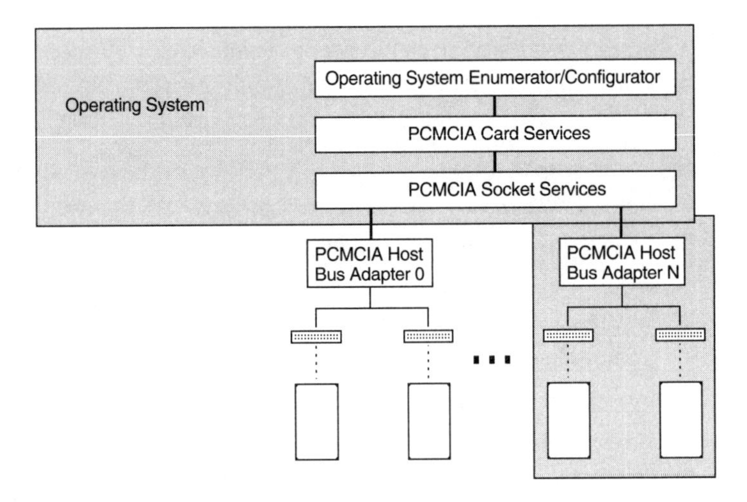

FIGURE 2.6.
The PCMCIA architecture.

NOTE

Both card and Socket Services are defined in detail by the PCMCIA Committee's *PCMCIA Socket Services Specification* and *PCMCIA Card Services Specification* documents, respectively. For more information contact the following:

Personal Computer Memory Card International Association
1030 East Duane Avenue, Suite G
Sunnyvale, CA 94086

Functionality of the PCMCIA Bus

At the hardware level, the PCMCIA bus consists of one or more controllers, each of which can support one or more sockets into which PCMCIA cards are inserted. PCMCIA resources fall into one of two general categories: those used by the controller and those used by the PCMCIA cards.

The PCMCIA controller is a stand-alone legacy ISA, systemboard, Plug and Play ISA or PCI device, and its resource usage is governed by the Plug and Play interface for the particular bus on which the controller resides. If the controller resides on a Plug and Play ISA compliant adapter, for example, the Plug and Play BIOS enumerates the controller during POST as it would with any Plug and Play ISA adapter. As you learned already, the Plug and Play BIOS first isolates the device, and then interrogates its assigned and possible resource blocks, and finally assigns resources to the adapter based on what's available in the system.

The PCMCIA card, on the other hand, is only capable of residing on the PCMCIA bus. The task of managing PCMCIA card resources is limited by the fact that the system must first enumerate and configure the PCMCIA controller before it is able to communicate with individual cards on the bus.

For this and other reasons, PCMCIA software almost always resides at the operating system level and executes only after the operating system has begun its boot process.

The PCMCIA software suite is broken down into the following layers:

> *Socket Services*—The lowest layer in the PCMCIA software architecture. Socket Services provides a hardware independent interface for configuring and interrogating PCMCIA sockets and controllers in a system. The functions that Socket Services provides are vendor-independent and are described in the PCMCIA committee's *Socket Services Specification.*
>
> *Card Services*—A client of Socket Services, this layer translates card-specific information among applications and PCMCIA controllers or cards plugged into the controllers' sockets. Importantly, the Card Services driver is the recipient of card status change interrupts, which signal that a PCMCIA card has either been inserted in, or removed from a socket. When a card insertion or removal occurs, the Card Services layer is responsible for allocating or deallocating resources for the socket in which the status change occurred.
>
> *Client Drivers*—Client drivers provide operating system and device specific support beyond what is possible via the Card Services interface. The FFS (Flash File System) driver, for example, establishes itself as a block device driver within the operating system, and manages installed Flash ROM PCMCIA cards in such a way that they appear to be additional removable drives.
>
> *Memory Technology Drivers* (MTDs)—MTDs are Card Services clients that handle erase/write cycles for various vendors' Flash RAM PCMCIA cards. Installed MTDs communicate with both the Flash File System and Card Services layers. Also, because Flash RAM cells have a limited write cycle lifetime, MTDs provide erase leveling algorithms that distribute data reads and writes to all regions within the RAM cards storage space.
>
> *ATA Drivers*—This Card Services' client, like the FFS client driver, establishes itself as a block device driver within the operating system, and logically structures any installed ATA drive-compatible rotating or RAM-based PCMCIA devices as additional system drives.

When discussing resource allocation for PCMCIA devices, you need to be able to differentiate between adapters and cards. An *adapter* is a systemboard or bus-resident circuit that provides sockets with an interface to the system's host bus. A PCMCIA *card* is the credit card-sized peripheral that the user inserts into any of the system's sockets.

Resource requirements for PCMCIA adapters and cards differ in many respects. The adapter requires one or more I/O ranges for communicating adapter configuration parameters back and forth to the system's Socket Services. Additionally, the adapter uses a single IRQ to signal clients of Socket Services that a `card status change` event has occurred. Finally, the adapter reserves one or more memory ranges that it will allocate to those cards that communicate via memory-mapped RAM.

NOTE

Card status change is fancy terminology that simply means the user has inserted or removed a card.

The resource requirements of a PCMCIA card varies from case to case. PCMCIA modems, for example, typically require a single IRQ and I/O range while network adapters usually require one IRQ channel and one or more memory windows for swapping packet information.

The process by which PCMCIA cards are assigned is as follows. When a user inserts a PCMCIA card into one of the adapter's sockets, the adapter's controller issues a `card status change` interrupt. Card Services intercepts this interrupt and calls Socket Services to determine whether the status change occurred as a result of a card insertion or removal.

If the status change signals a removal event, Card Services invokes the system's Configuration Manager to return the device's resources to the system pool. Otherwise, Card Services invokes Socket Services to read the device's tuples and identify its resource requirements. These tuples (identification records) are records within the card that reveal to Card Services such information as Vendor ID strings, device capabilities, and resource requirements.

Once Card Services has determined the resource needs of the newly installed card, it issues a call to the OS Configuration Manager to determine which system resources remain. If there is a match between the card's needs and the system's leftover resources, then Card Services configures the PCMCIA card and notifies the Configuration Manager of which resources the card now is assigned. The Configuration Manager, in turn, removes these resources from the available system pool.

Enumerating the PCMCIA Bus

Card Services, the primary Socket Services client, maintains a complete record of system resource usage, and updates this record each time a PCMCIA card is inserted or removed from the machine.

Card Services assumes the role of a small scale system enumerator in order to service its client drivers that have no mechanism for calling the system's Configuration Manager driver to manage their card's resources. When the user inserts or removes a card from one of the system's PCMCIA sockets, the PCMCIA controller issues a card status change, which Card Services intercepts.

Upon intercepting a `card status change` interrupt, Card Services invokes the `call-back` function for each client driver that has registered as a Card Services client. Each client driver in the call-back list examines the CIS (Card Information Structure) that belongs the card that was just inserted or removed. If the client driver is responsible for the PCMCIA card undergoing a status change, it issues a series of calls to Card Services to acquire or release resources for that particular card.

In the current implementation of Plug and Play, it is not necessary for any outside resource allocation monitoring application to be able to determine those resources currently allocated to a particular PCMCIA card. Instead, Card Services acts as a client of the system's Configuration Manager, and allocates resources using the same calls that the monitoring program would use.

If you are writing a PCMCIA client driver, Card Services will handle the chore of allocating resources to your card. This solution is superior one in which individual client drivers trying to manage resources for their own cards because the task of enumerating remaining system resources falls on the shoulders of a central process, the Configuration Manager. If client drivers were to communicate directly with the Configuration Manager, this would violate the state of Card Services' resource information, and the resource allocation process for other active PCMCIA cards might fail.

3

The Plug and Play BIOS

The Plug and Play BIOS is a new, integral member of the PC/AT system firmware space, with importance equal to that of the system BIOS, PCI BIOS, power management firmware, and video BIOS. In addition to participating in the POST, or Power On Self Test sequence, the Plug and Play BIOS reports system events, such as docks and undocks, and provides runtime event handling and resource reporting services to operating system components such as the configuration manager.

Plug and Play BIOS Installation Check

Every compliant Plug and Play system contains an *installation check header*, a table that serves two important purposes. First, it signals to the operating system that the target system supports Plug and Play, and second, it supplies the operating system with the physical location and capabilities of the system's Plug and Play BIOS.

The installation check header resides on a 16-byte (paragraph) boundary within the `F0000H-FFFF0H` region. It may be separate from or part of the system's actual Plug and Play BIOS. Figure 3.1 details the location of the Plug and Play BIOS within the system's firmware address space.

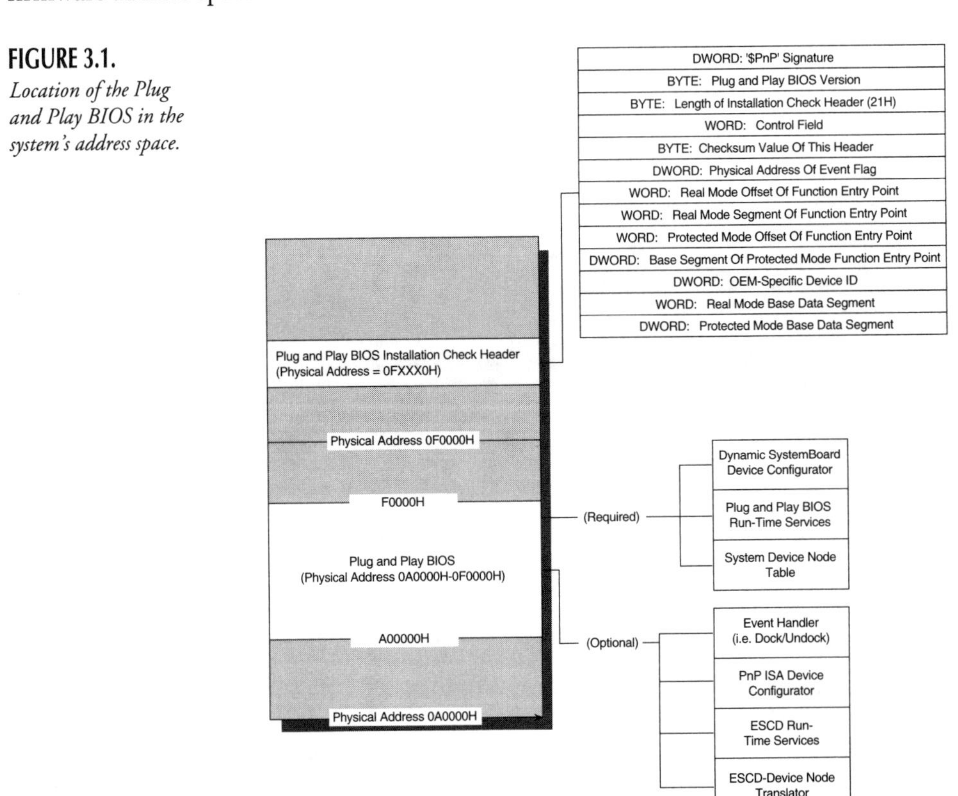

FIGURE 3.1.
Location of the Plug and Play BIOS in the system's address space.

Table 3.1 displays the format of the Plug and Play BIOS Installation Check Header.

Table 3.1. The Plug and Play BIOS Installation Check Header.

Offset	*Size*	*Description*
00H	DWORD	Plug and Play BIOS Signature, `$PnP`
04H	BYTE	Plug and Play BIOS Version Adherence
05H	BYTE	Length of installation check header (`021H`)
06H	WORD	Control Field (Supported Plug and Play BIOS features)
08H	BYTE	`Checksum` byte for this structure (in a valid installation check header, the `checksum` should equal `0`)
09H	DWORD	Physical address of the Plug and Play BIOS event flag
0DH	WORD	Real-mode offset of Plug and Play BIOS API entry point
0FH	WORD	Real-mode segment of Plug and Play BIOS API entry point
11H	WORD	Protected-mode offset of Plug and Play BIOS API entry point
13H	DWORD	Base segment of 16-bit protected mode Plug and Play BIOS entry point
17H	DWORD	OEM-specific system information
1BH	WORD	Real-mode base data segment
1DH	DWORD	Protected-mode base data segment
21H	BYTE	Reserved

You can determine whether a Plug and Play BIOS is present by searching for the string `$PnP` on each 16-byte boundary within the region `F0000H-FFFF0H`. When you find this structure, you should verify that it has a valid `checksum` by adding each of the bytes within the structure. If the sum of the `21H` bytes is zero, you can assume that the header and its contents are valid. The following code locates the Plug and Play Installation Check Header within the `F0000H` segment of the system's address space:

```
void far * GetFuncEntry() {
     (unsigned long)PNPHdr = 0x0F0000000;
     do {
      if (!_fstrncmp("$PnP",PNPHdr->Signature,4))
      return ((unsigned long far *) PNPHdr->RealEntry);
      (unsigned long)PNPHdr += 0x10000;
     } while (PNPHdr);
     return(0);
}
```

The Plug and Play BIOS Device Node

Device nodes are records that the Plug and Play BIOS and operating system use to communicate systemboard device configuration and resource allocation. The device node is a structure that consists of two basic parts—a 12-byte header field and a variable length group of three resource records. The system's legacy ISA information is stored in a structure that effectively is a headerless device node. Many of the resource descriptor definitions described here apply not only to device nodes, but to the legacy ISA resource information descriptor as well.

The form in which the Plug and Play BIOS stores legacy ISA information and system device nodes within the BIOS and its associated NVRAM is at the discretion of the developer. During the static resource enumeration process, the Plug and Play BIOS is only responsible for transferring compliant device node and legacy information to operating system-supplied buffers.

Similarly, applications never examine the Plug and Play BIOS' contents directly. This storage independence is crucial for Plug and Play BIOS implementations that support the ESCD extensions because it frees BIOS developers from having to directly maintain and translate between two completely different resource structures—the ESCD slot record and the device node.

TIP

Systems equipped with the optional ESCD function set may internally contain no device nodes; however, their ESCD slot records contain the information necessary to build a simulated group of device node records. ESCD-equipped systems may maintain both the ESCD and device node structure groups, or they might build device node records on-the-fly and copy these nodes into an operating system-supplied buffer during enumerator-issued `GetNode` calls.

Table 3.2 details the fields within a systemboard device node.

Table 3.2. The format of the systemboard device node.

Offset	*Field Name*	*Size*
0	NodeSize	WORD
2	NodeHandle	BYTE
3	DeviceID	DWORD
7	DevBaseClass	BYTE

Offset	*Field Name*	*Size*
8	DevSubType	BYTE
9	DevInterfaceType	BYTE
10	DevAttribute	WORD
11	ResAlloc	VARIABLE
11+	PossibleConfig	VARIABLE sizeof(ResAlloc)
11+	CompatibleIDs	VARIABLE sizeof(ResAlloc)+sizeof(PossibleConfig)

Following are the fields within a device node:

`NodeSize` Size of this device node in bytes

`NodeHandle` A unique number assigned to this node by the Plug and Play BIOS for purposes of identifying this node

`DeviceID` A compressed 7-byte EISA-style product ID string that identifies the device to which this node corresponds. See the list entitled Device IDs in Appendix A.

The four bytes within an EISA ID adhere to the format shown in Table 3.3.

Table 3.3. The four bytes within an EISA ID.

Offset	*Description*
0	Bits [7]—Always 0
	Bits [6:2]—First character of the three character manufacturer code
	Bits [1:0]—Upper two bits of the second manufacturer code character
1	Bits [7:5]—Lower three bits of the second manufacturer code character
	Bits [4:0]—Third character of the manufacturer code
2	Bits [7:4]—First hexidecimal digit of the product ID number
	Bits [4:0]—Second hexidecimal digit of the product ID number
3	Bits [7:4]—Third and final hexidecimal digit of the product ID number
	Bits [4:0]—One digit product revision character

In their uncompressed form, EISA-style product ID's appear as three uppercase ASCII digits followed by four hexadecimal digits, such as `PNP0303`, which is the device ID for the system keyboard controller device.

The following C function uncompresses EISA IDs into string form:

```
char * DecodeID(char * buffer, DWORD EISAID) {
     buffer[0] = (char) (((EISAID & 0x007CL) >> 2) + 0x40);
     buffer[1] = (char) ((((EISAID & 0x0003L) << 3) |
          ((EISAID & 0x0000E000L) >> 13) ) + 0x40);
     buffer[2] = (char) (((EISAID & 0x1F00L) >> 8) + 0x40);
     sprintf(buffer+3, "%02X%02X",
          (BYTE) ((EISAID & 0x00FF0000L) >> 16),
          (BYTE) ((EISAID & 0xFF000000L) >> 24));
     return(buffer) ;
}
```

`DevBaseType`

In addition to the `DeviceID` field, the `DevBaseType` serves as a mechanism for identifying the type of device to which the device node belongs. The `DevBaseType` is used in conjunction the `DevSubType` and `DevInterfaceType` bytes that follow it. The `DevBaseType` describes the most general class of devices to which the device belongs. A base type of `7`, for example, signifies that the device is a communications device. In order to determine exactly what type of communications device to which the node belongs, you also must examine the `DevSubType` and `DevInterfaceType` bytes. A complete listing of the device base type, sub-base type, and device interface type class codes appears in Appendix A.

`DevSubType`

As mentioned earlier, the `DevSubType` field identifies a subtype for the device to which the node belongs. If `DevBaseType = 7` and `DevSubType = 1`, for example, you know that the device is some kind of parallel device. By looking at the `DevInterfaceType`, you can determine exactly what kind of parallel device the node belongs to.

`DevInterfaceType`

The `DevInterfaceType` field most explicitly defines the class of device to which the node belongs. If you take the device mentioned previously, you know that the node belongs to some kind of a parallel device. Currently there are three types of parallel devices identifiable by class codes. For the purpose of example, following is a list of the various types of parallel port devices and the three class codes that correspond to each device.

NOTE

Enumerator applications can identify devices via either the EISA-style device ID field or the device class codes contained in the device node header. As shown in Appendix A, class codes describe the capabilities of a particular device in a generic fashion, with no regard to the device's manufacturer. Device IDs, which also appear in Appendix A, sometimes identify the device's manufacturer or OEM and the exact model number for a particular device.

It may surprise you to learn that some devices appear only in the device class code list, or alternatively, only in the device ID list. For example, the device class code list from Intel provides entries for 386-class and newer CPU's, whereas the device node list supplied by Microsoft indicates no such devices. Your best strategy for identifying devices is to first try to match the device node's class bytes to those shown in Appendix A. If the information you obtain from the device class list is inadequate, you should next try to find the device's ID in the Microsoft list. Should the device not appear in either list, it may be non-compliant.

Table 3.4 Device Class Code example, the currently available parallel port device class codes.

Device Description	`DevBaseType`	`DevSubType`	`DevInterfaceType`
Generic AT Parallel Port	7	1	0
PS/2 Parallel Port	7	1	1
ECP Capable Parallel Port	7	1	2

`DevAttribute`—The device attribute field describes various capabilities and properties of the device to which the node belongs. These bits are defined as follows:

Bit	*Description*
Bits `[15:9]`	Unused (`0`)
Bits `[8:7]`	(`00`) = Device is configurable; however, the configuration parameters only take effect when the system is rebooted
	(`01`) = Device is configurable at runtime
	(`10`) = Unused/Reserved
	(`11`) = Device can only be configured at runtime

continues

Bit	*Description*
Bit [6]	0 = Device is non-removable
	1 = Device is removable
Bit [5]	0 = Device is not a docking station
	1 = Device is a docking station
Bit [4]	0 = Device cannot be the primary IPL device
	1 = Device is capable of being the primary IPL device
Bit [3]	0 = Device cannot be the primary input device
	1 = Device is capable of being the primary input device
Bit [2]	0 = Device cannot be the primary output device
	1 = Device is capable of being the primary output device
Bit [1]	0 = Device is not configurable
	1 = Device is configurable
Bit [0]	0 = Device cannot be disabled
	1 = Device is capable of being disabled

As you might expect, some of the fields within the `DevAttribute` word deserve better description.

Bits `[8:7]`, for example, describe devices that can be configured at runtime as opposed to devices that can be configured *only* at runtime. On-board PCMCIA controllers are good examples of devices that can be configured *only* at runtime because their resource allocation is handled by device drivers that execute only after the Plug and Play operating system has loaded them. Devices such as on-board multimedia controllers might be configured during the Plug and Play BIOS POST sequence, however, the operating system is free to reconfigure these devices and notify their associated drivers of any resource reconfigurations.

Bit `[4]` signals whether the device is capable of being the primary IPL device for the system. The Plug and Play BIOS gives the highest priority to IPL devices when allocating resources during POST. To do otherwise might prevent the system from booting at all. If a device is not capable of being the system IPL device, the Plug and Play BIOS assigns it resources after all IPL-capable devices have been successfully configured.

Bit `[0]` in the `DevAttribute` word may at first seem equally puzzling. This bit specifies whether the device can be disabled. This feature is crucial in describing devices that cannot or do not participate in the IPL sequence. By disabling a device, the Plug and Play BIOS is free to allocate that device's resources to other, higher priority devices, such as boot devices.

This does not mean that the device will not be able to operate properly in a Plug and Play system. Instead, the Plug and Play BIOS leaves the task of assigning resources to this type of device to the much more sophisticated Plug and Play operating system device enumerators and configurators, which exhaustively check and cross-check resource allocations for all devices in the system. Assuming that there are any resources left in the system at boot time, the success of a disable-able device to configure and operate properly depends solely on the range of configurations it can support:

Resource Descriptors

Resource descriptors are variable-length structures that reveal exactly the resources a device has been, or can be configured to use. This type of structure can appear in both the Allocated Resource Descriptor Block and the Possible Resource Descriptor Block within a device node. Resource descriptors also appear in the configuration header within Plug and Play ISA adapters and devices. As a result, the descriptor definitions shown here also apply to this book's discussion of Plug and Play ISA adapters, which occurs in Chapter 5.

System resources invariably fall into one of four specific categories: IRQs, I/O ranges, memory ranges, and DMA levels. Table 3.5 outlines the conventions to which future discussions of resources will adhere.

Table 3.5. Conventions for referring to system resources.

IRQ Level 0-15	Interrupt ReQuest level 0 through 15 (decimal)
DMA Level 0-7	DMA level 0 through 7
I/O Range `0-3FFH`	I/O Range `0` through `3FFH` (Hexadecimal)
Memory Range *xxxxxxxx*H-*yyyyyyyy*H	Any memory range in the physical address space between *xxxxxxxx*H and *yyyyyyyyy*H (Hexadecimal)

Because device nodes contain a section to describe the currently allocated device configuration as well as a section outlining possible configurations, the range within a resource descriptor can have two meanings. When it appears in the allocated resource block, the range signifies resources currently being used by the device. In the block of possible configurations, the range applies to alternate configurations to which the device could be programmed.

Remember that the format for resource descriptors is shared between system device nodes, Plug and Play ISA adapters, and the legacy ISA resource node. The use of a common format simplifies the task of enumerating system resource usage. Other Plug and Play devices, such as PCI and PCMCIA adapters, cannot be represented by resource descriptors because they return resource usage information that doesn't fit within the framework of the device node structure.

For the sake of flexibility, resource descriptors have a short and long format that are distinctly different. A short format descriptor is distinguishable by a `0` in its tag bit, or bit `7` of the first byte of the descriptor. In all long format descriptors, the tag bit permanently is set to a `1`. If you are writing an enumerator that parses resource descriptors, you first must test the tag bit and then switch to a short or long format descriptor parser. The following code excerpt performs this fundamental test.

```
typedef struct {

     WORD Size;
     BYTE Handle;
     DWORD ProductID;
     BYTE BaseType;
     BYTE SubType;
     BYTE InterfaceType;
     WORD Attribute;
      BYTE Variable[128];

} DevNode;

void ParseResource(DevNode * pNode) {

   // pResource Is void Until We Know Descriptor Format

   void * pResource ;

   // ... Some Other Code Here

   pResource = &pNode -> Variable ;
   if ((*pResource) & 0x80) {
     //  Parse Large Resource Descriptor
   }
   else {
     //  Parse Small Resource Descriptor
   }

}
```

Small Format Resource Descriptors

Small format resource descriptors have a maximum size of eight bytes, not including byte `0`, which is referred to as the descriptor's tag byte. In addition to the tag bit mentioned previously, the tag byte of a small format resource descriptor contains the descriptor's type and size as shown in Table 3.6.

Table 3.6. Byte 0 of the small format resource descriptor.

Offset	*Description*
0	Bit [7]—Tag Bit (Always 0 in a small format resource descriptor)
	Bits [6:3]—Small item name
	Bits [2:0]—Size *n* of descriptor in bytes, not including byte 0
1 to *n*	Actual resource information

Bits [6:3] of the first byte in a small item resource descriptor contain the item's name. This bit field describes what type of resource descriptor is present, according to Table 3.7.

Table 3.7. Small item names.

Value	*Descriptor*	*Small Item Name*
x0x01	x0001xxB	Plug and Play Version Number
x0x02	x0010xxB	Logical Device ID
x0x03	x0011xxB	Compatible Device ID
x0x04	x0100xxB	IRQ Resource Descriptor
x0x05	x0101xxB	DMA Resource Descriptor
x0x06	x0110xxB	Start of a Dependent Function
x0x07	x0111xxB	End of a Dependent Function
x0x08	x1000xxB	I/O range Resource Descriptor
x0x09	x1001xxB	Fixed I/O range Resource Descriptor
x0x0A to 0x0D	N/A	Reserved
x0x0E	x1110xxB	Vendor Defined Resource Descriptor
x0x0F	x1111xxB	End Tag

The following section briefly describes the meaning and usage of each type of resource descriptor.

Plug and Play Version Number

The Plug and Play Version Number resource descriptor specifies the Plug and Play ISA specification with which the device node's Plug and Play ISA adapter is compatible. Table 3.8 shows the Plug and Play Version Number resource descriptor.

Table 3.8. The format of the Plug and Play Version Number descriptor.

Offset	*Description*
0	Value always 00001010B (Small Format, Length 2 Bytes, Small Item Name = 1)
1	Bits [7:4]—Packed BCD digit representing Plug and Play Major Version
	Bits [3:0]—Packed BCD digit representing Plug and Play Minor Version
2	Vendor-definable adapter revision

Logical Device ID

A *logical device ID descriptor* contains a four-byte EISA-style ID that is identical in format to that contained in the Vendor ID field within a device node. This compressed ID string signals to enumeration software the device to which this particular device is equivalent.

The logical device ID field is provided so that enumeration software can distinguish between multiple devices located on a single adapter. A multi-I/O adapter might have separate logical device IDs for each of its two serial ports, a parallel port, and a game port. If the serial ports are identical, the logical device descriptors also are identical.

The logical device ID provides no means for differentiating among identical devices on a single adapter. Likewise, it provides no mechanism for equating devices on this particular adapter to any existing devices. This task is left for the compatible device ID descriptor, which is described in the following section. Logical device IDs, such as the Adaptec 1534 Plug and Play ISA SCSI adapter, which contains, in addition to a SCSI controller, a PC/AT-compatible floppy disk controller, whose logical device ID is PNP0700, are included solely for aiding the system software to properly enumerate adapters equipped with more than one device.

In addition to its compressed EISA-style ID, the logical device descriptor contains an attribute byte that signals whether the adapter can participate in the system's boot sequence, as well as a bit field that indicates which Plug and Play ISA adapter registers in the range 31H to 37H are supported by this particular adapter.

Table 3.9 displays the format of the logical device ID descriptor.

Table 3.9. The format of a logical device ID descriptor.

Offset	*Description*
0	Value always = to 00010101B or 00010110B for a logical device ID descriptor (Small format, Length = 5 or 6 bytes, Small item name = 2)
1	Bits [7:0]—Byte 0 of the device's EISA-style ID
2	Bits [7:0]—Byte 1 of the device's EISA-style ID
3	Bits [7:0]—Byte 2 of the device's EISA-style ID
4	Bits [7:0]—Byte 3 of the device's EISA-style ID
5	Bits [7:1]—Each bit represents support present for Plug and Play ISA registers 31H to 37H as described in Chapter 5. Bit 1 signifies support for register 31H, bit 2 for register 32H, and so on.
	Bit [0]—1 = device can participate in the boot process
	0 = device does not participate in the system's boot process
6	Bits [7:0]—A value of 1 in any bit signifies Plug and Play ISA register support for each register in the range 38H to 3FH. Bit 0 signifies support for register 38H, bit 1 for register 39H, and so on.

For a full explanation of Plug and Play ISA registers, refer to Chapter 5.

Compatible Device IDs

Compatible device IDs, if present, indicate that the device is compatible with an existing device for which an EISA-style compressed ID has been assigned. The compatible device ID is similar to the logical device ID in that it contains a compressed EISA-style ID; however, the similarity ends there. Compatible device IDs contain no Plug and Play ISA register support because it is assumed that the system software enumerators already have access to this information.

Although the logical device ID provides no means for differentiating among identical devices on a single adapter, it does provide a mechanism by which the adapter's devices can be equated to common, existing industry devices.

In other words, rather than creating a situation in which every manufacturer has its own device ID for well-documented devices such as a PS/2-compatible parallel port, the logical device ID enables you to take a shortcut by identifying PS/2-compatible parallel ports from a variety of manufacturers. In cases in which the device is vendor-specific, it is up to the manufacturer to obtain a unique logical device from an ID provider, such as Microsoft.

The IRQ Resource Descriptor

The Plug and Play BIOS reports system IRQ usage in a device node by means of one or more *IRQ resource descriptors.* As mentioned previously, resource descriptors reside in the Allocated Resource Block, or the Possible Resource Allocation Block. If you encounter an IRQ resource descriptor in the Allocated Resource Block, its contents describe an IRQ channel currently assigned to the device to which that particular device node belongs. Otherwise, if the IRQ descriptor appears in the Possible Resource Allocation Block, it describes an IRQ channel that can be assigned to the device.

Table 3.10 displays the format of the IRQ resource descriptor.

Table 3.10. The format of the IRQ resource descriptor.

Offset	*Size*	*Description*
0	BYTE	Value always = 00100001XB for an IRQ descriptor (Small Type, Length = 2 or 3 bytes, name = 0x04)
1	WORD	IRQ mask field. Bits [15:0] represent IRQs 15 through 0, respectively. A 1 in any bit position signals the use of that IRQ
3	BYTE	Device-specific IRQ capabilities. This optional field is used only if the device supports non-traditional active-high, edge-triggered ISA interrupts Bits [7:4]—Reserved (must be 0) Bit [3]—Level triggered, active low Bit [2]—Level triggered, active high Bit [1]—Edge triggered, active low Bit [0]—Edge triggered, active high

The DMA Channel Resource Descriptor

Each DMA descriptor that appears within a systemboard device node or Plug and Play ISA device header describes the number and capabilities of a single DMA channel. If the device supports, or has been assigned more than a single DMA channel, it will report one DMA descriptor for each of these channels.

Table 3.11 displays the format of the DMA Channel Resource Descriptor.

Table 3.11. The format of the DMA Channel Resource Descriptor.

Offset	*Size*	*Description*
0	BYTE	Value always = 00101010B (Small Type, Length = 2, name = 0x05)
1	BYTE	DMA Channel Mask. Bit [0] = DMA Channel 0, Bit [1] = DMA Channel 1, and so on
2	BYTE	DMA Channel Description Field
		Bit [7]—Reserved, always 0
		Bits [6:5]—DMA channel timing
		00B = Compatible 8237 DMA controller timing
		01B = Type A EISA DMA timing
		10B = Type B DMA timing
		11B = Type F DMA timing
		Bits [4:3]—DMA count modes supported
		00B = Reserved
		01B = Device's DMA supports byte count only
		10B = Device's DMA supports word count only
		11B = Device's DMA supports word or byte count
		Bit [2]—Device bus mastering status
		1 = Device is a bus master
		0 = Device is not a bus master
		Bits [1:0]—Device's preferred DMA transfer type
		00B = 8-bit transfers only
		01B = 8-or 16-bit transfers
		10B = 16-bit transfers only
		11B = Reserved

The Start Dependent Functions Descriptor

Dependent functions are groups of resource descriptors that detail alternate resource allocation schemes for a device. The *Start Dependent Functions Descriptor* provides an optional configuration priority byte that describes the optimality of the particular resource configuration follows it.

For example, a device node may contain five dependent functions, each one containing a valid resource configuration for a device. If the configuration priority byte is missing, or is identical for each of these five configurations, then the currently executing enumerator prioritizes the configurations according to the order in which they appear in the device node. Otherwise, the enumerator assigns resources to the configuration with the highest priority until it has exhausted all combinations.

Dependent functions appear in a device node only if the corresponding device is configurable. In its basic one-byte form, the Start Dependent Functions Descriptor merely signals that a series of descriptors comprising a complete device configuration follows. The two-byte form of the Start Dependent Functions descriptor includes the optional, configuration priority byte as shown in Table 3.12.

Table 3.12. The Start Dependent Functions Descriptor.

Offset	*Size*	*Description*
0	BYTE	Value always = 0011000XB (Small type, length = 0 or 1 byte(s), name = 0x06)
1	BYTE	Optional configuration priority byte. Following are possible values: 0 = Preferred, optimal configuration for this device 1 = Acceptable configuration 2 = Sub-optimal, yet functional configuration

The End Dependent Functions Descriptor

The *End Dependent Functions Descriptor* signals the end of all dependent functions for a particular device. Table 3.13 shows its format.

Table 3.13. The End Dependent Functions Descriptor.

Offset	*Size*	*Description*
0	BYTE	Value always = 00111000B (Small type, length = 0, name = 0x07)

The Variable I/O Descriptor

The *Variable I/O Format Descriptor* is the first of two types of I/O resource descriptors. Unlike Fixed I/O Format Descriptors, Variable I/O Format Descriptors allow full 16-bit addresses for the base and limit addresses of an individual I/O range.

Variable I/O Descriptors are used to describe I/O ranges used by both programmable ISA devices (such as Plug and Play ISA and dynamic systemboard devices) and legacy ISA adapters whose I/O range exists above the 10-bit (03FFH) limit of standard ISA devices. When used for 16-bit legacy ISA device I/O ranges, Variable I/O Descriptors appear within the legacy ISA node with the descriptors' minimum and maximum range base addresses set to the same value.

Table 3.14 displays the format of the Variable I/O Format Descriptor.

Table 3.14. The Variable I/O Format Descriptor.

Offset	*Size*	*Description*
0	BYTE	Value always = 01000111B (Small type, length = 7 bytes, name = 08H)
1	BYTE	ISA Range Qualifier Bits [7:1]—Reserved (must be 0) Bit [0] 0H = Device decodes a full 16-bit I/O address 1H = Device decodes only a 10-bit ISA I/O address
2	WORD	16-bit minimum base address of I/O range
4	WORD	16-bit maximum base address of I/O range
6	BYTE	Minimum base address alignment in 1-byte increments
7	BYTE	Length of I/O range in bytes

The Fixed I/O Descriptor

Fixed I/O Descriptors usually appear in systemboard device nodes or in the legacy ISA device node. This type of descriptor defines a single, 10-bit ISA I/O range.

If a systemboard device uses more than one 10-bit I/O range, its device node contains several Fixed I/O Descriptors. If a legacy ISA device uses more than one 10-bit I/O range, the legacy ISA resource node contains one fixed I/O descriptor for each of these ranges.

The format of the legacy ISA device node is described more fully in the section that describes the process of enumerating system device nodes.

Table 3.15 displays the format of a Fixed I/O Range Descriptor.

Table 3.15. The Format of a Fixed I/O Range Descriptor.

Offset	*Size*	*Description*
0	BYTE	Value always = 01001011B (Small type, length = 3 bytes, name = 09H)
1	WORD	Base address of 10-bit I/O range (Bits [15:12] must be 0)
3	BYTE	Length of I/O range in bytes

The Vendor-Specific Descriptor

The Plug and Play BIOS specification allows for *Vendor-Specific Descriptors* whose use is left to adapter and device vendors. Vendor-Specific Descriptors allow for as many as seven OEM or vendor-defined bytes. Vendors or OEMs who desire more than seven bytes simply include more than one of these descriptors. The Plug and Play BIOS and operating system enumerators normally ignore this type of descriptor. Vendor-Specific Descriptors adhere to the format shown in Table 3.16.

Table 3.16. The format of the Vendor-Specific Descriptor.

Offset	*Size*	*Description*
0	BYTE	Value always = 01110xxxB (Small type, length = 1-7 bytes, name = 0EH)
1	1-7 bytes	Vendor or OEM-specific

The End Tag Descriptor

The End Tag Descriptor signals that there are no more descriptors remaining in the current section of the Plug and Play ISA configuration header or device node block. It contains a single byte that is the checksum of all preceding resource data. If the checksum byte is 0, then the resource enumerator should assume that the contents of all preceding descriptor blocks are valid. Table 3.17 displays the format of the End Tag Descriptor.

Table 3.17. The End Tag Descriptor format.

Offset	*Size*	*Description*
0	BYTE	Value always = 01111001B (Small type, length = 1 byte, name = 0FH)
1	BYTE	checksum byte (If 0, all preceding information within the current block is assumed to be valid)

Large Format Resource Descriptors

Large Format Resource Descriptors contain a 16-bit length field which enables each individual descriptor to contain as much as 64KB of resource information. The format of the Large Resource Descriptor is quite similar to that of the Small Descriptor. The first byte in each Large Descriptor contains the item's name. The second and third bytes contain the length of the descriptor. Any information following the length field is actual resource information. Table 3.18 displays the format of the Large Resource Descriptor. Table 3.19 shows the currently defined Large Resource Descriptor Names.

Table 3.18. The format of the Large Resource Descriptor.

Offset	*Size*	*Description*
0	BYTE	Value = 1*xxxxxxx*B (Large type, item name = *xxxxxxx*B)
1	WORD	Length of actual resource data
3	*Varies*	Actual resource data

Table 3.19. The Large Resource Descriptor Names.

Value	*Description*
01H	16-bit memory range descriptor
02H	ANSI identifier string
03H	Unicode identifier string
04H	Vendor-defined
05H	32-bit memory range descriptor
06H	32-bit fixed location memory range descriptor
07H-7FH	Reserved/Unused

Table 3.20 displays the format of the 16-bit Memory Range Descriptor.

Table 3.20. The 16-bit Memory Range Descriptor.

Offset	*Size*	*Description*
00H	BYTE	Tag Byte, Value always = 81H (Large type, name = 01H)
01H	WORD	Size, always = 09H
03H	BYTE	Memory range information
04H	WORD	Range minimum address bits [23:8]
06H	WORD	Range maximum address bits [23:8]
08H	WORD	Base alignment increment value
0AH	WORD	Range length

The 16-bit memory descriptor most commonly describes expansion ROM firmware located on the systemboard or Plug and Play ISA adapters. The use of this type of memory range descriptor is limited to those devices whose expansion firmware address can be described by a 24-bit address. For this reason, a device node that describes systemboard or Plug and Play ISA whose memory range resides above the 16 MB boundary must use the 32-bit resource descriptor, which is described later in this section.

The third field in the memory range descriptor deserves special explanation, since it contains a variety of dissimilar bit fields.

Table 3.21 displays the format of the range information field within a 16-bit Memory Range Descriptor.

Table 3.21. The range information field of the 16-bit Memory Range Descriptor.

Bit(s)	*Value*	*Description*
[7]	0	Reserved
[6]	0	Memory is not an expansion ROM
	1	Memory is an expansion ROM
[5]	0	Memory is non-shadowable
	1	Memory is shadowable
[4:3]	00	Memory is byte-addressable only
	01	Memory is word-addressable only

Bit(s)	*Value*	*Description*
	10	Memory is either byte or word-addressable
	11	Reserved
[2]	0	Device decodes range length
	1	Device decodes high address
[1]	0	Memory range is non-cacheable
	1	Memory range is cached in write-through fashion
[0]	0	Region is non-writeable
	1	Region is writeable

The 32-Bit Memory Range Descriptor

Device nodes and Plug and Play ISA adapters will use the 32-bit form of the memory range descriptor when any memory range used by the device can reside beyond the 24-bit address limit of the 16-bit descriptor. Among those adapters that might use the 32-bit descriptor are Plug and Play ISA VGA adapters, whose frame buffers might appear anywhere within the 32-bit address 4 GB region accessible to processors based on the 80386 architecture.

The format of the 32-bit memory range descriptor is simply a "stretched" version of the 16-bit descriptor. Its format appears in Table 3.23.

Table 3.22. The format of the 32-bit Memory Range Descriptor.

Offset	*Size*	*Description*
00H	BYTE	Value always = 85H (Large type, name = 0x05)
01H	WORD	Length of descriptor (= 11H bytes)
03H	BYTE	Range information (identical to 16-bit descriptor)
05H	DWORD	Range minimum address bits [31:0]
09H	DWORD	Range maximum address bits [31:0]
0DH	DWORD	Range alignment value bits [31:0]
11H	DWORD	Range length value bits [31:0]

Plug and Play BIOS During POST

The Plug and Play BIOS is an active participant in booting the system. By the time the operating system validates the contents of the installation check header and begins to issue calls to the runtime Plug and Play services, the Plug and Play BIOS will have already enumerated and configured many of the devices within the system and helped the system BIOS to launch the operating system itself. Figure 3.2 describes how the Plug and Play BIOS participates in the system's POST, or Power On Self Test sequence.

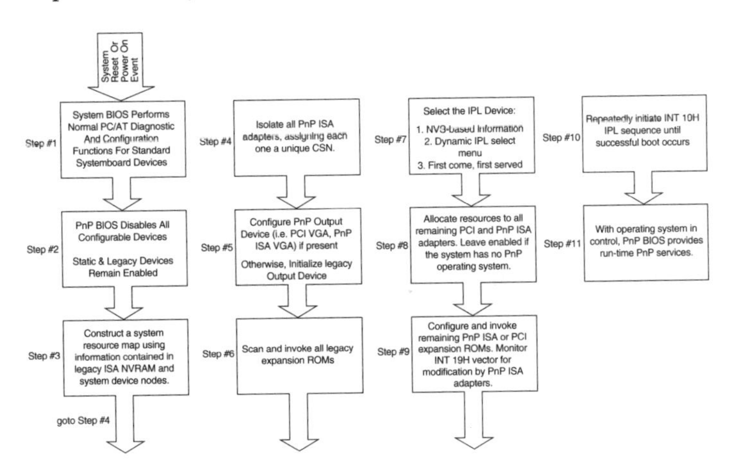

FIGURE 3.2.
The Plug and Play BIOS' participation in the system POST.

The Plug and Play BIOS executes in two different contexts: reset-time and runtime. The reset-time context is referred to as POST because the Plug and Play BIOS is executing in conjunction with the system BIOS to perform the machine's POST (Power On Self Tests).

State of the System at Reset

As a rule, when the system resets or first powers on, all Plug and Play devices are disabled. Directly after a system reset or power on, only legacy ISA and static systemboard devices are enabled.

> **NOTE**
>
> There is one exception to the rule just mentioned. Plug and Play ISA devices that may be required to boot the system (such as bootable network or SCSI

adapters) may power on with their expansion ROM firmware visible in the system's reserved memory area. This is at the discretion of the adapter's designer; however, any Plug and Play device that powers on in the active state must support the Plug and Play ISA disable bit within its own register space. This bit allows the Plug and Play BIOS to selectively enable and disable Plug and Play ISA adapter's ROM if it needs to balance address space requirements with other configurable, expansion ROM-equipped devices.

Plug and Play BIOS Participation Early in POST

Early in the POST sequence, the PC/AT-compatible portion of the system's BIOS enables and tests various legacy systemboard devices, such as the DMA controller, PIC (Programmable Interrupt Controller), keyboard controller, and system timer.

Next, the Plug and Play BIOS disables all systemboard devices and constructs an available resource map based on its NVS-based legacy ISA device resource information and device node table.

NOTE

There is no need for the Plug and Play BIOS to record those resources allocated to Plug and Play-compliant devices because the operating system enumerator can retrieve this information from the devices themselves, with no assistance from the Plug and Play BIOS. The situation is different with dynamic systemboard devices because the operating system enumerator cannot directly interrogate these devices to determine their resource usage. Instead, the operating system retrieves device node records from the Plug and Play BIOS by issuing Plug and Play BIOS `GetNode` call for each systemboard device.

After the Plug and Play BIOS creates its available resource map, it has a clear picture of which resources have been assigned to the system's statically configured devices. With this resource information in hand, the Plug and Play BIOS then isolates any Plug and Play ISA devices present in the system and assigns each of these a unique CSN (Card Select Number). The Plug and Play BIOS performs the Plug and Play ISA isolation sequence in preparation to search for an output device such as a video adapter.

Selecting the Default Output Device

If a legacy output device exists, the Plug and Play BIOS searches for and configures only those output devices which, if enabled, would not conflict with the legacy device. If the system contains a legacy-style ISA VGA adapter, for example, the Plug and Play BIOS does not have the option of disabling this device. If, however, the Plug and Play BIOS detects another output device whose resource needs do not conflict with those used by the legacy VGA adapter, then it may assign resources to and configure this secondary, Plug and Play output device.

After locating and configuring the system's output devices, the Plug and Play BIOS locates and invokes each legacy expansion ROM it encounters in the system's reserved address space between `C8000H` and `E0000H`. The Plug and Play BIOS skips all Plug and Play ISA expansion ROMs that either have not yet been enabled, or contain a valid Plug and Play expansion ROM header. If the Plug and Play BIOS encounters an active Plug and Play ISA expansion ROM, it will attempt to set that device's disable bit in case there exists another legacy expansion ROM in the same physical address space. Once the Plug and Play BIOS has scanned each legacy expansion ROM, it assigns memory space to and scans each Plug and Play ISA expansion ROM.

Selecting the System IPL Device

After the system's legacy expansion ROMs have been initialized, the Plug and Play BIOS selects an IPL device from which it will attempt to launch the operating system. The IPL device selection occurs in one of the following three ways:

- In the first case, the Plug and Play BIOS supports either the ESCD or its own optional, proprietary extensions. This type of Plug and Play BIOS will search for an NVS-based record when it chooses which IPL device to launch first, whether the NVS specifies a Plug and Play-compliant or legacy boot device. The BIOS will store this information until the actual IPL sequence begins, then discard it.
- In the second case, the Plug and Play BIOS searches for all possible IPL devices in the system and presents the user with an IPL device selection menu. A non-ESCD equipped system may not be able to provide selections for legacy IPL devices, but will default to booting from a legacy device if the user does not choose a Plug and Play IPL device from the selection menu.
- The third type of IPL device selection occurs on systems that provide neither ESCD support nor an IPL device selection menu. In this type of system, the IPL boot device is selected on a first come, first served basis beginning with installed legacy boot devices such as an IDE drive.

After having selected the system's IPL device, the Plug and Play BIOS assigns resources to any remaining Plug and Play devices, such as PCI and Plug and Play adapters not involved in the IPL sequence. If the Plug and Play BIOS has been made aware that the IPL device contains a Plug and Play operating system, it will disable all non-IPL Plug and Play adapters immediately after assigning them resources, thereby leaving the task of dynamic device configuration to the OS. If the Plug and Play BIOS has been configured to launch a non-Plug and Play operating system, it will leave all Plug and Play adapters configured and enabled.

NOTE

There exists no exact method by which the Plug and Play BIOS can determine whether the operating system loaded on the IPL device is Plug and Play-compliant. This introduces an interesting issue because the Plug and Play BIOS specification requires that all non-IPL devices remain disabled if the target operating system is Plug and Play-capable.

If the Plug and Play BIOS were to unconditionally disable all Plug and Play devices, they might never get enabled in an environment such as DOS, in which the operating system does not support the Plug and Play architecture. For this reason, many Plug and Play BIOS vendors add a Plug and Play-Active option to their system setup utilities to enable end-users to specify the capabilities of the target operating system. If the Plug and Play BIOS is operating in "PnP-Active" mode, it disables all non-IPL Plug and Play devices prior to launching the operating system. Otherwise, it leaves these devices enabled.

Plug and Play BIOS Performs the Initial Program Load Sequence

At the completion of POST, the Plug and Play BIOS assists the system BIOS in activating and launching the IPL sequence. If the IPL device is a legacy device, the OS launch occurs as it would on a standard PC/AT, via INT 19H. Otherwise, the OS launch follows special protocols detailed in the chapters on PCI and Plug and Play ISA devices.

Once the IPL sequence has successfully begun, both the system BIOS and Plug and Play BIOS transfer control of execution to the operating system. If the operating system supports Plug and Play, then the responsibility of the Plug and Play BIOS shifts to providing the runtime services described in the next section.

Plug and Play BIOS Runtime Services

The Plug and Play BIOS provides a variety of runtime services that bridge the gap between the machine's low-level firmware and operating system. The following sections describe the Plug and Play BIOS runtime services according to the functionality they offer. Generally, Plug and Play BIOS runtime services belong to one of the following categories:

- System resource enumeration
- System resource configuration
- System event signaling

All Plug and Play BIOS function calls use the C language style of parameter passing. The calling application pushes all arguments from right to left and is responsible for removing the calling arguments from the stack upon return from the function. All Plug and Play BIOS functions are of type `int FAR`, meaning that the calling application invokes the function via a `far` call, and receives a 16-bit integer return value in the `AX` register.

The Plug and Play BIOS installation check header provides you with two base data segments that describe where its device nodes reside in both real and protected mode (refer to Figure 3.1). If your application is executing in protected mode, you will have to create a read/write data selector for the Plug and Play BIOS' protected mode data segment and pass this selector into both the `GetNode` and `GetNodeCount` functions.

If your application is executing in real mode, you simply pass the real mode segment that you retrieved from the installation check header earlier on. The Plug and Play BIOS functions independently of the current processor mode and simply will load its segment or selector registers with whatever value you pass in the `BiosSelector` field. The Plug and Play BIOS functions use the `DataSelector` to access both device node tables and global data private to the Plug and Play BIOS itself.

Enumerating Static Devices

During POST, the Plug and Play BIOS enumerates its own internal table of device nodes or ESCD slot records as a reference for determining which system resources have been spoken for at any given point in the POST. After the BIOS has launched the Plug and Play operating system, an OS enumerator performs a series of Plug and Play BIOS `GetNode` calls to retrieve the system device nodes, and creates its own, RAM-based device map called the *device node tree.*

The OS device node tree contains nodes for all devices currently active in the system, and is a superset of the Plug and Play BIOS' systemboard device node table. In addition to system device nodes, the OS device node tree contains nodes for each Plug and Play-compliant and legacy adapter installed in the system. When the system has been successfully configured, the resource information for the systemboard device entries in the OS' device node tree exactly mirrors that contained in the Plug and Play BIOS.

Static resources are those that have been allocated either to systemboard devices or legacy ISA devices. The Plug and Play operating system enumerates static resource usage to determine which resources are available for Plug and Play-compliant devices. It does this by invoking Plug and Play BIOS functions `00H` (`GetNodeCount`), `01H` (`GetNode`), and `0AH` (`GetStaticResInfo`). If the Plug and Play BIOS also supports the ESCD extensions, the operating system may issue functions `41H` (`GetESCDInfo`) and `42H` (`ReadESCDData`) to get information about devices in addition to their resource usage.

NOTE

The contents of ESCD are a superset of those contained in the legacy ISA information block and system device node records. ESCD is an optional storage mechanism whose main purpose is to provide the operating system and Plug and Play BIOS a mechanism for locking the resources assigned to a particular Plug and Play device.

Alternatively, the Plug and Play BIOS may support only the ESCD interface and return the error code `USE_ESCD` in response to functions `09H` and `0AH`. In this case, it is the task of the OS profiler to determine the mechanism by which the Plug and Play BIOS reports static resource allocation.

ESCD-equipped systems support both the device nodes and ESCD functions detailed in the Plug and Play BIOS specification. The method by which such systems support both ESCD slot records and device nodes internally is completely at the discretion of the system's developer.

The format and implementation of the ESCD BIOS extensions is described in Chapter 8. The specification governing ESCD is the *Extended System Configuration Data Specification* available through the Plug and Play Association, whose address appears in Chapter 1.

The non-ESCD Plug and Play BIOS enumeration functions appear in the following section.

Plug and Play BIOS Function *0—GetNodeCount*

Function 0, or GetNodeCount, returns the number of systemboard devices as well as the size of the largest device node in bytes. In order to correctly call GetNodeCount, your application should retrieve the offset of the Plug and Play services entry point from the Plug and Play BIOS installation check header and then get either the 16-bit protected mode base selector, or the real mode base segment, depending on the mode in which your application is currently executing.

In order to invoke GetNodeCount, your application first builds and then calls a far function pointer to the Plug and Play BIOS service entry point. The example program SHOWRES.C, included later, shows the correct sequence for invoking GetNodeCount from real mode.

Following is the C language declaration for the GetNodeCount function:

```
int FAR (pFuncEntry)(Function, NodeCount, MaxNodeSize, DataSelector) ;
int Function ;                     // Always = 0 for GetNodeCount
unsigned char far * NodeCount ;  // Number of system device nodes
unsigned int far * NodeSize ;     // Size in bytes of the largest node
unsigned int DataSelector ;       // App-Supplied R/W data seg/selector.
```

Plug and Play BIOS Function *1—GetNode*

Function 1, the GetNode function, copies a single, caller-specified node into a buffer within the caller's application. Following is the declaration for the C language GetNode function:

```
int FAR (pFuncEntry)(Function, WhichNode, NodeBuffer, Flag, DataSelector);
int Function;                                   // Always 1 for GetNode
unsigned char far * WhichNode;  // Number of which node to retrieve
struct DevNode far * NodeBuffer;  // Pointer to buffer big enough to store the largest
➥node
unsigned int Flag;  // Signals whether to retrieve Now or Next Boot information
unsigned int DataSelector;  // Real or protected mode base data segment from
➥installation check header
```

For each system device represented by a device node, the Plug and Play BIOS maintains a Now configuration and a Next configuration. The Now configuration describes how the device currently is configured, while the Next configuration specifies how the device will be configured the next time the system is booted. If the device is static, the Now and Next configurations should be identical. To get the Now configuration, set Bit 0 in the Flag parameter. To get the Next configuration, set Bit 1. You must select either Bit 0 or Bit 1. All other bits are reserved and should be left as zeroes.

Plug and Play BIOS Function 2—*SetNode*

Function 2, or SetNode, is the opposite of GetNode. The application that calls SetNode supplies the Plug and Play BIOS with a far pointer to a buffer containing a complete device node reflecting the Now or Next boot settings for a particular dynamic, systemboard device.

Following is the C language declaration for the SetNode function:

```
int far (pFuncEntry)(Function, WhichNode, NodeBuffer, Flag, DataSelector) ;
int Function;                     // Always 02H for SetNode
unsigned char WhichNode           // Index of caller-selected device node
struct DevNode far * NodeBuffer   // far pointer to caller-supplied device node
unsigned int Flag;                // Signals whether to set Now or Next Boot
➥information
unsigned int DataSelector;  // Real or protected mode base data segment from
➥installation check header
```

The application that calls SetNode is responsible for ensuring that the resource configuration for the device specified by the argument WhichNode is supported by the device and is in the correct form for a device node. The safest way for applications to ensure that the format of the device node is correct is to modify the BIOS-supplied device node rather than building the node from scratch. The application first invokes GetNode to get a copy of the device node into NodeBuffer. Next, the application modifies the resource allocation block within the device node to reflect the resource configuration changes and writes the device node back via SetNode.

Bits [2:0] of the caller-supplied control variable Flag signify whether the changes are to take place immediately, or during the next system boot sequence. If the calling application sets bit 1 to a value of 1, the resource assignments contained in NodeBuffer will take effect during the next boot. If bit 0 is set to 1, the Plug and Play BIOS reconfigures the device immediately.

NOTE

The caller may set both control bits in the variable Flag in order to cause the desired device reconfiguration to occur both immediately and during subsequent boots of the system. If the target system is unable to record the new device node configuration for future system boot sequences, SetNode may return the value NOT_SET_STATICALLY.

Function 0AH—GetStaticResInfo

Following is the C language declaration for the `GetStaticResInfo` function:

```
int FAR (pFuncEntry)(Function, pBuffer, DataSelector);

int Function;                   // Always 0AH for GetStaticResInfo
unsigned char far * pBuffer;    // Buffer To Receive ISA Info
unsigned int DataSelector;      // Real or protected mode base data segment from
➥installation check header
```

The `GetStaticResInfo` function returns to the user a table of all static resources currently allocated to non-Plug and Play, non-systemboard devices. Plug and Play engineers refer to this information as the system's *old*, or *legacy* ISA information.

The Plug and Play BIOS maintains legacy ISA information in its Non-Volatile Storage (NVS). Legacy ISA information enters the Plug and Play BIOS NVS via utilities like Intel's ICU (ISA Configuration Utility) which allow users to "teach" the system about resources that are being used by non-Plug and Play compliant add-in boards. For more information about Intel's ICU, see Chapter 8.

Legacy ISA information is stored in a single structure that resembles the allocated resource descriptor block of a systemboard device node. The legacy node, however, has no device node header, nor does it have the possible resource descriptor block or compatible device blocks that normally follow the allocated resource block in a standard device node. The legacy node is simply a list of individual resource descriptors followed by an end tag byte. The other device node components are not needed and, therefore, are omitted from the legacy node.

You can, however, treat the legacy ISA node as if it were a true device node by adding dummy versions of the header, possible resource block, and compatible device block. This is useful in cases in which you would like your application to use a single resource descriptor parser for both the legacy ISA information and the system device nodes. The example program SHOWRES.C in this chapter shows how to create a dummy legacy ISA device node that will work properly with a standard device node parser.

System Event Signaling—More Runtime Services

A Plug and Play system should support event signaling in its BIOS if it needs to communicate system events such as docks and undocks with the Plug and Play operating system. *Event signaling* is an optional Plug and Play BIOS feature because many systems have no mechanism by which runtime events can occur. Bits `[1:0]` of the control word field in the Plug and Play BIOS installation check header notify applications if the system can support event handling, and if so, which of the two event signaling mechanisms the system supports. These control word bits are defined as follows:

Bit `[0]`—If set, the system supports polled event signaling

Bit `[1]`—If set, the system supports asynchronous event signaling

Both event signaling methods notify the operating system or one of its components that a potentially important event has happened at the hardware or firmware level. For example, if the user is about to undock his or her notebook from its convenience base, it's crucial that the operating system be notified of this event in order for it to close any open files, log out from a network, and so on.

Polled Event Signaling

Polled event signaling is the simpler of the two mechanisms. If a system's Plug and Play BIOS supports polled event signaling, it sets bit `0` of the Event Notification Flag each time a system event occurs. The operating system, which has retrieved the physical address of the Event Notification Flag from the Plug and Play BIOS installation check header, periodically polls bit `0` of the notification flag to determine whether a system event has occurred.

When a system event occurs, the operating system detects a change in the value of the `poll` flag and issues a `GetEvent` (Plug and Play BIOS function `03H`) call to determine why the Plug and Play BIOS has set the event flag. If the Plug and Play BIOS processes the `GetEvent` function without error, it will clear the Event Notification Flag before returning control to the operating system.

If you are writing a Plug and Play BIOS that supports the polled event signaling method, you also need to support Plug and Play BIOS function `04H`, `SendMessage`. When a Plug and Play operating system loads, it will pass the message `PNP_OS_ACTIVE` to the Plug and Play BIOS. This message tells the Plug and Play BIOS to wait indefinitely for the operating system to issue a `GetEvent` call and retrieve the system event message. Otherwise, the Plug and Play BIOS may, at its own discretion, clear the Event Notification Flag after a certain amount of time has passed.

Asynchronous Event Signaling

The *asynchronous* method of event signaling uses a hardware interrupt to signal events to the operating system or its device drivers. Currently, there are two different types of asynchronous event notification: the generic method and the OEM-specific method.

In systems that support the generic method, the Plug and Play BIOS will contain a special device node whose uncompressed identifier is `PNP0C03`. This event notification device node contains resource descriptors specifying the IRQ level on which system events might occur, and a single I/O address that the operating system uses to both verify and clear the event IRQ.

Asynchronous event signaling occurs in this manner. First, the event (such as a system dock) causes the event notification IRQ to occur. The operating system's event notification interrupt handler then reads the I/O address specified in the system's event notification device node. If bit `0` of the value read is set, this signals to the operating system that the interrupt occurred as a result of a system event. According to the Plug and Play BIOS specification, the operating system can clear the event by writing the I/O address with bit `0` clear. As with polled event detection, once the operating system has determined that a system event has occurred, it then will invoke the Plug and Play BIOS `GetEvent` function to determine the exact nature of the event.

The OEM-specific asynchronous event signaling mechanism is more loosely defined. In a system that supports OEM-specific event signaling, the method for broadcasting that a system event has occurred is via an interrupt as it is in the generic method; however, once the interrupt has occurred, the task of handling and clearing the event interrupt is left completely to an OEM-supplied device driver or application.

Enumerating Static Devices

The example shown here, SHOWRES.C, retrieves the resources used by both system and legacy devices in much the same fashion as a Plug and Play operating system's static resource enumerator.

After first detecting that the system has a Plug and Play BIOS, SHOWRES reads the system's device nodes and calls `GetNodesResources` to parse and sort the nodes' allocated resource descriptor information into four separate arrays: `IOMap`, `IRQMap`, `MemMap`, and `DMAMap`.

Before you start entering any code, SHOWRES.C and its two Plug and Play-specific `#include` files, PNPBIOS.H and PLUGPLAY.H, appear on the disk that accompanies this book.

```
#include <string.h>
#include "plugplay.h"
#include "pnpbios.h"

DEVNODE Nodes [30] ;

unsigned char * resptr = 0, output_buffer[200] ;

int IONum=0, DMANum=0, IRQNum=0, MemNum=0, NumNodes=0, inside=0;

IOMapDef IOMap[MAX_IO];
IRQMapDef IRQMap[MAX_IRQ];
MemMapDef MemMap[MAX_MEM];
DMAMapDef DMAMap[MAX_DMA] ;

PLUGNPLAYHEADER far *PNPHdr = (PLUGNPLAYHEADER far *) 0xf0000000;
```

```
int (far * _based(_segname("_CODE")) FuncEntry)() = (unsigned long) 0L ;

static char * EStrings [] = {
   "\n",                          // OK
   "No PnP BIOS Found",           // Couldn't Find A PnP BIOS
} ;

int main(int argc, char ** argv) {

   unsigned int    loop = 0, whichnode = 0, NodeSize ;
   unsigned char   CheckSum = 0, * pLegacy, NodeHandle = 0 ;

   printf("\nSHOWRES.EXE—PnP Static Resource Viewer") ;

   if (((void far *)FuncEntry = GetFuncEntry()) == NULL)

      ErrorExit(ERROR_NO_PNP_BIOS) ;

   // We Have A PnP BIOS—Let's Keep Going

   for (loop=CheckSum=0;loop < sizeof(PLUGNPLAYHEADER);loop++)

           CheckSum += *((char far *) PNPHdr + loop) ;

      printf("\n$PnP Header found at %lX", PNPHdr) ;
      printf("\n$PnP Header checksum = %02xH", CheckSum);
      printf("\n$PnP Runtime Dispatcher at %lX",FuncEntry);

   //
   // Function 0 - Get System Device Node Count
   //

   printf("\nFunction 0 - Get Number of System Device Nodes :");

   (*FuncEntry)(FGET_SYSTEM_NODE_COUNT,
               (unsigned int far *) &NumNodes,
               (unsigned int far *) &NodeSize,
               PNPHdr->RealDataSeg) ;

   printf("\nNumber Of Static Nodes : [%u]", NumNodes) ;
   printf("\nMax Node Size   : [%u]", NodeSize) ;

   //
   // Function 1 - Get System Device Nodes
   //

   NodeHandle=0;
   printf("\nFunction 1 - Get System Device Nodes :");

   do {
      (*FuncEntry)(FGET_SYSTEM_DEVICE_NODE,
                  .(unsigned char far *) &NodeHandle,
                   (FPDEVNODE) &Nodes[NodeHandle],
                   SET_NEXTBOOT,
                   PNPHdr->RealDataSeg) ;

      } while (NodeHandle != 0xFF);
```

```
//
// OK, we're going to play a little game here—since the ISA
// legacy info is identical to a device node except for the PnP
// ISA header, we will prepend to it a special header that
// identifies it as the legacy stuff.  That way we can print
// it out using standard functions.
//

if ((*FuncEntry)(FGET_OLD_ISA_ALLOCATED,
            (FPDEVNODE) &Nodes[NumNodes].Variable,
            PNPHdr->RealDataSeg) == SUCCESS) {

pLegacy = (BYTE *) &Nodes[NumNodes] ;
EncodeID((BYTE *)&Nodes[NumNodes].ProductID, "PNP9999") ;

// Stick Some End-Tags At The End Of The Legacy "Node"

loop = 0 ;

do { loop++; } while ((BYTE)((*pLegacy++) & 0x78) != 0x78) ;

Nodes[NumNodes++].Size = loop + 5 ;
*(pLegacy + 1) = *(pLegacy + 3) = 0x79 ;

}

GetNodesResources();

for(loop = 0; loop < MAX_DMA, DMAMap[loop].owner != 0; loop++)
   printf("\nDMA %02Xh Owned By Node [%02Xh]",
         DMAMap[loop].num, DMAMap[loop].owner);

for(loop = 0; loop < MAX_IRQ, IRQMap[loop].owner != 0; loop++)
   printf("\nIRQ %02Xh Owned By Node [%02Xh]",
         IRQMap[loop].num, IRQMap[loop].owner);

for(loop = 0; loop < MAX_IO, IOMap[loop].owner != 0; loop++)
   printf("\nI/O %04Xh To %04Xh Owned By Node [%02Xh]",
         IOMap[loop].start, IOMap[loop].end, IOMap[loop].owner);

for(loop = 0; loop < MAX_MEM, MemMap[loop].owner != 0; loop++)
   printf("\nMEM %08lXh To %08lXh Owned By Node [%02Xh]",
        MemMap[loop].start, MemMap[loop].end, MemMap[loop].owner);

  ErrorExit(SUCCESS) ;
}

///////////////////////////////////////////////////////////////////
//
// Name:          void far * GetFuncEntry() ;
// Passed:        Nothing
// Purpose:       Returns Real Mode PnP BIOS Entry Point
// Description:   Searches E0000H-FFFF0H For PnP Installation
//                Header, If Found, Returns Real Mode Entry Point
//
///////////////////////////////////////////////////////////////////

void far * GetFuncEntry() {
   (unsigned long)PNPHdr = 0x0F0000000;
   do {
```

```
        if (!_fstrncmp("$PnP",PNPHdr->Signature,4))
           return ((unsigned long far *) PNPHdr->RealEntry);

        (unsigned long)PNPHdr += 0x10000;
    } while (PNPHdr);
  return(0);
}

//////////////////////////////////////////////////////////////////
//
// void GetNodesResources()
//
// Passed:      Nothing
// Returns:     Nothing
// Purpose:     Sort system device node contents by resource
// Description: This function parses the allocated descriptor
//              blocks in each device node and transfers
//              resource usage information to resource map
//              arrays which can be used to print resource
//              usage by type.
//
//////////////////////////////////////////////////////////////////

void GetNodesResources()  {

   WORD j, k, ct, w1, w2, allocated ;
   DWORD dw1,dw2;

   IONum = IRQNum = DMANum = MemNum = 0 ;

   for(ct = 0; ct < NumNodes; ct++) {

      resptr = Nodes[ct].Variable;
      allocated = TRUE;

      while((resptr <= (char *) ((DEVNODE *) &Nodes[ct]) +
Nodes[ct].Size))
      {

      // Skip Any Vendor-Info Descriptors

      if ((*resptr & 0xF8) == SMALL_VENDOR)  {
           resptr += (*resptr & 0x07) + 1;
           continue;
         }

      // Skip All Descriptors After Allocated Block

      if(allocated == FALSE) { resptr++; continue; }

      switch(*resptr++) {

         case IRQ_DESC_WITHOUT_FLAGS:
         case IRQ_DESC_WITH_FLAGS:
            for(j = 1,k = 0; k < 15; j *= 2, k++) {
               if(*((WORD *)resptr) & j) {
                  IRQMap[IRQNum].num = k;
                  IRQMap[IRQNum].owner = ct;
                  if(IRQNum < MAX_IRQ-1) IRQNum++;
```

```
            }
          }
          resptr += 2;
          if (*resptr == IRQ_DESC_WITH_FLAGS) resptr++ ;
          break;

        case DMA_DESC:
          for(j = 1,k = 0; k < 8; j *= 2, k++) {
            if(*resptr & (BYTE) j)
             {  DMAMap[DMANum].num = k;
                DMAMap[DMANum].owner = ct;
                if(DMANum < MAX_DMA-1) DMANum++;
             }
          }
          resptr += 2;
          break;
        case IOPORT_DESC:
          w1 = (WORD) *(resptr+1) + (*(resptr+2) << 8);
          w2 = w1 + (WORD) *(resptr+6) - 1;
          IOMap[IONum].start = w1;
          IOMap[IONum].end = w2;
          IOMap[IONum].owner = ct;
          if(IONum < MAX_IO-1) IONum++;
          resptr += 7;
          break;
        case IOPORT_FIXED_DESC:
          w1 = (WORD) *resptr + (*(resptr+1) << 8);
          w2 = w1 + (WORD) *(resptr+2) - 1;
          IOMap[IONum].start = w1;
          IOMap[IONum].end = w2;
          IOMap[IONum].owner = ct;
          if(IONum < MAX_IO-1) IONum++;
          resptr += 3;
          break;
        case MEMORY_DESC:
          resptr += 2;      // Skip Length Field
          dw1 = (DWORD) (*(resptr+1) + (*(resptr+2) << 8)) << 8;
          dw2 = dw1 + ((DWORD) (*(resptr+7) + (*(resptr+8) << 8))
<< 8);

          MemMap[MemNum].start = dw1;
          MemMap[MemNum].end = —dw2;
          MemMap[MemNum].owner = ct;
          if(MemNum < MAX_MEM-1) MemNum++;
          resptr += 9;
          break;
        case DF_START:
        case DF_START_WITH_PRIORITY:
        case END_TAG:
        case END_TAG_SUM:
          allocated = FALSE;
      }     // switch(*resptr)
    }   // while
  }  // for

}

//
// ErrorExit—void ErrorExit(int ErrorNumber) ;
```

```
//
// Purpose : Exit W/Error Condition & Simple Diagnostic Message
// Passed  : int ErrorNumber—Return Code & Message Offset
// Returns : Doesn't
// Description : Supply DOS W/Exit Code — 0 = SUCCESS, See EStrings[] ;
//

void ErrorExit(int ErrorNumber) {
if (ErrorNumber)
printf("\nPNPBIOS Error — %s\n", EStrings[ErrorNumber]) ;
exit(ErrorNumber) ;
}

/////////////////////////////////////////////////////////
//
// void EncodeID(BYTE * Target, BYTE * Source) ;
//
// Purpose:  Encode a PnP Device ID Into Compressed EISA Form
// Passed:   BYTE * Target—Pointer To Target Location
//           BYTE * Source—Source Device ID String
// Returns:  Nothing
// Description:  Opposite Of DecodeID, can be used to stuff
//           device IDs into nodes that don't have one, such
//           as legacy ISA info node.
//
/////////////////////////////////////////////////////////


void EncodeID(BYTE * Target, BYTE * Source) {
    BYTE Dummy ;

    // Don't Optimize This Code, Some Compilers Get Confused!!

    Dummy = *Source ; Dummy -= 0x40 ;
    Dummy = (BYTE) ((BYTE) Dummy << 2) ;
    *Target = Dummy ; Source++ ;

    Dummy = *Source ; Dummy -= (BYTE) 0x40 ;
    Dummy = (BYTE) ((BYTE) Dummy >> 3) ;
    *Target |= Dummy ; Target++ ;

    Dummy = *Source ;
    Dummy = Dummy - (BYTE) 0x40 ;
    Dummy = (BYTE) ((BYTE) Dummy << 5) ;
    *Target = Dummy ; Source++ ;

    Dummy = *Source ;
    Dummy = (BYTE) ((BYTE) Dummy - (BYTE) 0x40) ;
    *Target |= Dummy ;

    Source++ ;

    Target++ ;
    *Target = ASCII_To_Hex(*Source++) ;
    *Target += (ASCII_To_Hex(*Source++) << 4) ;
    Target++ ;
    *Target = ASCII_To_Hex(*Source++) ;
```

```
    *Target += (ASCII_To_Hex(*Source) << 4) ;

}

BYTE ASCII_To_Hex(BYTE Character) {
  if ((Character >= 'A') && (Character <= 'F')) return(Character - 'A') ;
  if ((Character >= '0') && (Character <= '9')) return(Character - '0') ;
    return(0) ;
}
```

Plug and Play BIOS Support for Docking Stations

Once a system has docked to its convenience base, it more than likely has new devices that require additional system resources. Also, the docking station has capabilities that the Plug and Play operating system must be able to understand. For example, the operating system must be able to distinguish between "Surprise-style" docking stations that allow the user to remove the notebook system at any time, and "VCR-style" docking stations that allow the operating system to physically lock the notebook unit in place until such time that it is safe to undock.

The operating system has no control over systems that support "Surprise-style" docking only. On "VCR-style" systems, however, the Plug and Play BIOS will warn the system via its event notification interface that an undock event is about to occur by sending the message `ABOUT_TO_CHANGE_CONFIG`. After the operating system receives the `ABOUT_TO_CHANGE_CONFIG` message, it initiates some type of orderly shutdown sequence.

Upon completing its shutdown sequence, the operating system will signal to the Plug and Play BIOS that an undock now can occur by invoking the Plug and Play BIOS `SendMessage` function with the message `UNDOCK_DEFAULT_ACTION`. Only when the Plug and Play BIOS receives the `UNDOCK_DEFAULT_ACTION` message will it release the notebook system from the VCR-style docking station.

NOTE

Because the Plug and Play BIOS clears the event notification following a successful `GetEvent` call, any application that issues the Plug and Play BIOS `GetEvent` call must be able to handle whatever message the Plug and Play BIOS returns. If you are writing user applications, you should allow the operating system to handle any and all event notifications. Otherwise, you run the risk of "stealing" messages from the operating system and the system might perform erratically.

4

PCI Bus Overview

Intel introduced the PCI, or Peripheral Component Interconnect bus, in 1992 with the intention of breaking through the I/O bottlenecks of the choked PC/AT ISA bus and creating a high-speed, processor-independent bus that would supply the continually evolving PC architecture with the performance and interoperability so crucial to its future viability.

Although Intel did not design the PCI bus specifically for either the PC or Plug and Play architectures, growing industry acceptance of the Plug and Play technology has helped Intel steer the PCI technology in such a direction that it fits well within the Plug and Play framework. The PCI bus architecture is outlined in detail by the following documents:

- *PCI Local Bus Specification*
- *PCI BIOS Specification*
- *PCI IDE Specification*
- *PCI-PCI Bridge Specification*

Each of these documents is available from the PCI SIG (Special Interest Group) at the following address:

PCI Special Interest Group
P.O. Box 14070
Portland, OR 97214

Telephone (International) (503)797-4297

Fax (503)234-6762

As a Plug and Play programmer, you need to understand how the PCI bus and its supported devices fit within the framework of the PC/AT system. Also, you should learn how to configure PCI devices both directly and via the PCI BIOS interface. Both the PCI BIOS and register level programming interfaces appear throughout this chapter. The following section describes the overall architecture of the PCI bus.

The PCI Bus Architecture

Compliant PCI systems support multiple bus instances in a hierarchical fashion. In simpler terms, this means that a PCI-equipped system may contain one PCI bus, or it may contain several (up to 255). The primary bus (bus `0`) is called the *root bus*. The root bus is connected to the system's CPU and DRAM by a device called the *host controller*. The host controller can support at most three or four PCI devices. This limit is not arbitrary; it is derived from the electrical loading characteristics of the high-speed bus.

If the PCI bus could support only three or four devices, it would be of little use to the world of PC designers and consumers. In order to break the four device limit, designers install *bridge devices*, which introduce additional PCI buses downstream from the root bus.

Some bridge devices connect other, secondary system buses to the CPU via the root node bus. A PCI-EISA bridge, for example, allows EISA devices to execute on an EISA bus located behind the host PCI controller.

PCI bridge devices support one of a variety of secondary buses, including EISA, ISA, and PCMCIA. A special bridge device called a *PCI-PCI bridge* creates a secondary PCI bus. Like the root bus, any secondary PCI bus introduced by the PCI-PCI bridge is capable of supporting up to three or four PCI devices, including bridge devices. Figure 4.1 displays two possible bus topologies within a PCI-equipped system.

FIGURE 4.1.
Two sample PCI bus topologies.

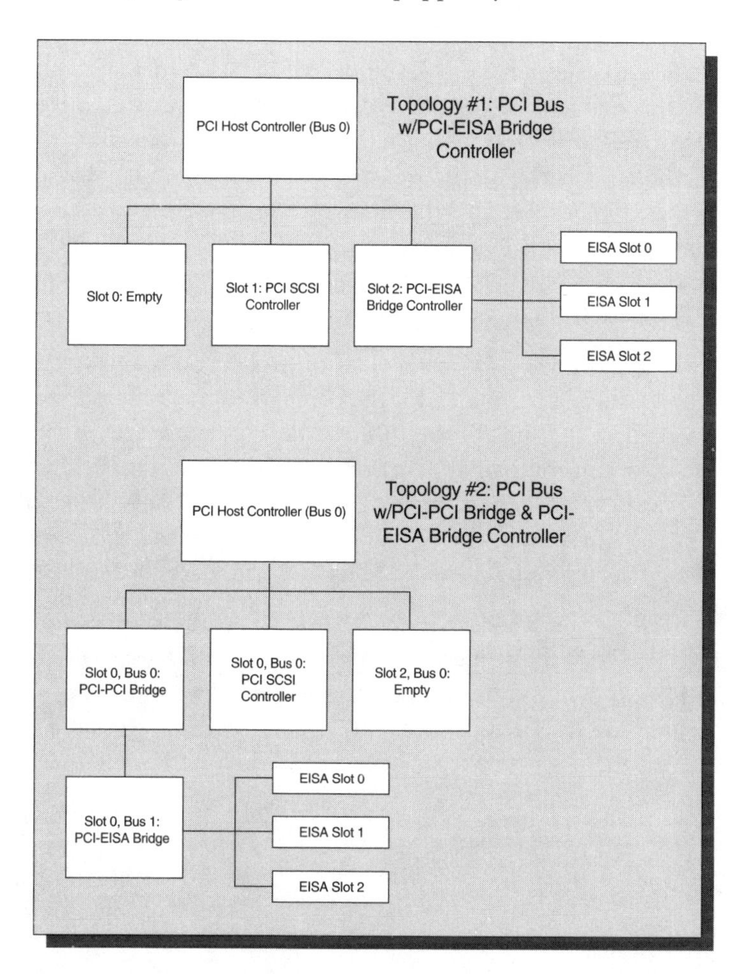

PCI Device Resource Usage

Because the PCI bus is not designed specifically for the PC architecture, the resource needs of its devices differ slightly from standard PC buses. The *PCI Local Bus Specification* defines how PCI devices support I/O ranges, memory ranges, and interrupt channels, but makes no assumptions about the platform within which the PCI device is currently operating.

The PCI bus, for example, provides each physical slot four interrupt channels, `INTA#`-`INTD#`. In a PC/AT-compatible system, special interrupt steering hardware routes the four PCI bus `INTx#` lines to a subset of the PC/AT system's 16 IRQ channels inside the system's PIC. On a non-PC/AT system, the `INTx#` to interrupt request conversion mechanism most likely is very different.

PCI Service I/O Address Range Usage

PCI devices support a full 32-bit decode of I/O read and write addresses, as opposed to the ISA bus standard 12-bit address. As a result, the majority of ISA devices are only able to decode I/O addresses in the `0-3FFH` range, as detailed in Chapter 2. PCI devices, on the other hand, can decode all I/O addresses ranging from `0-0FFFFFFFFH`. This enhanced I/O decode capability allows BIOS an OS configuration software to assign PCI devices I/O ranges that do not conflict with existing systemboard or plug-in ISA adapters. Of course, the software that assigns I/O ranges to PCI devices must check that the PCI device I/O ranges do not conflict with one another.

Additionally, many PCI hosts and controllers offer a programmable *I/O base register.* The PCI host controller adds the contents of the I/O base register to each I/O operation on the PCI bus. If the I/O base register is configured to `3000H`, for example, the PCI host controller will not perform any I/O operations below `3000H`. By programming the host controller's I/O base register to a value above `03FFH`, the system's PCI BIOS can easily prevent conflicts between PCI devices and legacy, or static systemboard devices that are incapable of decoding I/O addresses above `03FFH`.

Some legacy devices decode a full 16-bit I/O address and could potentially conflict with PCI devices if the host controller's base register has been programmed to a value in the `1000H-F000H` range. In this case, the user must execute a Plug and Play resource viewer, such as the Intel ICU (ISA Configuration Utility), to find an I/O range that satisfies the capabilities of the legacy device and does not conflict with any installed PCI devices.

PCI Device DMA Channel Usage

The *PCI Local Bus Specification* prohibits third-party DMA support on the PCI bus. Consequently, neither the PCI host controller, nor any of the devices on the PCI bus, consume any DMA channels.

Some systems contain a PCI-ISA bridge that allows DMA to occur on the ISA bus located behind the system's host controller. DMA that occurs behind a host controller passes through the PCI bridge via a sideband mechanism, such as special cycles, and not as PCI-based DMA. This type of implementation is highly chipset-specific, and does not impact the allocation of PCI device resources. The system's BIOS and configuration software cannot distinguish between an ISA bus behind a PCI-ISA bridge and a standard ISA bus connected directly to the CPU via a standard ISA controller chipset.

PCI Device IRQ Usage

The PCI bus provides four individual, level-triggered interrupt lines: `INTA#`, `INTB#`, `INTC#`, and `INTD#`. Each `INTx#` line is routed to each slot on every PCI bus in the system. In the case of on-board PCI devices, designers may opt to route only the `INTA#` line to each device because the number of interrupt lines needed by each on-board device is known at design time.

The PCI system designer is responsible for deciding which PC IRQ channels connect to the PCI bus `INTx#` lines that appear in the system's adapter slots. He or she may connect IRQ and `INTx#` lines directly, or provide some type of programmable steering hardware that allows the PCI BIOS to dynamically configure the system's `INTx#`-IRQ translation.

At the firmware level, the PCI BIOS configures and allocates system IRQ channels based on its intimate knowledge of a particular systemboard. If the hardware supports programmable IRQ steering, the PCI BIOS might allocate IRQ channels based on IRQ requirements of legacy, or other Plug and Play adapters installed in the system. If the system connects IRQ channels directly to PCI slots or devices, and does not support interrupt steering, the IRQ channels should appear in a static Plug and Play BIOS device node.

Operating system enumerator/configurator applications can determine the IRQ mapping strategy for a particular system by issuing `GET_IRQ_ROUTING_INFO` and `SET_PCI_IRQ` calls to the PCI BIOS. These functions are explained in the PCI BIOS portion of this chapter.

According to the *PCI Local Bus Specification*, devices with a single function must only assert interrupt request signals on the `INTA#` line. The other three `INTx#` lines are reserved for *multifunction devices*, and do not apply to single function devices. Devices on a multifunction adapter may share a single `INTx#` line; however, each function on a multifunction device may only assert interrupts on a single `INTx#` line.

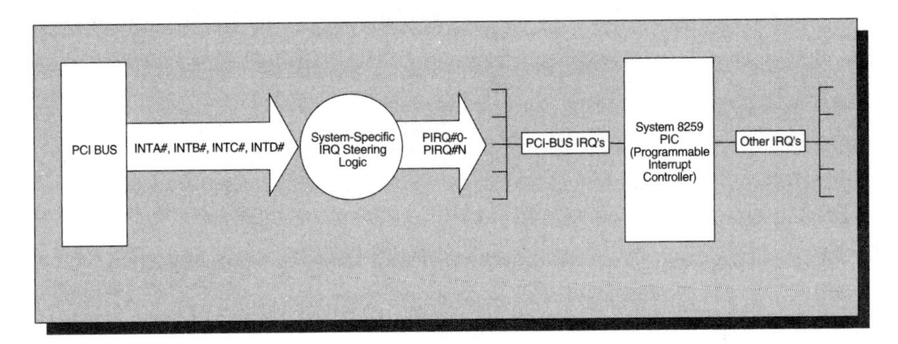

FIGURE 4.2. *Translation of PCI interrupts to PC IRQ channels.*

Unless you are writing a PCI BIOS, you probably don't care how the system's underlying interrupt steering hardware has been implemented. You can always determine which IRQ the system BIOS has allocated to a particular PCI device by examining the contents of that device's `Interrupt Line` register. The `Interrupt Line` register, which resides at offset `03CH` in the device's configuration space, contains the ordinal value of the IRQ channel that the system BIOS has assigned that device. In a PC/AT compatible system, the legal values for the `Interrupt Line` register are `00H-0FH`. A value of `0FFH` in this 8-bit register signifies that the PCI device uses no IRQ channel.

PCI Device Address Range Usage

PCI devices consume many of the same memory space resources as legacy ISA devices. They can have expansion ROMs, frame buffers (PCI video devices), and memory mapped I/O.

The configuration space for each PCI device provides six *base address registers* through which system software communicates and configures PCI device memory range resource needs. Base address registers are 32-bits wide for I/O ranges and either 32- or 64-bits wide for memory ranges.

The minimum granularity for I/O ranges is 4 bytes, and the maximum allowed size for a single I/O range is 256 bytes. The minimum granularity for a memory address range is 16 bytes, and the maximum allowed size is limited by the register's size, which can be either 32 or 64 bits. Each 64-bit memory range uses two of the six possible base address registers. A device or function that uses three 64-bit memory ranges has no leftover registers.

Each device or device function may request a single expansion ROM memory address range. If the device has an on-board expansion ROM, it requests an address range for the ROM image via the `Expansion ROM Base Address` register located at offset `30H` within its configuration space header.

During the system boot sequence, the PCI BIOS queries the base address registers within each device's configuration space to determine the granularity and type of memory range that the device requires. If an appropriate memory range is available, the configurator then writes the device's base address registers with the base address of a unique, conflict-free address range.

Both the `Base Address` registers and `Expansion ROM Base Address` register are discussed more fully in the following section, which outlines each register in a PCI device's configuration space.

PCI Device Configuration Space

The PCI bus is based on the concept of slots. Each PCI compliant device on a PCI bus occupies a single PCI slot. To each PCI slot, the PCI controller assigns `100H` I/O locations, called the slot's *configuration space*. The `Header Type` register, located at offset `0EH` within a device's configuration space, specifies the format to which the first `40H` registers in that device's configuration space registers adhere. The most common header type is `00H`. The format of a type `00H` configuration space header, as outlined in the *PCI Local Bus Specification*, appears in Figure 4.3.

NOTE

Like any other PCI device, the system's host controller communicates with system configuration software through a configuration space. The host controller's `Vendor ID`, `Device ID`, and `Device Class Code` registers identify the device as a host controller, and also reveal the manufacturer of the controller.

The PCI BIOS and system BIOS configure the system's host controller by writing both the `Command` register and device-specific registers located above `offset 3FH` within the host controller's configuration space. In order to correctly program a system's host controller, you need to know its slot location and the format of its device-specific registers, which normally appear in the device's data sheet.

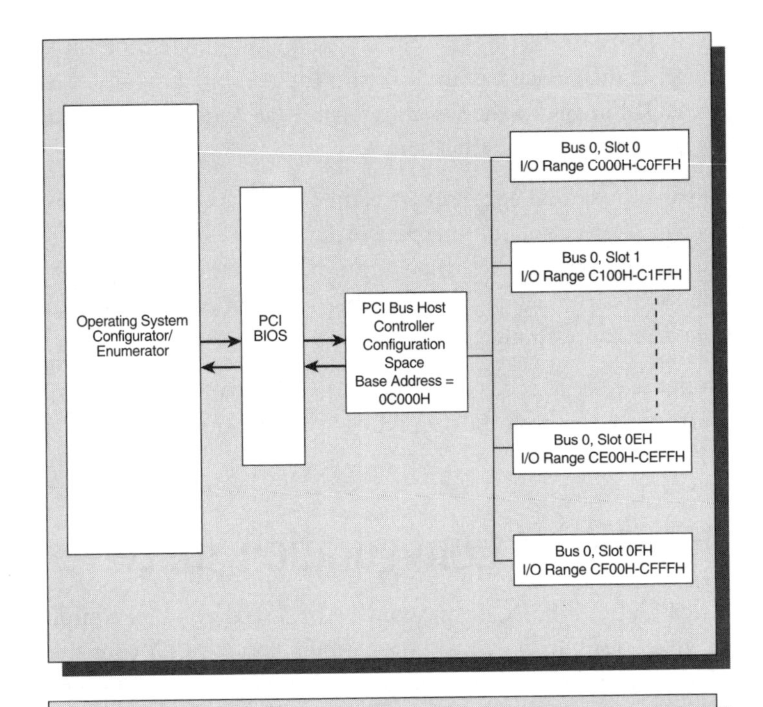

FIGURE 4.3.

The type `00H` PCI device configuration space header.

Bit 31	Bit 16	Bit 15	Bit 0	
Device ID		Vendor ID		00H
Status Register		Command Register		04H
Device Class Code			Revision ID	08H
BIST	Header Type	Latency Timer	Cache Line Size	0CH
Base Address Registers				10H–24H
Reserved				28H, 2CH
Expansion ROM Base Address				30H
Reserved				34H, 38H
Max Latency	Min Grant	Interrupt Pin	Interrupt Line	3CH

Device Identification Fields Within Configuration Space

A PCI device's configuration space consists of 100H registers. The first 10H locations within configuration space apply to all PCI devices and are not optional. Devices that do not properly support the first 10H locations within configuration space are non-compliant. The contents of registers 10H-3FH vary according to the Header Type value in configuration space register 0EH.

If the Header Type register reports 00H, then the configuration space header adheres to the format outlined in Figure 4.3. If the Header Type is 01H, then the device is a PCI-PCI bridge, and its contents are detailed in the *PCI to PCI Bridge Specification.* Currently, all other values within the Header Type register are reserved. Registers 40H-0FFH within configuration space are device-specific; their contents and usage are not controlled by the *PCI Local Bus Specification*, regardless of the value in the Header Type Register.

Offset *00H— Vendor ID* (*WORD,* Read Only)

The Vendor ID register returns a 16-bit value that identifies the vendor that produced the PCI device. A value of 0FFFFH in this field signifies that no device exists in this slot. Vendor IDs are allocated and maintained by the PCI Special Interest Group. The list of such IDs changes as the PCI SIG adds or removes vendors. A current list of Vendor IDs appears in Appendix B.

Offset *02H—Device ID* (*WORD,* Read Only)

The Device ID register contains a vendor-defined, 16-bit identifier that identifies this particular device. For example, a vendor may outfit three different SCSI controllers with device IDs 0000H, 0001H, and 0002H. The device ID enables application and driver software to differentiate between a series of products that are otherwise indistinguishable in function and interface.

During its hardware profiling sequence, the operating system enumerator first queries the Device Class Code register to determine the functionality of a PCI device. If the OS provides device- or vendor-specific support for PCI devices, it then reads the Vendor ID and Device ID registers to determine the original manufacturer or vendor of that device. Similarly, device drivers that support a family of devices read the Device Class Code registers to decide exactly which device to support.

Offset *08H—Revision ID* (*BYTE,* Read Only)

The Revision ID register provides an 8-bit, vendor-defined revision value for a particular PCI device.

Offset *0EH—Header Type* (*BYTE*, Read Only)

The `Header Type` register specifies the format of bytes `10H-3FH` in a PCI devices configuration space header, which in turn consists of the first `40H` registers within the header. Currently, the PCI SIG has defined only two values for the `Header Type` register. A value of `00H` in the `Header Type` register signals that the device's configuration space header adheres to the format shown in Figure 4.3. A value of `01H` means that the device is a PCI-PCI bridge, and the format of its configuration space header is explained in the *PCI to PCI Bridge Specification.*

Device Class Code Registers (Offset *09H-0BH, 3*BYTE*)

The `Device Class Code` registers identify the exact function that the PCI device performs. The `Device Class Code` register contains three one-byte fields identical to those found in system device nodes and Plug and Play ISA devices. Offset `0BH` provides the base class code for the device. Offset `0AH` contains the subclass code, and offset `09H` the device interface code.

Device class codes assist the OS enumerator and configurator in determining the capabilities of all devices installed in the system. For example, if a PCI device reports a value of `080301H` in the class code register, it signals to the operating system that it contains an ISA RTC (Real Time Clock) controller. A value of `080300H` is less specific, and specifies only a generic RTC controller. A complete list of device class codes appears in Appendix A.

Device-Independent Status and Control Registers in Configuration Space

PCI device configuration space provides two device-independent registers, the `Command` register and `Status` register, for controlling and monitoring the status of any PCI device. Support for these registers is mandatory and is described in the next sections.

The *Command* Register (Offset *04H, WORD*)

The `Command` register is a 16-bit, read/write register that controls how a PCI device generates and responds to various cycles on the PCI bus. Writing a value of `00H` to this register signals that a device should neither generate nor respond to PCI bus signals, and effectively disconnects the device from the PCI bus. With the exception of the address/data stepping bit (bit `7`), all bits in this register default to `0` after a `RST#` (PCI bus reset) signal occurs.

Table 4.1 displays the format of the PCI configuration space `Command` register.

Table 4.1. The format of the PCI configuration space `Command` register.

Bit(s)	*Description*
`[15:10]`	Reserved
`[09]`	Fast Back-to-Back Enable—This bit applies to bus masters only. If it is set, the bus mastering device may perform fast back-to-back address and data cycles. PCI Bus configuration software sets this bit in master devices only if all target devices on the bus are capable of performing address/data stepping.
`[08]`	`SERR# Enable`—Setting this bit to `1` enables the device to drive the `SERR#` (`System Error`) pin when conditions such as parity errors occur. If this bit is clear, the device cannot drive `SERR#`.
`[07]`	Wait cycle control—If this bit is `0`, the device is incapable of performing fast back-to-back address and data stepping. If this bit is set, it must be read/write and signifies that the device is capable of supporting fast back-to-back address and data stepping.
`[06]`	Parity Error Response—If this bit is clear, the device ignores parity errors. Otherwise, the device is required to perform its normal response to a parity error. All devices are required to generate parity, but only those that implement parity checking need to implement this bit.
`[05]`	VGA Palette Snoop—This bit applies only to graphics devices that support VGA palette registers. If this bit is set, graphics devices snoop the contents of all writes to VGA palette registers, but do not respond to these writes. If this bit is clear, graphics devices treat accesses to palette registers like any other I/O access.
`[04]`	Memory Write and Invalidate Enable—A value of `1` enables bus mastering devices to perform writes via the `Memory Write and Invalidate` command. If the value of this register is `0`, bus masters must perform writes via the `Memory Write` command. These commands are detailed in the *PCI Local Bus Specification.*

continues

Table 4.1. continued.

Bit(s)	*Description*
`[03]`	Special cycle enable/disable—A value of `1` enables the device to monitor all special cycles that occur on the PCI bus.
`[02]`	Bus mastering capabilities enable/disable—A value of `1` enables the device to act as a PCI bus master if the device is so capable.
`[01]`	Memory space enable/disable—A value of `1` enables the device's response to all memory ranges specified in the device's configuration space base address registers.
`[00]`	I/O space enable/disable—A value of `1` enables the device's response to all I/O ranges specified in the device's configuration space base address registers.

HANDLING DEVICES THAT DON'T RESPOND TO THE COMMAND REGISTER

Bits `0` and `1` within the `Command` register control whether a PCI device responds to memory and I/O range accesses. Both the PCI BIOS and OS configurators use these bits as the fundamental mechanism for enabling and disabling devices. Older or non-compliant PCI devices may not respond correctly to values written to bits `0` and `1`. The PCI BIOS and OS configurators need to take additional steps for handling non-responsive or non-compliant devices.

There are two methods for handling devices that fail to respond to `Command` register enable/disable bits. In Method #1, the configuration software reads each device's Vendor ID and Device ID and attempts to match these values against a list of known non-compliant devices. If a match occurs, the configuration software records the presence of the non-compliant device(s) and proceeds accordingly.

In Method #2, the configuration software selectively disables each device and then attempts to snoop out the device's registers. If the device in question is a PCI IDE controller, the PCI BIOS might write bit `0` of that device's `Command` register to `0` to disable its I/O range, and then attempt to read and write standard IDE registers to see if an IDE controller responds.

Method #2 is effective only in the absence of similar controllers on other buses in the system. For example, the PCI BIOS might disable the PCI IDE controller, and then during its snoop algorithm detect a second IDE controller on the system's ISA bus. At this point, the PCI BIOS would leave the PCI IDE disabled with the assumption that either the PCI device is non-configurable, or that a second non-configurable IDE device (such as a plug-in ISA card) is present in the system.

The *Status* Register (Offset *06H, WORD*)

The `Status` register signals various device capabilities and PCI bus events that the device detected. The contents of this register have no effect on the Plug and Play aspects of configuring a system but are included for the purpose of completeness (see Table 4.2).

Table. 4.2. The format of the PCI configuration space `Status` register.

Bit(s)	*Description*
`4:0`	Reserved
`5`	If set, the device is capable of running at 66MHz. Otherwise, the device is capable of running at 33MHz. This bit is optional, and must be `0` if the device does not support it.
`6`	If set, the device, or one of its functions, supports UDF (User Definable Features) about which the user must be made aware. User Definable Features are described in the *PCI Local Bus Specification*, revisions 2.1 and above. This bit is optional, and must be `0` if the device does not support it.
`7`	If set, the device can accept fast back-to-back transactions from different agents (masters) when it acts as a target (slave). This bit is optional, and must be `0` if the device does not support it.
`8`	Data Parity Error detected. This bit is supported only by bus mastering devices. A bus mastering device sets this bit if the following three conditions are met: 1) the bus agent (master) asserts the `PERR#` (`Parity ERRor`) signal or detects that another device has asserted `PERR#`; 2) the agent that asserted `PERR#` was the bus master during the operation that

continues

Table. 4.2. continued.

Bit(s)	*Description*
	caused the parity error; 3) the device's parity error reporting is currently enabled via the Parity Response bit in the device's `Command` register.
`10:9`	`DEVSEL#` timing. (`00B` = Fast, `01B` = Medium, `10B` = Slow)
`11`	`Signaled Target Abort`. The PCI device sets this bit if it was acting as a target and aborted a transaction via the Target-Abort bus signal.
`12`	`Received Target Abort`. The PCI device sets this bit if it was acting as a master and its target aborted a transaction via the Target-Abort bus signal.
`13`	`Received Master Abort`. The PCI device sets this bit if it was acting as a master and its transaction was aborted via a Master-Abort bus signal.
`14`	`Signaled Error`. The PCI device sets this bit if it asserted the `SERR#` (System ERRor) bus signal.
`15`	`Parity Error Detected`. The PCI device sets this bit if it detected a parity error, regardless of the state of its `Command` register Parity Response bit.

Device Configuration Registers Within Configuration Space

PCI device configuration registers enable bus configuration software such as the PCI BIOS and OS configurator to map PCI device resource needs into the PC architecture. These registers fall into one of three categories: base address configuration, expansion ROM handling, and interrupt configuration.

The *Interrupt Line* Register (Offset *3CH, BYTE*)

In a PC system, the `Interrupt Line` register indicates which physical PC IRQ channel has been assigned to the device. Any PCI device that uses interrupts must support this read/write register. During POST, the PCI BIOS writes this register with the ordinal value that it has assigned to the device. For example, if the PCI BIOS assigns IRQ `14` to a device, then it writes the device's `Interrupt Line` register with the value `0EH`.

Device drivers and operating systems use the contents of this register primarily to determine which interrupt vector corresponds to the device. If the device's `Interrupt Line` register contains the value `0FFH` at power-on, the device uses no interrupts.

The PCI BIOS supplies the functions `GET_IRQ_ROUTING_INFO` and `SET_PCI_IRQ` for applications that want to monitor or change the system's PCI IRQ routing at runtime. These functions are described in the PCI BIOS section at the end of this chapter.

The *Interrupt Pin* Register (Offset *3DH, BYTE*)

The `Interrupt Pin` register is read-only, and can contain only one of five values. A value of `0` means that the device or function uses no interrupts. A value of `1` indicates that the device or function generates interrupts on the `INTA#` signal, `2` signifies usage of `INTB#`, `3` signifies `INTC#`, and `4 INTD#`.

Each function on a multifunction device may assert interrupts on a single `INTx#` line. In this case, the `Interrupt Line` register for each function that generates interrupts contains the same value. Individual devices may assert interrupts only on a single channel. This makes sense if you consider that individual devices and functions are assigned only one `Interrupt Line` register, via location `3CH` within their configuration space. Any device that asserts interrupts on more than a single `INTx#` channel must be a multifunction device.

As mentioned previously, the PCI BIOS provides `GET_IRQ_ROUTING_INFO` and `SET_PCI_IRQ` functions to applications that want to monitor or change the system's PCI IRQ routing at runtime. These functions are described in the PCI BIOS section at the end of this chapter.

PCI Device *Base Address* Registers (Offset *10H, 6*DWORD*)

PCI devices support six 32-bit base address registers, each of which specifies one I/O or memory address range. If bit `0` in the `base address` register is a `1`, the `base address` register pertains to an I/O range. Otherwise, the `base address` register pertains to a memory address range. Bit 0 in each `base address` register is read-only.

The first `base address` register always resides at offset `10H` within configuration space. Because memory base addresses may be 64-bits wide, the second `base address` register may reside at either offset `14H` or `18H`, depending on the width of the first base address. I/O range base addresses are always 32-bits wide. If the first `base address` register corresponds to an I/O range (bit `0 = 1`), the next `base address` register begins at offset `14H`. If the first `base address` register corresponds to a memory range, the configuration software then checks bits `[2:1]` within the register to determine the width of the register.

The *Memory Range Base Address* Register

If bit `0` of a `base address` register is clear, then the register specifies a memory range. The lower four bits of this register describe the size of the memory range and whether the range is prefetchable. Table 4.3 shows the format of the `Memory Range Base Address` register.

Table 4.3. The format of the `Memory Range Base Address` register.

Bit(s)	*Description*
`[0]`	Always `0` for a `memory range base address` register
`[2:1]`	Size attribute for the memory range as follows: `00B`—Base register is 32-bits wide and the memory range can be assigned anywhere within physical 32-bit address space. `01B`—Base register is 32-bits wide; however, the memory range can be assigned only below 1MB in the system's address space. `10B`—Base register is 64-bits wide and the memory range can be assigned anywhere within physical 64-bit address space. `11B`—Reserved
`[3]`	Prefetchability of the memory range—This bit is set to `1` if the memory range meets the following qualifications: ■ Reads to this memory range produce no ill side effects ■ Reads to this memory range return all bytes in a single read operation, regardless of the state of the PCI bus `BE#` (`Byte Enable`) signals. ■ The host controller may perform byte-merged write operations to this memory range. (See the following Note on byte merging.)

Bits `[31:4]` within the `Memory Range Base Address` register define bits `[31:4]` of the physical location of the memory range. In order to determine the granularity of memory address ranges that the register supports, configuration software writes a value of all `1`'s to the register, and then reads back the contents of the register. The value read back contains `0`'s in all the "don't-care" bits for the memory range. For example, if the configurator reads back a value of `0FFFF0000H`, then the granularity of the address range is 64KB and the configurator should assign this device an address range on a 64KB boundary. Bits `[3:0]` within a `Memory Range Base Address` register are non-writeable; therefore, the minimum granularity for any memory range is one memory paragraph, or 16 bytes.

BYTE MERGING

Byte merging is a PCI bus-specific technique whereby the host controller can improve bus throughput by writing non-contiguous memory locations in a single operation. The data path on the PCI bus is 32-bits, or 4-bytes wide. The host controller only accesses memory space on four-byte boundaries, and asserts the `BE0#-BE3#` signals to indicate which of the four bytes are significant.

If a device supports byte merging, the PCI bus host controller will perform writes to that device with non-contiguous `BE#` signals asserted, the assumption being that the device will examine the bus' byte-enable signals and use only those bytes for which a byte-enable line is active.

For example, if an application writes to locations `0xxxxxxx1H` and `0xxxxxxx3H`, the host controller has two choices for performing the write operation. If the target device does not support byte merging, the bus controller performs two separate writes; during the first write, `BE1#` is asserted to indicate that only byte `1` on the data bus is significant, and during the second write `BE3#` is asserted to indicate that byte `3` is significant. If the target device supports byte merging, the host controller performs a single write with both the `BE1#` and `BE3#` byte-enable signals asserted. The device receiving the data then merges the bytes on the data bus, rather than quitting after detecting the first non-asserted `BE#` signal.

The I/O *Range Base Address* Register

If bit `0` in a `base address` register is set, the register defines an I/O range for the PCI device. As is the case with `Memory Range Base Address` registers, application software performs a range size inquiry by first writing a pattern of all `1`'s to the register and then reading back the contents of the register. Any bytes set to `0` in the value read signify "don't-care" bits. Table 4.4 shows the format of the I/O `Range Base Address` register.

Table 4.4. The format of the I/O `Range Base Address` register.

Bit(s)	*Description*
`0`	Always `1` for an I/O `range base address` register
`1`	Reserved
`31:2`	Bits `31:2` of the base address for this I/O range

Devices are not allowed to consume more than 256 I/O locations via a single I/O range `base address` register. Therefore, it is illegal for an I/O range `Base Address` register to report a value of `0` in any bits beyond bit `7` in the I/O range size inquiry process. Devices that use more than 256 bytes of I/O space do so either by supporting more than one I/O Range Base Address, or by equipping the device with memory-mapped I/O locations and requesting the I/O space via a `Memory Range Base Address` register, which is not subject to the 256-byte limitation.

The *Expansion ROM Base Address* Register (Offset *30H, DWORD*)

The purpose of the `Expansion ROM Base Address` register is to provide configuration software the capability to selectively enable and configure expansion ROMs for those PCI devices requiring this support. The *PCI Local Bus Specification* allows for just one `Expansion ROM Base Address` register in a type `00H` configuration space header. Therefore, PCI devices that support the type `00H` header are limited to a single on-board expansion ROM. Table 4.5 shows the format of the `Expansion ROM Base Address` register.

Table 4.5. The format of the `Expansion ROM Base Address` register.

Bit(s)	*Description*
`0`	Expansion ROM address decode enable/disable.
`10:1`	Reserved
`31:11`	Bits `31:11` of the expansion ROM Base Address

The `Expansion ROM Base Address` register is similar both in format and functionality to the `Memory Range Base Address` register described previously. In order to determine the granularity of the requested expansion ROM base address, configuration software

performs a range size inquiry by first writing this register with a value of all 1's, and then reading back its contents. In the value read back, bits [31:11] represent the top 21 bits in the required expansion ROM range. Any bits read back as 1's are "don't-care" bits. For example, a device that requires 16KB for its expansion ROM returns a value of 0FFFFC000H during the inquiry process.

A PCI device may share its allocated address space between its expansion ROM and one or more memory ranges specified in the memory range base address registers. If both the expansion ROM range and an overlapping memory range or ranges are enabled, then the memory range takes precedence.

Because the PCI bus is system architecture-independent, the PCI device may contain expansion ROM images for each of a variety of system and processor architectures. For this reason, each expansion ROM within the PCI device's EPROM contains a ROM header and a PCI Data Structure that identify the ROM's contents.

The PCI Expansion ROM Header

A ROM header resides at location 0 within each expansion ROM image that the PCI device contains. If you have worked with PC-compatible expansion ROMs, the header's 55AAH signature word at location 0H should look familiar. Unlike in a PC expansion ROM, the 55AAH signature in PCI expansion ROM header signals not only the start of the ROM image, but also the location of the *PCI Data Structure* within a particular image. Locations 02H through 05H, which normally specify the length of, and entry point into a PC-compatible expansion ROM are initially invalid. The correct length and entry point appear after the PCI BIOS has successfully copied the device's *x*86-compliant expansion ROM image into the system's shadow RAM.

Figure 4.4 displays the contents of a PCI ROM that contains *N* separate expansion ROM images. Table 4.6 shows the format of the PCI expansion ROM header.

Table 4.6. The format of the PCI expansion ROM header.

Offset	*Size*	*Description*
00H	WORD	Value = 55AAH if an expansion ROM is present; otherwise, the device has no expansion ROM
02H-17H	16H	Unused/Reserved
18H	WORD	16-bit offset of PCI data structure within the PCI device's ROM

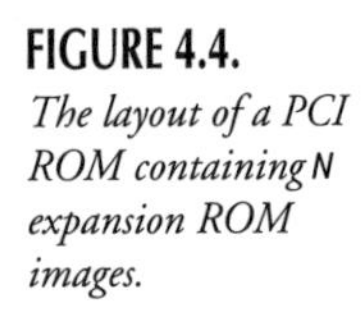

FIGURE 4.4.
The layout of a PCI ROM containing N *expansion ROM images.*

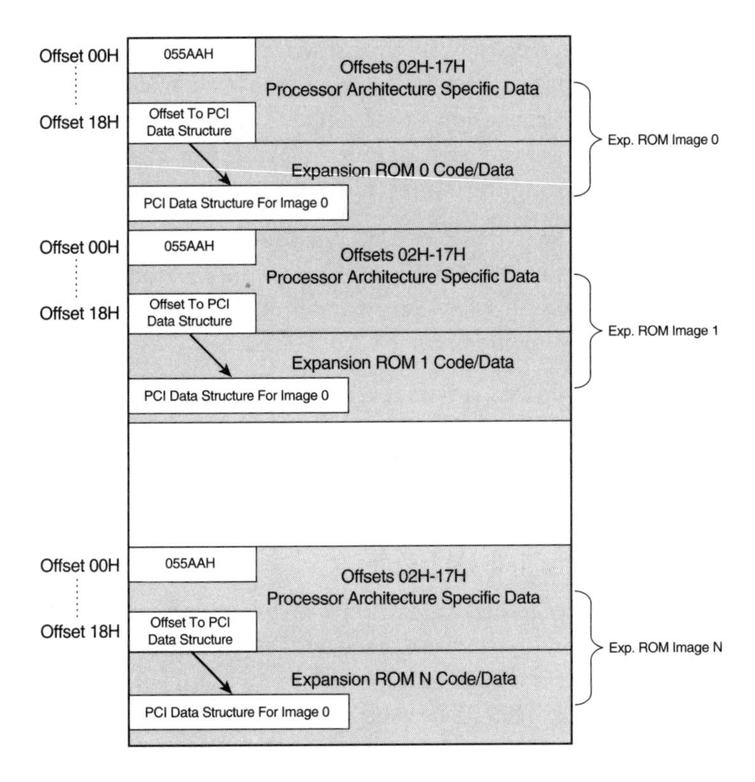

The PCI Data Structure

The *PCI Data Structure* is an 18H-byte, DWORD-aligned table that resides within the first 64KB of each expansion ROM image within a PCI device's ROM. The purpose of the PCI Data Structure is to provide information about the expansion ROM image inside which it resides. PCI Data Structures are both processor and architecture independent. Table 4.7 show the format of the PCI Data Structure.

Table 4.7. The format of the PCI Data Structure within a PCI expansion ROM image.

Offset	*Size*	*Description*
00H	DWORD	PCI Data Structure signature PCIR Byte 0 = ASCII character P Byte 1 = ASCII character C, and so on
04H	WORD	Vendor ID—Matches the Vendor ID reported in the PCI device's configuration space header

Offset	*Size*	*Description*
06H	WORD	Device ID—Matches the Device ID reported in the PCI device's configuration space header
08H	WORD	Pointer to VPD (Vital Product Data) structure. This structure had not been defined as of Revision 2.1 of the PCI Local Bus Specification.
0AH	WORD	Length of the PCI Data Structure
0CH	WORD	PCI Data Structure Revision Level. The only defined value, 0, indicates that the structure adheres to this format
0DH	3*BYTE	The PCI device Class Code as reported in this device's configuration space header
12H	WORD	Length of the expansion ROM image in 512-byte increments
14H	BYTE	Code type as follows: 00H—PC/AT, Intel *x*86-compatible expansion ROM 01H—Open Firmware standard for PCI format 02H-FFH—Reserved
15H	BYTE	Indicator Byte. A value of 1 in bit 7 indicates that this is the last expansion ROM image in the PCI device's ROM. Bits [6:0] are reserved.

It is the task of the system configuration software (in the case of the PC, its PCI BIOS) to search for an expansion ROM that matches the architecture and processor of the host system. In a PCI-equipped Plug and Play system, the PCI BIOS iteratively examines each expansion ROM image within a PCI device's ROM until it either finds an *x*86-compatible expansion ROM, or exhausts all images within the PCI ROM.

PCI Expansion ROM Initialization Sequence

During POST, the PCI BIOS and Plug and Play BIOS maintain a complete map of all available memory ranges within the C0000H-EFFFFH expansion ROM area. With the exception of video adapter ROMs, the PCI BIOS performs its expansion ROM scan after the PC/AT portion of the system BIOS has completed its scan of legacy ISA expansion ROMs. The BIOS configures and scans both PCI and legacy video ROMs much earlier in the POST sequence in order to maintain PC/AT compatibility.

The PCI BIOS assigns memory ranges to PCI expansion ROMs either based on user-supplied ESCD information, or on a first-come, first-served basis.

The process of configuring and scanning PCI device expansion ROMs differs from that used for standard PC/AT-style ROMs. When dealing with PCI expansion ROMs, the first task of the PCI BIOS is to locate an Intel *x*86-compatible ROM image within the PCI device's ROM.

After the PCI BIOS has located the expansion ROM image, it writes the `Expansion ROM Base Address` register within the device's configuration space header with a value that maps the expansion ROM image to a memory location that conflicts with no other memory-mapped devices in the system. A safe method for isolating the PCI expansion ROM is to map it to the top of system address space, while leaving enough room for the expansion ROM image to appear in its entirety.

Next, the PCI BIOS locates the expansion ROM's PCI Data Structure, verifies that the device identification matches that reported in the device's configuration space header registers, and calculates the length of the expansion ROM image. In an ESCD-equipped system, the Plug and Play BIOS NVRAM already may contain a record that details where the device's expansion ROM should be mapped. In a non-ESCD system, the PCI BIOS searches its POST-time memory map for an area large enough to receive the expansion ROM image.

After the PCI BIOS has determined the target region for the expansion ROM image, it copies the image from the PCI device ROM (still mapped to the top of addressable memory space) into shadow RAM inside the target region. Then, without write protecting the shadow RAM, the PCI BIOS invokes the expansion ROM's initialization routine by performing a `far` call to offset three within the newly "shadowed" ROM image.

By leaving the shadow RAM within the target region unprotected, PCI BIOS allows the expansion ROM initialization to perform such tasks as discarding initialization code, adjusting the ROM image length stored in the expansion ROM header, and storing any initialization-time data within its image area. When the initialization procedure has returned control to the PCI BIOS, the BIOS write-protects the ROM image shadow RAM and continues on to the next PCI device. It is the responsibility of the PCI expansion ROM to ensure that prior to returning control to the PCI BIOS, the `checksum` of its image is `0`.

TIP

Each PCI expansion ROM has associated with it three lengths: an image length, an initialization length, and a runtime length. The *image length* is the total length of the ROM image within the PCI device's ROM. This length must be greater than the initialization length. The *initialization length* is the 8-bit value located at offset `02H` of the *x*86 non-shadowed expansion ROM header. This value tells the PCI BIOS how many 512 byte blocks to copy into shadow RAM in the expansion ROM's target region.

The initialization length must be greater than or equal to the runtime length. The *runtime length* is the 8-bit value located at offset `02H` of the shadowed ROM image upon return from its initialization code. The expansion ROM initialization code may adjust the value of its length field in cases in which it discards initialization code. Upon return from the expansion ROM's initialization code, the runtime length field may not be larger than the value that existed when the PCI BIOS first invoked the ROM.

Performing I/O Within PCI Configuration Space

The *PCI Local Bus Specification* defines two configuration space register I/O mechanisms, appropriately named Mechanism #1 and Mechanism #2.

The PCI BIOS is the only application that directly accesses PCI `Configuration Space` registers. Other applications, such as system configurators and enumerators, have no knowledge of the PCI chipset and may only read and write `Device Configuration Space` registers by issuing calls to the PCI BIOS.

CONFIGURATION SPACE I/O MECHANISMS #1 AND #2

Individual PCI chipsets support at least one of the two different mechanisms that exist for programming registers within device configuration space.

Chipsets that support Mechanism #1 reserve two `DWORD` I/O locations in system address space specifically for writing device configuration space. The first location, `CONFIG_ADDRESS`, resides at location `0CF8H` in the system's I/O map. The second, `CONFIG_DATA`, resides at location `0CFCH`. The PCI BIOS performs a Mechanism #1 I/O operation by first writing a value to the `CONFIG_ADDRESS` register, and then reading or writing the contents of `CONFIG_DATA`.

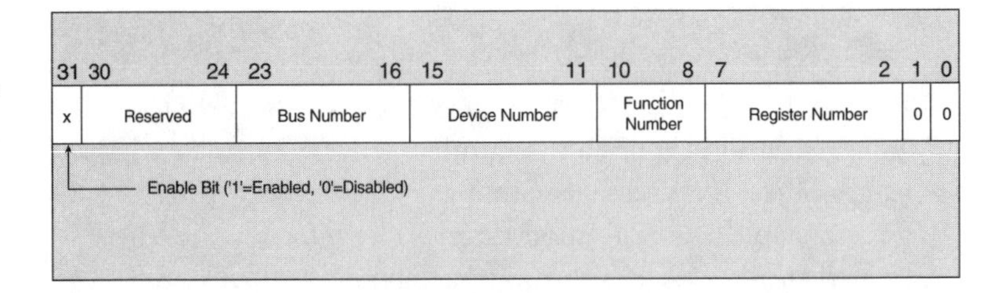

FIGURE 4.5.
The format of the `CONFIG_ADDRESS` *register.*

In a Mechanism #2 chipset, the PCI BIOS unlocks PCI configuration space by writing a non-zero value to bits `[7:4]` of the `CSE (Configuration Space Enable)` register at location `0CF8H` in normal I/O space. When configuration space has been unlocked, the host controller is in Configuration Mode, and the configuration spaces for each PCI device appear as if in normal I/O space in the range `C000H-CFFFH`.

For example, after the PCI BIOS has unlocked configuration space, it could read the `Vendor ID` register of slot 4 simply by performing a `WORD` read of location `C400H`. After having performed its I/O operation, the PCI BIOS writes zeros to bits `[7:4]` of the `CSE` register to relock configuration space and remove the host controller from Configuration Mode. When configuration space is locked, the PCI host controller treats all I/O accesses to the range `C000H-CFFFH` as normal I/O cycles.

Although Mechanism #2 chipsets are much simpler to program, they quickly are being phased out because of multiprocessor systems. In a multiprocessor environment, it's costly and slow to synchronize the state of configuration space read/writes between the system's processors and the Mechanism #2 chipset. For example, if processor #1 enables configuration space on the PCI bus, and processor #2 performs an I/O operation in the range `CXXXH`, then the chipset must consult a complicated and slow synchronization circuit to decide if the I/O cycle pertains to configuration space, or normal I/O space.

Revision 2.1 of The PCI Local Bus Specification states that future host controllers must support Mechanism #1 and should support Mechanism #2 only for reasons of backward compatibility.

The PCI BIOS Runtime Interface

The PCI BIOS provides applications with a function interface by which to communicate with devices on a system's PCI bus or buses. PCI BIOS services are available in real, virtual mode, and 16-bit protected via a set of software INT `1AH` extensions, or in

32-bit protected mode via a physical entry address contained in the system BIOS' 32-bit services directory. Regardless of the calling mechanism it uses, the application driver or program should verify that the system's firmware supports PCI BIOS prior to invoking any PCI BIOS functions.

PCI BIOS Calling Conventions

PCI BIOS functions pass both arguments and return values in *x*86 CPU registers. The functions require 1KB of stack space, and also require that the stack segment and code segment are the same size (for example, both 16-bit, or both 32-bit). Regardless of processor mode, the PCI BIOS executes as if the code segment `CS` is execute-only, and the data segment `DS` is read-only.

Each PCI BIOS function preserves all register contents except `CF` (Carry Flag), which is used to signal function success or failure and those registers that return values to the calling application. PCI BIOS functions never modify the value of the CPU interrupt-enable flag; however, they may enable hardware interrupts within the interrupt controller. In protected mode environments, the caller must ensure that the PCI BIOS has full access to I/O space, including interrupt controller registers.

Real, virtual, and 16-bit protected mode applications invoke PCI BIOS functions via the INT `1AH` mechanism. Protected mode 32-bit applications first locate and verify the PCI BIOS flat-mode entry point (as described in Chapter 2), and then call PCI BIOS functions indirectly, through a 32-bit function pointer.

Complete Listing of PCI BIOS Functions

Applications and device drivers access devices on the PCI bus via the following PCI BIOS functions rather than directly reading or writing configuration space registers. This allows the chipset register mechanism to be transparent to OS level software. If the system did not support PCI BIOS functions, applications would have to contain code to support both mechanism #1 and mechanism #2 chipsets.

Function *01H—PCI_BIOS_PRESENT*

The primary purpose of this function is to signal the presence and revision level of the system's PCI BIOS. Additionally, `PCI_BIOS_PRESENT` reports the actual hardware mechanism that the PCI BIOS uses to read and write configuration space registers, as well as what type of special cycle support exists in the chipset.

Passed

```
AH   B1H (PCI_FUNCTION_ID)
AL   01H (PCI_BIOS_PRESENT)
```

Returns

EDX	20494350H (4-byte ASCII string PCI) if PCI BIOS present
AH	If 0, and CF and EDX are correct, PCI BIOS is present
AL	Supported hardware mechanism
BH	BCD-encoded major revision of interface supported
BL	BCD-encoded minor revision of interface supported
CL	Zero-based number of last PCI bus in the system
CF	If clear, and AH and EDX are correct, PCI BIOS is present If set, no PCI BIOS is present

If the PCI_BIOS_PRESENT function returns successfully, the AL register contains chipset-specific information regarding special cycle support and the programming mechanism that the system's chipset supports. Table 4.7 shows the AL register upon return from a successful call to PCI_BIOS_PRESENT.

Table 4.7. The AL register upon return from a successful call to PCI_BIOS_PRESENT.

Bit(s)	*Description*
[7:6]	Reserved
[5]	1—Special cycles are supported via Mechanism #2
[4]	1—Special cycles are supported via Mechanism #1
[3:2]	Reserved
[1]	1—System chipset supports Mechanism #1
[0]	1—System chipset supports Mechanism #2

Function *02H—FIND_PCI_DEVICE*

Given a Vendor ID, Device ID, and an Index N, the function FIND_PCI_DEVICE will find the Nth device or function whose Vendor ID and Device ID match those passed into the function. Additionally, FIND_PCI_DEVICE will return the Bus Number, Device Number, and function number of the device if it successfully finds a match.

Passed

AH	B1H (PCI_FUNCTION_ID)
AL	02H (PCI_FIND_DEVICE)
CX	16-bit Device ID

DX 16-bit Vendor ID

SI Index *N* (*N*th occurrence of PCI device)

Returns

BH Bus Number of device (0-based)

BL Bits [7:3] = Device number

Bits [2:0] = Function number within located device

AH Function return status code

SUCCESSFUL

DEVICE_NOT_FOUND

BAD_VENDOR_ID

CF Function completion status

Clear—Device was located

Set—An error occurred, AH register contains error code

This function is useful for locating all PCI devices in the system that perform the same function. The first return value of DEVICE_NOT_FOUND indicates that there are no more devices of the type specified in the system.

Function 03H—FIND_PCI_CLASS_CODE

The function FIND_PCI_CLASS_CODE returns the *N*th occurrence of the device or device function whose class code matches the value passed in the ECX register.

Passed

AH B1H (PCI_FUNCTION_ID)

AL 03H (FIND_PCI_CLASS_CODE)

ECX Class Code in lower three bytes

SI Index *N* (*N*th occurrence of PCI device or function whose Class Code matches that passed in the ECX register)

Returns

BH Bus Number of device (0-based)

BL Bits [7:3] = Device number

Bits [2:0] = Function number within located device

AH Function return status code

SUCCESSFUL

DEVICE_NOT_FOUND

CF Function completion status

Clear—Device was located

Set—An error occurred, AH register contains error code

The FIND_PCI_CLASS_CODE function is useful for locating all system PCI devices that belong to the same device class. The first return value of DEVICE_NOT_FOUND indicates that there are no more devices in the system with the specified Class Code.

Function 06H—GENERATE_SPECIAL_CYCLE

The PCI host controller has the capability to broadcast messages across the entire bus by issuing special cycles. When a special cycle occurs, devices on the bus may monitor the message, but must not acknowledge the message by asserting their DEVSEL#, or Device Select signal. PCI devices do not have to respond to special cycles. If a device is capable of responding to special cycles, the system configurator or PCI BIOS enables this capability in a device by setting bit 3 of its Configuration Space Command register to a 1.

Passed

AH B1H (PCI_FUNCTION_ID)

AL 06H (GENERATE_SPECIAL_CYCLE)

BH Number of bus on which to assert the cycle (0-FFH)

EDX Special Cycle Data

Bits [15:0] = Special cycle message

Bits [31:16] = Message specific data

Returns

AH Function return status code

SUCCESSFUL

FUNC_NOT_SUPPORTED

CF Function completion status

Clear—Function completed successfully

Set—An error occurred, AH register contains error code.

Special cycle messages consist of a 16-bit message field, which the host controller asserts on Address/Data lines AD[15:0], and a message field, which is asserted in signals AD[31:16]. The meaning of each message field is determined by the PCI SIG and a list of all valid special cycles appears in *The PCI Local Bus Specification.* Revisions 2.0 and 2.1 of the PCI Local Bus Specification define the following special cycle messages:

`0000H`	System shutdown
`0001H`	PCI Bus Halt
`0002H`	Intel *x*86 Architecture-Specific message.
`0003H-FFFFH`	Reserved

One useful application of special cycle messages is to broadcast a pending system shutdown to PCI bus devices. For example, a PCI network controller should immediately abort its current network activity in the event of a system shutdown. It is the responsibility of the operating system to issue a PCI BIOS call to generate the system shutdown message (`0000H`).

NOTE

The PCI BIOS provides applications and drivers six functions for reading and writing configuration space registers:

- Function `08H—READ_CONFIG_BYTE`
- Function `09H—READ_CONFIG_WORD`
- Function `0AH—READ_CONFIG_DWORD`
- Function `0BH—WRITE_CONFIG_BYTE`
- Function `0CH—WRITE_CONFIG_WORD`
- Function `0DH—WRITE_CONFIG_DWORD`

If you are reading or writing a `DWORD`-sized value in configuration space, then the `Register Number` you specify in the function `WRITE_CONFIG_DWORD` or `READ_CONFIG_DWORD` must be on a `DWORD` boundary, such as `00H`, `04H`, `08H`, and so on. Similarly, if you are reading or writing a `WORD`-sized value in configuration space, the `Register Number` you specify in the function `WRITE_CONFIG_WORD` or `READ_CONFIG_WORD` must be on a `WORD` boundary, such as `00H`, `02H`, `04H`, and so on. The remaining functions, `READ_CONFIG_BYTE` and `WRITE_CONFIG_BYTE` operate correctly on any register boundary within configuration space.

If the calling program attempts an illegal I/O operation, such as a `DWORD` read of configuration space location `02H`, the PCI BIOS returns the value `87H` (`BAD_REGISTER_NUMBER`) in the `AH` register and sets the `carry` flag.

PCI BIOS return values are listed in Appendix B.

Function *08H—READ_CONFIG_BYTE*

This function reads one byte from the configuration space of the caller-specified PCI device.

Passed

AH B1H (PCI_FUNCTION_ID)

AL 08H (READ_CONFIG_BYTE)

BH Number of bus on which the device resides

BL Bits [7:3] = Device number

Bits [2:0] = Device function number

DI Register index (0-FFH) within the device's or function's configuration space

Returns

AH Function return status code

CL Byte read from configuration space

CF Function completion status

Clear—Function completed successfully

Set—An error occurred

Function *09H—READ_CONFIG_WORD*

This function reads one word from the configuration space of the caller-specified PCI device.

Passed

AH B1H (PCI_FUNCTION_ID)

AL 09H (READ_CONFIG_WORD)

BH Number of bus on which the device resides

BL Bits [7:3] = Device number

Bits [2:0] = Device function number

DI Register index (0-FFH) within the device's or function's configuration space

Returns

AH Function return status code

SUCCESSFUL

BAD_REGISTER_NUMBER

CX Word read from configuration space

CF Function completion status

Clear—Function completed successfully

Set—An error occurred, AH register contains error code

Function *0AH—READ_CONFIG_DWORD*

This function reads one double word from the configuration space of the caller-specified PCI device.

Passed

AH	B1H (PCI_FUNCTION_ID)
AL	0AH (READ_CONFIG_DWORD)
BH	Number of bus on which the device resides
BL	Bits [7:3] = Device number
	Bits [2:0] = Device function number
DI	Register index (0-FFH) within the device's or function's configuration space

Returns

AH	Function return status codes
	SUCCESSFUL
	BAD_REGISTER_NUMBER
ECX	Double word read from configuration space
CF	Function completion status
	Clear—Function completed successfully
	Set—An error occurred, AH register contains error code

Function *0BH—WRITE_CONFIG_BYTE*

This function writes one byte to the configuration space of the caller-specified PCI device.

Passed

AH	B1H (PCI_FUNCTION_ID)
AL	0BH (WRITE_CONFIG_BYTE)
BH	Number of bus on which the device resides
BL	Bits [7:3] = Device number
	Bits [2:0] = Device function number

CL Byte value to write to configuration space

DI Register index (0-FFH) within the device's or function's configuration space

Returns

AH Function return status code

SUCCESSFUL

CF Function completion status

Clear—Function completed successfully

Set—An error occurred, AH register contains error code

Function *0CH—WRITE_CONFIG_WORD*

This function writes one word to the configuration space of the caller-specified PCI device.

Passed

AH B1H (PCI_FUNCTION_ID)

AL 0CH (WRITE_CONFIG_WORD)

BH Number of bus on which the device resides

BL Bits [7:3] = Device number

Bits [2:0] = Device function number

CX Word value to write to configuration space

DI Register index (0-FFH) within the device's or function's configuration space

Returns

AH Function return status code

SUCCESSFUL

BAD_REGISTER_NUMBER

CF Function completion status

Clear—Function completed successfully

Set—An error occurred

Function *0DH—WRITE_CONFIG_DWORD*

This function writes one double word to the configuration space of the caller-specified PCI device.

Passed

AH B1H (PCI_FUNCTION_ID)

AL 0DH (WRITE_CONFIG_DWORD)

BH Number of bus on which the device resides

BL Bits [7:3] = Device number

Bits [2:0] = Device function number

DI Register index (0-FFH) within the device's or function's configuration space

ECX Double word value to write to configuration space

Returns

AH Function return status code

SUCCESSFUL

BAD_REGISTER_NUMBER

CF Function completion status

Clear—Function completed successfully

Set—An error occurred, AH register contains error code

Function *0EH—GET_IRQ_ROUTING_INFO*

The GET_IRQ_ROUTING_INFO function fills a caller-supplied buffer with one IRQ routing information table for each PCI slot and motherboard device in the system. Table 4.8 shows the format of the IRQ Routing Table.

Table 4.8. The format of the IRQ Routing Table.

Offset	*Size*	*Description*
00H	BYTE	PCI Bus number for this device
01H	BYTE	Bits [7:3] = physical PCI Device number. The PCI BIOS assigns each PCI device in the system a unique number. The number that the PCI BIOS has assigned to a device is arbitrary, yet guaranteed to be unique.
02H	BYTE	INTA# Link Value
03H	WORD	INTA# IRQ Connectivity bit map
05H	BYTE	INTB# Link Value

continues

Table 4.8. continued.

Offset	*Size*	*Description*
06H	WORD	INTB# IRQ Connectivity bitmap
08H	BYTE	INTC# Link Value
09H	WORD	INTC# IRQ Connectivity bitmap
0BH	BYTE	INTD# Link Value
0CH	WORD	INTD# IRQ Connectivity bitmap
0EH	BYTE	Device Slot Number. This value is 00H for motherboard devices, and is otherwise OEM-specific. The *PCI BIOS Specification* recommends that the PCI BIOS should assign Device Slot Numbers to physical slots in such a way that it is easy for the user to correlate this value to the actual motherboard slot.
0FH	BYTE	Reserved

The routing information table provides a Link Value and IRQ Connectivity bitmap for each of the four PCI INTx# lines. OS level enumerator and configurator applications wanting to reconfigure PCI devices at runtime first invoke the GET_IRQ_ROUTING_INFO function to retrieve an IRQ routing information table for each PCI device installed. They then interpret the table entries and issue a corresponding call to SET_PCI_IRQ if an appropriate new configuration is possible.

The IRQ Connectivity bitmaps within a device's routing information table specify the IRQ channels to which the PCI BIOS can connect that device's INTA#-INT#D outputs. Bit 0 in the bitmap corresponds to IRQ 0, bit one corresponds to IRQ 1, and so on. A value of 08000H in the INTB# availability bitmap, for example, signals that the INTB# output for the device can only connect to IRQ 15.

The Link Values within each IRQ routing information table specify which INTx# lines are wire ORed together on the systemboard. A link value of 00H indicates that the INTx# line is not connected to the system interrupt controller. Otherwise, any two INTx# lines whose Link Values are identical are assumed to share the same IRQ channel.

The caller supplies the function GET_IRQ_ROUTING_INFO with a RoutingBuffer structure that adheres to the following format:

```
typedef struct {
WORD SizeOfBuffer ;  // Size of caller allocated buffer in bytes
BYTE far * pBuffer ;  // Far pointer to caller-allocated buffer
} IRQRoutingBuffer ;
```

Passed

AH B1H (PCI_FUNCTION_ID)

AL 0EH (GET_IRQ_ROUTING_INFO)

BX 0000H

DS Segment/Selector of PCI BIOS data

In 16-bit real and protected modes, this value should resolve to a 64KB limit read/write segment based at F0000H physical. In 32-bit mode, the selector should satisfy the length/address fields supplied in the PCI BIOS' 32-bit services directory.

ES Segment/Selector of caller-supplied RoutingBuffer structure

DI Offset of RoutingBuffer structure (16-bit real/protected mode only)

EDI Offset of RoutingBuffer structure (32-bit protected mode only)

Returns

BX Bit map of IRQ channels permanently dedicated to PCI

AH Function return status code

SUCCESSFUL

BUFFER_TOO_SMALL

FUNC_NOT_SUPPORTED

CF Function completion status

Clear—Function completed successfully

Set—An error occurred, AH register contains error code

In addition to providing the caller with interrupt routing tables, the function GET_IRQ_ROUTING_INFO returns in the BX register a bitmap that specifies all system IRQs that have been permanently allocated to the PCI bus. As is the case with the IRQ Connectivity bitmaps within a device's IRQ routing information table, bit 0 in the returned BX register corresponds to IRQ 0, bit 1 pertains to IRQ 1, and so on. If the BX register contains the value 0C000H upon return from a call to GET_IRQ_ROUTING_INFO, for example, the caller should assume that IRQs 14 and 15 belong exclusively to the PCI bus.

The function GET_IRQ_ROUTING_INFO returns the error condition BUFFER_TOO_SMALL if the caller's buffer is inadequate for receiving the IRQ routing information tables from the PCI BIOS. A list of PCI error codes appears in Appendix B.

Function 0FH—SET_PCI_IRQ

The function SET_PCI_IRQ allows the caller to specify that a particular IRQ be connected to the device specified in the caller's BX register. This function assumes three things. First, the function assumes that the caller understands the IRQ routing topology of the target system. Second, it assumes that the IRQ to which the caller wants to connect the PCI device does not conflict with other, currently installed devices. Finally, SET_PCI_IRQ assumes that the caller will update the contents of the Interrupt Line register for each device that is currently using the IRQ line that is to be rerouted.

Passed

AH	B1H (PCI_FUNCTION_ID)
AL	0FH (SET_PCI_IRQ)
BH	Number of bus on which the device resides
BL	Bits [7:3] = Device number
	Bits [2:0] = Device function number
CH	Number of IRQ to connect to target device
CL	Number of the Interrupt Pin (INTA#-INTD#) line to reprogram. Values of 0AH through 0DH indicate lines INTA# through INTD#, respectively
DS	Segment/Selector of PCI BIOS data.

In 16-bit real and protected modes, this value should resolve to a 64K limit read/write segment based at F0000H physical. In 32-bit mode, the selector should satisfy the length/address fields supplied in the PCI BIOS' 32-bit services directory.

Returns

AH	Function return status code
	SUCCESSFUL
	SET_FAILED
	FUNC_NOT_SUPPORTED
CF	Function completion status
	Clear—Function completed successfully
	Set—An error occurred

Example DOS Device Driver for a PCI Device

This section presents, of all things, a real-life DOS device driver example designed specifically for users and programmers who want to provide support for interrupt-driven PCI devices within the DOS environment.

To activate the example driver PCITSR.SYS, first create the driver using the following simple commands:

```
ML PCITSR.ASM
EXE2BIN PCITSR.EXE PCITSR.SYS
```

Add the following command to your DOS-based system's CONFIG.SYS file:

```
DEVICE=C:\path\PCITSR.SYS
```

During the processing of the system's CONFIG.SYS file, DOS installs the `PCITSR.SYS` driver in its device chain under the name `$PCITSR$`. During DOS' initialization sequence, the `$PCITSR$` driver first looks for a PCI BIOS in the system, and then searches for any occurrences of the PCI device specified by `MYDEVICEID` and `MYVENDORID` at the start of the `PCITSR.ASM` source module. You can customize these values and rebuild the driver to find your particular device.

If the `$PCITSR$` driver finds both its intended PCI device and a PCI BIOS, it will terminate and stay resident by supplying DOS with a driver length and success status code in the driver request header. Each of the following two books provides a good explanation of DOS device driver format:

Writing MS-DOS Device Drivers, Robert Lai, The Waite Group, 1987, 466 pp. (ISBN 0-201-13185-4)

IBM Disk Operating System Technical Reference—Version 4.00, Application Programming, First Edition, 1988, International Business Machines Corp.

The following listing for PCITSR.ASM presents a working DOS device driver example whose function is to locate the adapter for which it is intended (in this case, a Digital Equipment Corporation Ethernet controller). The device driver aborts its installation if the system contains no PCI BIOS, or if the driver cannot locate the DEC device.

```
;****************************************************************
;*
;* PCITSR.ASM: Simple DOS Driver That Handles Finds A PCI
;*       Device And Determines Its Assigned IRQ Channel
;*
;* To Build, Type: ML PCITSR.ASM
;*         EXE2BIN PCITSR.EXE PCITSR.SYS
;*
;****************************************************************


;
; The following equates apply to your device. For the purpose
; of example, these values correspond to a DEC Ethernet adapter.
; Note: Pre-2.10 device do not support the Device Sub-Type
; configuration space register. Any Ethernet adapter that uses
; the DEC chip whose Device ID = 0002H will be found by this
; driver, regardless of who is the actual vendor.
;

 MYDEVICEID     EQU 0002H
 MYVENDORID     EQU 1011H
 MYCLASSCODE    EQU 020000H
```

```
;
; PCI BIOS Function Values
;

PCI_FUNCTION_ID    EQU 0B1H
PCI_BIOS_PRESENT   EQU 001H
FIND_PCI_DEVICE    EQU 002H
FIND_PCI_CLASS_CODE EQU 003H
READ_CONFIG_BYTE   EQU 008H
READ_CONFIG_WORD   EQU 009H
READ_CONFIG_DWORD   EQU 00AH
WRITE_CONFIG_BYTE   EQU 00BH
WRITE_CONFIG_WORD   EQU 00CH
WRITE_CONFIG_DWORD EQU 00DH

;
; PCI BIOS Return Values
;

SUCCESS        EQU 000H
FUNC_NOT_SUPPORTED EQU 081H
BAD_VENDOR_ID     EQU 083H
DEVICE_NOT_FOUND   EQU 086H
BAD_REGISTER_NUMBER EQU 087H
SET_FAILED       EQU 088H
BUFFER_TOO_SMALL   EQU 089H

;
; PCI Signature (EDX = 'PCI ' Upon Successful Return From PCI_FUNCTION_ID)
;

PCI_INSTALL_SIG EQU ('P'+(100H*'C')+(10000H*'I')+(1000000H*' ')) ; 'PCI '

;
; DOS Device Driver-Specific Request Header EQUates
;

RQ_LEN EQU 0           ;BYTE - Length field
RQ_UCD EQU 1           ;BYTE - Unit code field
RQ_CCD EQU 2           ;BYTE - Command code field
RQ_STA EQU 3           ;WORD - Status code field
RQ_RES EQU 5           ;Reserved area field
RQ_NUNI EQU 13+0         ;BYTE - Number of units for device
RQ_BRKA EQU 13+1         ;DWORD - Break address for this device
RQ_BPBP EQU 13+5         ;DWORD - Pointer to BPB ARRAY
RQ_ARGP EQU 13+5         ;DWORD - Pointer to arg list in CONFIG.SYS
RQ_DRVN EQU 13+9         ;BYTE - Drive number (block dev DOS 3.10)
RQ_MDAB EQU 13+0         ;BYTE - Media descriptor
RQ_TRSA EQU 13+1         ;DWORD - Transfer address
RQ_BSCT EQU 13+5         ;WORD - BYTE/SECTOR count
RQ_SSEC EQU 13+7         ;WORD - Starting sector number
RQ_VLID EQU 13+9         ;DWORD - Pointer to volume label (DOS 3.10)

NOERROR      EQU 0
NOTREADY     EQU 2

; Some Possible Device Attributes For DOS Device Header
```

```
BLKDEV EQU 0000H
CHRDEV EQU 8000H

;
; DEVICE_STAT: A MACRO To Set Device Return Status In
; A DOS Device Driver Request Header. Assumes ES:BX
; Points To The Driver's Request Header.
;

DEVICE_STAT Macro STATE, DEVERR
  ifidn <STATE>,<DONE>
   or es:word ptr RQ_STA[bx],0100H  ; Done Bit
  endif
  ifidn <STATE>,<BUSY>
   or es:word ptr RQ_STA[bx],0300H  ; Busy And Done Bits
  endif
  ifidn <STATE>,<ERROR>
   or es:word ptr RQ_STA[bx],8100H  ; Error And Done Bits
  endif
  or es:word ptr RQ_STA[bx],DEVERR
Endm

;
; A Quick HEX To ASCII Character MACRO
;

HEX_2_ASCII Macro INREG
  local  l1, l2

  cmp   INREG, 0FFH
  je   NoInterrupt

  cmp   INREG, 0AH
  jae   l1

  add   INREG, '0'
  jmp   l2

l1: add   INREG, 'A' - 10
l2:
Endm


    .MODEL   SMALL
    .code
    .386

NxtDeviceOff:  jmp short EXEEntry   ; If .EXE, jump over this header
NxtDeviceSeg   dw -1          ; Pointer to next device
DevAttrib     dw CHRDEV        ; Device attributes (CHAR Only)
DevStrat      dw OFFSET CS:_PCIStrat ; Strategy routine address
DevInt       dw OFFSET CS:_PCIEntry ; Entry point address
DevName      db "$PCITSR$"      ; Name Of Example Driver

EXEEntry:
   MOV  AX, 4C00H     ; if user runs this as an .exe
   INT  21H        ; exit to DOS w/no error code
```

```
reqptr   dw  0       ; store pointer to DOS' device
      dw  0      ; driver request header here

OldInt   dw  0       ; store old interrupt vector
      dw  0      ; here

FUNTBL   label word    ; JMP offsets for device routines
   dw PCIInit       ; initialization
   dw Not_Supported    ; media check
   dw Not_Supported    ; build BPB
   dw Not_Supported    ; I/O control input
   dw Not_Supported    ; input
   dw Not_Supported    ; input status
   dw Not_Supported    ; input flush
   dw Not_Supported    ; output
   dw Not_Supported    ; output/verify
   dw Not_Supported    ; ** output status
   dw Not_Supported    ; ** output flush
   dw Not_Supported    ; ** I/O control output
   dw Not_Supported    ; ** open (DOS 3.xx)
   dw Not_Supported    ; ** close (DOS 3.xx)
   dw Not_Supported    ; ** removeable (DOS 3.xx)

;************************************************************
;*
;* PCIStrat: Strategy Routine For DOS' Driver Initialization
;*
;* DOS invokes this function once during the initialization
;* phase of the device driver (during CONFIG.SYS processing)
;*
;* DOS passes ES:BX, which points to a dedicated request
;* header that DOS builds prior to each call into the driver.
;*
;* The driver stores ES:BX locally in reqptr. When DOS issues
;* a call into the driver, the PCIEntry routine restores
;* ES:BX from the reqptr variable and retrieves the DOS
;* command code from the request header. Upon exit, the
;* driver stores various status information back in the header
;*
;************************************************************

_PCIStrat proc near
   mov   word ptr CS:reqptr+2,es ; save segment of request header
   mov   word ptr CS:reqptr,bx  ; save offset of request header
   retf
_PCIStrat endp

;************************************************************
;*
;* PCIEntry: The Standard Entry Point For DOS Driver Requests
;*
;* DOS Passes
;*
;************************************************************

_PCIEntry proc near
```

```
    push  ax
    push  bx
    push  es
    push  si

    les   bx, dword ptr cs:reqptr ; Get Pointer To DOS Request Header

    xor   ax,ax          ; Clear AH For Dispatch
    mov   al,es:RQ_CCD[BX]    ; AL = DOS Function Code
    shl   ax,1          ; Mul By 2 To Index Function Table
    mov   si,ax          ; SI Points Into Function Table

    pusha               ; Save All Regs Around This Call
    push  ds
    push  es
    call  word ptr FUNTBL[si]   ; Dispatch To Correct Function
    pop   es
    pop   ds
    popa               ; We'll Crash On 8086's Probably

    jc   SignalError       ;

    DEVICE_STAT NOERROR, NOERROR  ; Signal To DOS' Request Header
    jmp   ExitInit        ; That The Call Succeeded & Exit

 SignalError:
   DEVICE_STAT ERROR, NOTREADY  ; Signal To DOS' Request Header
                  ; That The Call Failed & Exit
 ExitInit:
   pop   si
   pop   es
   pop   bx
   pop   ax
   retf
_PCIEntry endp

;************************************************************
;*
;* Stub Routine For Non-Supported Device Driver Functions
;*
;************************************************************

Not_Supported proc near
  stc
  ret
Not_Supported endp

;************************************************************
;*
;* Output Strings Used By PCIInit Function
;*
;************************************************************

 ;
 ; If there's no PCI BIOS, tell the user and get out
 ;

NoPCIMess  db 'MYDEVICE or PCI BIOS Not Found ... Aborting !!'
```

```
     db 0DH, 0AH, '$'

;
; If we find a PCI BIOS, display its major/minor revisions
;

YesPCIMess db 'Version '
VerString  db '[x.x]'
      db ' PCI BIOS Detected'
      db 0DH, 0AH, '$'
;
; Once we find a PCI BIOS, display the number of buses supported
;

BusCntMess db 'System Contains '
CntString  db '[x]'
      db ' PCI bus(es)', 0DH, 0AH, '$'

;
; Once we found MYDEVICE, display it's bus and occurrence #'s
;


DevFoundMess db 'Found MYDEVICE On Bus '
BusNumber  db '[x] (', 01H, ') Device Index = '
DevIndex   db '[x]', 0DH, 0AH, 07H, '$'

DevIntMess  db 'Device Uses Interrupt '
IntNumber  db '[x]', 0DH, 0AH, '$'

IntLevel   db 0

;************************************************************
;*
;* PCIInit: Check For PCI Installed In System
;*
;* If System Supports PCI BIOS:
;*  o Find Our Device
;*  o Read Interrupt Line For MYDEVICE
;*  o Intercept Our Device's IRQ Vector (You Add This Code)
;*  o Terminate & Stay Resident, Return No Error
;*
;* Else:
;*  o Print Message
;*  o Abort With Error Condition, No TSR
;*
;************************************************************

PCIInit proc near
  mov   word ptr cs:NxtDeviceOff, -1 ; Fix The Device Link Field
                    ;
  mov   ah, PCI_FUNCTION_ID      ; Check For PCI BIOS Present
  mov   al, PCI_BIOS_PRESENT     ;
  int   1AH              ;

  jc   NoPCI              ; Carry Set — No PCI BIOS

  cmp   edx, PCI_INSTALL_SIG     ; Second Check For EDX = 'PCI '
```

```
    jne   NoPCI              ; If Not, We Fail The Call

    ;
    ; Print Out PCI BIOS Version Supported And Bus Count.
    ; Save Bus Count So We Can Iteratively Scan For Our Device
    ;

    HEX_2_ASCII bh              ; If Found, Convert Versions
    HEX_2_ASCII bl              ; To ASCII Characters And Store
    mov   byte ptr VerString + 1, bh  ; In Sign-On String
    mov   byte ptr VerString + 3, bl  ;

    inc   cl                 ;
    HEX_2_ASCII cl              ; Save Bus Count For Display
    mov   byte ptr CntString + 1, cl  ;

    mov   dx, offset YesPCIMess     ; Print Sign-On Message
    call  PrintMessage          ;

    mov   dx, offset BusCntMess     ; Print # Of Installed Buses
    call  PrintMessage          ;

    ;
    ; Now, we'll go scan for all occurrences of our device. This
    ; operation aborts once the PCI BIOS returns DEVICE_NOT_FOUND
    ;

    mov   si, 0              ; si = device index

NextOccurrence:
    push  si

    mov   ah, PCI_FUNCTION_ID      ; Call PCI BIOS To Find
    mov   al, FIND_PCI_DEVICE      ; The Nth Occurrence Of
    mov   cx, MYDEVICEID        ; MYDEVICE (SI Holds N)
    mov   dx, MYVENDORID        ;
    int   1AH              ;
    jc   FindDeviceError        ;

    cmp   ah, DEVICE_NOT_FOUND     ; If DEVICE_NOT_FOUND,
    je   FindDeviceError        ; We're Done, Get Out

    pop   si
    inc   si

    mov   dl, bh
    HEX_2_ASCII dl
    mov   BusNumber + 1, dl

    mov   ax, si
    HEX_2_ASCII al
    mov   DevIndex + 1, al

    ;
    ; Here, you might want to take over the interrupt vector for
    ; your device if it supports interrupts. This code determines
    ; which interrupt has been assigned to the device, if any,
    ; by reading the Interrupt Line Register at location 03CH
```

```
; within the device's configuration space.
;

mov   di, 03CH              ; Get Device's Interrupt Line
mov   ah, PCI_FUNCTION_ID         ; Register, BH & BL Already
mov   al, READ_CONFIG_BYTE        ; Identify MYDEVICE
int   1AH                   ;
jc   ReadError              ;

cmp   cl, 0FFH              ; Interrupt Line Register = 0FFH
je   NoInterrupt             ; Means Device Uses No IRQ's

mov   cs:IntLevel, cl           ;
HEX_2_ASCII cl               ; Store Int # While We Have It
mov   IntNumber + 1, cl         ;

mov   dx, offset DevFoundMess     ; Print Our Happy
call  PrintMessage           ; "Device Found" Message

mov   dx, offset DevIntMess      ;
call  PrintMessage           ; Print Contents Of Interrupt
jmp   NextOccurrence          ; Line Register For MYDEVICE

NoInterrupt:
  mov   dx, offset DevFoundMess
  call  PrintMessage
  jmp   NextOccurrence

ReadError:
FindDeviceError:
  pop   si                 ;
  or   si, si               ; If SI == 0, We were unable
  jz   NoPCI                ; to find MYDEVICE, so abort

  ;
  ; Set DOS Break Address For Terminate-Stay-Resident Action.
  ; Store Offset Of End Of This Program To Tell DOS How
  ; Large We Are In Resident Mode. (Pad w/10H Bytes For Safety)
  ;

  les   bx, dword ptr cs:reqptr
  mov   word ptr es:RQ_BRKA+0[bx], offset EndLabel + 10H
  mov   word ptr es:RQ_BRKA+2[bx], cs
  clc
  ret

NoPCI:
  mov   dx, offset NoPCIMess
  mov   ax, cs
  mov   ds, ax
  mov   ax, 0900H
  int   21H

  les   bx, dword ptr cs:reqptr
  mov   word ptr es:RQ_BRKA+0[bx], 00H
  mov   word ptr es:RQ_BRKA+2[bx], cs
  stc
  ret
```

```
PCIInit endp

;***********************************************************
;*
;* PrintMessage: Invoke DOS Function 09H To Print A String.
;* Only DOS Functions < 0CH are OK In A Device Driver. This
;* Function Assumes DX Is The Offset Of The String To Print
;*
;***********************************************************

PrintMessage proc near
  push  ds
  mov   ax, cs
  mov   ds, ax
  mov   ax, 0900H
  int   21H
  pop   ds
  ret
PrintMessage endp

;***********************************************************
;*
;* MyDeviceIRQ: Sample Interrupt Handler For MYDEVICE
;*
;* Note: Since PCI uses level sensitive interrupts, this
;*    routine MUST check to see if the interrupt belongs
;*    to MYDEVICE. Also, if the IRQ was greater than
;*    IRQ 7, we must issue an EOI to both PIC's
;*
;***********************************************************

MyDeviceIRQ proc far
  push ax

  ;
  ; Figure out if our device generated the interrupt signal.
  ; If another device did, we'll chain the interrupt.
  ;

  ; pushf
  ; call dword ptr cs:OldInterrupt
  ;

  mov  al, 20H
  out  20H, al
  cmp  byte ptr cs:IntLevel, 07H
  jbe  PrimaryPICOnly

  out  0A0H, al

PrimaryPICOnly:
  pop  ax
  iret
MyDeviceIRQ endp

EndLabel:

  END   NxtDeviceOff
```

5

Plug and Play ISA

Since its introduction in the original IBM PC, the ISA (Industry Standard Architecture) bus has undergone just two modifications—the 1984 addition of a 16-bit extension adapter and a subsequent increase in the frequency of the bus' SYSCLK to 8 MHz on later models of the AT. The ISA bus architecture continues to thrive because it is simple and inexpensive, it offers adequate performance for system devices such as serial ports, parallel ports, and audio cards, and because of the sheer volume of adapters, chipsets, and tooling that manufacturers have designed to support the architecture.

Faced with the challenge of facilitating the PC industry's transition to auto-configurable systems, Plug and Play architects at Microsoft and Intel introduced the Plug and Play ISA model, which enables Plug and Play-compliant ISA devices to coexist with legacy devices on existing ISA bus implementations. The *Plug and Play ISA Specification* provides designers with a relatively simple and inexpensive method for converting existing ISA designs to a Plug and Play-compliant form.

A WORD ABOUT EXISTING LEGACY ISA SYSTEMS...

A legacy system might contain both Plug and Play ISA adapters and Plug and Play-aware drivers or application programs capable of initializing and configuring specific adapters. The process of configuring this mixed-model system might be simpler than that for a similar legacy system containing only legacy ISA devices. The mixed-model system is not, however, Plug and Play compliant because it lacks a Plug and Play BIOS. If a system lacks a Plug and Play BIOS, operating system level applications executing in that system lack an accurate method for enumerating and configuring those resources assigned to system-board or legacy devices, regardless of the flexibility offered by any Plug and Play devices installed on its ISA bus.

The methods involved in programming Plug and Play ISA devices at the register level apply largely to both legacy and Plug and Play-compliant systems. In order to provide a cohesive, system-level approach to programming in a Plug and Play environment, this chapter proceeds as if your target system is Plug and Play-compliant, including a Plug and Play BIOS and POST-time Plug and Play ISA device support.

Plug and Play ISA devices operate on a standard ISA bus through a combination of additional system software and device-resident hardware. Plug and Play ISA software support is distributed among the system's firmware, its operating system enumerator/configurator, and any operating system level runtime device-management interface.

A Plug and Play ISA device's hardware layer consists of its normal ISA function, and a new set of logic that introduces the Plug and Play ISA-specific `READ_DATA`, `ADDRESS`, and `WRITE_DATA` registers and controls the Plug and Play ISA adapter's current state.

As described in Microsoft's *Plug and Play ISA Specification*, all Plug and Play ISA adapters installed in a system respond to I/O reads and writes to `READ_DATA`, `ADDRESS`, and `WRITE_DATA`. Additionally, all installed Plug and Play ISA adapters are capable of transitioning between any of four states, namely Wait For Key state, Sleep state, Isolation state, and Configuration state. These registers and states are described in detail in this chapter. Figure 5.1 displays the additional software/hardware interface that exists in a Plug and Play system equipped with Plug and Play ISA device support.

FIGURE 5.1
Displays the system hardware and software support for Plug and Play ISA devices.

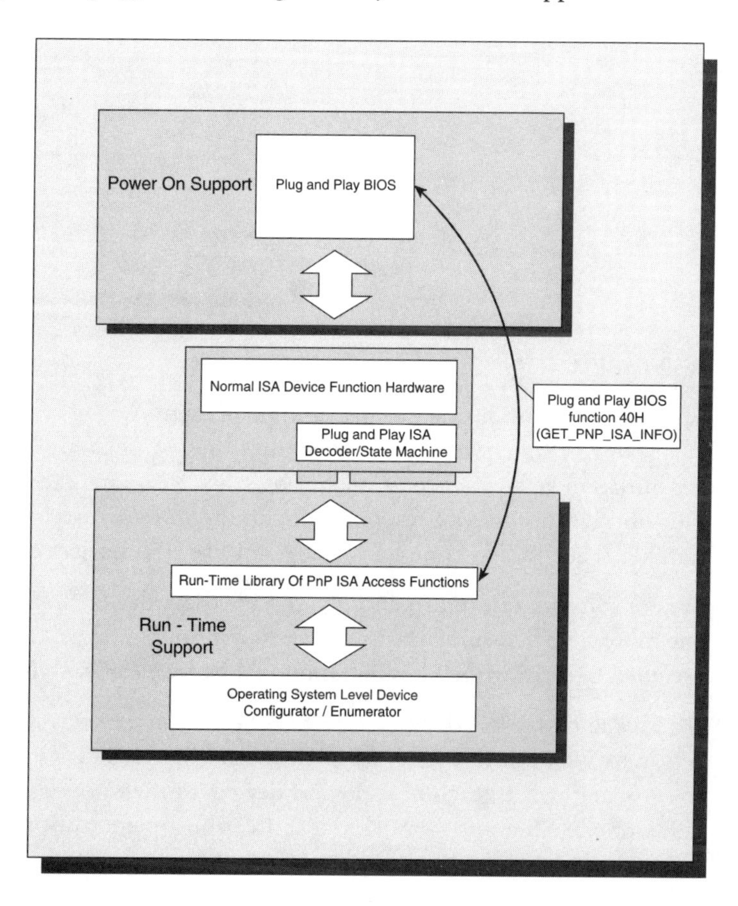

Plug and Play ISA Device States

As Figure 5.2 shows, Plug and Play ISA devices operate in one of four defined states: *Wait For Key*, *Sleep*, *Isolation*, or *Configuration* state.

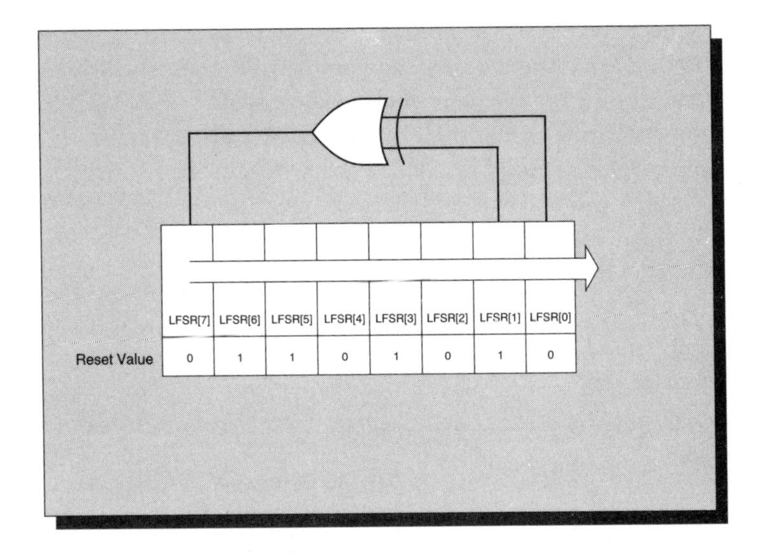

FIGURE 5.2.
The initiation key LFSR register.

Wait For Key State

At system reset, or during normal runtime operation, Plug and Play ISA devices are in Wait For Key state, where they remain until system software, such as the BIOS, issues the initiation key sequence. While in Wait For Key state, the Plug and Play logic on a Plug and Play ISA device responds only to the *initiation key sequence.* Once the initiation key sequence has completed, Plug and Play ISA devices enter *Sleep state.*

System software can return all Plug and Play ISA devices to Wait For Key state from any other state by issuing the `Wait For Key` command. The `Wait For Key` command is executed by writing the Configuration Control register with bit `1` set.

If a Plug and Play ISA device receives the `RESET_DRV` ISA bus signal, it will immediately return to Wait For Key state, set its own `CSN` (Plug and Play ISA Card Select Number) to zero, and default each of its logical devices to their power-on configurations. Revisions of the Plug and Play ISA specification up to, and including revision 1.0a, mentioned that the software `Reset` command, which is executed by writing the `Configuration Control` register with bits `0`, `1`, and `2` set, has the same effect on Plug and Play ISA devices as a total system reset. This requirement has since been dropped; only `RESET_DRV` truly resets the system's Plug and Play ISA adapters.

Sleep State

While in Sleep state, Plug and Play ISA devices are in a holding pattern, waiting for a `Wake[CSN]`, `Wait For Key`, or `Reset` command from system software. A Plug and Play ISA device can enter Sleep state in one of the following ways:

- The device is currently in Wait For Key state, and the BIOS or operating system issues the Initiation Key Sequence.
- The device "drops-out" of the current *isolation sequence* (the process that system software performs during power on to separately enable and configure Plug and Play ISA adapters).
- The device is in Isolation state and the BIOS or operating system issues the `Wake[CSN]` command with a `CSN` (`Card Select Number`) that differs from the device's own `CSN`.
- The device is in Configuration state and the BIOS or operating system issues the `Wake[CSN]` command with a `CSN` that differs from the device's own `CSN`.

The BIOS and operating system leave devices in Sleep state only during their corresponding Plug and Play ISA device isolation and configuration processes. Prior to booting the system, the BIOS returns all devices to Wait For Key state. Similarly, once the operating system has completed its enumeration and configuration of Plug and Play ISA devices, it too returns them to Wait For Key state—a state in which they can operate normally without the risk of being accidentally disabled or reconfigured.

The `Wake[CSN]` command awakens Plug and Play ISA devices from Sleep state. The BIOS or operating system awakens a particular device by writing an 8-bit `CSN` number to Plug and Play register `03H`, the `Wake[CSN]` register. If the value written is `0`, the `Wake[CSN]` command will force into Isolation state all adapters that have not yet been assigned a `CSN`. Otherwise, the adapter whose `CSN` matches that written to the `Wake[CSN]` register enters Configuration state.

Isolation State

Plug and Play ISA devices enter Isolation state from Sleep state. When a Plug and Play ISA device is in Isolation state, it is the only active Plug and Play ISA device. System software forces a Plug and Play ISA device into Isolation state in order to separate it from the system's other installed Plug and Play ISA devices for the purpose of configuring the device's resources. Only those devices whose `CSN` has not yet been configured, meaning the device's `CSN` is still `0` from a power on or reset, can enter Isolation state. As part of its normal POST sequence, a Plug and Play BIOS issues the initiation key sequence and a `Wake[0]` command to put all Plug and Play ISA devices into Isolation state.

In addition to placing all uninitialized Plug and Play ISA devices into Isolation state, the `Wake[0]` command resets each uninitialized device's `Serial Identification` register pointer to the beginning of the device's serial ID data. Serial ID data is unique to a particular Plug and Play ISA adapter. Its uniqueness guarantees correct completion of the system software's isolation protocol, which is described later. By resetting a device's serial ID register pointer, the `Wake[0]` command effectively prepares a Plug and Play ISA device for the system software's next isolation sequence.

TIP

If a Plug and Play operating system is executing on a legacy system, or on a system whose Plug and Play BIOS neither isolates nor configures Plug and Play ISA adapters, the operating system must perform the isolation sequence during its boot sequence because all Plug and Play ISA devices are still in their power-on, Wait For Key state.

Regardless of whether the host system is Plug and Play compliant, the Plug and Play operating system must detect whether the system's Plug and Play ISA devices have already been isolated and configured by a device driver.

For example, the Intel Configuration Manager, which may be installed via DOS' CONFIG.SYS file, will isolate and configure the system's Plug and Play ISA devices by itself. A Plug and Play environment operating on top of DOS must detect that the Intel Configuration Manager driver is installed, and avoid performing a `Reset` command, as this destroys any existing device resource assignments.

After having successfully located the system's first Plug and Play ISA device, the system BIOS or operating system will configure the address of the `READ_DATA` register via the `SET_READ_DATA` register, which is located at offset `00H` in each device.

When the system BIOS or operating system assigns the value of the `READ_DATA` register, every Plug and Play ISA device in the system simultaneously configures its own internal logic to respond to `READ_DATA` at the address written to the first device. Additionally, some Plug and Play ISA devices record a copy of `READ_DATA` in their own I/O space. By recording the address of `READ_DATA` in hardware, designers provide a back door method by which their own device drivers and applications can communicate with a particular device.

In a Plug and Play-compliant system, the BIOS configures the `READ_DATA` register to an 8-bit I/O location between `203H` and `3FFH` that it knows to be free from conflict with other I/O range consuming devices. In a non-Plug and Play-compliant system, the

operating system or OS driver that performs the Plug and Play ISA isolation/configuration process will make a guess toward choosing a non-conflicting address for READ_DATA. The SET_READ_DATA register allows system software to specify bits [9:2] of the READ_DATA address. Bits [1:0] are assumed to both be 1. Therefore, the READ_DATA port always resides on an odd, 4-byte boundary in the range 203H-3FFH. Sample READ_DATA addresses include 203H, 207H, 20BH, and so on.

It's important that the Plug and Play BIOS or operating system assigns a conflict free value for READ_DATA to the installed Plug and Play ISA adapters. If the I/O address used for READ_DATA is incorrect, the system's Plug and Play ISA adapters may fail. In order to avoid this, the Plug and Play BIOS and operating system carefully search the system's device nodes, PCI adapters, and legacy device resource information to guarantee that READ_DATA does not conflict with other, installed adapters.

In a Plug and Play-compliant system, the operating system determines the address of READ_DATA, as well as the number of installed Plug and Play ISA devices by calling Plug and Play BIOS function 40H (GET_PNP_ISA_INFO).

The entire process of isolating and enumerating Plug and Play ISA devices appears in the example program RDPNPISA.C at the end of this chapter.

Configuration State

Devices can enter *Configuration state* only from Sleep state or Isolation state. A Plug and Play ISA device enters Configuration state in one of two ways:

- System software awakens a device that already has been assigned a CSN by first generating the Initiation Key Sequence, and then issuing a Wake[CSN] command with the target device's CSN.
- A device in Isolation state is successfully isolated by the BIOS or operating system. At the end of each isolation cycle, the device that remains automatically enters configuration state.

At any given time, at most one device may be in Configuration state. The *Plug and Play ISA Specification* guarantees this in two ways. First, if the device enters Configuration state from Sleep state via a Wake[CSN] command, all other devices whose CSN is not equal to the CSN issued during the Wake[CSN] command must return to, or remain in Sleep state. Second, if the device enters Configuration state from Isolation state, the contents of its Serial Identification register will have guaranteed that by the time the isolation sequence completed, it was the only remaining participant in the isolation sequence.

When a Plug and Play ISA device is in configuration mode, system software may read its possible resource allocations from the Resource Data register, or configure its resource usage via either its logical device control or logical device configuration registers, which are discussed later in this chapter.

Configuring Plug and Play ISA Devices

The system's Plug and Play BIOS provides operating system level applications with a single Plug and Play ISA-specific function—function 40H. The format of Plug and Play BIOS function 40H appears in the next section.

Plug and Play BIOS Function *40H—GET_PNP_ISA_INFO*

Following is the C language declaration for the GET_PNP_ISA_INFO function:

```
int FAR (pFuncEntry)(Function, pBuffer, DataSelector) ;

int Function;       // Always 40H for GET_PNP_ISA_INFO
unsigned char far pBuffer ;  // Buffer to receive Plug and Play ISA Info
unsigned int DataSelector ; // Real or protected mode base data segment
                 // from Plug and Play BIOS installation check header
```

The GET_PNP_ISA_INFO function returns to the caller a structure containing the address of the Plug and Play ISA READ_DATA port and the total number of CSN's that the Plug and Play BIOS has assigned to Plug and Play ISA adapters in the system. Table 5.1 shows the format of the Plug and Play ISA Configuration structure.

Table 5.1. The format of the Plug and Play ISA Configuration structure.

Offset	*Size*	*Description*
00H	BYTE	Structure revision—This value reflects the revision of the structure itself, and does not imply adherence to a particular revision of the Plug and Play ISA specification. Currently, the only defined value for this field is 01H.
01H	BYTE	CSN Count—The value indicates the number of Card Select Numbers that the system BIOS has allocated to installed Plug and Play ISA devices. If no Plug and Play ISA devices exist in the system, this field contains 00H.
02H	WORD	The address of the Plug and Play ISA READ_DATA port. If the CSN count is 0, this value is meaningless.
04H	WORD	Reserved, must contain 00H
Returns		
If successful	AX = SUCCESS, CF = 0	
Otherwise	AX = FUNCTION_NOT_SUPPORTED, CF = 1	

Systems capable of supporting Plug and Play ISA devices must support function 40H, even if the system's ISA bus is not currently installed. For example, a portable system that can receive an ISA docking station should return zeros in the CSN Count and READ_DATA port fields if the system is currently undocked. Systems that are incapable of containing Plug and Play ISA devices return to the caller with the Carry Flag (CF) set and an error code of FUNCTION_NOT_SUPPORTED.

Like PCI devices and many systemboard devices, Plug and Play ISA devices are dynamically reconfigurable at the hardware level. Plug and Play ISA devices differ from PCI and systemboard devices in that the operating system can directly read and write each Plug and Play ISA device's configuration registers. Once the operating system has retrieved the READ_DATA register address from the Plug and Play BIOS, it is free to reconfigure Plug and Play ISA devices without system firmware intervention.

By default, Plug and Play ISA devices power on in a disabled state unless required for system boot. In a non-Plug and Play system, those Plug and Play ISA devices that are active at power on may conflict with existing legacy ISA devices, or other bootable Plug and Play ISA devices installed in the system. For this reason, some vendors of Plug and Play ISA adapters provide jumpers or switches that enable the adapter to operate in either legacy ISA or Plug and Play ISA mode.

In a Plug and Play system, the BIOS takes the following steps to identify and configure Plug and Play ISA devices.

Power On/Reset

After a system power on or reset, Plug and Play ISA devices required for boot default to an active state. All other Plug and Play ISA devices remain disabled. No Plug and Play ISA device provides access to its on-board configuration or control registers.

Initiation Key Sequence

The BIOS performs the *Initiation Key Sequence* to enable the Plug and Play logic on each Plug and Play ISA device and remove Plug and Play ISA devices from Wait For Key state. The sequence consists of 32 8-bit writes to the ADDRESS register. Plug and Play ISA devices contain a special LFSR (Linear Feedback Shift register) that resets to a value of 6AH. Each of the 32 values that the BIOS writes must match the current value of the LFSR register, or the Plug and Play ISA device will remain in Wait For Key state. Both the BIOS and the LFSR register calculate the next write value as a function of the current write value according to the following steps:

1. Perform XOR of LFSR[0] and LFSR[1]. Set this value aside as NEXT_BIT7.
2. Perform 1-bit arithmetic right shift of LFSR.
3. Set LFSR[7] to NEXT_BIT7 value.

NOTE

Refer to Figure 5.2 to see a logical diagram of the initiation key LFSR register.

The following code fragment correctly performs the Plug and Play ISA initiation key sequence:

```
ADDRESS_REG      EQU 279H
START_KEY        EQU 6AH

  mov  dx, ADDRESS_REG ; Plug & Play ISA ADDRESS Register
  mov  cx, 32          ; Number of writes to perform
  mov  al, START_KEY   ; LFSR resets to 6AH

NextWrite:
  mov  bh, al          ; Get AL Bits [1:0] Into BX
  mov  bl, al          ;
  shr  bl, 1           ; BL = LFSR[1]
  and  bl, 1           ;
  and  bh, 1           ; BH = LFSR[0]
  xor  bh, bl          ; BH = LFSR[0] XOR LFSR[1]
  shl  bh, 7           ;
  out  dx, al          ; Write This Initiation Key Value
  shr  al, 1           ; Shift Out Old LFSR[0]
  or   al, bh          ; OR In New LFSR[7]
  loop NextWrite       ; Keep going 32 times
```

Isolation Sequence

During the isolation sequence, the system BIOS iteratively locates, enumerates, and assigns a unique CSN (Card Select Number) to each Plug and Play ISA device in the system. As soon as a Plug and Play ISA adapter has been isolated, its on-board logic enters Configuration state. At this point, no other adapter is in Configuration state.

While the device is in Configuration state, the system BIOS reads and stores that device's resource information and assigns the device its CSN. Once the device has been assigned a CSN, system software may, in the future, use the CSN to place that device in and out of Configuration state, thereby alleviating the software from having to perform the isolation sequence each time it wants to communicate with a single Plug and Play ISA device.

The Isolation sequence takes place via a succession of 72 pairs of reads to the adapter's `Serial Identification` register located in the adapter's Plug and Play ISA logic hardware. Each adapter's `Serial Identification` contains a unique, 72-bit field called its *Serial Identifier.* Figure 5.3 shows the order in which the `Serial ID` register's contents appear during the enumeration of a Plug and Play ISA adapter's `RESOURCE_DATA` information.

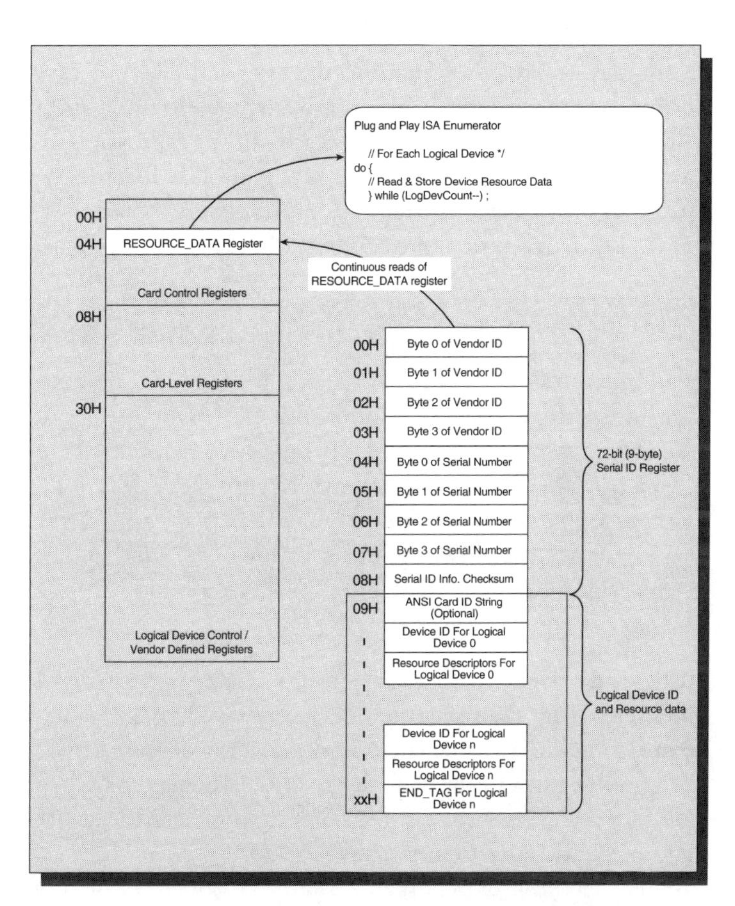

FIGURE 5.3.
The Plug and Play ISA `Serial ID` *register during the enumeration of an adapter.*

During a single isolation sequence, each Plug and Play ISA device shifts the next bit of its 72-bit serial identifier into an internal current bit register. Devices whose current bit is a `1` will drive `055H` on the bus during the first of each pair of reads, and `AAH` during the second read. Any device whose current-bit register is a `0` examines the bus during both reads to determine whether any other devices drove the bus first with 055H and then with AAH. If a device whose current bit is a 0, detects 55H and AAH on successive reads, it "drops-out" of the current iteration of the isolation sequence and participates in the next one. Otherwise, the device shifts its serial identifier by one position and prepares to respond to the next pair of read cycles. In this fashion, when a single iteration of the isolation sequence completes, only a single adapter remains. This remaining adapter automatically enters Configuration state.

In addition to providing input to the Plug and Play ISA isolation process, the Serial Identification register contains the adapter's Manufacturer Device Code and serial number. Once a device has been placed in Configuration state, either as a result of a Wake[CSN] command or the system's Plug and Play ISA isolation sequence, the first nine I/O reads of the device's RESOURCE_DATA register (Offset 04H, Plug and Play ISA Card Control registers) return the contents of the serial ID register.

NOTE

In order to simplify Plug and Play ISA hardware implementations, devices whose current bit is a 0 examine only bits [1:0] of the system data bus during isolation sequence read cycles. If the device detects a value of 01B during the first of a pair of reads, then it assumes that another device is currently driving the value 055H on the bus. Similarly, if the device detects a value of 10B during the second of a pair of reads, then it assumes that another device is currently driving the value 0AAH on the data bus.

At the end of each isolation sequence, a single Plug and Play ISA device remains. Prior to enumerating the remaining device, the system software performing the isolation sequence verifies that the checksum byte of the device's serial isolation register matches the value the software has built during this particular isolation pass. If the checksum values do not match, the system software assumes that the READ_DATA port conflicts with an unknown, existing I/O port elsewhere in the system. At this point, the system software assigns a new READ_DATA port and restarts the isolation sequence. If the isolation sequence fails repeatedly, the system software assumes either that there are no Plug and Play ISA devices in the system, or that the checksum values within all installed Plug and Play ISA devices are invalid.

Plug and Play ISA Device Enumeration

After isolating a Plug and Play ISA adapter, the system BIOS reads the adapter's configuration information from the adapter's RESOURCE_DATA register and stores this information in system RAM for use after the isolation sequence for each installed Plug and Play ISA adapter is complete. The system BIOS must not assign resources to Plug and Play ISA devices until it has read and stored the contents of each one's resources via its READ_DATA register. Only after the isolation process is complete, and each Plug and Play ISA adapter has been assigned a CSN does the system BIOS have a complete picture of Plug and Play ISA device resource needs.

The format in which the system BIOS stores Plug and Play ISA device information is at the discretion of the BIOS designer. Once the BIOS has configured the system's Plug and Play ISA adapters, it can discard its RAM-based device information tables.

After each Plug and Play ISA adapter has been assigned a CSN, system software can easily place each adapter in Configuration state by first generating the Initiation Key sequence and issuing the Wake[CSN] command with the desired adapter's CSN number. The Wake[CSN] command is described in the section that outlines programming Plug and Play ISA devices.

Plug and Play ISA Device Resource Allocation and Configuration

Plug and Play ISA devices consume the same types of resources as legacy ISA devices—I/O ranges, DMA channels, IRQ channels and memory address ranges.

System software communicates with Plug and Play devices via the three Plug and Play ISA auto-configuration registers.

The Plug and Play ISA Auto-Configuration Registers

The Plug and Play ISA specification reserves three 8-bit auto-configuration registers within the system's I/O address space. Operating system and firmware level enumerators and configurators perform all communication with Plug and Play ISA devices through these three I/O registers.

The Plug and Play ISA *ADDRESS* Register

The Plug and Play ISA ADDRESS register is a write-only, 8-bit register located at I/O address 0279H. The ADDRESS register resides at the same address as the LPT3 printer port status register, which by no coincidence is read-only. This address sharing reduces the number of I/O address locations that Plug and Play ISA devices consume within the system's I/O address space. Enumeration and configuration software set the contents of the ADDRESS register to specify a configuration register within the Plug and Play ISA device's card control, logical device control, or logical device configuration register groups. After setting the ADDRESS register, the configurator or enumerator application either performs a read from READ_DATA or a write to WRITE_DATA.

The Plug and Play ISA *WRITE_DATA* Register

The WRITE_DATA register is a write-only, 8-bit register that resides at I/O address 0A79H, an alias of the LPT3 printer status port address 0279H. Values written to WRITE_DATA are directed to the Plug and Play ISA register specified by the ADDRESS register. Writes to WRITE_DATA take effect only if the target Plug and Play ISA device is currently in Configuration state.

The Plug and Play ISA *READ_DATA* Register

The READ_DATA register is a read-only, 8-bit register whose I/O address is relocatable within the range 0203H-03FFH. A read of the READ_DATA register returns an 8-bit value from the Plug and Play ISA register specified in the ADDRESS register. In a Plug and Play compliant system, the system BIOS sets aside a single, conflict-free READ_DATA I/O address within the range 0203H-03FFH. The order in which the system BIOS searches for, and locates a conflict free address for READ_DATA is at the discretion of the BIOS designer.

During the POST's Plug and Play isolation sequence, the BIOS supplies all of the system's Plug and Play ISA devices with the correct value of READ_DATA by writing its address to the SET_READ_DATA register in the first Plug and Play ISA device. All installed Plug and Play ISA cards respond to the SET_READ_DATA register, regardless of which Plug and Play ISA adapter currently is in isolation mode. Operating system Plug and Play ISA enumeration and configuration software determines the address of READ_DATA (and the number of installed Plug and Play ISA devices) by invoking function 40H of the system's Plug and Play BIOS.

Plug and Play ISA Device Registers

Plug and Play ISA devices support a 256-byte configuration space. This configuration space consists of 30H standard and vendor-defined card control registers that apply to the entire adapter and C0H logical device control and logical device configuration and control registers for each logical device. Although the Plug and Play ISA adapter provides 0C0H (208) registers for each of its on-board logical devices, only a single set of logical device control/configuration registers is visible at any given time.

Each Plug and Play device may contain as many as 256 individual logical devices. System software selects individual logical devices by writing a zero-based value to the Logical Device Number register located at offset 07H in the device's card control register section.

Figure 5.4 displays the register mapping for a Plug and Play ISA device.

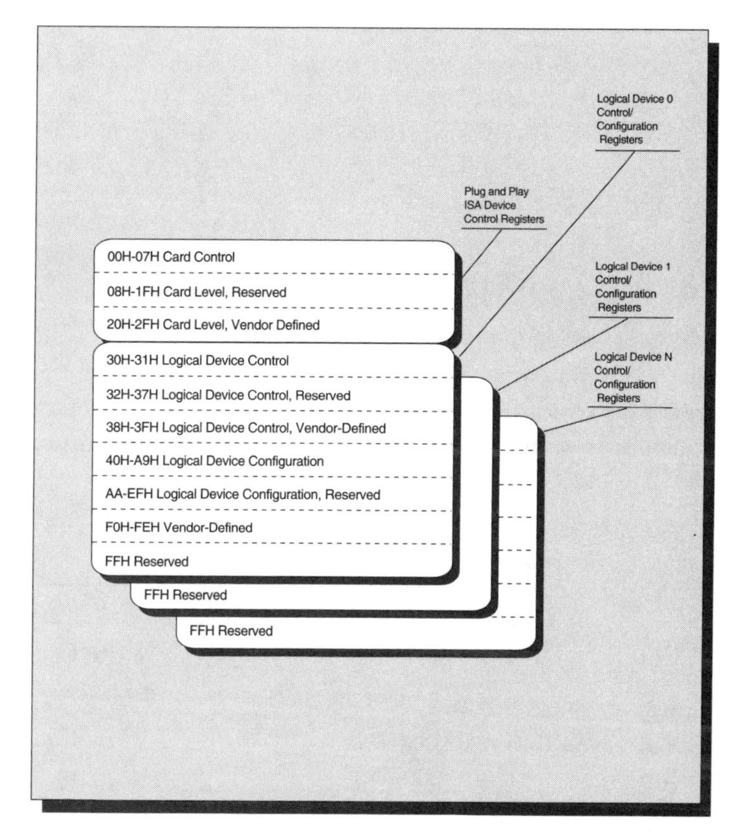

FIGURE 5.4.
The Plug and Play ISA device configuration/ control registers.

To access a device's configuration registers, the BIOS or operating system places the device in Configuration state, either by isolating the device or issuing a `Wake[CSN]` command.

NOTE

If the device has entered Configuration state by having just been isolated, it may not yet have been assigned a `CSN`. If the device's Card Select Number register is `00H`, the BIOS or operating system that isolated the device immediately assigns it a `CSN` by writing a unique, non-zero value to the Card Select Number register. System software assigns `CSN`'s in the order 1, 2, 3, and so on.

Often, the software that performed the isolation sequence records the `CSN` that it assigned to each device. If the software wants to configure the device at a later time, it can issue a `Wake[CSN]` command with the device's `CSN` number rather than re-isolating each Plug and Play ISA device.

An enumerator or driver that does not know the CSN for a particular device first retrieves the system CSN count from Plug and Play BIOS function 40H. Next, the software iteratively issues a Wake[CSN] to each Plug and Play ISA device until it finds the device whose serial number or Device ID matches its search condition.

The Plug and Play ISA Card Control Registers

The first 30H registers within a Plug and Play ISA device are 8-bit, card level registers. Regardless of whether they are vendor-definable, card level registers pertain to the Plug and Play ISA adapter as a whole, and not to its individual functions or logical devices. The following table details the card level Plug and Play ISA registers. Table 5.2 shows the Plug and Play ISA card level registers.

Table 5.2. The Plug and Play ISA card level registers.

Offset	*Name*	*Attributes*
00H	SET_READ_DATA	Write-Only
01H	SERIAL_ISOLATION	Read-Only
02H	CONFIG_CONTROL	Write-Only
03H	WAKE[CSN]	Write-Only
04H	RESOURCE_DATA	Read-Only
05H	STATUS	Read-Only
06H	CSN (Card Select Number)	Read/Write
07H	LOG_DEV_NUMBER	Read/Write
08H-1FH	Reserved for future use	N/A
20H-2FH	Vendor-defined	Vendor-defined

The *SET_READ_DATA* Register (Offset *00H*, Write-Only)

Bits [7:0] of this register contain bits [9:2] of the offset of the Plug and Play ISA READ_DATA register within system I/O space. Bits [1:0] of the READ_DATA address are always 1. The Plug and Play BIOS programs this register within each Plug and Play ISA device's configuration space to a conflict free I/O address between 203H and 03FFH. The following code excerpt sets the system's READ_DATA register to 207H.

```
MOV  DX, ADDRESS       ;
MOV  AL, SET_READ_DATA  ;
```

```
OUT  DX, AL            ;
MOV  DX, WRITE_DATA    ;
MOV  AL, 010000001B    ; Bits [9:2] of 207H (Bits [1:0] are always 1)
OUT  DX, AL            ; Write it
```

Plug and Play operating systems retrieve the address of READ_DATA by issuing a call to Plug and Play BIOS function 40H. If a Plug and Play operating system is executing on a legacy system, it assigns devices a best-guess, conflict-free READ_DATA address. In turn, the Plug and Play operating system may provide a dynamically callable function by which applications and device drivers can retrieve the address of the Plug and Play ISA READ_DATA register.

The *SERIAL_ISOLATION* Register (Offset *01H*, Read-Only)

The SERIAL_ISOLATION register reports the data that the system's Plug and Play ISA devices assert on the system's data bus during a single step of the Isolation sequence, which is described earlier in this chapter. Importantly, a single read to the SERIAL_ISOLATION register triggers those devices currently in Isolation state to perform the next comparison of their serial identifier register against other devices on the bus.

The *CONFIG_CONTROL* Register (Offset *02H*, Write-Only)

The CONFIG_CONTROL register contains three significant, write-only bits whose intended action occurs when the particular bit is written with the value 1.

Bit [2]	Resets each installed Plug and Play ISA adapter's CSN to 0
Bit [1]	Forces each installed Plug and Play ISA adapter to Wait For Key state
Bit [0]	Returns each logical device on all installed adapters to its default state

System software sets CONFIG_CONTROL reset bits when it wants to disable or re-isolate the system's Plug and Play ISA adapters and their corresponding logical devices. On a system with no firmware-based Plug and Play ISA support, for example, the OS enumerator needs to perform the Plug and Play ISA isolation protocol during the system boot. Also, the Plug and Play BIOS will reset the system's Plug and Play ISA adapters during a warm boot because the warm boot does not generate the hardware RESET_DRV signal needed to reset these adapters at a hardware level.

The *WAKE[CSN]* Register (Offset *03H*, Write-Only)

Writing a non-zero value to WAKE[CSN] causes the adapter whose CSN matches the value written to transition to Configuration state. A Wake[CSN] with CSN = 0 forces only those devices that have not yet been assigned a CSN to switch to Isolation state.

A device that has already been assigned a CSN responds to a Wake[0] command in one of two ways. If the device is in Configuration state when the Wake[0] command occurs, it returns to Sleep state. If the same device is already in Sleep state when the Wake[0] command occurs, the device remains in Sleep state and ignores the Wake[0] command. The Wake[CSN] command is valid only after system software has issued the Initiation Key sequence to all Plug and Play ISA devices.

The *RESOURCE_DATA* Register (Offset *04H*, Read-Only)

RESOURCE_DATA returns the contents of the serial identification register followed by the Plug and Play ISA logical device's resource descriptor block, one byte at a time. Reads of RESOURCE_DATA are valid only after the device has successfully completed its isolation sequence and entered Configuration state, or after the device has been awoken by a Wake[CSN] command specifying that device's CSN. Both the completion of the isolation sequence and the Wake[CSN] command have the effect of resetting the device's Plug and Play logic to point to the start of its internal serial identification/resource descriptor information.

The RESOURCE_DATA register returns the device's serial identification register contents and resource information in byte format, rather than in the bit-by-bit format that the SERIAL_ISOLATION register produces during the device's isolation sequence.

After a Plug and Play ISA device has entered Configuration state, the first nine 8-bit reads produce the device's Vendor ID, serial number, and serial identification register checksum byte. If the enumerator has already correlated this information to the device's CSN, it may discard it.

All bytes read from RESOURCE_DATA following the serial identification register information, up to and including and END_TAG byte comprise the device's resource descriptor block. Both the END_TAG byte and the possible contents of the resource descriptor block appear in Chapter 3 because the format of the Plug and Play ISA device's resource descriptor is identical to that used in the possible resource allocation block of Plug and Play BIOS device nodes.

If a Plug and Play device has more than one function, the resource descriptor block returned by RESOURCE_DATA pertains to the logical device specified in the LOGICAL_DEV_NUM register (see the following section). When the enumerator has retrieved the resource descriptor for a particular device, it parses the contents of the descriptor and determines what resources are available to the device based on its knowledge of resource usage elsewhere in the system. The system configurator then configures the device by assigning resources to the device's logical device configuration registers.

OVERVIEW OF RESOURCE ASSIGNMENT STRATEGIES

If the configurator resides at the firmware level, it assigns resources to Plug and Play ISA devices according to one of the following methods:

First come, first served—The BIOS allocates resources to Plug and Play ISA devices as it isolates them. As the BIOS allocates a single resource, it deletes the resource from an overall map of system resources. Once a particular resource, such as DMA channels, has been depleted, any devices yet to be isolated may not receive the resources they require to function properly.

Predefined priority basis—The BIOS provides the user an interface for specifying the order in which devices will receive resources. For example, some system BIOSes supply a menu in which the user can select the system's IPL device from among several Plug and Play ISA IPL devices. The BIOS ensures that the currently selected IPL device is first to receive its required resources, followed in priority by non-active IPL devices, non-IPL devices and unknown devices.

Locked configurations—The system BIOS allocates resources to Plug and Play ISA devices on the basis of locked configuration records stored within the system's ESCD database. Locked configuration records are configuration records that guarantee a particular configuration for an adapter during each system boot sequence. This type of record is only available on an ESCD-capable system, as described in Chapter 8. In non-ESCD systems, the Plug and Play BIOS allocates resources to Plug and Play ISA devices on a first-come, first-served basis.

The *STATUS* Register (Offset *05H*, Read-Only)

The `STATUS` Register simply indicates that the device is prepared to respond to another read of its `RESOURCE_DATA` register. If set, bit `[0]` in the `STATUS` register indicates that the device is ready for the next read of `RESOURCE_DATA`.

The *CSN* Register (Offset *06H*, Read/Write)

The system configurator iteratively assigns each Plug and Play ISA device a unique `CSN` during the Plug and Play ISA device isolation process. The default value of the `CSN` register is `0`. Once the configurator has isolated a particular Plug and Play ISA device, that device enters Configuration state, at which time its card control register become active. The configurator assigns a unique, 8-bit `CSN` (starting from `1` and assigning subsequent `CSN`s in ascending order) for the newly isolated card and writes that value to the card's `CSN` register.

System software issues Wake[CSN] commands to quickly place Plug and Play ISA devices in Configuration state, once those devices have been isolated and assigned a CSN valued. The Wake[CSN] mechanism allows system software to instantly places devices in Configuration state, while bypassing the more time-consuming device isolation process.

Operating system-level software determines the number of assigned CSN's by issuing a call to function 40H in the system's Plug and Play BIOS, which returns the number of CSN's that the BIOS assigned to Plug and Play ISA devices during its isolation process. The operating system assumes that the system BIOS assigned CSN numbers to Plug and Play ISA devices in numerical order, starting with the value 1.

The first time the operating system issues a Wake[CSN] command to a particular Plug and Play ISA device, it records the device's serial number and Vendor ID and correlates this information to the CSN. This allows the operating system to register the device, so that it can associate future references to a particular CSN to the exact device to which the CSN belongs.

The *LOGICAL_DEV_NUM* Register (Offset *07H*, Read/Write)

If a Plug and Play ISA device contains more than one logical device, the value written to LOGICAL_DEV_NUM selects which logical device is currently the focus of the configuration operation.

Cards with only one logical device must implement LOGICAL_DEV_NUM in read-only fashion; the register always returns the value 00H.

The value that has been programmed into the LOGICAL_DEV_NUM register determines the logical device to which logical device configuration register values apply. For example, if the configuration software programs the value 01H into the LOGICAL_DEV_NUM register of a multifunction device, subsequent writes to the device's memory range, I/O range, DMA channel or IRQ channel configuration registers pertain to logical device 1, and no other logical devices located on that adapter. Similarly, any subsequent writes to the IO_RANGE_CHECK and ACTIVATE registers apply to device 01H. This register correspondence continues until either the LOGICAL_DEV_NUM register is programmed to a different value, or the device exits Configuration state.

Card Level Registers, Reserved (Offsets *08H-1FH*)

As of revision 1.0a of the *Plug and Play ISA Specification*, the function of these registers had not yet been defined. Plug and Play ISA-specific software that adheres to revisions 1.0a and older should make no assumptions about the contents or function of these or any other reserved registers.

Card Level Registers, Vendor-Defined (Offsets *20H-2FH*)

The purpose of these registers is wholly vendor-defined and is not governed by the Plug and Play ISA specification.

For example, some vendors use Card Level registers to provide extra I/O space for their adapters, such as performance features, initialization registers, and so on. This frees up more normal I/O space for the actual function that the adapter and its logical devices perform.

The Plug and Play ISA Logical Device Control Registers

Plug and Play ISA adapters may contain one or several logical devices. For each logical device, the Plug and Play ISA adapter provides a set of control registers. System software uses a logical device's control registers to activate and deactivate the device or perform I/O conflict detection on the device's assigned I/O ranges. Currently, the *Plug and Play ISA Specification* requires adapters to support two Logical Device Control registers—the `ACTIVATE` and `IO_RANGE_CHECK` registers. These registers are described in the next few sections. Table 5.3 shows the Plug and Play ISA Logical Device Control registers.

Table 5.3. The Plug and Play ISA Logical Device Control registers.

Offset	*Name*	*Attributes*
`30H`	`ACTIVATE`	Read/Write
`31H`	`IO_RANGE_CHECK`	Read/Write
`32H-37H`	Reserved Logical Device Control Registers	N/A
`38H-3FH`	Reserved Vendor-Defined Logical Device Control	N/A

ACTIVATE (Offset *30H*, Read/Write)

Bit `[0]` of the `ACTIVATE` register determines whether this logical device is active on the ISA bus. If bit `[0]` is set, the logical device becomes active. Devices that can participate in the system boot sequence power on in active state with bit `[0]` of their `ACTIVATE` register set to `1`. Bits `[7:1]` must be `0` during reads of this register.

Prior to activating a logical device, the system software must disable that device's I/O range checking by clearing bit [1] of the device's IO_RANGE_CHECK register.

IO_RANGE_CHECK (Offset *31H*, Read/Write)

The IO_RANGE_CHECK provides system software with a mechanism for verifying that the logical device's assigned I/O range does not conflict with those used by other system devices. The IO_RANGE_CHECK register is organized as follows:

Bit [7:2]	Reserved, must return 0 on a read
Bit [1]	I/O Range Check Enable/Disable. Bit [1] in IO_RANGE_CHECK enables and disables IO range checking on the current logical device. If bit [1] is set, any reads to the device's assigned I/O range or ranges cause the device to drive either 055H or AAH onto the system's data bus, depending on the state of bit [0] in the IO_RANGE_CHECK register.
Bit [0]	I/O Read Pattern Select. If both bit [1] and bit [0] are set, the device will assert the pattern 055H on the system data bus during a read of any of its assigned I/O ports. If bit [1] is set and bit [0] is clear, the device will assert the pattern 0AAH on the data bus during a read of any of its I/O ports. Other system devices that conflict with the Plug and Play ISA device's assigned I/O range will assert system bus data that corrupts at least one of the selected patterns during reads of the Plug and Play ISA device's assigned I/O ranges.

In order to perform I/O range checking on a particular, configured Plug and Play ISA logical device, the system software first selects the device by writing its logical device number to the adapter's LOGICAL_DEV_NUM register, and then clears bit [0] of the device's ACTIVATE register to disable the device's normal ISA bus activity. Next, the system software enables I/O range checking on the device and performs two sets of I/O reads to each I/O port assigned to the device. During one set of reads, bit [0] of IO_RANGE_CHECK is clear, and during the other it is set.

The following code fragment assigns an I/O range starting at 300H to a logical device and performs I/O range checking on RangeLength locations within this single range. In practice, the system BIOS or operating system would implement, in place of Check300H(), a general purpose routine capable of checking each range assigned to the logical device.

```
// #define's for Logical Device Control Registers

#define Check55 0x03
#define CheckAA 0x02
#define CheckOff 0x00
```

```
#define DevDisable 0x00

// #define's for Plug and Play ISA Registers

#define ADDRESS 0x279
#define WRITE_DATA 0xA79
#define LOGICAL_DEV_NUM 0x07
#define ACTIVATE 0x30
#define IO_RANGE_CHECK 0x31
#define IO_BASE0_HIGH 0x60
#define IO_BASE0_LOW 0x61

#define SUCCESS 0x00
#define FAILURE !SUCCESS

//
// ToggleIOCheck — Set up caller-specified I/O Range
//  checking (Check55, CheckAA, CheckOff)
// Note:  Logical Device Is Disabled During I/O Checking
//

void ToggleIOCheck(unsigned char CheckType) {

    outp(ADDRESS, ACTIVATE) ;
    outp(WRITE_DATA, DevDisable) ;
    outp(ADDRESS, IO_RANGE_CHECK) ;
    outp(WRITE_DATA, CheckType) ;

}

//
// IORangeCheck — Perform Actual I/O Checking
// Read RangeLength bytes from BaseAddress first with
//  055H pattern enabled, then AAH pattern enabled.
// Note:  If an I/O conflict exists, device could pass
//  Check55 or CheckAA, but not both.
//

int IORangeCheck(int BaseAddress, int RangeLength) {

int i ;

ToggleIOCheck(Check55) ;

for (i = BaseAddress; i < BaseAddress + RangeLength; i++) {
    if (inp(BaseAddress + i++) != 0x55) return(FAILURE) ;
}

ToggleIOCheck(CheckAA) ;

for (i = BaseAddress; i < BaseAddress + RangeLength; i++) {
    if (inp(BaseAddress + i++) != 0xAA) return(FAILURE) ;
}

return(SUCCESS) ;

}
```

```
//
// AssignDeviceIO — Activate Logical Device and assign
// an I/O range to the specified I/O Base Register pair
//

void AssignDeviceIO(unsigned char DeviceNumber,unsigned char IODescriptor,unsigned int
IOBaseAddress) {

outp(ADDRESS, LOGICAL_DEV_NUM) ;
outp(WRITE_DATA, DeviceNumber) ;

outp(ADDRESS, IODescriptor) ;
outp(WRITE_DATA, (IOBaseAddress >> 8)) ;

outp(ADDRESS, IODescriptor + 1) ;
outp(ADDRESS, (IOBaseAddress & 0xFF)) ;
}

//
// Check300H() — Check I/O Range at 300H for conflicts
// Caller retrieves RangeLength from I/O Range Descriptor
// Note: for purpose of example, assigns I/O range to and
//   checks only the range contained in the first pair
//   of I/O Base registers. (IO_BASE0_HIGH & IO_BASE0_LOW)
// Returns:  SUCCESS if no conflicts, FAILURE if conflicts
//

int Check300H(unsigned char DeviceNumber,unsigned int RangeLength) {

AssignDeviceIO(DeviceNumber, IO_BASE0_HIGH, 0x300) ;
return (IORangeCheck(0x300, RangeLength) ;

}
```

`IO_RANGE_CHECK` especially is useful to a Plug and Play operating system or driver that is running in a non-Plug and Play system because in a legacy system the operating system is unable to retrieve Plug and Play BIOS device nodes to detect those I/O ranges already allocated to systemboard or legacy ISA devices.

The Plug and Play ISA portion of the BIOS might use `IO_RANGE_CHECK` to double check the I/O ranges it has assigned to Plug and Play ISA devices for conflicts. In a Plug and Play-compliant system that supports Plug and Play ISA devices, the decision to support I/O range checking is at the discretion of the system's firmware designer.

Reserved Logical Device Control Registers (Offsets *032H-037H*)

Per the *Plug and Play ISA specification*, these registers are reserved for future use.

Logical Device Control, Vendor-Defined (Offsets *038H-03FH*)

The purpose of these registers is wholly vendor-defined and is not governed by the *Plug and Play ISA Specification*.

Logical Device Configuration Registers (Offsets 40H-EFH)

Logical Device Configuration registers provide system software the mechanism for assigning system resources to Plug and Play ISA devices. A Plug and Play ISA adapter provides one complete set of Logical Device Configuration registers for each of its logical devices. The value of the LOGICAL_DEV_NUM register determines the logical device to which the Logical Device Configuration registers currently apply.

As you might expect, Logical Device Configuration registers belong to one of four categories: DMA channel configuration, IRQ channel configuration, I/O range configuration, and memory space configuration.

You may be surprised to learn that there are two types of memory range configuration registers. The first group of memory range registers, which resides between offsets 40H-5FH in the logical device configuration space, supports 24-bit address ranges. The second group of memory range registers resides between offsets 76H and A8H and supports 32-bit address ranges. Plug and Play ISA logical devices may support either the 24-bit or the 32-bit address range registers, but cannot mix the two on a single adapter. The type of the first memory descriptor that appears in the adapter's resource data descriptor indicates which type of memory range descriptor the card supports for all of its logical devices.

Each logical device on a Plug and Play ISA adapter can support up to four separate memory ranges (24- or 32-bit), eight I/O ranges, two IRQ channels, and two DMA channels. Table 5.4 shows the Plug and Play ISA Logical Device Configuration registers.

Table 5.4. The Plug and Play ISA Logical Device Configuration registers.

Offset	*Name*
40H-44H	24-bit Memory Descriptor 0
44H-47H	Reserved
48H-4CH	24-bit Memory Descriptor 1
4DH-4FH	Reserved
50H-54H	24-bit Memory Descriptor 2
55H-57H	Reserved
58H-5CH	24-bit Memory Descriptor 3
5DH-5FH	Reserved
60H-61H	I/O Range 0

continues

Table 5.4. continued

Offset	*Name*
62H-63H	I/O Range 1
64H-65H	I/O Range 2
66H-67H	I/O Range 3
68H-69H	I/O Range 4
6AH-6BH	I/O Range 5
6CH-6DH	I/O Range 6
6EH-6FH	I/O Range 7
70H-71H	IRQ Channel Select 0
72H-73H	IRQ Channel Select 1
74H	DMA Channel Select 0
75H	DMA Channel Select 1
76H-7EH	32-bit Memory Range 0
7FH	Reserved
80H-88H	32-bit Memory Range 1
89H-8FH	Reserved
90H-98H	32-bit Memory Range 2
99H-9FH	Reserved
A0H-A8H	32-bit Memory Range 3
A9H-AFH	Reserved

The 24-Bit *Memory Range Configuration* Registers (Offsets *40H-44H, 48H-4CH, 50H-54H, 58H-5CH*)

Each Plug and Play ISA device can support four separate 24-bit memory ranges via its 24-bit `Memory Range Configuration` registers provided the Plug and Play ISA adapter on which the logical device resides supports 24-bit memory ranges. The system Plug and Play ISA configuration software in the BIOS or operating system configures an adapter's logical device `Memory Range Configuration` registers after first having examined read the adapter's resource data descriptor and scanned each of its logical device entries for memory range requirements.

Writing a value of `00H` to each register within a single group of `Memory Range Configuration` registers disables that memory range. Unless otherwise noted, `Memory Range`

Configuration registers are read/write and adhere to the following structure. Table 5.5 shows the format of the Memory Range Configuration register group.

Table 5.5. The format of the Memory Range Configuration register group.

Byte	*Description*
00H	Memory Address High Bits. Address bits [23:16] of the memory range base address
01H	Memory Address Low Bits. Address bits [15:8] of the memory range base address
02H	Memory Range Control
03H	Memory Limit High Bits. [23:16] of the memory range upper limit address, or bits [23:16] of range length in bytes, according to bit [0] of the Memory Range Control register
04H	Memory Limit Low Bits. [15:8] of the memory range upper limit address, or bits [15:8] of the range length in bytes, according to bit [0] of the Memory Range Control register

Memory Address High Bits (Offsets 40H, 48H, 50H, 58H, Read/Write)

This Memory Address High Bits register contains address bits [23:16] of the memory range base address. Bits [7:0] are assumed to be zero, therefore the minimum granularity for a 24-bit memory range is 256 bytes. For example, if the Memory Address High Bits register contains 0DH, and its corresponding Low Bits register contains 00H, the base address of the memory range is 0D0000H, or the real mode address D000:0H.

Memory Address Low Bits (Offsets 41H, 49H, 51H, 59H Read/Write)

The Memory Address Low Bits register contains bits [15:8] of the memory range base address. As mentioned, bits [7:0] in a memory range are set to 0 and are not programmable.

Memory Range Control (Offsets 42H, 4AH, 52H, 5AH Read/Write or Read-Only)

The Memory Range Control register serves two purposes. First, it defines the meaning of the two Memory Limit registers that follow it, and second, it provides a mechanism for configuring the type of memory located on the logical device. Following are descriptions of operations of the Memory Range Control register's bits:

Bits [7:2]	Reserved
Bit [1]	Memory control—If set, this bit indicates that the device's memory is 16-bit memory. Otherwise, the device's memory is 8-bit memory. If the logical device supports only a single type of memory, bit [1] can be read-only.
Bit [0]	Limit Type—If set, bit [0] indicates that the Memory Limit registers contain bits [23:8] of the upper limit address for the memory range. Otherwise, the Memory Limit registers contain bits [23:8] of the memory range size in bytes.

Memory Limit High Bits (Offsets *43H, 4BH, 53H, 5BH* Read/Write, or Read-Only)

If bit [0] of the Memory Control register is set, the Memory Limit High Bits register contains bits [23:16] of the physical address limit for the memory range. Otherwise, the Memory Limit High Bits register contains bits [23:16] of the memory range size mask.

Memory Limit Low Bits (Offsets *44H, 4CH, 54H, 5CH* Read/Write or Read-Only)

If bit [0] of the Memory Control register is set, the Memory Limit High Bits register contains bits [15:8] of the physical address limit for the memory range. Otherwise, the Memory Limit High Bits register contains bits [15:8] of the memory range size mask.

> **NOTE**
>
> When used to specify a memory range's size, the Memory Limit High Bits and Low Bits registers form a 24-bit mask, rather than an actual byte count. Those bits that are set to 0 indicate don't-care bits in the device's address decoder. For example, if the Memory Limit High Bits and Low Bits registers contain the values 0FFH and F0H, respectively, together they indicate a 24-bit mask equal to 0FFF000H. The value 0FFF000H indicates that the device requires a memory range whose lower 12 bits are don't-care bits, and whose granularity, or size is 4KB.
>
> If a device has a memory range whose granularity is equivalent to its size, the Memory Limit registers for that range can be read-only. For example, if the device requires a 4KB memory range on a 4KB boundary, the Memory Limit High Bits and Low Bits registers contain the values 0FFH and 00H, respectively, to form a 24-bit mask value of 0FF0000H. In this case, bit [0] of the Memory Range Control register is clear to indicate that the Memory Limit registers contain a range size value, and not an upper limit address.

A logical device's Memory Limit registers contain an upper limit if the device requires memory at an absolute, physical location. For example, if a Plug and Play ISA video adapter requires a 64KB frame buffer just below the 16MB boundary, bit [0] of its Memory Control register is set, and its Memory Limit Upper Bits and Lower Bits registers contain the values 0FFH and 0FFH, respectively, to indicate and upper limit address of 0FFFF00H physical, the largest allowed in these registers.

The *I/O Range Configuration* Registers (Offsets *060H-6FH*)

Plug and Play ISA devices support up to eight individual I/O ranges. The system's Plug and Play ISA configuration software first scans each logical device entry in the adapter's resource data block to determine the I/O range needs of the adapter's logical devices, then assigns each logical device its required I/O ranges via the I/O Range Configuration registers.

A logical device's I/O Range Configuration registers consists of eight pairs of I/O base address registers. The first register in each pair specifies bits [15:8] of a single I/O range, and the second specifies bits [7:0] of the same range. Writing a value of 00H to both base address registers in an I/O Range Configuration register pair disables the corresponding I/O range. Table 5.6 shows the format of the I/O Range Configuration register group.

Table 5.6. The format of the I/O Range Configuration register group.

Byte	*Description*
00H	I/O Range High Bits. Bits [15:8] of the I/O range base address
01H	I/O Range Low Bits. Bits [7:0] of the I/O range base address

I/O Range High Bits (Offsets *60H, 62H, 64H, 66H, 68H, 6AH, 6CH, 6EH*, Read-Write)

The I/O Range High Bits register contains bits [15:8] of the I/O range base address. Together with the I/O Range Low Bits register that follows it, this register forms a 16-bit I/O range base address.

I/O Range Low Bits (Offsets 61H, 63H, 65H, 67H, 69H, 6BH, 6DH, 6FH, Read-Write)

The `I/O Range Low Bits` register contains bits `[7:0]` of the I/O range base address. Together with the `I/O Range High Bits` register that precedes it, this register forms a 16-bit I/O range base address.

IRQ Channel Configuration Registers (Offsets 70H-73H)

Plug and Play ISA devices can use as many as two IRQ channels. A logical device's configuration space contains two groups of `IRQ Channel Configuration` registers, each of which consists of two bytes. The system's Plug and Play ISA configuration software first scans each logical device entry in the adapter's resource data block to determine the IRQ needs of the adapter's logical devices, and then assigns each logical device its IRQ channels via the IRQ `Channel Configuration` registers. Table 5.7 shows the format of the `IRQ Channel Configuration` register group.

Table 5.7. The format of the `IRQ Channel Configuration` register group.

Byte	*Description*
`00H`	`IRQ Number` (See the following description)
`01H`	`IRQ Type` (See the following description)

IRQ Channel Number Register (Offsets 70H, 72H, Read-Write)

The two `IRQ Channel Number` registers each specify the ordinal value of the IRQ channel assigned to the current device.

Bits `[7:4]`	Reserved
Bits `[3:0]`	IRQ channel number. Bits `[3:0]` are read-write and contain the zero-based, ordinal value of the selected IRQ channel. A write of `0` to this register indicates that no interrupt is selected.

IRQ Type Register (Offsets 71H, 73H, Read-Write or Read-Only)

If the Plug and Play adapter on which the logical device resides can support more than one style of interrupt, the register is read-write; otherwise this register can be read-only. The following shows the format of each of the two IRQ type registers.

Bits [7:2] Reserved

Bits [1:0]

00B—Edge triggered, active-low

01B—Level triggered, active low

10B—Edge triggered, active high

11B—Level triggered, active high

The PC/AT architecture reserves IRQ channel 0 for its timer tick interrupt. IRQ channel 0 is also non-shareable. Because the channel cannot be used by Plug and Play ISA devices, Plug and Play ISA designers chose the value 0 to indicate no interrupt selection in the IRQ Number register.

DMA Channel Select Registers (Read/Write, Offsets *74H-75H*)

Plug and Play ISA devices can use as many as two DMA channels. A logical device's configuration space contains two, 8-bit DMA Channel Select registers. The system's Plug and Play ISA configuration software first scans each logical device entry in the adapter's resource data block to determine the DMA channel the adapter's logical devices, and then assigns each logical device its DMA channels via the DMA Channel Select registers. Table 5.8 shows the format of the DMA Channel Select register.

Table 5.8. The format of the DMA Channel Select register.

Byte	*Description*
00H	DMA Channel Select (See the following description)

The *DMA Channel Select* Register (Offsets *74H, 75H*, Read-Write)

The following table displays the format of the DMA Channel Select register.

Bits [7:3] Reserved

Bits [2:0] Contain the zero-based, ordinal value of the selected DMA channel. A value of 04H, *not* 00H signifies that no channel is selected.

The PC/AT architecture reserves DMA channel four for cascading DMA requests from the secondary DMA controller to the primary controller. This channel cannot be used by Plug and Play ISA devices. For this reason, Plug and Play designers chose the value 04H to signify no channel selected.

32-bit *Memory Range Configuration* Registers (Offsets *76H-7EH, 80H-88H, 90H-98H, A0H-A8H)*

Not surprisingly, the 32-bit `Memory Range Configuration` registers are similar to their 24-bit counterparts described previously. The Plug and Play ISA committee introduced 32-bit `Memory Range Configuration` registers to satisfy ISA-like devices, such as VL-bus adapters that, other than having the capability to decode 32-bit addresses, conform to the Plug and Play ISA model. The 32-bit `Memory Range Configuration` registers are a superset of the 24-bit `Memory Range` registers and are functionally backward-compatible. In other words, the newer 32-bit `Memory Range` registers can describe all memory ranges in the older, 24-bit `Memory Range` registers.

Each Plug and Play ISA device can support four separate 32-bit memory ranges via its 32-bit `Memory Range Configuration` registers. The system Plug and Play ISA configuration software in the BIOS or operating system configures an adapter's logical device `Memory Range Configuration` registers after first having examined the adapter's resource data descriptor and scanned each of its logical device entries for memory range requirements.

Writing a value of `00H` to each register within a single group of `Memory Range Configuration` registers disables that memory range. Unless otherwise noted, `Memory Range Configuration` registers are read/write and adhere to the following structure. Table 5.9 shows the format of the `Memory Range Configuration` register group.

Table 5.9. The format of the `Memory Range Configuration` register group.

Byte	*Description*
`00H`	`Memory Address [31:24]`. Address bits `[32:24]` of the memory range base address
`01H`	`Memory Address [23:16]`. Address bits `[23:16]` of the memory range base address
`02H`	`Memory Address [15:8]`. Address bits `[15:8]` of the memory range base address
`03H`	`Memory Address [7:0]`. Address bits `[7:0]` of the memory range base address
`04H`	`Memory Range Control`
`05H`	`Memory Limit [31:24]`. Bits `[31:24]` of the memory range upper limit address, or bits `[31:24]` of range length in bytes, according to bit `[0]` of the `Memory Range Control` register

06H	Memory Limit [23:16]. Bits [23:16] of the memory range upper limit address, or bits [23:16] of the range length in bytes, according to bit [0] of the Memory Range Control register
07H	Memory Limit [15:8]. Bits [15:8] of the memory range upper limit address, or bits [15:8] of the range length in bytes, according to bit [0] of the Memory Range Control register
08H	Memory Limit [7:0]. Bits [7:0] of the memory range upper limit address, or bits [7:0] of the range length in bytes, according to bit [0] of the Memory Range Control register

Memory Address [31:24] (Offsets *76H, 80H, 90H, A0H,* Read/Write)

The Memory Address [31:24] register contains address bits [31:24] of the memory range base address.

Memory Address [23:16] (Offsets *77H, 81H, 91H, A1H,* Read/Write)

The Memory Address [23:16] register contains address bits [23:16] of the memory range base address.

Memory Address [15:8] (Offsets *78H, 82H, 92H, A2H,* Read/Write)

The Memory Address [15:8] register contains address bits [15:8] of the memory range base address.

Memory Address [7:0] (Offsets *79H, 83H, 93H, A3H* Read/Write)

The Memory Address [7:0] register contains address bits [7:0] of the memory range base address.

Memory Range Control (Offsets *7AH, 84H, 94H, A4H,* Read/Write or Read-Only)

As in the case of 24-bit memory ranges, the 32-bit Memory Range Control register serves two purposes. First, it defines the meaning of the four Memory Limit registers that follow it, and second, it provides a mechanism for configuring the type of memory located on the logical device. The Memory Range Control register's bits operate as follows:

Bits [7:3]	Reserved
Bits [2:1]	Memory Type Control. The 32-bit Memory Control register supports the following types of memory: 00B—8-bit memory

	`01B`—16-bit memory
	`10B`—Reserved
	`11B`—32-bit memory
Bit `[0]`	`Limit Type`. If set, bit `[0]` indicates that the 32-bit `Memory Limit` registers contain the 32-bit physical upper limit address for the memory range. Otherwise, the 32-bit `Memory Limit` registers contain the range's size mask.

Memory Limit [31:24] (Offsets *7BH, 85H, 95H, A5H,* Read/Write)

If bit `[0]` of the `Memory Control` register is set, the `Memory Limit [31:24]` register contains bits `[31:24]` of the physical address limit for the memory range. Otherwise, the `Memory Limit High Bits` register contains bits `[31:24]` of the memory range size mask.

Memory Limit [23:16] (Offsets *7CH, 86H, 96H, A6H,* Read/Write)

If bit `[0]` of the `Memory Control` register is set, then the `Memory Limit [23:16]` register contains bits `[23:16]` of the physical address limit for the memory range. Otherwise, the `Memory Limit High Bits` register contains bits `[23:16]` of the memory range size mask.

Memory Limit [15:8] (Offsets *7DH, 87H, 97H, A7H,* Read/Write)

If bit `[0]` of the `Memory Control` register is set, the `Memory Limit [15:8]` register contains bits `[15:8]` of the physical address limit for the memory range. Otherwise, the `Memory Limit High Bits` register contains bits `[15:8]` of the memory range size mask.

Memory Limit [7:0] (Offsets *7EH, 88H, 98H, A8H,* Read/Write)

If bit `[0]` of the `Memory Control` register is set, the `Memory Limit [7:0]` register contains bits `[7:0]` of the physical address limit for the memory range. Otherwise, the `Memory Limit High Bits` register contains bits `[7:0]` of the memory range size mask.

> **NOTE**
>
> When used to specify a memory range's size, the `Memory Limit` registers form a mask, rather than an actual byte count. Those bits that are set to `0` indicate don't-care bits in the device's address decoder. For example, if the `Memory Limit` registers collectively contain the value `0FFFFF000H`, together they indicate that the device requires a memory range whose lower 12-bits are don't-care bits, and whose granularity, or size is 4KB.

Logical Device Configuration Registers, Reserved (Offsets *0A9H-0EFH*)

As of version 1.0a of the *Plug and Play ISA Specification*, the value of these registers was yet undefined.

Logical Device Configuration Registers, Vendor-Defined (Offsets *0F0H-0FEH*)

The use of these registers is completely at the discretion of the adapter vendor.

Logical Device Mystery Register (Offset *0FFH*)

As of version 1.0a, the use of the Mystery register was yet undefined.

Actually, the register has no official name; it's the reserved `Logical Device` register located at offset `0FFH`.

The Plug and Play Expansion ROM

Expansion ROMs are adapter, or systemboard-based firmware modules that initialize, test and provide interface functions for additional system hardware, such as SCSI and VGA controllers. Whether located on a PCI adapter, a legacy ISA adapter, a Plug and Play ISA adapter, or within the system's built-in firmware, all expansion ROMs reside on a 2KB boundary and contain at offset `0` a header that provides the system BIOS with a signature, length and initialization entry point. Table 5.10 shows the format of the standard IBM PC expansion ROM header.

Table 5.10. The format of the standard IBM PC expansion ROM header.

Offset	*Size*	*Description*
`00H`	`WORD`	`55AAH` Signature
`02H`	`BYTE`	Length of expansion ROM in 512 byte increments
`03H`	`3*BYTE`	Vendor-defined initialization entry point. Usually contains a near `JMP` instruction to ROM `init` code.

During POST, the system BIOS scans for and initializes any expansion ROMs that it encounters in the system address range from `C0000H-EE000H`. The BIOS' ROM scan allows individual adapters to initialize on-board registers and attached devices prior to the system's operating system launch.

Figure 5.5 shows the format of the Plug and Play Expansion ROM.

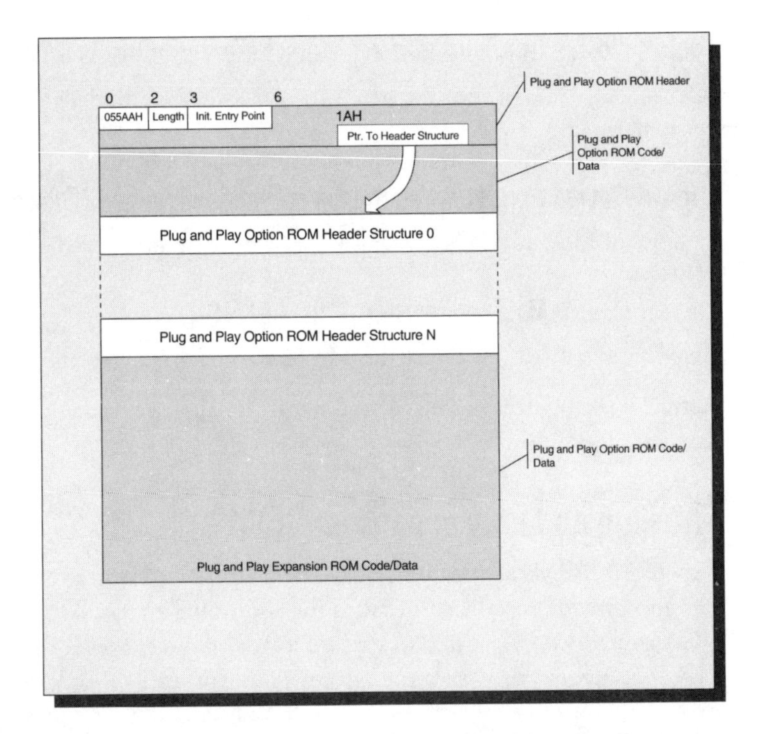

FIGURE 5.5.
The format of the Plug and Play Expansion ROM.

AUTHOR'S NOTE

In case you're wondering, the format of Plug and Play-compliant expansion ROMs appears in the Plug and Play BIOS Specification, and not the *Plug and Play ISA Specification.* From the standpoint of the authors of the *Plug and Play BIOS Specification,* it is possible for non-Plug and Play ISA devices to support pseudo-Plug and Play functions, such as reporting device resource consumption via the Static Resource Information vector; therefore, the issues involved in defining Plug and Play-compliant option ROMs extend beyond the scope of the *Plug and Play ISA Specification.*

In practice, though, very few legacy ISA adapters support the Plug and Play Option ROM format, whereas all expansion ROM-equipped Plug and Play ISA devices are required to support the Plug and Play Option ROM format in their on-board firmware. Despite the fact that the Plug and Play Option ROM format applies mainly to Plug and Play ISA devices, the reader should refer to the *Plug and Play BIOS Specification* to obtain the industry definition of the Plug and Play Option ROM format.

In addition to the information contained in a standard IBM PC expansion header, the expansion ROM header on Plug and Play ISA devices contains at location 1AH the offset to the Plug and Play Expansion Header Structure. Table 5.11 shows the format of the Plug and Play Option ROM Header.

Table 5.11. The format of the Plug and Play Option ROM header.

Offset	*Size*	*Description*
00H	WORD	55AAH Signature
02H	BYTE	Length of expansion ROM in 512 byte increments
03H	3*BYTE	Vendor-defined initialization entry point. Usually contains a near JMP instruction to ROM init code.
06H	14H * BYTE	Reserved
1AH	WORD	Offset to first Plug and Play Expansion Header Structure

In order to adhere to the Plug and Play BIOS specification, a Plug and Play ISA adapter equipped with an expansion ROM must supply both a Plug and Play Option ROM Expansion Header and Expansion ROM Header Structure in its on-board firmware. However, both legacy and Plug and Play ISA adapters can contain Plug and Play Expansion Headers and Expansion Header Structures. Legacy ISA devices that contain Plug and Play Expansion Headers and Expansion Header Structures are considered to be "polite," in that they report resource consumption via their Static Resource Information Vector, but these devices are by no means Plug and Play devices because the process of configuring the device's resources requires that the user change jumpers, switches, and so on.

The format of both the Plug and Play Option ROM Expansion Header and the Expansion ROM Header Structure is the same for both legacy and Plug and Play ISA compliant devices. Table 5.12 shows the format of the Plug and Play Expansion Header Structure.

Table 5.12. The format of the Plug and Play Expansion Header Structure.

Offset	*Size*	*Description*
00H	DWORD	Expansion Header Signature
04H	BYTE	Expansion Header Revision (01H)
05H	BYTE	Expansion Header Length in paragraphs
06H	WORD	Next Header Offset
08H	BYTE	Reserved (00H)
09H	BYTE	Expansion Header checksum
0AH	DWORD	Compressed EISA Device ID
0EH	WORD	Offset of Manufacturer ID string
10H	WORD	Offset of Product ID string
12H	3*BYTE	Device Class Code
15H	BYTE	Device Attributes
16H	WORD	Boot Connection Vector
18H	WORD	Disconnect Vector
1AH	WORD	Bootstrap Entry Point
1CH	WORD	Reserved (00H)
1EH	WORD	Static Resource Information Vector

Expansion Header Signature—This four-byte field contains the ASCII string $PnP. The Option ROM enumerator checks this field to confirm that the Expansion Header Offset located either at location 1AH within the expansion ROM or at location 06H within a previous expansion ROM header points to a valid Expansion Header Signature.

Expansion Header Revision—This field identifies the revision of the Expansion Header Structure. Expansion ROMs that utilize the structure shown here contain the value 01H in the Expansion Header Revision field.

Expansion Header Length—The Expansion Header Length contains the length of the Expansion Header Structure in paragraphs. System software uses the Expansion Header Length to determine the number of bytes on which to perform its structure checksum verification.

Next Header Offset—Devices whose expansion ROM adheres to the *Plug and Play Option ROM Specification* can contain one or several Expansion ROM Header structures. If this field contains 00H, the current header is the last in the

device's expansion ROM. Otherwise, the Next Header Offset field contains the 16-bit offset of the next Expansion ROM Header Structure relative to location 00H within the firmware image.

Expansion Header Checksum—Filled in during the expansion ROM build process, the Expansion Header Checksum byte contains a value such that the sum of all bytes in the Expansion Header is `0`. System software considers those Expansion Headers whose checksum is not `0` to be invalid.

Compressed EISA Device ID—The four-byte Compressed EISA Device ID is identical in format to those used in the Plug and Play ISA serial identification register, Plug and Play BIOS device nodes and PCI configuration space. In its uncompressed form, the Device ID is a seven-character ASCII string that uniquely identifies the device upon which the expansion ROM resides. For example, the Device ID `04H`, `09H`, `32H`, `15H` (which appears in decompressed form as `ADP1532`) signifies that the device is an Adaptec 1532-compatible SCSI adapter.

Offset of Manufacturer ID String—If non-zero, this field contains the offset to a Manufacturer-supplied ASCIIZ (null-terminated) string that identifies the adapter's manufacturer. Often, the Manufacturer ID String is the same string that the adapter firmware displays when the adapter "signs-on" during the expansion ROM initialization sequence.

Offset of Product ID String—If non-zero, this field contains the offset to a Manufacturer-supplied ASCIIZ (null-terminated) string that describes the product's function. Often, the Product ID string appears with the Manufacturer ID String during the adapter's sign-on process.

Device Class Code—The three-byte Device Class Code is an alternative to the Device ID for purposes of identifying the capabilities of a particular device. The format of the Device Class Code field is identical to that used within Plug and Play BIOS device nodes and PCI device configuration space. A complete list of Device Class Codes appears in Appendix A.

Device Attributes—The Device Attribute field identifies various capabilities of the device as outlined in Table 5.13. A description of each device attribute also appears here.

Table 5.13. The format of the Device Attributes field.

Bit	*Description*
7	If set, the ROM supports DDIM (Device Driver Initialization Model)
6	If set, the ROM can execute properly in system shadow RAM

continues

Table 5.13. continued

Bit	Description
5	If set, reads of this ROM can be cached
4	If set, the ROM is required only if the device is chosen as a boot device.
3	Reserved (00H)
2	If set, the device is an IPL (Initial Program Load) device
1	If set, the device is a primary Input device
0	If set, the device is a primary Output device

Bit 7—If set, the adapter's expansion ROM adheres to the DDIM (Device Driver Initialization Model). DDIM-compliant expansion ROMs assume that the system BIOS has copied the ROM image into write-enabled shadow RAM prior to invoking the ROM's initialization vector.

The purpose for making an expansion ROM DDIM-compliant is to aid the system BIOS in conserving UMB (Upper Memory Block) space. If the expansion ROM's initialization code executes in write-enabled shadow RAM, the expansion ROM can discard its initialization code and adjust the expansion ROM size value at offset 02H within the ROM image prior to returning control to the system BIOS, thereby reducing the amount of address space that the ROM image consumes at runtime.

The expansion ROM recalculates the checksum of its own contents before returning to the BIOS because applications assume that the checksum of a valid ROM image is 0. Support for DDIM is optional and conserves upper memory address space only if both the system BIOS and expansion ROM are DDIM-aware. The DDIM-aware BIOS increases the effectiveness of UMB space conservation by packing DDIM-capable expansion ROM images into the closest available 2KB shadow RAM boundary.

Bit 6—If set, the device is capable of executing in shadow RAM. Many system BIOS implementations are capable of copying expansion ROM contents to shadow RAM, in which case the expansion ROM's runtime code executes much more quickly. In fact, many BIOS authors assume they can shadow the system's video BIOS without side effects.

Designers that implement memory-mapped I/O on their adapters should set this bit to 0. If the adapter's expansion ROM has been shadowed, the system's chipset simply discards any reads or writes to the adapter's system address space.

Bit 5—If set, the contents of the adapter's expansion ROM are read-cacheable. The adapter's expansion ROM contents are read-cacheable if the adapter always returns the same value for a read of any location within the ROM's address space. An adapter is not read-cacheable, for example, if contains readable, memory-mapped registers whose value changes at runtime.

Bit 4—When set, the expansion ROM is required only if the device on which the ROM resides has been chosen as a boot device. If the system BIOS does not choose the device as a boot device, it checks this bit in order to determine if the adapter's expansion ROM is discardable. If the system BIOS determines that the adapter's expansion ROM is discardable, it will attempt to disable the adapter's ROM by unconfiguring its memory space registers.

Bit 2—If set, the device is capable of acting as the system's IPL (Initial Program Load) or boot device. If the system BIOS detects that the device can act as the IPL device, it issues a far call to the device's Boot Connection Vector, if one is present. When the BIOS calls the device's Boot Connection Vector, the expansion ROM "hooks" any interrupts (such as INT 09H, INT 13H, and INT 19H) that the device will use to take over control of the system's boot sequence.

Bit 1—If set, the device is capable of acting as an input device, such as the keyboard. If the system BIOS detects that the device can act as an input device, it issues a `far` call to the device's Boot Connection Vector, if one is present. As is the case with IPL devices, when the BIOS calls the device's Boot Connection Vector, the expansion ROM "hooks" any interrupts (such as INT 09H, INT 14H, and INT 15H) that the device will use to take over control of the system's input.

Bit 0—If set, the device is capable of acting as an output device, such as the system's video controller. If the system BIOS detects that the device can act as an output device, it issues a `far` call to the device's Boot Connection Vector, if one is present. As is the case with IPL and input devices, when the BIOS calls the device's Boot Connection Vector, the expansion ROM "hooks" any interrupts (such as INT 10H and INT 14H) that the device will use to take over control of the system's output.

Boot Connection Vector—During POST, the system BIOS calls the device's Boot Connection Vector if any of the lower three bits of the device's Attribute byte are set to 1. The BIOS calls a device's Boot Connection Vector to allow the device to hook any interrupts it needs to initiate the system IPL sequence. Many Plug and Play SCSI controllers, for example, have bit 2 of their Attribute byte set indicating that they can act as an IPL device. During the BIOS' Boot Connection call to the device, most SCSI controllers intercept both INT 13H and INT 19H.

By intercepting INT 13H, the SCSI controller's firmware can replace the BIOS's calls to system BIOS resident INT 13H boot sector load functions with SCSI-device specific calls located within the SCSI controller's firmware.

Similarly, SCSI devices intercept the system's INT 19H vector during the Boot Connection Sequence. Plug and Play SCSI controller expansion ROMs intercept INT 19H so that they can restore the system's original INT 19H vector and return control to the system BIOS in case the SCSI device boot sequence fails.

Disconnect Vector—If the device fails its IPL sequence, the system BIOS will call the device's Disconnect Vector, provided the value of the Disconnect Vector is non-zero. Within its Boot Disconnect code, the device's expansion ROM should restore any vectors it hooked during its Boot Connect Vector sequence, and perform any other clean up operations that will prevent its device from interfering with the continuation of the system's boot.

Bootstrap Entry Point—The Bootstrap Entry Point serves primarily as a mechanism for passing control of the system boot sequence to an RPL (Remote Program Load) device. Remote Program Load devices differ from IPL devices in that they don't support the standard INT 13H calls that the system BIOS invokes to read the system's boot sector. The system BIOS will invoke the Bootstrap Entry Point vector of an RPL device if the Bootstrap Entry Point vector is non-zero, and if the lower three bits of the Device Attribute byte within the device's Plug and Play Option ROM header structure are clear.

Static Resource Information Vector—The Static Resource Information Vector provides a mechanism by which non-Plug and Play ISA devices report their resource consumption in the form of a system device node. While not truly Plug and Play compliant, devices that report their resource usage via the Static Resource Information Vector assist the system BIOS in determining the total system resource map and mapping configurable resources so as not to conflict with those consumed by the device supplying the Static Resource Information Vector.

When the BIOS invokes a device's Static Resource Information Vector, it loads the `ES:DI` register with a far pointer to a 1KB buffer designed to receive the static device's system device node. Within its Static Resource Information Vector code, the device's expansion ROM copies a system device node-like data structure into the caller's buffer. The static resource information device node is identical in format to a system device node, as described in Chapter 3, with the following exceptions:

- The Device Node Number is 0.
- The possible resource allocation block contains a single END_TAG descriptor. Since the device's resource consumption is static, the device has no possible resource allocation alternatives.

THE PLUG AND PLAY EXPANSION ROM CALLING SEQUENCE

Prior to calling a Plug and Play expansion ROM, the Plug and Play-compliant system BIOS loads the CPU registers with the following values:

ES:DI	Far pointer to the system's Plug and Play Installation Check Header
BX	CSN for the Plug and Play ISA adapter. If the adapter is not Plug and Play ISA-compliant, yet contains a Plug and Play Option ROM header, the BIOS loads BX with 0FFFFH
DX	Address of the system's Plug and Play ISAREAD_DATA register. If the adapter is not Plug and Play ISA-compliant, yet contains a Plug and Play Option ROM header, the BIOS loads DX with 0FFFFH.

The Plug and Play system BIOS supplies Plug and Play expansion ROMs with the information listed above in order to facilitate the expansion ROM's process of initializing its on-board functions. Once the Plug and Play ISA device's expansion ROM knows the CSN and READ_DATA port addresses assigned to its adapter, it issues a WAKE[CSN] command to enable the device's configuration space registers. From the device's configuration space registers, the Plug and Play expansion ROM retrieves the adapter's IRQ, DMA, I/O range and memory range configuration. Armed with its device's resource information, the Plug and Play expansion ROM accurately initializes its device's on-board functions prior to returning control to the system BIOS.

If the system in which the Plug and Play adapter is installed is not Plug and Play compliant, the value of the CPU registers are undefined upon entry to the device's expansion ROM initialization vector. In this case, the expansion ROM may "snoop" for its on-board functions and attempt to isolate the system's Plug and Play devices. The results of this operation are unpredictable.

Example Program

The following example program, RDPNPISA.C, gives you a good look at a working example of the Initiation Key Sequence, the `Wake[CSN]` command, and a simple logical device enumerator. RDPNPISA.EXE requires that the host system be equipped with a Plug and Play BIOS, as it uses Plug and Play BIOS function `40H` (`GET_PNP_ISA_INFO`) to determine the address of the `READ_DATA` register and the total number of `CSN`'s that the system BIOS has allocated to Plug and Play ISA adapters.

```
//
// RDPNPISA.C — Read & Print Plug and Play ISA Adapter
//              Resource Data Block and Print Contents
//
// To Compile:  CL /Zp RDPNPISA.C
// NOTE:  You Must compile with structure packing (/Zp) enabled,
//        otherwise 'C' compiler will word-align the pldd structure
//

#include <malloc.h>
#include <string.h>

#define BYTE   unsigned char
#define WORD   unsigned int
#define DWORD  unsigned long
#define FPCHAR char far *
#define FPVOID void far *

//
// Descriptor groups within PnP ISA configuration space regs.
//

#define Num_Mem_Descriptors      4  // 4 24-bit and 32-bit Memory ranges
#define Num_IO_Descriptors       8  // 8 IO ranges
#define Num_IRQ_Descriptors      2  // 2 IRQ channels
#define Num_DMA_Descriptors      2  // 2 DMA channels

//
// Return Values For PnP BIOS Function 0x40
//

#define SUCCESS                     0x00
#define NO_ISA_PNP_CARDS            0x88

//
// Some resource format types used in this program.
// A complete listing appears in PLUGPLAY.H
//

#define PNP_VERSION_DESC            0x0A
#define LOGICAL_DEVICE_DESC         0x15
#define LOGICAL_DEVICE_DESC_FLAGS   0x16
#define END_TAG_CHECKSUM            0x79
#define ANSI_STRING_DESCRIPTOR      0x82
#define LRD_ANSI_STRING_ID          0x82
```

```
//
// Plug and Play ISA Auto-Configuration Fixed Ports
//

#define PNPISA_ADDRESS           0x279
#define PNPISA_WRITE_DATA        0xA79

//
// Some PnP ISA Configuration Space Registers
//

#define CONFIG_CONTROL           0x02  // Bit [0]-Reset all devices
                                       // Bit [1]-Return to Wait for Key
                                       // Bit [2]-Reset all CSNs to 0
#define WAKE_CSN                 0x03  // 0 => Isolation; == => config
#define RESOURCE_DATA            0x04  // read the next byte of res.data
#define STATUS                   0x05  // Bit [0] ok to read next byte
#define LOGICAL_DEV_NUM          0x07  // Selects the current log.device
#define MEM24_BASE_HIGH          0x40  // selected base bits [23:16]

//
// Plug and Play Header — Format of the Installation Check Header
//   located on a 16-byte boundary in the F0000H segment of
//   a Plug and Play system.
//

typedef struct PlugnPlay_Header {

     BYTE   Signature[4] ;          // '$PnP'
     BYTE   Revision ;              // 01
     BYTE   HdrLength ;
     WORD   Control ;
     BYTE   ChkSum ;
     FPVOID EventFlag ;
     FPVOID RealEntry ;
     WORD   ProtEntryOffset;
     DWORD  ProtEntrySeg;
     DWORD  OEMDeviceID;
     WORD   RealDataSeg;
     DWORD  ProtDataSeg;

} PLUGNPLAYHEADER;


#define SendWaitForKey() outp(PNPISA_ADDRESS, CONFIG_CONTROL);\
                         IODelay();\
                         outp(PNPISA_WRITE_DATA, 2)

#define SendWakeCSN(p)   outp(PNPISA_ADDRESS, WAKE_CSN);\
                         IODelay();\
                         outp(PNPISA_WRITE_DATA, p)

#define SetLogicalDev(n) outp(PNPISA_ADDRESS,LOGICAL_DEV_NUM);\
                         IODelay();\
                         outp(PNPISA_WRITE_DATA,n);
```

```
#define ResetLFSRReg()    outp(PNPISA_ADDRESS, 0);\
                          IODelay();\
                          outp(PNPISA_ADDRESS, 0)

//
// HEX2ASCII — Convert InChar to printable ASCII HEX digit
//

BYTE HEX2ASCII(BYTE InChar) {

   if (InChar <= 9) return (InChar += '0') ;
   return (InChar += 'A' - 10) ;

}

//
// ErrorExit — Exit w/Error Code & ErrString Message
//

void ErrorExit(int ErrNum, BYTE * ErrString) {

   printf("\n%s", ErrString) ;
   exit(ErrNum) ;

}

//
// LogDeviceData — struct that holds one logical device's
//   configuration space registers.  It's convenient to store
//   device's settings in the same format as its registers.
//

typedef struct LogDeviceData {

   // 4 memory descriptors per log dev      (config regs 40-5F)

   struct {
      WORD  base;
      BYTE  control;
      WORD  length;
      BYTE  filler[3];
   } mem[Num_Mem_Descriptors];

   // 8 I/O descriptors per log dev         (config regs 60-6F)

   WORD  iop[Num_IO_Descriptors];

   // 2 IRQ descriptors per log dev         (config regs 70-73)

   struct {
      BYTE channel;
      BYTE type;
   } irq[Num_IRQ_Descriptors];

   // 2 dma channel descriptors per log dev (config regs 74-75)

   BYTE dmac[Num_DMA_Descriptors];
```

```
    // 4 memory32 descriptors per log dev    (config regs 76-a8)
    // first Mem descriptor has only one filler byte (76-7F)

    struct memdesc {
       DWORD base;      // base
       BYTE control;     // control
       DWORD length;     // length
       BYTE filler;     // filler (just one on descriptor 0 ref 7F)
    } mem32a;

    // other Mem descriptors have seven filler bytes (80-A8)

    struct {
       DWORD base;      // base
       BYTE control;     // control
       DWORD length;     // length
       BYTE filler[7];  // filler  9 seven on descriptors 1, 2, 3)
    } mem32b[Num_Mem_Descriptors-1];

    // values for PNPISA Allocate & Deallocate

    WORD  iol[Num_IO_Descriptors];

    } LOGDEVICEDATA;

typedef struct PlugNPlay_Runtime_Data {

   WORD  PNPISA_READ_DATA;  // assigned PNPISA read port
   BYTE  PNPISA_CSN;        // number of PNPISA cards

} PNP_RUNTIME_DATA;

typedef PNP_RUNTIME_DATA far *FPRTD;

// BYTE HEX2ASCII(BYTE InChar) ;
// void ErrorExit(int ErrNum, BYTE * ErrString) ;
// void DecodeID(BYTE * buffer, DWORD value) ;

//
// PnP BIOS Dispatch Entry Point From Installation Check Header
//

int (far * _based(_segname("_CODE")) FuncEntry)() = (DWORD) 0L ;

//
// PLUGNPLAYHEADER — Pointer To PnP BIOS Installation Check Header
//

PLUGNPLAYHEADER far *PNPHdr = (PLUGNPLAYHEADER far *)0xf0000000;

//
// Insert a delay between Read Status ready, and write for read register
//

void Read_Delay() {

     _asm       mov     cx, 200
```

```
     _asm  XXX: out     0EDh, al
     _asm       loop    XXX

}

void IODelay() {

   _asm out 0EDH, al
   _asm out 0EDH, al

}

//
//  Read_Resource_Data — Read A Single BYTE From The
//  RESOURCE_DATA register.  Notice The 2mSec Delay Between
//  Successive Reads/Writes To Allow The Device To Recover
//

void Read_Resource_Data(FPRTD fprtd, FPCHAR b) {

    do {
        Read_Delay();
        outp(PNPISA_ADDRESS, STATUS);
        Read_Delay();
    } while (!(inp(fprtd->PNPISA_READ_DATA) & 1));

    outp(PNPISA_ADDRESS, RESOURCE_DATA); Read_Delay();
    *(b)=inp(fprtd->PNPISA_READ_DATA);   Read_Delay();

}

//
// IssueInitiationKey — Initiate The LFSR Register Sequence
// To Enable Plug and Play logic on installed devices
//

void IssueInitiationKey() {

     register WORD i, lfsr;

     // Reset the LFSR with a sequence of two write cycles of 0x00
     // to the PNPISA_ADDRESS register

     ResetLFSRReg();

     // Issue the Initiation Key as — First write is 6A then...

     lfsr = 0x6a;
     outp(PNPISA_ADDRESS, lfsr);

     //  ...31 writes of LFSR >> 1 WITH LFSR[7] = LFSR[0] XOR LFSR[1]

     for (i=1; i<32; i++ ) {
       lfsr = (lfsr>>1) ¦ (((lfsr &1) ^ ((lfsr>>1)&1) )<<7);
       outp(PNPISA_ADDRESS, lfsr);
     }
}
```

```
//
// PNPISA_GetRegs -- Read Plug and Play ISA Configuration Space
// registers into pldd (pointer to logical device data).
// Registers beyond 0xA8 are reserved or OEM-defined.
//

void PNPISA_GetRegs(FPRTD fprtd, FPCHAR pldd ) {

   WORD ReadPort = fprtd->PNPISA_READ_DATA,\
        reg_index = MEM24_BASE_HIGH ;

   do {
      outp(PNPISA_ADDRESS, reg_index++) ;
      IODelay() ;
      * pldd++ = inp(ReadPort) ;
   }  while (reg_index <= 0xA8) ;
}

//
// GetFuncEntry — Find system's Plug and Play Installation Check Header
// to retrieve the real mode entry point for Plug and Play services.
//

FPVOID GetFuncEntry() {

   // look for the $PnP Installation Check in F000:0

   (DWORD)PNPHdr = 0x0F0000000;

   do {
       if (!_fstrncmp("$PnP",PNPHdr->Signature,4))
         return (PNPHdr->RealEntry) ;
       (DWORD) PNPHdr += 0x10;
   } while ((WORD)PNPHdr);

   return (0) ;

}

//
// ReadConfigurationData — Read logical device's resource
// allocation descriptor via RESOURCE_DATA register.  The
// first 9 reads of RESOURCE_DATA return the adapter's
// serial number, Device ID and serial header checksum.
//

WORD ReadConfigurationData(register FPRTD fprtd, register FPCHAR fpBuff) {

   WORD count, i, firstbyte = 1, reslen ;
   BYTE datatype;

   //
   // First, Read In The Header (Device ID & Serial Number)
   // Ignore The CheckSum Byte
   //

   count = 8;
   for (i=0; i<8; i++) Read_Resource_Data(fprtd, &fpBuff[i]);
```

```
Read_Resource_Data(fprtd, &datatype) ;  // Discard Checksum (9th byte)

//
// Now, read the board's configuration data
//

do {

   // read the Resource Data Type

   Read_Resource_Data(fprtd,&datatype);

   //
   // This is a patch for early PnP ISA adapters whose very
   // first byte is garbage.  If the current byte is not
   // the PNP_VERSION_DESC, something's out of synch, try
   // to read one more byte and get back in synch, else give up
   // Also, we'll fix the Device ID & Serial # display strings.
   //

   if ((count == 8) && (datatype != PNP_VERSION_DESC)) {

         for (i=0; i<7; i++) fpBuff[i]=fpBuff[i+1];
           Read_Resource_Data(fprtd,&datatype);
         if (datatype != PNP_VERSION_DESC) return (0) ;
   }

   fpBuff[count++] = datatype;

   //
   // Figure Out Length reslen Of Resource Data From Byte[0]
   // If It's A Large Data Type, reslen Is Byte[1] & Byte[2]
   // Else It's A Small Data Type, reslen Is Bits [2:0] of Byte[0]
   //

   if (datatype & 0x80) {

       Read_Resource_Data(fprtd,&fpBuff[count]);
       Read_Resource_Data(fprtd,&fpBuff[count+1]);
       reslen = fpBuff[count] + (fpBuff[count+1] << 8);
       count+=2;
   }
   else reslen = datatype & 7;

   //
   // Using reslen, Read In Remainder Of Resource Data Structure
   //

   for (i=0; i<reslen; i++) Read_Resource_Data(fprtd,&fpBuff[count++]);

   //
   // Don't Read Forever In Case Resource Data Has No End Tag
   //

   if (count > 2048) { count = 0 ; break ; }

 } while (datatype != END_TAG_CHECKSUM);
```

```
   return(count);

}

//
// PNPISA_CountLogicalDevices -- Return the number of logical devices
// on a particular adapter.  This function uses a union of a memory
// range and a logical Device ID format in order to correctly
// calculate the length of the descriptor it's currently examining
//

typedef struct LRD_Memory_Range {

   BYTE  TagByte ;
   WORD  MemLength ;
   BYTE  Information ;
   WORD  RangeMinimum ;
   WORD  RangeMaximum ;
   WORD  Alignment ;
   WORD  RangeLength ;

} LRDMEMORYRANGE;

typedef struct SRD_Logical_Device_ID {

   BYTE TagByte ;
   BYTE ID_0_7 ;
   BYTE ID_8_15 ;
   BYTE ID_16_23 ;
   BYTE ID_24_31 ;
   BYTE Flag1 ;
   BYTE Flag2 ;

} SRDLOGICALDEVICEID ;

WORD PNPISA_CountLogicalDevices(FPCHAR PNPISA_Data) {

     WORD reslen;
     BYTE DevCount = 0, Type ;

     //
     // Create A Pointer for all Small/Large Data Types
     //

     union {
       LRDMEMORYRANGE      far *pMem ;
       SRDLOGICALDEVICEID  far *pLog ;
       FPCHAR                  pChar ;
     } Ptr ;

   // scan the resource data looking for LOGICAL DEVICE DESCRIPTORS

   Ptr.pChar = PNPISA_Data ;

   do {

      if ((Type = *(Ptr.pChar)) == END_TAG_CHECKSUM) return(DevCount) ;
```

```
        // Calculate the length of the resource type data (once)

        reslen = Type & 0x80 ? Ptr.pMem->MemLength + 3 : (Type & 7) + 1 ;

        // Increment Count If It's A Boot Device
        // And Select Next Logical Device

        switch (Type) {

           case LOGICAL_DEVICE_DESC:
           case LOGICAL_DEVICE_DESC_FLAGS:

              SetLogicalDev(++DevCount);
              break ;

           case END_TAG_CHECKSUM:

              return((WORD)DevCount) ;

        } // End switch

        Ptr.pChar += reslen;

    } while ((Ptr.pChar - PNPISA_Data) < 1024) ; // Don't Do Forever

    return(0) ;

}

//
// SerialNum -- Convert 8-digit serial number to ASCII string
// Note:  Serial number nibbles appear in left-to-right order
//

void SerialNum(FPCHAR buffer, DWORD SerialNumber) {

    WORD count ;
    BYTE niblet ;

    for (count = 0; count < 8; count++) {

        niblet = (BYTE) ((SerialNumber & 0xF0000000L) >> 28) ;
        buffer[count] = HEX2ASCII(niblet) ;
        SerialNumber = SerialNumber << 4 ;

    }
    buffer[count] = 0 ;
}

//
// DecodeID -- Convert compressed EISA style Device ID
//  to readable, uncompressed ASCII string form
//

void DecodeID(BYTE * buffer, DWORD EISAID) {

      buffer[0] = (char) (((EISAID & 0x007CL) >> 2) + 0x40);
```

```
    buffer[1] = (char) ((((EISAID & 0x0003L) << 3) ¦
              ((EISAID & 0x0000E000L) >> 13) ) + 0x40);
    buffer[2] = (char) (((EISAID & 0x1F00L) >> 8) + 0x40);
    sprintf(buffer+3, "%2x%2x",
              (BYTE) ((EISAID & 0x00FF0000L) >> 16),
              (BYTE) ((EISAID & 0xFF000000L) >> 24));
    return(buffer) ;
}

//
// SwapShort -- swap bytes of int values to send to PNP ISA
//  memory range config registers which are programmed
//  hi byte first ... very un-Intel !
//

unsigned short SwapShort(unsigned short temp) {

   _asm  mov   ax, word ptr temp // Implicitly, unsigned short
   _asm  xchg  al, ah            // function return value is in AX

}

//
// SwapLong -- swap bytes of long values to send to PNP ISA
//  memory range config registers which are programmed
//  hi byte first ... very un-Intel !
//

DWORD SwapLong(DWORD temp) {

   _asm  mov   dx, word ptr temp+2
   _asm  xchg  dl, dh
   _asm  mov   ax, word ptr temp
   _asm  xchg  al, ah
}

int main(int argc, BYTE ** argv) {

   PNP_RUNTIME_DATA   rtd;
   FPRTD              fprtd=(FPRTD)&rtd;
   LOGDEVICEDATA      ldd, far *pldd=&ldd;
   WORD               CurrentCSN, ld, i, j;
   BYTE               far *fpBuff, cardstring[80], PNPISA_Config[8];

   //
   // 1. Check For PnP BIOS Installed
   // 2. Query Plug and Play BIOS for # of PNP ISA cards
   //

   if (!((FPVOID)FuncEntry=GetFuncEntry()))
      ErrorExit(1, "No PnP BIOS!!!") ;

   if ((*FuncEntry)(0x40,
                   (FPCHAR)&PNPISA_Config[0],
                   PNPHdr->RealDataSeg) == NO_ISA_PNP_CARDS)

      ErrorExit(2, "No Plug and Play ISA Cards Found") ;
```

```
//
// 3. Set up a run-time data buffer to store the CSN count
//    and READ_DATA values from PnP BIOS function 40H
//

rtd.PNPISA_READ_DATA = *(PNPISA_Config+3) * 0x100 + *(PNPISA_Config+2);
rtd.PNPISA_CSN = *(PNPISA_Config+1);

//
// 4. Get a buffer to hold each device's registers
//

if (!(fpBuff = (FPCHAR) malloc(2048))) ErrorExit(2, "Malloc Error") ;

//
// 5. Get everybody out of Wait For Key state by issuing
//    the Initiation Key sequence.  Afterward, all Plug
//    and Play ISA adapters are in Sleep state
//

IssueInitiationKey();

//
// 6. Loop through currently assigned CSN's.  Wake each card,
//    read its logical device registers and display their contents
//

for (CurrentCSN=0; CurrentCSN < rtd.PNPISA_CSN; CurrentCSN++) {

   SendWakeCSN(CurrentCSN+1);
   ReadConfigurationData(fprtd, fpBuff);
   j=PNPISA_CountLogicalDevices(fpBuff+8);

   for (ld=0;ld<j;ld++) {

      cardstring[0] = 0 ;

      //
      // Check For ANSI String Descriptor
      //

      if (fpBuff[11]==LRD_ANSI_STRING_ID) {
         for (i=0;i<fpBuff[12];i++)
             cardstring[i]=fpBuff[i+14];
         cardstring[fpBuff[12]]=0;
         printf("ANSI ID: %s\n",cardstring);
      }
      else printf("No Available Device Description\n");

      //
      // First two DWORDs in fpBuff are the adapter's
      // Device ID and the Serial #
      //

      DecodeID(&cardstring[0],*(DWORD far *)&fpBuff[0]);
      SerialNum(&cardstring[10],*(DWORD far *)&fpBuff[4]);

      printf("Device ID: %s Serial Num: %s\n",cardstring,&cardstring[10]);
```

```
SetLogicalDev(ld);
PNPISA_GetRegs( fprtd, (FPCHAR)&pldd->mem[0]);

printf("Logical Device %X:\n",ld);

// IRQ Descriptors

for (i=0; i<Num_IRQ_Descriptors; i++) {
   printf("IRQ %d:\tLevel %X\tType %s%s\n",i,pldd->irq[i].channel,
            pldd->irq[i].type & 1 ? "level/" : "edge/",
            pldd->irq[i].type & 2 ? "high" : "low");
}

// DMA Descriptors

for (i=0; i<Num_DMA_Descriptors; i++) {
   printf("DMA %d:\tChannel ",i);

   // channel 4 is flag for disabled

   if (pldd->dmac[i] == 4) printf("none\n");
   else                     printf("%d\n",pldd->dmac[i]);
}

// I/O Descriptors

for (i=0; i<Num_IO_Descriptors; i++)
   printf("IO %d:\tBase %.04X\n",i,SwapShort(pldd->iop[i]));

// Memory 24-bit Descriptors

for (i=0; i<Num_Mem_Descriptors; i++) {
   printf("MEM24 %d: Base %.04X\tUpper/Range %.04X\tControl %X ",
           i,
           SwapShort(pldd->mem[i].base),
           SwapShort(pldd->mem[i].length),
           pldd->mem[i].control);

   if (pldd->mem[i].base)
      printf("= %s, %s",pldd->mem[i].control & 2 ? "16bit " : "8bit ",
           pldd->mem[i].control & 1 ? "Range" : "Upper Limit");

   printf("\n");
}

//
// Memory 32-bit Descriptors -- Note:  We handle the first
// 32-bit descriptor differently, since it appears on
// a different boundary in PnP ISA configuration space.
//

printf("MEM32 %d: Base %.08lX\tUpper/Range %.08lX\tControl %X ",
        i,
        SwapLong(pldd->mem32a.base),
        pldd->mem32a.length,
        pldd->mem32a.control);
```

```
        if (pldd->mem32a.base) {
           printf("= %s ",pldd->mem32a.control & 1 ? "Range" : "Upper Limit");
           if (pldd->mem32a.control & 6 == 6 ) printf(",32bit ");
           if (pldd->mem32a.control & 6 == 2 ) printf(",16bit ");
           if (pldd->mem32a.control & 6 == 0 ) printf(",8bit ");
        }

        printf("\n");

        // The remaining three 32-bit memory descriptors

        for (i=0; i<Num_Mem_Descriptors-1; i++) {
           printf("MEM32 %d: Base %.08lX\tUpper/Range %.08lX\tControl %X ",
                  i,
                  SwapLong(pldd->mem32b[i].base),
                  pldd->mem32b[i].length,
                  pldd->mem32b[i].control);

          if (pldd->mem32b[i].base) {
           printf("= %s ",
              pldd->mem32b[i].control & 1 ? "Range" : "Upper Limit");

           if (pldd->mem32b[i].control & 6 == 6 ) printf(",32bit ");
           if (pldd->mem32b[i].control & 6 == 2 ) printf(",16bit ");
           if (pldd->mem32b[i].control & 6 == 0 ) printf(",8bit ");
          }
        printf("\n");
        }

        printf("Press the any key ..."); getch(); system("CLS");

        } // logical device
     } // CSN

  // 7. Politely return all Plug and Play ISA devices
  //    to Wait For Key state

  SendWaitForKey();

  ErrorExit(0, "Done!!!") ;

}
```

6

The PCMCIA Model

Strictly speaking, the *PCMCIA* (*Personal Computer Memory Card International Association*) is a governing body that defines the mechanical, electrical, and software interface characteristics of PC cards—a growing family of credit card-sized, hot-swappable PC adapters and peripheral devices.

As you might guess from its name, the PCMCIA has its roots in add-on memory adapters, such as SRAM (Static RAM) and FLASH cards, the original intent of which was to expand the storage capacity of portable systems via external adapter slots. In 1989, the PCMCIA adopted a physical pinout and form factor that had been designed earlier by JEIDA, the Japanese Electronics Development Association. Later, the PCMCIA joined forces with Intel's ExCA (Exchangeable Card Architecture) group to form what we now recognize as the *PC Card Architecture.*

Currently, the PCMCIA committee provides the following specifications for the PCMCIA architecture and its related topics:

- *PCMCIA PC Card Standard*, revision 2.0
- *PCMCIA Card Services Specification*, revision 2.1
- *PCMCIA Socket Services Specification*, revision 2.0

Additionally, in early 1995, the PCMCIA committee expects to release a specification for CardBus that, among other things, defines DMA and multi-function adapters for future PC Cards and PCMCIA Host Bus Adapter implementations.

To receive information regarding committee membership or availability of the specifications listed above, contact the PCMCIA committee at the following address:

> The Personal Computer Memory Card International Association
> 1030 East Duane Avenue, Suite G
> Sunnyvale, CA 94086
>
> Telephone (408)720-0107
>
> Fax (408)720-9416

The PCMCIA Software Suite

Users and system integrators typically deal with a third-party vendor-supplied suite of PCMCIA software that has been designed to recognize, provide resources for, and configure the majority of PC Cards available on the market today. Once installed, a PCMCIA software suite consists of at least the following components:

> *Socket Services*—Socket Services is a firmware, or operating system level module, that provides an interface for recognizing and configuring the system's particular PCMCIA Host Bus Adapter and its associated socket or sockets.

Card Services—Card Services is an operating system level module that provides an interface by which client drivers receive notification of PC Card insertion and removal events. Similarly, during card status change events, client drivers call Card Services functions to request or configure system resources for specific PC Cards. Card Services does not directly configure PC Cards; rather, it relies on its registered client and super-client drivers to recognize and initialize any installed PC Cards.

Client Drivers—Client drivers are operating system level driver modules that register as clients of Card Services in order to support specific PC Cards. Registered Card Services clients receive a variety of event notifications from Card Services via the call-back address they supply to Card Services during the registration process. Client drivers most often are supplied by vendors who want custom configuration support for the PC Cards they produce.

Super-Client Drivers—Like Card Services client drivers, super-clients register as Card Services clients and receive a variety of event notifications via their call-back address. Unlike normal client drivers, which support just one PC Card, or one small family of similar PC Cards, super-client drivers recognize and configure a wide variety of PC Cards, ranging from modems and LAN cards to SRAM cards and ATA-compatible storage devices.

Block Device Drivers—Block device drivers provide support for IOCTL and operating system block device driver commands directed toward installed PC Card mass storage devices, such as ATA drives SRAM PC Cards that have been formatted with a FAT file system.

During the operating system boot sequence, the block device driver creates and reserves logical drive letters (such as `E:`, `F:`, and so on) for installed block device PC Cards. At runtime, the block device driver processes operating system read, write, verify, and other commands, and allocates and deallocates logical drive letters to mass storage PC Cards as they are inserted or removed by the user.

Memory Technology Drivers—Memory Technology Drivers (or MTDs) provide vendor, or device-specific support for reading, writing, and formatting non-standard types of mass storage devices, such as FLASH ROM-equipped PC Cards. During the operating system load, MTDs register as Card Services clients. At runtime, file system Card Services clients pass read/write requests to Card Services, which in turn translates the file system driver's Card Services call to an MTD-specific call.

File System Drivers—File System Drivers, such as Microsoft's FFS (FLASH File System), provide the operating system with an INT `2FH` file redirector interface similar to that used to perform file operations between a network server and a DOS-based PC client.

Because they are not designed specifically for PCMCIA applications, File System Drivers typically require an intermediate Card Services client driver that translates FFS commands to Card Services calls. In the case of FFS, the intermediate client uses Card Services to forward FFS read, write, and copy commands to the MTD driver that corresponds to the installed FLASH storage device. Figure 6.1 displays the architecture of the PCMCIA software suite.

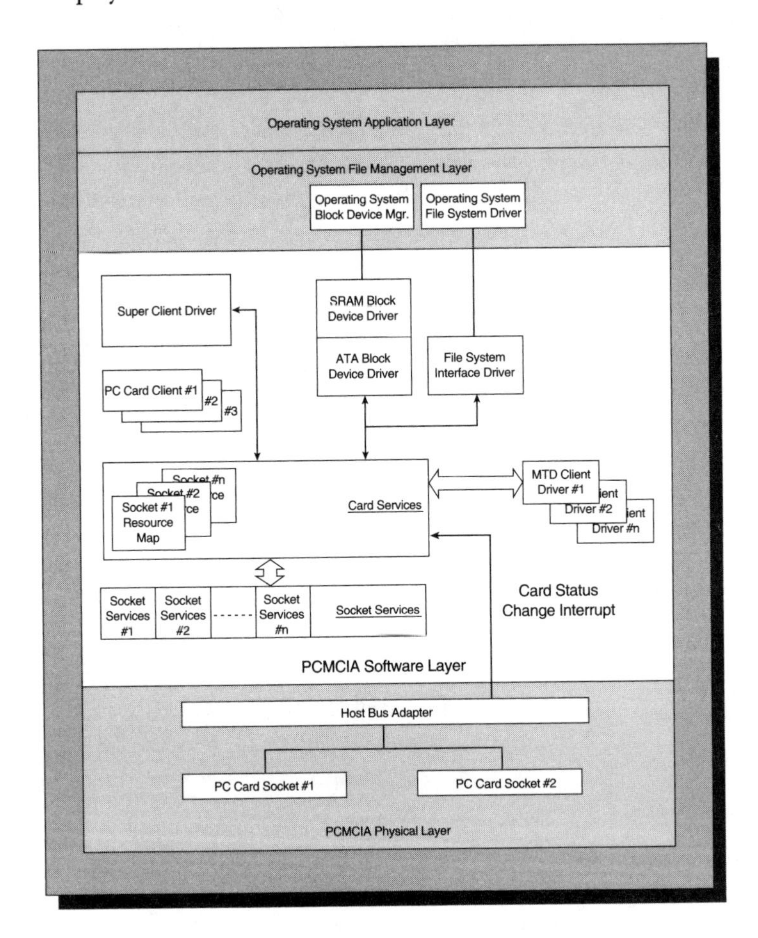

FIGURE 6.1.
The PCMCIA software architecture.

Most engineers that develop Plug and Play software will never write PCMCIA-specific applications or drivers. This chore belongs primarily to the handful of third-party system software providers (such as SystemSoft, AMI, Phoenix Technologies, and Award Software) who produce a full suite of Socket Services, Card Services, FLASH File systems, client drivers and other modules or applications. With the exception of Socket Services and client drivers, PCMCIA drivers are not interchangeable among different vendors' products.

Plug and Play engineers should, however, understand the types of resources that the PCMCIA subsystem uses, and the manner in which PCMCIA software requests and allocates system resources to its PCMCIA Host Bus Adapter and PC Cards. For this reason, this chapter details the workings of PCMCIA from a system approach, describing each of the PCMCIA software suite components mentioned previously, as well as providing an overview of the physical hardware, beginning with a description of PC Cards.

The PC Card

Currently, the PCMCIA defines three types of adapters, which are distinguishable only by their physical shape. *Type I* adapters are 3.3 mm thick, *type II* adapters are 5.0 mm thick, and *type III* adapters are 10.5 mm thick. The 68-pin PC Card interface provides each PC Card access to I/O space, memory space, and interrupt channels (like PCI adapters, PC Cards cannot use DMA channels), allowing designers to create adapters and peripherals that very closely mimic those available for the ISA and PCI buses.

Because of size constraints, designers most often use the type I form factor for non-mechanical storage media, such as FLASH and SRAM devices, while reserving the type II and III packages for less miniaturized devices such as modems, SCSI adapters, and ATA-compatible fixed disks. Many portable systems incorporate two type II slots, which are located one above the other. This arrangement allows a mixture of two type I or type II PC Cards, or a single type III card, which, when inserted, occupies both the upper- and lower-card bays.

As outlined by the PCMCIA committee, the PC Card Architecture consists of five separate layers called the *PC Card Metaformat.* At the lowest level of the Metaformat, the *Physical Layer* includes the system's individual card sockets, PCMCIA Host Bus Adapter, and electrical connections.

Directly above the Physical Layer, the *Compatibility Layer* consists of a CIS (Card Information Structure) that resides within each 2.0 compliant PC Card. The Card Information Structure describes the function, resource requirements, and OEM, or device-specific characteristics of the PC Card.

Like the Compatibility Layer, layers three through five (the *Data Recording Format Layer, Data Organization Layer,* and *System-Specific Layer,* respectively) reside on the PC Card. These layers appear almost exclusively in mass storage PC Card devices, and provide operating system configuration utilities and device drivers with the information necessary to apply OS file system, FLASH device File System (FFS) or other, application-specific data organization rules to the data that the device contains.

The PCMCIA Socket

PC Cards plug into PCMCIA *Host Bus Adapter sockets*, which provide the physical and electrical interface between the PC Card and the PCMCIA Host Bus Adapter.

Although the terminology "PCMCIA bus" appears quite often in industry literature, the individual sockets that a PCMCIA Host Bus Adapter supports are not part of a bus. Instead, the PCMCIA Host Bus Adapter provides 68 discreet signals for each PCMCIA socket. Because of the large number of physical pins required to support a single PCMCIA socket, most PCMCIA Host Bus Adapters support a maximum of two sockets. Systems with more than two sockets usually require multiple PCMCIA Host Bus Adapters.

Each PCMCIA socket contains 26 address lines and 16 data lines. This allows each PC Card to operate in a 64MB address space and perform word-sized I/O and memory data transfers.

The 26-bit address lines within a PCMCIA socket form a linear offset within the PC Card's memory space. Because the Host Bus Adapter can remap physical system addresses into PCMCIA adapter address space, there often is no direct correlation between the address that appears on the PCMCIA bus and the physical system address in which the PC Card's data appears. When the user inserts a PC Card into a PCMCIA socket, the system's Card Services device driver layer configures the PCMCIA Host Bus Adapter with an appropriate memory mapping scheme for the PC Card's addressable space.

The PCMCIA socket can operate either in *memory-only mode* (in which case it can service only memory cards) or in *memory-I/O mode*, which supports both memory and I/O-based PC Cards. Figure 6.2 displays the pin definitions for each socket mode.

The PCMCIA Host Bus Adapter

The *PCMCIA Host Bus Adapter* is a discreet hardware circuit (usually a chip package) that introduces a single PCMCIA bus to the host bus on which it resides. Currently, PCMCIA Host Bus Adapters exist for the ISA, EISA, and PCI buses. Designers often refer to PCMCIA Host Bus Adapters as PCMCIA *bridges* because Host Adapters perform an electrical bridge between dissimilar buses.

The Intel 82092AA, or PPEC controller, for example, creates a bridge between the PCI bus on which it resides and the PCMCIA slots that it controls, thereby allowing software to communicate with PCMCIA devices across the system's PCI bus.

FIGURE 6.2.

The physical pinout of the PCMCIA socket.

Memory-I/O mode	Memory-only mode			Memory-only mode	Memory-I/O mode
GND	GND	35	01	GND	GND
CARD DET 1#	CARD DET 1#	36	02	DATA 3	DATA 3
DATA 11	DATA 11	37	03	DATA 4	DATA 4
DATA 12	DATA 12	38	04	DATA 5	DATA 5
DATA 13	DATA 13	39	05	DATA 6	DATA 6
DATA 14	DATA 14	40	06	DATA 7	DATA 7
DATA 15	DATA 15	41	07	CRD ENBL 1#	CRD ENBL 1#
CRD ENABLE 2#	CRD ENABLE 2#	42	08	ADDR 10	ADDR 10
REF/VS1#	REF/VS1#	43	09	OE#	OE#
IORD#	RESERVED	44	10	ADDR 11	ADDR 11
IOW#	RESERVED	45	11	ADDR 9	ADDR 9
ADDR 17	ADDR 17	46	12	ADDR 8	ADDR 8
ADDR 18	ADDR 18	47	13	ADDR 13	ADDR 13
ADDR 19	ADDR 19	48	14	ADDR 14	ADDR 14
ADDR 20	ADDR 20	49	15	WE#/PGM#	WE#/PGM#
ADDR 21	ADDR 21	50	16	RDY/BUSY#	INTR#
Vcc	Vcc	51	17	Vcc	Vcc
Vpp2	Vpp2	52	18	Vpp1	Vpp1
ADDR 22	ADDR 22	53	19	ADDR 16	ADDR 16
ADDR 23	ADDR 23	54	20	ADDR 15	ADDR 15
ADDR 24	ADDR 24	55	21	ADDR 12	ADDR 12
ADDR 25	ADDR 25	56	22	ADDR 7	ADDR 7
RESERVED/ VS2#	RESERVED/ VS2#	57	23	ADDR 6	ADDR 6
RESET	RESET	58	24	ADDR 5	ADDR 5
WAIT#	WAIT#	59	25	ADDR 4	ADDR 4
INPACK#	RESERVED	60	26	ADDR 3	ADDR 3
REG#	REG#	61	27	ADDR 2	ADDR 2
SPEAKER OUT#	BVD2	62	28	ADDR 1	ADDR 1
STATUS CHG#	BVD1	63	29	ADDR 0	ADDR 0
DATA 8	DATA 8	64	30	DATA 0	DATA 0
DATA 9	DATA 9	65	31	DATA 1	DATA 1
DATA 10	DATA 10	66	32	DATA 2	DATA 2
CARD DET 2#	CARD DET 2#	67	33	WRITE PROT.	I/O SENSE 16#
GND	GND	68	34	GND	GND

Like all PCMCIA Host Bus Adapters, the PPEC has two distinctly different "personalities." First, on the host bus side, the PPEC acts as a compliant PCI bridge device; at the hardware level, it interprets and responds to PCI bus signals and provides a 256 register PCI configuration space. Once the system software has configured the PPEC, the PPEC acts as a decoding gate, forwarding to its physical adapter slots only those memory and I/O transactions intended for the installed PC Cards. System software assigns resources to PC Cards by writing registers within the PPEC's PCI configuration space. Once the system software has configured the PPEC, the PPEC forwards to its physical adapter slots all memory and I/O transactions intended for its installed PC Cards.

Figure 6.3 displays a single PCMCIA Host Bus Adapter that provides two sockets.

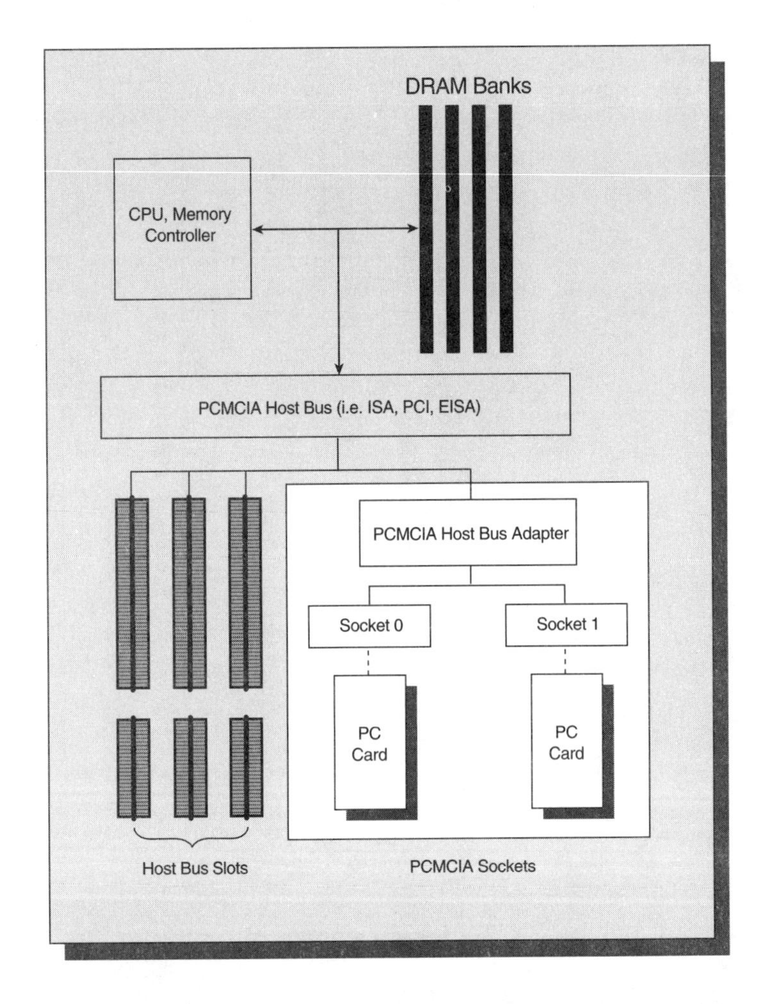

FIGURE 6.3.
PCMCIA Host Bus Adapter and sockets.

Similarly, ISA PCMCIA Host Bus Adapters act as both an ISA bus device and a PCMCIA socket controller. On the host bus side, the ISA PCMCIA Host Bus Adapter decodes I/O and memory transactions to its installed PC Cards as if the memory and I/O ranges assigned to the installed card belong to the PCMCIA Host Bus Adapter. On the PCMCIA socket side, the ISA PCMCIA Host Bus Adapter converts ISA cycles to PCMCIA cycles and translates ISA addresses into addresses within the PC Cards themselves.

If the ISA PCMCIA Host Bus Adapter conforms to the Plug and Play ISA model, it responds to the Plug and Play ISA `ADDRESS`, `READ_DATA`, and `WRITE_DATA` as described in Chapter 5, and provides a Plug and Play ISA card configuration space through which the system BIOS or operating system identifies, enumerates, and configures the PCMCIA Host Bus Adapter device.

PCMCIA Host Bus Adapter Usage of System Resources

The PCMCIA Host Bus Adapter is a consumer of system resources. PCMCIA Host Bus Adapters typically consume one I/O range and one IRQ channel. The I/O range that the PCMCIA Host Bus Adapter consumes allows operating system level drivers and applications to configure the PCMCIA Host Bus Adapter's performance features as well as assign system resources to each of its sockets. The PCMCIA Host Bus Adapter uses one IRQ channel to signal `card status change` events, such as card insertion and removal, to the operating system's Socket Services and Card Services driver layers.

Because the PCMCIA Host Bus Adapter may be a legacy ISA, PCI, Plug and Play ISA, or other type of device, the Plug and Play system tracks the PCMCIA Host Bus Adapter's resource usage in a variety of ways.

If the PCMCIA Host Bus Adapter is a legacy ISA device, for example, it may reside on the systemboard or on a plug-in adapter. Resources assigned to legacy ISA style PCMCIA Host Bus Adapters that reside on the systemboard appear in system BIOS device nodes because the system BIOS has intimate knowledge of the device's presence and the resources that it consumes. The system tracks resources assigned to plug-in style PCMCIA Host Bus Adapters via system NVRAM. In the case of plug-in legacy ISA PCMCIA Host Bus Adapters, the user or system integrator must run a utility such as the Intel ICU to record the adapter's resource usage in NVRAM.

If the PCMCIA Host Bus Adapter resides on the PCI bus, or is a Plug and Play ISA-compliant device, the system BIOS will assign resources to the PCMCIA Host Bus Adapter during the POST sequence and the Plug and Play operating system later enumerates the adapter's resource usage during its normal, boot-time hardware profiling and enumeration process.

During the system boot process, Socket Services drivers invoke Configuration Manager functions to detect the presence of, and determine the system resources allocated to their particular PCMCIA Host Bus Adapter. Later, Card Services issues the Socket Services `GetAdapter` call to each Socket Services driver in order to associate IRQ and I/O ranges with each installed PCMCIA Host Bus Adapter.

The system BIOS assigns resources to Plug and Play-compliant PCMCIA Host Bus Adapters based on the resource allocation strategies outlined in Chapters 4 and 5. For example, a Plug and Play system BIOS that adheres to version 1.0a of the Plug and Play BIOS specification might use a first-come, first-served approach to assigning resources to the PCMCIA Host Bus Adapter, or it may use a proprietary ordering scheme in which those Plug and Play adapters required for booting the system receive their resource allocations first.

Alternatively, if the system BIOS supports the optional ESCD BIOS extensions, the user or system integrator can run an operating system-level application such as the Intel ICU to assign "locked-configurations" to certain system peripherals, thereby fixing the exact resources that the system BIOS will assign to the PCMCIA Host Bus Adapter and other Plug and Play devices during POST.

NOTE

The device configuration space within a Plug and Play ISA or PCI-based PCMCIA Host Bus Adapter is not intended for configuring resources assigned to the adapter's installed PC Cards. Instead, the configuration space provides the mechanism by which system software, such as the BIOS or operating system configurator, can enable and disable the PCMCIA Host Bus Adapter and configure the PCMCIA Host Bus Adapter's card status change IRQ and I/O range.

To better understand this, imagine a PCMCIA Host Bus Adapter whose PCMCIA sockets currently are empty. Although no resources have been assigned to PC Cards (because none are installed), the PCMCIA Host Bus Adapter still requires its own system I/O range and card status change interrupt. System software assigns the PCMCIA Host Bus Adapter its card status change interrupt and I/O range within the adapter's Plug and Play ISA or PCI configuration space, thereby providing the adapter the basic resources it needs to operate correctly on the host bus.

Once the system software has provided the PCMCIA Host Bus Adapter with its card status change IRQ and I/O range, the Socket Services and Card Services layers in the operating system detect card insertions and removals via the card status change interrupt, and allocate and deallocate runtime resources to PC Cards via the PCMCIA Host Bus Adapter's normal I/O space registers.

PCMCIA Host Bus Adapter Mapping of Resources to PC Cards

The PCMCIA Host Bus Adapter's address decode and IRQ routing logic steers memory and I/O windows and system IRQ channels to the physical PC Card slots. Because the PCMCIA Host Bus Adapter operates downstream from the system's bus controller, its resource set is limited to those resources that the bus controller passes from the CPU.

For example, many PCI bus controllers, or OEM system implementations thereof, route only a subset of system IRQs to the PCI bus. Consequently, only those IRQs that pass across the PCI bus are available for either the PCI-resident PCMCIA Host Bus Adapter or its installed PC Cards.

The Card Services layer in a system equipped with a PCI-PCMCIA bridge must perform two separate enumerations when assigning IRQs to PC Cards. First, Card Services performs Configuration Manager calls to determine which IRQs are currently available in the system. Second, Card Services verifies that any available system IRQs currently are connected to the system's PCI bus.

TIP

Designers of PCI-PCMCIA Host Bus Adapter-aware Card Services often poll PCMCIA Host Bus Adapter registers for card status change conditions, rather than relying on an interrupt handler to detect PCI IRQ signals. Most implementations of Card Services support polled card status change for both PCI and ISA Host Bus Adapters.

Card Services' polling for card status change events within a PCI-PCMCIA environment has two distinct benefits. First, it frees up a PCI IRQ channel that would otherwise be tied to the PCMCIA Host Bus Adapter, and second, it bypasses the more complex problem of identifying and assigning a free PCI IRQ to the PCI-PCMCIA bridge device. The polling method does, however, detract from overall system performance because the Card Services layer "steals" processor cycles during the system's periodic interrupt to interrogate Card Status registers located in the PCMCIA Host Bus Adapter.

PC Card Resource Usage Within a PCMCIA Socket

PCMCIA sockets operate in two distinctly different modes: *memory-only mode* and *memory-I/O mode.* The electrical pin definitions differ depending on the mode in which the socket is currently operating. Refer to Figure 6.2 to see the pinout for each operational mode. At power on, all PC Cards default to memory-only mode.

PC Card client drivers select the current socket mode based on an examination of information *tuples* contained in the PC Card's *Card Information Structure.* If the socket contains an SRAM device, for example, the client driver examines the SRAM card's Card Information Structure tuples, determines that the device is an SRAM adapter, and configures the SRAM device's socket to operate in memory-only mode because the SRAM card is incapable of using I/O ranges.

PC Card Usage of IRQ channels

If a socket has been configured to operate in memory-I/O mode, it supports both memory and I/O operations and provides an INTR# pin, which allows PC Cards to issue interrupt requests to the PCMCIA Host Bus Adapter. Upon reaching the PCMCIA Host Bus Adapter, the socket's INTR# signal passes through PCMCIA Host Bus Adapter IRQ routing logic, which forwards the interrupt request to the physical IRQ channel on the host bus. The INTR# pin is not available to, and is not used by memory adapters that reside in a memory only socket.

Figure 6.4 displays the routing of PCMCIA socket INTR# signals to system IRQ channels for a single PCMCIA Host Bus Adapter.

FIGURE 6.4.
The routing of PCMCIA socket INTR# signals to system IRQ channels.

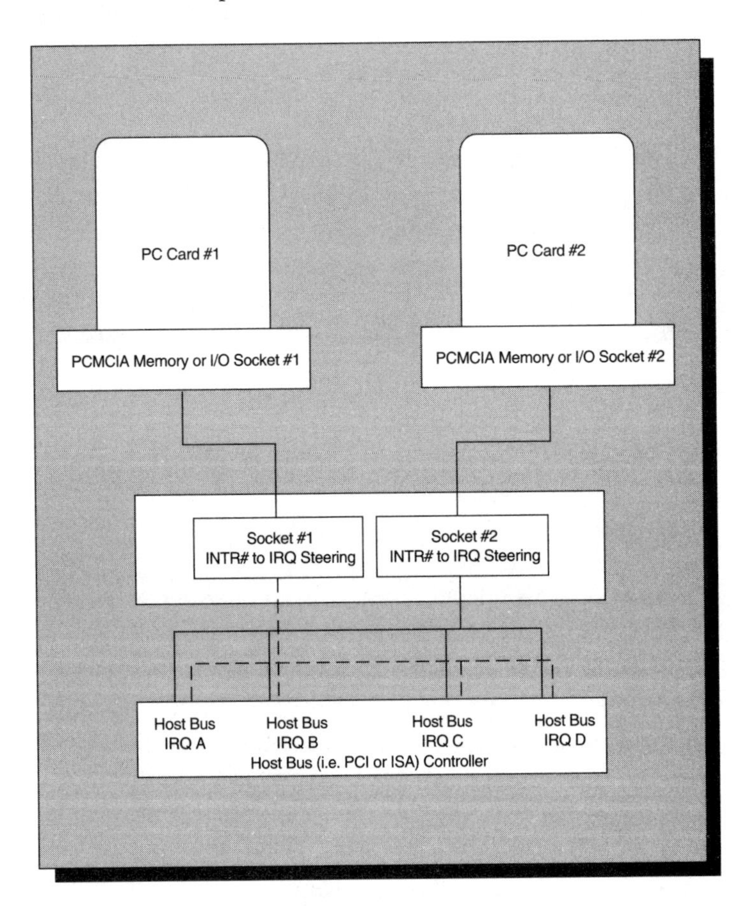

Card Services tracks PC Card IRQ usage by maintaining an internal resource map for each active socket. Additionally, most PCMCIA Host Bus Adapters provide *IRQ steering registers* for each socket. If a PC Card currently is installed in a socket, the IRQ steering register contains the physical IRQ to which the socket's `INTR#` pin has been routed, and Card Services need only examine this register to determine the socket's IRQ assignment.

During a card insertion, Card Services configures the target socket's IRQ usage based on a resource request by the PC Card client driver that responded to Card Services' insertion event broadcast. Upon receiving the resource request from the client, Card Services invokes the Configuration Manager to verify the availability of the resources that the client driver has requested. If the requested resources currently are available, Card Services issues `Socket Services` calls to assign those resources to the PC Card's socket.

PC Card Usage of Memory and I/O Ranges

The PCMCIA socket provides 26 address lines, which commonly are labeled `ADDR[25:0]`. The value that the PCMCIA Host Bus Adapter asserts on `ADDR[25:0]` represents a linear offset into the PC Card's memory or I/O space and is a translation of the address that the host bus controller (such as the PCI bus controller) asserted on the host bus.

Because the PCMCIA Host Bus Adapter translates host bus memory and I/O cycles to the PC Card's domain, the PC Card need not have any knowledge of the architecture of the system's host bus. As a result, PC Cards can and do function in non-PC environments because the task of mapping host bus signals to PC Card signals is handled by the PCMCIA Host Bus Adapter and not by PC Cards.

As with IRQ channels, client drivers request memory and I/O ranges for their supported PC Cards after having responded to Card Services' card insertion event. Once the client driver has requested I/O or memory ranges for its PC Card, Card Services invokes the Configuration Manager to determine the availability of those resources. If the requested resources currently are available, Card Services issues Socket Services calls to assign those resources to the PC Card's socket.

Translation of Host Bus I/O Ranges to PC Card I/O Ranges

PC Cards are limited to a maximum of two I/O ranges. When the PC Card is first inserted, the card's client driver parses the card's attribute memory tuples to determine its I/O range resource needs. Next, the client driver builds a structure of resources that its PC Card requires and invokes Card Services functions `SetIRQ` and `SetIO` to logically assign those resources to the card. If Card Services determines that the client-requested I/O range resources are available, then the client driver issues a Card Services `SetConfiguration` call to instruct Card Services to actually configure the PC Card's socket and contents.

Card Services configures the address of the requested I/O ranges in both the PCMCIA Host Bus Adapter and the PC Card. The PCMCIA Host Bus Adapter requires I/O range configuration in order to properly forward host bus I/O transactions to its sockets. Similarly, the PC Card has internal Card Configuration registers that determine how the card's I/O mapping hardware translates socket I/O addresses into internal PC Card I/O addresses.

Translation of Host Bus Memory Ranges to PC Card Memory Ranges

The PCMCIA socket's 26 `ADDR` lines can address up to 64MB of contiguous memory space. The PCMCIA socket's 64MB addressing capability almost invariably differs from the addressing limitations of the host bus. For example, the ISA bus's addressing capability is limited to the lower 16MB of system addresses, whereas the 32-bit PCI bus can address a full 4GB.

Because there is no one-to-one mapping of host bus addresses to PCMCIA socket addresses, PCMCIA Host Bus Adapters provide hardware that translates host bus addresses to PCMCIA socket addresses. Most often, PCMCIA memory cards appear in system address space either as extended memory resident past the limit of installed system DRAM, or as memory windows in which the PCMCIA Host Bus Adapter maps small portions of the PC Card's total address space. The following two sections provide examples of an SRAM card that appears first as extended memory, and then within PCMCIA Host Bus Adapter-supplied memory windows.

Memory Addressing Example #1—SRAM PC Card Used as Extended Memory

In this example, the user installs a 4MB SRAM PC Card into an ISA-based notebook machine in order to expand the total amount of system memory. The memory within the SRAM PC Card is contiguous, and linearly addressable from location `0` within the PCMCIA socket. Linearly-addressable PCMCIA-based RAM often is called `XIP`, or *eXecute In Place RAM,* because applications can execute directly out of RAM resident on the PCMCIA bus.

In order to make PC Card's SRAM resemble normal, extended system RAM, the Card Services layer configures the PCMCIA Host Bus Adapter to decode all addresses past the end of installed system RAM and translate them into linear offsets within the PC Card's on-board SRAM. This technique works because ISA-compatible memory controllers forward all memory reads and writes of addresses beyond installed DRAM to the system's host bus.

Memory Addressing Example #2—SRAM PC Card Configured as a Logical Block Device

PCMCIA software can expand the system's storage capacity by configuring SRAM PC Cards as logical block devices, rather than simply remapping the PC Cards' on-board RAM into extended system address space. One common method of configuring an SRAM PC Card as a logical block device involves organizing the PC Card's data into a FAT file structure, which is recognized by operating systems such as OS/2 and DOS.

In cases where the SRAM PC Card has been formatted with a FAT file system, the PC Card appears to the system as a removable block storage device, such as a floppy drive, and the system's overall storage capacity increases in the form of added file storage capacity, rather than additional extended memory. A device driver designed specifically for SRAM PC Cards installs into the operating system device chain and services the various IOCTL (I/O ConTroL) and block device calls that the operating system issues during file opens, closes, reads, and writes.

During an operating system block device call, the SRAM PC Card block device driver reads and writes the PC Card's RAM contents via a memory window, or group of memory windows that Card Services has configured within the PCMCIA Host Bus Adapter. PC Card block device drivers select memory regions within the SRAM card's address space by issuing Card Services calls to configure memory offset registers for each socket memory window.

The number of memory windows available to each socket depends on which type of PCMCIA Host Bus Adapter is installed in the system. Similarly, the granularity and location of socket memory windows vary with the installed controller. During the operating system boot process, the system's Card Services layer requests a system address region from the Configuration Manager, and then configures the PCMCIA Host Bus Adapter to decode its memory windows in the Configuration Manager-supplied address region. Typically, Card Services requests a memory window region below the 1MB boundary in order for memory window read/write operations to be carried out in real, virtual, and protected modes.

The Configuration Manager ensures that the memory region it supplies to Card Services does not conflict with any EMS (Expanded Memory) windows, expansion ROMs, UMBs (Upper Memory Blocks) or any other devices mapped into the system's 384KB reserved area.

Figure 6.5 displays a hypothetical PCMCIA Host Bus Adapter whose four, 16KB memory windows have been mapped into the `D0000H` segment of system address space.

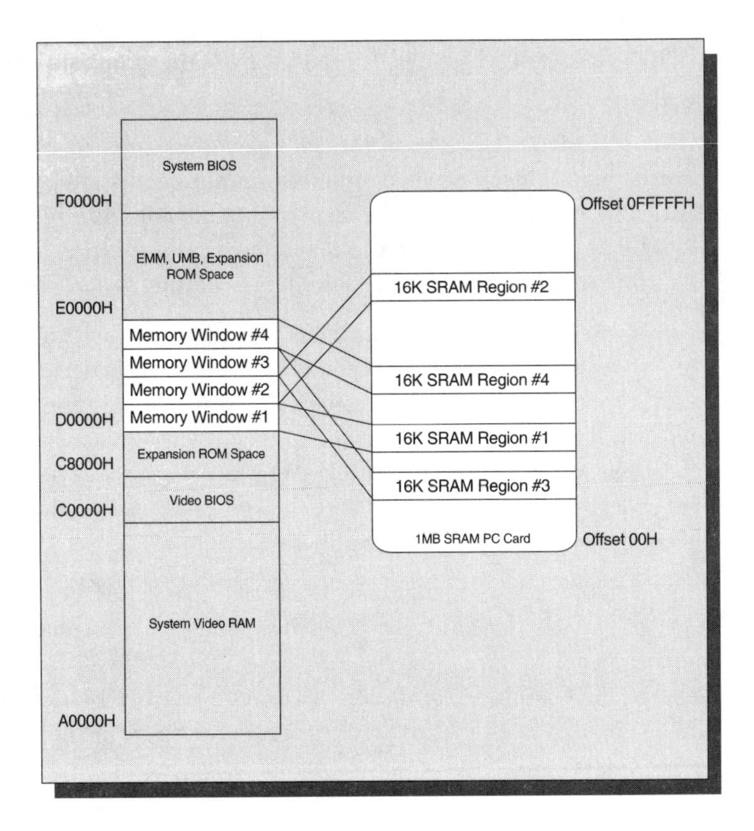

FIGURE 6.5.
Example mapping of PCMCIA Host Bus Adapter memory windows into an SRAM PC Card.

The Socket Services Layer

The Socket Services layer is a set of PCMCIA Host Bus Adapter-specific functions that resides either in the system firmware or in a resident operating system device driver. System designers often place Socket Services in firmware in order to conserve runtime driver space and eliminate the need to adapt Socket Services functions to a variety of operating system device driver formats. Conversely, other designers prefer that Socket Services exist in device driver format because the process of upgrading or fixing device drivers is much simpler than that of upgrading a system's firmware.

Systems that contain more than one PCMCIA Host Bus Adapter require one set of Socket Services for each installed adapter. One exception to this rule is that some versions of Socket Services can support multiple instances of the same type of PCMCIA Host Bus Adapter. During its load sequence, the system's Card Services driver locates and records all Socket Services drivers installed in the system. Once loaded, Card Services monitors and manages the configuration of the system's socket hardware by issuing Socket Services calls.

Socket Services Functions

Socket Services provides its client, normally Card Services, with an INT 1AH interface layer that abstracts the register-level specifics of the PCMCIA Host Bus Adapter, thereby allowing Card Services to execute on a variety of platforms and PCMCIA Host Bus Adapters with little or no modification. Because the Card Services layer relies on Socket Services to configure the PCMCIA Host Bus Adapter, Socket Services must be present by the time the operating system loads Card Services. In the DOS environment, this typically means that the Socket Services driver appears before the Card Services driver in the system's CONFIG.SYS file.

The Socket Services client, Card Services, invokes Socket Services functions to perform such tasks as the following:

- Assigning and configuring socket memory range windows
- Assigning and configuring socket I/O range windows
- Steering the PC Card's INTR# line to an available system IRQ channel
- Steering the PCMCIA Host Bus Adapter's card status change interrupt line to an available system IRQ channel

When Socket Services is present, its client Card Services has access to four types of functions, as follows. (A complete listing of Socket Services functions appears in the PCMCIA committee's *Socket Services Specification.*)

Adapter functions—Adapter functions apply either to an adapter's sockets as a group, or to features that pertain only to the adapter and not the adapter's sockets.

Socket-specific functions—Socket-specific functions provide Card Services a mechanism for configuring a particular socket: for example, Card Services calls Socket Services to toggle the socket's pinout between memory-only mode and memory or I/O mode.

Window management functions—Card Services invokes Socket Services window management functions to configure the size, granularity, and base address of memory and I/O windows within a socket's address space.

Error Detection and Correction (EDC) functions—As their name implies, the Error Detection and Correction Socket Services provide Card Services a mechanism for configuring and monitoring the EDC hardware associated with a particular socket.

Socket Services Event Notification

At load time, Socket Services assigns a card status change interrupt channel to each installed PCMCIA Host Bus Adapter. Card Services later intercepts the interrupt vector or vectors associated with each card status change IRQ channel.

When a card status change event occurs, the PCMCIA Host Bus Adapter generates a card status change IRQ signal that causes the system to transfer control to the Card Services status change interrupt handler. From within its status change interrupt handler, Card Services invokes each Socket Services driver to determine which socket caused the card status change event. Once Card Services has determined which socket caused the card status change event, it broadcasts the event to each registered Card Services client, thereby notifying all clients that a card needs attention.

Figure 6.6 displays the client call-back architecture for both the Socket Services and Card Services layers.

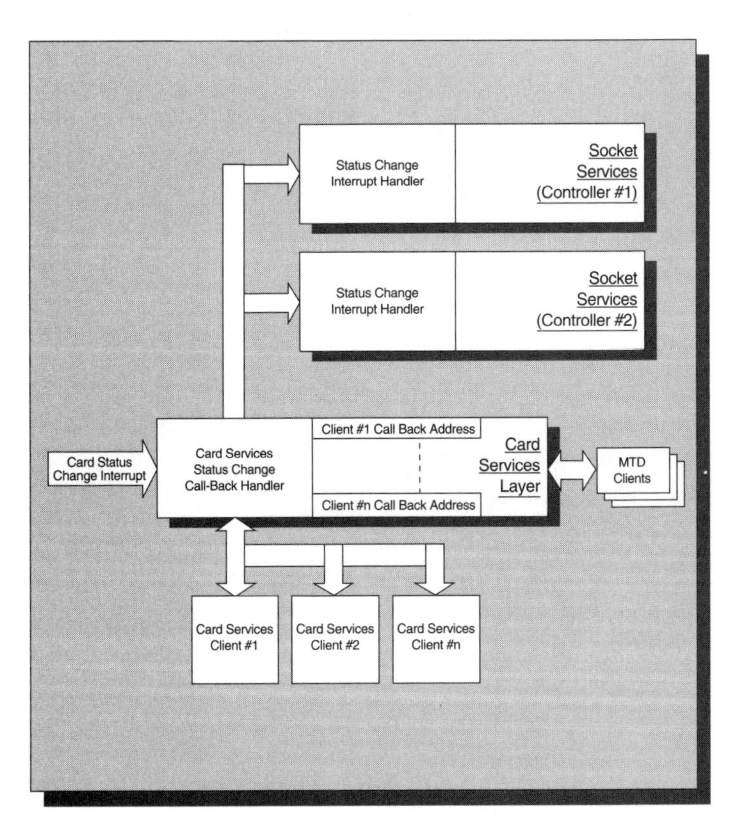

FIGURE 6.6.
The Socket Services Card status change client call-back mechanism.

NOTE

PCMCIA Host Bus Adapters do not require a card status change IRQ to function properly. As an alternative to the card status change IRQ, Card Services can poll each Socket Services driver for events during the system's timer tick interrupt, which occurs approximately every 55 milliseconds. Within systems in which Card Services is executing card status change detection in polled mode, if Card Services detects a status change event, it generates a "fake" status change IRQ in software, thereby initiating the normal Card Services status change call-back mechanism.

The Card Services Layer

Card Services' primary function is to process transactions between PCMCIA client drivers and physical sockets. It accomplishes this by internally tracking the status of the system's socket contents and current resource allocations, as well as balancing PC Card resource requirements against what is currently available in the system. At runtime, Card Services performs the following PCMCIA functions:

- Monitors the status and contents of each socket within the system
- Maintains a list of resources assigned to each socket
- Broadcasts PC Card and socket events to PCMCIA client drivers

Card Services as a Socket Monitor

During its load sequence, Card Services searches for and records all instances of Socket Services drivers in the system. Additionally, Card Services intercepts the card status change interrupt vector associated with each physical socket. By intercepting all status change events, Card Services is guaranteed to receive notification of all card status changes, such as insertions and removals.

During card status change events, Card Services issues Socket Services calls to assign or deassign resources from the socket in which the insertion or removal event occurred. In a Plug and Play system, Card Services notifies the Configuration Manager of any resources it has assigned to a newly installed PC Card, or recovered from a newly removed PC Card.

Card Services as a Resource Monitor

The Card Services driver is responsible for locating resources for, and supplying resources to its client drivers. Card Services never directly assigns resources to PC Cards; resource requests originate in PC Card Client drivers. Instead, Card Services broadcasts card insertions and removals to each installed client driver.

Upon receiving notification that its particular PC Card has been inserted, a client driver first determines the resource needs of its PC Card, and then issues a configuration request back to Card Services. At this point, Card Services may accept or reject the client driver's request, based on the availability of its requested resources in the system.

If Card Services accepts the client driver's request for system resources, it will generate Socket Services calls to configure the appropriate socket and the PC Card within the socket. Remember that Card Services is not directly configuring the socket or PC Card—it merely is forwarding client driver configuration requests to the appropriate PC Card and socket.

NOTE

After having successfully loaded, Card Services intercepts the Socket Services INT `1AH` interface and prevents client drivers from communicating directly with the Socket Services layer. Card Services "turns off" the Socket Services interface in order to better track system resource usage.

Because client drivers are unable to communicate with the Socket Services layer directly, they must perform all resource usage requests via Card Services calls. In this way, the Card Services system resource map does not become inaccurate due to client drivers that try to short-circuit the PC Card configuration process.

Some PCMCIA software suites include a Card Services client driver whose sole function is to create and/or provide Card Services with a map of system resource usage.

The SystemSoft PCMCIA suite, for example, loads its CSALLOC.EXE driver subsequent to Card Services in the system's CONFIG.SYS file. During its load process, `CSALLOC` builds a map of system resource usage and passes this resource map into the resident Card Services driver. Similarly, Phoenix Technologies supplies the driver PCMRMAN.SYS, which provides the PMCS.EXE module with an overall system resource map.

Card Services as an Event Broadcaster

From a Plug and Play standpoint, Card Services acts as a miniature Configuration Manager, servicing only the PCMCIA bus. When a card insertion event occurs, Card Services immediately issues a series of operating system Configuration Manager calls to build a map of all available resources within the system. Next, Card Services broadcasts the card insertion to each of its client drivers by iteratively invoking the call-back address that each client driver supplied during its load-time Card Services registration sequence.

If the client driver detects the insertion of the PC Card for which it is responsible, then the client requests from Card Services a group of resources for its PC Card. If the resources are available, then Card Services configures the PC Card's socket to decode the requested set of resources. Before returning control to the operating system, Card Services notifies the Configuration Manager that the resources it selected for its client driver have been allocated to a PCMCIA socket, and are no longer available to other adapters within the system.

CARD INFORMATION STRUCTURE

PC Cards contain a special configuration header called the *CIS* (*Card Information Structure*) that details, among other things, those resources that the PC Card is capable of using. When a PC Card is inserted, its attribute memory contains the card's CIS, as defined in the PCMCIA committee's PC Card Standard specification. The CIS contains a series of tuples, or PCMCIA-specific variable-length records detailing the PC Card's possible resource configurations, vendor-specific information and device-specific information.

During a PC Card insertion, it is the responsibility of the client driver to accurately parse the CIS and request from Card Services a set of resources that the PC Card is capable of using. During a card insertion event, Card Services contains a complete map of system resource usage from which it determines whether it can satisfy the client driver's resource requests.

If Card Services cannot satisfy the resource needs of its client, it rejects the PC Card and returns control to the foreground task. Otherwise, it notifies the client driver that the resource allocation succeeded, and prior to returning control to Card Services, the client driver configures its PC Card with those resources allocated by Card Services.

Card Services also broadcasts events not related to resource usage. For example, FLASH File System drivers rarely perform direct reads or writes of a FLASH PC Card's contents. Instead, the FLASH File System driver calls Card Services with a request to read, write, or copy the contents of a FLASH PC Card. Alternatively, some implementations of Card Services broadcast MTD read, write, and copy commands to all installed MTD drivers. In this type of implementation, the MTDs to which a particular memory read/write/copy event does not pertain simply ignore that call-back event.

The PCMCIA Client Driver Layer

Client and super-client drivers logically reside one layer above the Card Services layer. Following are the primary purposes of client drivers:

- Recognize individual PC Cards or families of PC Cards
- Determine resource needs for newly inserted PC Cards
- Request PC Card system resources from Card Services
- Configure PC Cards to use Card Services-supplied system resources
- Initialize and configures PC Cards

Once a client driver has initialized a PC Card, control of the PC Card's operation then becomes the responsibility of the foreground application that is using the PC Card, and the client driver's job is complete until another PC Card insertion event occurs. If the user inserts a PC Card modem, for example, the Card Services client or super-client driver that provides modem recognition capabilities recognizes the modem, assigns it system resources, and initializes its standard registers. As soon as the modem has been initialized, it becomes available to the user's foreground serial communications program.

The Card Services Super-Client

Super-client drivers, such as SystemSoft's CARDID.EXE and Phoenix Technologies' PCMSCD.EXE, recognize and configure a wide variety of PC Cards and act as a default client driver for PC Cards that do not require OEM, vendor-specific recognition, or configuration. Remember, Card Services neither recognizes nor configures PC Cards; rather, it broadcasts card insertion events to its registered clients, including the super-client driver, and expects a client to both recognize and initialize the PC Card.

Because most PC Cards are compliant, it makes no sense to require the user to install tens or hundreds of drivers to identify and configure each PC Card available on the market. Instead, the super-client acts like hundreds of client drivers in one by

recognizing, requesting resources for, and configuring the majority of available PC Cards. If the super-client is incapable of either recognizing or configuring a particular card, it rejects the Card Services' call-back, and Card Services broadcasts the event to the next client in its call-back chain. If all clients reject a newly inserted card, the card remains unconfigured and is unusable.

The Card Services Client Driver

As mentioned previously, client drivers are responsible for identifying and configuring specific PC Cards. Client drivers serve two purposes. First, if a PC Card is non-compliant, the default Card Services client is not able to properly recognize and configure the card and only the card-specific client driver knows how to properly recognize and configure the card. Second, the vendor might provide a client driver that tweaks the performance of a PC Card by writing registers about which the default super-client driver is unaware.

Some PCMCIA LAN adapters, for example, can function in either I/O-based or memory-mapped mode. Only the LAN adapter driver has enough knowledge about the card to choose one mode over the other; therefore, the LAN adapter client driver services all Card Services call-back events for those LAN cards that it recognizes, and prevents these events from passing through to the more generic super-client driver.

Client drivers load only after both Socket Services and Card Services have successfully installed. During its load sequence, a client driver registers as a client of Card Services and provides Card Services with a call-back address. Card Services invokes client driver call-back functions when it needs to broadcast events to its clients. A full list of Card Services events appears in the PCMCIA Card Services specification. Client drivers respond only to those events that pertain to the PC Card or Cards for which the driver provides support.

The process of creating a working client driver is one that rarely appears in published form, and yet it is the one area in which Plug and Play developers are most likely to develop PCMCIA-specific code. Generally, the client driver for a memory-I/O card adheres to the rules outlined in the following sections.

Card Services Detection

During load, the client calls `GetCardServicesInfo` to check the Card Services presence and version. If Card Services is absent or reports a version that the client does not support, the client driver aborts its installation and does not stay resident in RAM.

Client Registration

Also during its load sequence, the client driver calls `RegisterClient` to register itself as a Card Services client, which includes the driver supplying Card Services with its call-back address.

Unrecognized Call-Back Events

For each call-back event that the client does not recognize, it returns `SUCCESS`.

Card Insertion

When the client driver receives the `CARD_INSERTION` message, it attempts to identify the newly inserted PC Card. If the client driver recognizes the PC Card, it attempts to configure the card via its standard and alternate possible configurations until the card configures properly, or the client driver has exhausted the card's possible configurations.

PC Card Configuration

When configuring a PC Card, the client driver calls `RequestIRQ` to request an IRQ for the card if the card needs one, and then calls `RequestIO` to request an I/O range if the card needs an I/O range. Finally, the client driver calls `RequestConfiguration` to set the configuration for the PC Card. If the card's IRQ is to be enabled immediately, the client driver marks this in the IRQ attribute field. If the card does not use an IRQ, the client driver simply makes no call to the `RequestIRQ` function.

Releasing Resources

If the `RequestConfiguration` fails, the client driver calls `ReleaseIO` and `ReleaseIRQ` to release any resources allocated to it by Card Services.

Pin Replacement Register

If the client driver's card has a Pin Replacement Register, the client driver sets the Present field to `0FH` prior to its call to `RequestConfiguration` to clear the pin-change bits that may have been set differently for a previously installed PC Card.

Card Removal

When the client driver receives a `CARD_REMOVAL` event for one of its installed PC Cards, it releases the card's configuration and all IRQ and I/O resources assigned to the card. If the client driver fails to release the card's configuration and resources, they cannot be

assigned to newly inserted cards because Card Services never releases configurations or resources itself; instead, it relies on client drivers to perform this task.

Resource "Over-Requests"

In order to preserve system resources, the client driver never "over-requests" resources; it only requests resources that PC Card absolutely requires to operate.

Memory Window Requests

The client driver makes no assumptions about the size of memory or I/O windows supplied to it by Card Services, except that the size of a memory window is always a multiple of 4KB. Importantly, if Card Services cannot supply a particular size of memory window, the client driver should issue further memory window requests using a size requirement that is a smaller multiple of 4KB.

Aborting Installation

If a driver aborts installation, it must call `DeregisterClient` to prevent Card Services from continuing to issue call-backs to its now-invalid call-back function.

The MTD (Memory Technology Driver)

MTDs (*Memory Technology Drivers*) constitute a special class of clients, whose only function is to provide hardware level read, write, and copy operations for various types of FLASH devices. FLASH devices contain special programmable memory chips that are capable of retaining data without battery backup, even after power has been removed from the system. MTD drivers abstract the operating system from the techniques involved in programming devices whose algorithms differ according to both vendors and individual chip models.

By itself, a single MTD generally supports all FLASH cards produced by one vendor, such as Intel or AMD. This modular approach allows PCMCIA users to upgrade their FLASH device capabilities simply by adding MTD drivers. Likewise, users of a single vendor's FLASH cards reduce their memory overhead by loading only a single MTD driver.

In the same manner that client drivers respond only to events that pertain to their particular PC Card or cards, MTD drivers respond only to those read, write, and copy operations targeted for the type of FLASH device the MTD supports. If Card Services broadcasts a read of an Intel FLASH device to its MTD clients, for example, only the Intel-specific MTD responds to the call-back event.

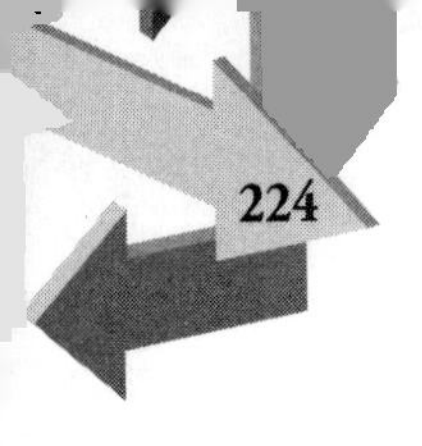

The Block Device Driver Layer

PCMCIA Block Device Drivers enable block devices such as ATA-compatible storage devices and SRAM storage devices to appear to the operating system as additional, logical system drives.

ATA-compatible devices, such as IDE fixed disks, contain registers that adhere to the ATA committee specification. Some vendors, such as IBM, produce SRAM-based PC Cards that, although they have no rotating storage media inside, respond to system I/O commands in a manner identical to that of an IDE fixed disk.

The category of block device drivers has little effect on resource usage because the allocation of resources to ATA and SRAM devices occurs in the client driver layer, not the block device layer. In a more general Plug and Play sense, however, PCMCIA block device drivers provide operating systems, such as DOS and OS/2, truly hot-swappable block storage devices.

The FFS (FLASH File System) Layer

The *FFS* (*FLASH File System*) layer provides a redirector interface to specially formatted PCMCIA FLASH cards. FFS drivers allow the operating system to read, write, and copy the contents of FLASH PC Cards by forwarding these requests through Card Services to device-specific MTD drivers.

Like block device drivers, FFS has little effect on the resource allocation within a system, other than the fact that FFS drivers require that a Card Services client has provided memory windows for the target FLASH storage devices. FFS, like PCMCIA block device drivers, makes hot-swappable mass storage devices available to DOS and other operating systems.

The Role of the PCMCIA Software Suite in a Plug and Play System

If you're still unclear about how the PCMCIA software suite "fits" into the Plug and Play environment, read on because this section offers a brief review of the technology.

PCMCIA Suite as a Miniature Configuration Manager

Unlike the devices described in previous chapters, PCMCIA devices operate within the framework of a self-contained software suite. PCMCIA devices differ from their PCI, ISA, Plug and Play ISA, and other counterparts because they can be "hot-swapped," or inserted and removed at runtime.

The "hot-swappability" of PCMCIA devices places special constraints on the operating system's capability to reliably monitor system resource usage. Whereas PCI, Plug and Play ISA, legacy ISA, EISA, and static systemboard devices already have been configured by the time the Plug and Play operating system begins its enumeration process, PC Cards rely on the pool of remaining system resources for their configuration needs.

The Card Services driver fills the gap between asynchronous card insertions and removals and the operating system's maintenance of an overall system resource map. During card insertion and removal events, Card Services performs like a miniature Configuration Manager, deciding the availability of system resources for PC Cards by performing "snapshot" calls to the Plug and Play operating system's Configuration Manager.

PC Card client drivers and super-client drivers do not attempt to invoke the Configuration Manager in order to balance and assign system resources; instead, they allow Card Services to act as a focal point for all runtime resource allocation and deallocation.

PCMCIA Device Driver Ordering Constraints

Socket Services drivers are the first drivers among the PCMCIA software suite to load. As Socket Services drivers load, they search for and "chain" to previously loaded Socket Services drivers. The complementary procedure of drivers chaining to each other simplifies Card Services' determination of how many Socket Services drivers exist in the system.

Card Services loads immediately following all Socket Services drivers. The first task Card Services performs is to locate and initialize each physical PCMCIA Host Bus Adapter and socket within the system. Card Services' socket initialization process consists of invoking the `GetAdapter` function within each Socket Services' driver to determine the type and quantity of installed sockets. Next, Card Services examines each PCMCIA Host Bus Adapter in order to determine whether the system BIOS or Plug and Play operating system already has assigned the PCMCIA Host Bus Adapter its card status change interrupt channel or configuration register I/O range.

If any PCMCIA Host Bus Adapters have not yet been initialized, Card Services invokes the operating system Configuration Manager to identify those resources that are still available to system devices. From the pool of unclaimed system resources, Card Services supplies each PCMCIA Host Bus Adapter with its card status change interrupt channel and configuration register I/O range. If Card Services has been instructed (via an .INI file, command line argument, or other means) to configure a particular PCMCIA Host Bus Adapter to report status change events in polled rather than interrupt driven mode, it skips the process of finding and assigning a status change interrupt for that controller.

NOTE

In some cases, Plug and Play-aware PCMCIA software executes in an environment in which the operating system does not provide a Configuration Manager. In this case, Card Services may postpone its socket configuration process until a time that a PCMCIA resource manager, (such as SystemSoft's CSALLOC.EXE or Phoenix Technologies' PCMRMAN.SYS) has loaded and provided Card Services with its own version of the system's resource map.

Once the Card Services driver has successfully loaded and configured the system's physical sockets, it is capable of supporting client drivers that might request resources for their own installed PC Cards. (Remember that the user might power-on a system that already contains PC Cards).

Upon loading, client drivers register as a Card Services client and supply Card Services with an event call-back address. From this point forward, Card Services notifies any installed client drivers of card insertion and removal events. Installed block device or FLASH File System PC Cards, such as ATA storage devices and SRAM devices, receive resource configurations from their client drivers. Although configured, block device, and FLASH File System PC Cards do not fully participate in the operating system until the appropriate block device or FLASH File System device drivers have successfully loaded.

Finally, the MTDs, FLASH File System, and block device drivers load and install as Card Services clients, and the PCMCIA software suite becomes active within the Plug and Play operating system environment.

The Runtime PC Card Environment

Once a PC Card has successfully received its configuration, it appears in system address space much in the same way as an ISA or PCI device, with the exception that current PC Cards are incapable of utilizing DMA channels.

If the system contains a PCMCIA modem that has been configured as COM1, for example, the modem responds to normal system I/O at registers `3F8H-3FBH`. Rarely, if ever, do applications invoke the modem's client or super-client driver to reconfigure the modem. Bear in mind also that once the PCMCIA software has configured a PC Card, the card retains its configuration until a time that the user removes power from the system, or physically removes the PC Card from its socket; therefore, applications have little or no control over a PC Card's configuration once the client driver has completed the card's configuration and initialization process.

And yet, in the event that the user re-inserts the modem or introduces a new and different modem PC Card to the system, the client driver that identified and initially configured the modem PC Card remains resident in system RAM. For many users, the overhead of resident client drivers most often is offset by the unique hot-swappability and portability of the PCMCIA devices themselves.

PCMCIA Device Resource Usage

As mentioned previously, the usage of system resources by PCMCIA devices belongs to one of two categories.

First, the PCMCIA Host Bus Adapter typically consumes one IRQ channel for signaling card status change events, and one I/O range through which Card Services configures the adapter's sockets, memory windows, I/O windows, and socket IRQ channels.

Second, PC Cards consume resources based on the configuration tuples they contain within on-card attribute memory. In the same way the system BIOS or operating system Configuration Manager parses the configuration space within a PCI or Plug and Play ISA device to determine the device's resource needs, PCMCIA client drivers parse the PC Card's attribute memory tuples, and then make Card Services configuration calls based on the PC Card's tuple contents.

Each time Card Services supplies resources to a client driver's PC Card, it records the resource usage locally in its internal socket map and notifies the Configuration Manager that the resources now are being used by an installed device. Likewise, when the user removes a PC Card, Card Services reverses its resource tracking process, first by removing the resources from its socket map, and then by notifying the Configuration Manager that the newly removed PC Card's resources are again available to other system devices.

When Card Services allocates a client's requested resources to a PC Card, it configures those resources, both in the PCMCIA Host Bus Adapter and in the PC Card itself. Card Services configures the PCMCIA Host Bus Adapter with the PC Card's resources in order to enable decoding of these resources from the host bus to the PCMCIA socket. At the same time, Card Services configures the PCMCIA card in such a way that the card's internal resource mapping logic responds to the cycles that the PCMCIA Host Bus Adapter forwards from the host bus to the PC Card via its physical socket.

7

Other Plug and Play Programming Topics

Previous chapters have mainly focused on the letter "P" technologies—PCI, Plug and Play ISA, Plug and Play BIOS, and PCMCIA. While these technologies are the building blocks in a Plug and Play system, other components such as serial/parallel ports, APM (Advanced Power Management) firmware, and docking stations, have Plug and Play specific requirements as well. With the exception of the Intel Plug and Play solution, which appears in Chapter 8, this chapter is designed to briefly cover the following Plug and Play major remaining system components:

- Plug and Play system requirements
- Plug and Play BIOS support for APM
- Plug and Play BIOS support for docking stations
- Enhanced IDE and INT 13H system BIOS extensions
- Miscellaneous Plug and Play Hardware

Plug and Play System Requirements

This might lead you to wonder about one important question that this book has so far left unanswered—"What type of hardware makes a system Plug and Play compliant?"

As of yet, there is no single document that defines, at an industry level, the "official" hardware/software requirements of a Plug and Play system.

Currently, the book *Hardware Design Guide for Microsoft Windows 95*, from Microsoft Press, defines those components that designers and vendors must incorporate into their systems in order to pass the Microsoft Windows 95 compliance tests. Similarly, Intel has launched its DTEP (DeskTop Enhancement Program) as a means of introducing new features to the PC architecture via its DTIK (DeskTop Integration Kit).

If the personal computer industry's history is any indicator of its future, system vendors will at first rush to gain Windows 95 compliance as soon as they discover that "the other guys have it." Therefore, Microsoft's hardware design guide will likely serve as the first Plug and Play system specification with the assistance of those existing Plug and Play specifications mentioned throughout this book.

Later, as the PPA (Plug and Play Association) and Intel's DTEP team mature, these groups may provide further definitions of Plug and Play system requirements.

The book *Hardware Design Guide for Microsoft Windows 95* details Plug and Play system requirements according to this table.

Feature	*Logo Requirement*	*Recommendation*
Plug and Play BIOS 1.0a	Yes	Yes
All resources readable	Yes	Yes
All resources soft-settable	No	Yes
All expansion cards	No	Yes, individually Windows 95 certified
16-bit I/O decode for all	No	Yes, ISA systemboard devices
APM 1.1 (Desktop)	No	Yes
APM 1.1 (Portable)	Yes	Yes
Option ROMs use `PnP` option	Yes	Yes, ROM header format

Plug and Play BIOS support for APM

APM (*Advanced Power Management*) 1.1 support consists of a set of firmware resident functions through which the operating system controls the power consumption within a desktop or portable system. Support for APM 1.1 is crucial in portable systems for the purpose of prolonging battery life, as it supplies the only mechanism by which the operating system can notify the system's firmware that the system currently is idle. Figure 7.1 displays the structure of a system whose firmware supports APM 1.1 BIOS extensions and Plug and Play BIOS services.

In an APM-equipped legacy or Plug and Play system, operating system drivers manage the power consumption of individual devices by invoking APM 1.1 BIOS functions with a particular device's APM device ID. The *APM 1.1 BIOS Specification* is available from Intel.

Plug and Play systems extend this standard APM 1.1 functionality through Plug and Play BIOS function `0BH` (`GetAPMIDTable`), which correlates the APM device ID of each power-manageable device to its equivalent Plug and Play EISA style device ID.

Plug and Play BIOS Function *0BH—GetAPMIDInfo*

Function `0BH`, or `GetAPMIDInfo`, returns in a caller-supplied buffer the APM device ID and corresponding Plug and Play logical device ID for each power-manageable device within the system. Third-party APM aware device drivers use the contents of this table to determine which Plug and Play devices have a corresponding APM ID.

GetAPMIDInfo returns a variable length array of six-byte structures, each of which adheres to the format in Table 7.1.

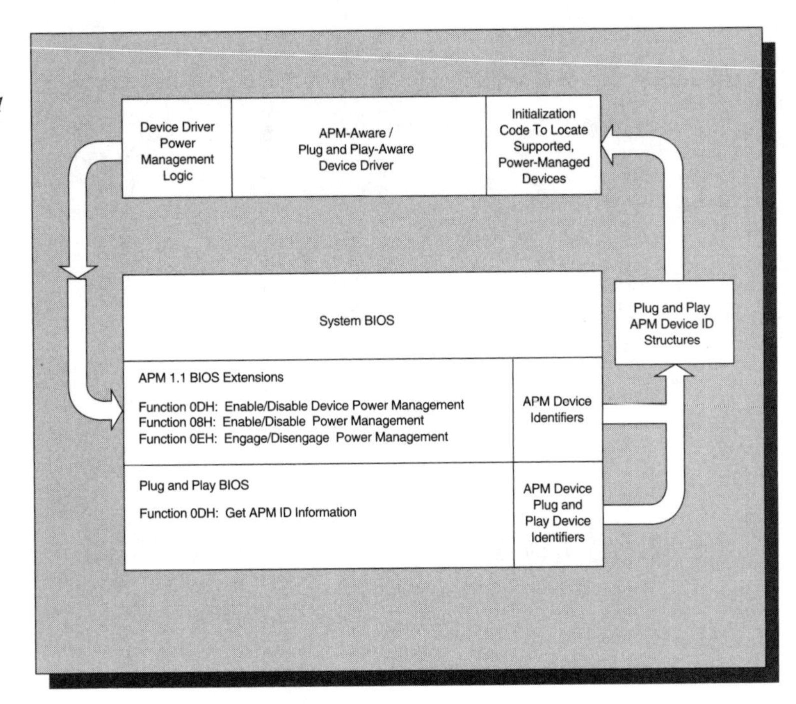

FIGURE 7.1.
System firmware support for APM 1.1 BIOS and Plug and Play BIOS.

Table 7.1. The format of a single APM ID structure.

Offset	*Size*	*Description*
00H	4*BYTE	Plug and Play logical device ID for device #n
04H	2*BYTE	APM ID for device #n

Following is the C language declaration for the GetAPMIDInfo function:

```
int FAR (pFuncEntry)(Function, fpBuffer, ESCDSelector, DataSelector) ;

int Function ;                      // Always = 0BH for GetAPMIDInfo
unsigned int far *pBuffSize;        // ptr to size of caller's buffer
unsigned char far *pBuffer;         // ptr to caller-supplied buffer
unsigned int DataSelector;          // Caller-Supplied R/W BIOS data
                                    // segment/selector.
```

Following are the arguments for the function GetAPMIDInfo:

Function—Function is the index to select the Plug and Play BIOS function and always equals 0BH for GetAPMIDInfo.

`pBuffSize`—`pBuffSize` is the caller-supplied, far pointer to an integer variable specifying the size of the buffer pointed to by `pBuffer`.

`pBuffer`—`pBuffer` is the far pointer to a caller-supplied buffer to receive APM ID structures.

`DataSelector`—`DataSelector` is the 16-bit, caller-supplied segment or selector that enables the Plug and Play BIOS to read and write its own local variables and ESCD data if that data is stored in a memory mapped fashion. If the calling application is executing in real mode, it retrieves the `DataSelector` value from the Plug and Play BIOS installation check header. Protected mode applications must build a CPU descriptor table selector for the Protected Mode Base Data Segment that appears in the BIOS' Installation Check Header (refer to Chapter 3).

Plug and Play BIOS Support for Docking Stations

A *docking station* or *convenience base* is a CPU-less unit that connects to a portable or notebook system. Docking stations primarily are used to transform a notebook system into a desktop system to save users the trouble of maintaining a complete office system and traveling system. The docking station may simply replicate devices already in the notebook (such as serial ports and VGA signaling hardware) or it may introduce new devices such as additional fixed disks, network connections, and multimedia capabilities.

Docking station equipped systems introduce new complexity to the Plug and Play model because they allow users to radically change the hardware profile of the entire system.

Additionally, some systems allow "hot-docking," or asynchronous runtime insertion or removal of the portable unit from its docking base. It's easy to imagine the issues that arise from hardware that suddenly appears or disappears as the user docks or undocks the portable system while the operating system is active. If the docking station contains a network adapter or fixed disk, for example, the operating system might have files open either on the fixed disk or network drive. The Plug and Play operating system and Plug and Play BIOS take special steps to ensure that docking and undocking sequences occur with no loss of user data.

Docking Methods

The industry currently defines the following three different methods for docking:

- *Cold docking*—The notebook is off when docked or undocked. The system BIOS detects the presence of the docking station during the normal BIOS

POST sequence, builds device nodes for the docking station's peripherals, and provides the operating system a copy of the docking station device node during the operating system launch.

- *Warm docking*—The notebook is in low power suspend mode when docked or undocked, allowing the user to quickly return to work after docking or undocking the notebook. Warm docking units are popular because they offer quick dock/undock capabilities without the extra protection circuitry required by the hot-docking system described below.
- *Hot docking*—The notebook is fully powered during the entire dock or undock sequence. Units that support hot docking require special hardware to prevent accidental electrical overloading when the notebook makes contact with the docking unit.

Styles of Docking Stations

Plug and Play docking station designers should take special care to ensure that users do not lose data as a result of docking or undocking a fully powered notebook system. For example, the operating system should be given the opportunity to close any files open on a fixed disk or network drive attached to the notebook system via its docking station. The industry defines three different types of docking stations whose hardware handles docking and undocking with varying degrees of data protection. Following is a description of each type of docking station:

- *Surprise-style Docking Station*—The user can remove the notebook system from its docking station at any time, regardless of whether any data files are open, thereby exposing the user to the danger of losing any unsaved data.
- *Honor System Docking Station*—The notebook system contains either an operating system applet, or a special undock button that the user activates to signal to the operating system that he or she is about to undock the system. Upon receiving the undock message, the operating system saves and closes all open files and logs out of the network, if one is attached. The OS applet or special undock LED light signals the user as soon as it is safe to physically remove the notebook from its docking station bay.

  Honor system docking stations represent a compromise between cost and functionality. Like the surprise-style docking station, the honor system docking station has no physical mechanism for preventing a user from removing a fully powered, active notebook unit from its docking bay. Unlike the surprise-style docking station, however, the honor system docking station coordinates notebook insertion and removal events with the operating system through its internal firmware and hardware. Assuming that the user adheres to the rules outlined in the system's technical literature, the honor-system `safe-to-undock` messages provide an additional, effective level of data protection.

- *VCR-style Docking Station*—The VCR-style docking station is similar to the honor system docking station described above, but adds VCR-like ejection hardware that physically locks the notebook unit inside its bay until the operating system's undock sequence has completed. When the operating system completes the undock sequence, it signals to the VCR hardware to physically eject the notebook system from its docking station bay.

Docking Station as a Port Replicator

Instead of, or in addition to, introducing completely new peripherals to the notebook system, many docking stations simply replicate hardware devices that already exist in the notebook. A docking station that replaces internal notebook devices with identical devices inside the docking station itself is called a *port replicator.*

Port replicator units serve two primary purposes. First, they allow the user to gain access to a variety of docking-station resident peripherals via a single dock operation rather than requiring him or her to connect several cables to the back of the notebook unit. Second, the port replicator provides duplicate connectors for devices that become physically hidden as a result of the dock operation.

Most notebook units, for example, have VGA, serial, parallel, and other connectors located on a panel at the rear of the system. These connectors often are physically inaccessible when the notebook unit is inserted in its docking bay and require identical connectors to be replicated at the rear of the docking station.

Plug and Play BIOS Support for Docking Stations

Within systems that support docking stations, the Plug and Play BIOS and operating system communicate docking and undocking sequences via three Plug and Play BIOS functions—functions `03H` (`GetEvent`), `04H` (`SendMessage`), and `05H` (`GetDockingStationInfo`).

Identifying Plug and Play BIOS Docking Station Support

In order to properly support dock and undock sequences, the Plug and Play BIOS must provide event notification services via the `GetEvent`, `SendMessage`, and `GetDockingStationInfo` functions mentioned previously. The `Control Field` located at offset `06H` within the Plug and Play BIOS Installation Check Header indicates what type (if any) of event notification the BIOS supports. The Installation Check Header Control Word adheres to the following format:

```
Bits [15:2]:  Reserved
Bits [1:0]:
    00B = Plug and Play BIOS does not support event notification
    01B = Plug and Play BIOS supports polled event notification
    10B = Plug and Play BIOS supports interrupt driven event notification
    11B = Reserved.
```

If the Plug and Play BIOS supports the Polled Event Notification method, the `DWORD`-size field at location `09H` within the Plug and Play BIOS Installation Check Header contains the physical address of the system's *Event flag*. It is the responsibility of the Plug and Play BIOS to set bit `0` of the Event flag each time a system event, such as a dock or undock occurs.

The Plug and Play operating system continuously polls the `Event` flag in the foreground, and upon detecting bit `0` set in the `Event` flag, it invokes Plug and Play BIOS function `03H` (`GetEvent`) to determine the type of system event that occurred. During the `GetEvent` call, the Plug and Play BIOS clears the `Event` flag, thereby allowing for subsequent system events to occur. If the operating system fails to issue a `GetEvent` call, the `Event` flag remains set indefinitely. The messages returned by `GetEvent` appear along with the following description of the function.

> **TIP**
>
> Remember that the `GetEvent` Plug and Play BIOS function clears upon exit the contents of the `Event` flag. Therefore, only the first application to invoke `GetEvent` receives notification of the event that occurred. In a Plug and Play operating system, only the OS polls the `event` flag. Plug and Play OS applications and device drivers receive event notification via their event call-back functions.
>
> In non-Plug and Play operating systems, however, the device driver call-back mechanism does not exist and system events are available on a first-come, first-served basis. Therefore, the event notification mechanism will only work properly if there is a single Plug and Play aware driver or application performing event polling.
>
> For example, if multiple device drivers and applications attempt simultaneously to poll the `Event` flag (such as during the system's periodic timer interrupt), each driver or application might detect that an event has occurred, but only the first to call `GetEvent` receives the actual system event value.

Plug and Play BIOS Function *03H—GetEvent*

Function `03H`, or `GetEvent`, enables operating system level software to retrieve messages posted by the Plug and Play BIOS. To indicate the presence of a message, the Plug and

Play BIOS sets bit `0` in the system `event` flag. The operating system polls the system `Event` flag in the foreground. When the operating system detects bit `0` set in the system `Event` flag, it invokes `GetEvent` to determine the cause of the system event.

Following is the C language declaration for the `GetEvent` function:

```
int FAR (*pFuncEntry)(Function, pMessage, DataSelector) ;

int Function ;                    // Always = 03H GetEvent
unsigned int far * pMessage       // ptr to caller's Message Variable
unsigned int DataSelector ;       // Caller-Supplied R/W data
                                  // segment/selector.
```

The following is an explanation of the arguments for the `GetEvent` function:

> `Function`—`Function` is the index to select the Plug and Play BIOS function and always equals `04H` for `GetEvent`.
>
> `pMessage`—`pMessage` is the Far pointer to caller-supplied variable to receive the Plug and Play BIOS message.
>
> `DataSelector`—`DataSelector` is the 16-bit, caller-supplied segment or selector that enables the Plug and Play BIOS to read and write its own local variables and ESCD data if that data is stored in a memory mapped fashion. If the calling application is executing in real mode, it retrieves the `DataSelector` value from the Plug and Play BIOS installation check header. Protected mode applications must build a CPU descriptor table selector for the Protected Mode Base Data Segment that appears in the BIOS' installation check header (refer to Chapter 3).

Following are the Plug and Play BIOS `GetEvent` messages:

`ABOUT_TO_CHANGE_CONFIG (01H)`

The preceding message indicates that an undock is pending.

`DOCK_CHANGED (02H)`

The preceding message indicates that the dock/undock action successfully has been completed.

`SYSTEM_DEVICE_CHANGED (03H)`

The preceding message indicates that the user has added or removed a hot-pluggable device from the convenience base, and that the system may need to be re-enumerated.

`CONFIG_CHANGE_FAILED (04H)`

The preceding message indicates that the dock or undock sequence has failed. If the Plug and Play BIOS can determine the cause of the failure, then it will post another event in the system event flag and will return to the operating system one of the following error codes shown in Table 7.2.

Table 7.2. The `CONFIG_CHANGE_FAILED` `GetEvent` Error Codes.

Value	*Name*	*Description*
89H	UNABLE_TO_DETERMINE_DOCK_CAPABILITIES	The system was unable to identify the docking station.
8AH	CONFIG_CHANGE_FAILED_NO_BATTERY	The system failed to undock because it detected no battery in the portable unit.
8BH	CONFIG_CHANGE_FAILED_RESOURCE_CONFLICT	The system failed to dock because it detected a conflict between a docking station device and an IPL (boot), primary input, or primary output device within the portable system.

`UNKNOWN_SYSTEM_EVENT (0FFFFH)`

The preceding message indicates that an unidentifiable system event occurred. By posting this message, the Plug and Play BIOS is warning the operating system that the system might have become unstable.

`OEM_DEFINED_EVENT (8000H-0FFFEH)`

The preceding message indicates that the Plug and Play BIOS returns an event that only an OEM-supplied device driver or operating system implementation is capable of interpreting. This allows the OEM to customize the Plug and Play BIOS operating system interface.

Plug and Play BIOS Function *04H—SendMessage*

Function `04H`, or `SendMessage`, allows operating system level software to send messages to the system's Plug and Play BIOS.

Following is the C language declaration for the `SendMessage` function:

```
int FAR (*pFuncEntry)(Function, Message, DataSelector) ;

int Function ;                      // Always = 04H For SendMessage
unsigned int Message                // Caller-supplied message
unsigned int DataSelector ;         // Caller-Supplied R/W data
                                    // segment/selector.
```

The following is an explanation of the arguments for `SendMessage`:

> `Function`—`Function` is the index to select the Plug and Play BIOS function and always equals `04H` for `SendMessage`.
>
> `Message`—`Message` is the caller-supplied message variable.
>
> `DataSelector`—`DataSelector` is the 16-bit, caller-supplied segment or selector that enables the Plug and Play BIOS to read and write its own local variables and ESCD data if that data is stored in a memory mapped fashion. If the calling application is executing in real mode, it retrieves the `DataSelector` value from the Plug and Play BIOS installation check header. Protected mode applications must build a CPU descriptor table selector for the Protected Mode Base Data Segment that appears in the BIOS' installation check header (refer to Chapter 3).
>
> The Plug and Play BIOS `SendMessage` function is capable of interpreting three types of messages. The first type of message, the *response message*, has a value in the range `0-3FH`. The second type of message, the *control message*, has a value residing in the range `40H-7FH`. The third type of message, the *OEM-specific message*, has a value ranging from `8000H-0FFFFH`.

Plug and Play BIOS Response Messages

The operating system sends *response messages* in response to a Plug and Play BIOS posted `ABOUT_TO_CHANGE_CONFIG` message in order to signal to the system firmware to continue with, or abort from its default undocking procedure. Currently, the only two defined response messages are `OK` and `ABORT` as shown in the Table 7.3.

Table 7.3. The Plug and Play BIOS Response Messages.

Value	*Name*	*Description*
`00H`	`OK`	Signal from the operating system to continue with the undock sequence. The Plug and Play BIOS waits for a `DEFAULT_UNDOCK_ACTION` control message before actually initiating an undock in hardware.
`00H`	`ABORT`	Signal from the operating system to abort the undock sequence. The Plug and Play operating system issues this message when it determines that an undock sequence is not safe or not possible, given the current operating environment.

Plug and Play BIOS Control Messages

The operating system issues *control messages* to the Plug and Play BIOS when it wants the Plug and Play BIOS or associated system firmware to carry out a specific event, such as initiating the system default undock sequence, or removing power from the system. The PNP_OS_ACTIVE active message is used by the Plug and Play BIOS to determine the degree to which the BIOS should configure non-boot devices during the POST. A related description of the PNP_OS_ACTIVE message appears in Chapter 8.

Table 7.4 shows the Plug and Play BIOS Specification control messages.

Table 7.4. The Plug and Play BIOS Control Messages.

Value	*Name*	*Description*
40H	DEFAULT_UNDOCK_ACTION	Instructs the Plug and Play BIOS to initiate a software-eject. During a software-eject, the Plug and Play BIOS broadcasts the message ABOUT_TO_CHANGE_CONFIG. If the Plug and Play operating system responds to the ABOUT_TO_CHANGE_CONFIG with an OK response message, the Plug and Play BIOS initiates the system's hardware undock sequence.
41H	POWER_OFF	The system BIOS should remove power from the system, if it is capable: otherwise, the Plug and Play BIOS returns the error MESSAGE_NOT_SUPPORTED.
42H	PNP_OS_ACTIVE	Upon receiving this message, the system firmware should adhere to the general guidelines of operating with a Plug and Play operating system. For example, the firmware should configure a minimum number of boot devices during POST if a Plug and Play operating system is active.
43H	PNP_OS_INACTIVE	Upon receiving this message, the system firmware acts as if a legacy operating system is executing. The firmware attempts to configure all devices during power on and dock sequences.

OEM-defined Messages

Any message whose value resides in the range `08000H-0FFFFH` is considered OEM-defined. This mechanism allows OEM-specific device drivers and applications to generate system events beyond those defined in the Plug and Play BIOS specification.

Plug and Play BIOS Function *05H—GetDockingStationInfo*

Function `05H`, or `GetDockingStationInfo`, provides the caller with information pertaining to the docking station or convenience base to which the portable system is currently connected.

Following is the C language declaration for the `GetDockingStationInfo` function:

```
int FAR (*pFuncEntry)(Function, pDockingInfo, DataSelector) ;

int Function ;                    // Always 05H For GetDockingStationInfo
unsigned char far * pDockingInfo // Caller-supplied Info Buffer
unsigned int DataSelector ;       // Caller-Supplied R/W data
                                  // segment/selector.
```

The following is a description of the arguments for `GetDockingStationInfo`:

> `Function`—`Function` is the index to select the Plug and Play BIOS function and always equals `05H` for `GetDockingStationInfo`.
>
> `pDockingInfo`—`pDockingInfo` is the caller that supplies a far pointer to a buffer large enough to receive the docking station information structure defined next.
>
> `DataSelector`—`DataSelector` is the 16-bit, caller-supplied segment or selector that enables the Plug and Play BIOS to read and write its own local variables and ESCD data if that data is stored in a memory mapped fashion. If the calling application is executing in real mode, it retrieves the `DataSelector` value from the Plug and Play BIOS installation check header. Protected mode applications must build a CPU descriptor table selector for the Protected Mode Base Data Segment that appears in the BIOS' Installation Check Header (refer to Chapter 3).

Table 7.5 displays the structure of the docking station information buffer returned by `GetDockingStationInfo`.

Table 7.5. The Docking Station Information Buffer.

Offset	*Size*	*Description*
00H	4*BYTE	EISA Style Docking Station ID
04H	4*BYTE	OEM-Defined Docking Station Serial # (must be 0 if no serial number is available for this docking station)
08H	WORD	Docking Station Capabilities

The Plug and Play BIOS is responsible for distinguishing between different docking stations and supplying a unique ID for each different docking station. The Plug and Play operating system, in turn, enumerates and records the devices within each type of docking station, thereby allowing the OS to bypass its enumeration process for known docking stations during future dock and undock sequences.

The Docking Station Capabilities entry in the `DockingInfo` buffer adheres to the following format:

Bits `[15:3]`	Reserved
Bits `[2:1]`	`00B` equals system supports cold docking only (system must be powered off to dock or undock)
	`01B` equals system supports warm docking only (system can dock or undock either in suspend mode, or when powered off)
	`10B` equals system supports hot (fully powered) docking or undocking
	`11B` equals Reserved
Bit `[0]`	Equals `1` if the system supports VCR-style docking
	Equals `0` if the system is a Surprise-style only docking station

`GetDockingStationInfo` returns the following values:

`FUNCTION_NOT_SUPPORTED`	The system supports no docking capabilities whatsoever.
`SYSTEM_NOT_DOCKED`	The system supports some type of docking, but currently is not docked.
`SUCCESS`	The system supports some type of docking, and currently is docked.

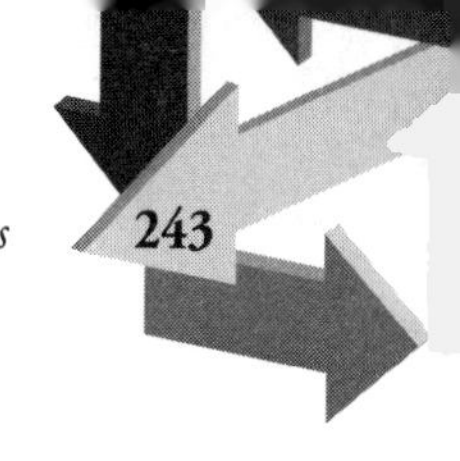

`UNABLE_TO_DETERMINE_DOCK_CAPABILITIES`	The system supports some type of docking, but is unable to identify the attached docking station.

The Dock/Undock Sequence

Docking station-equipped portable systems depend on close coordination between the system's hardware, firmware and operating system. The following sections detail the Plug and Play message handling that occurs during both a dock and undock sequence.

The Undocking Process

This section outlines the undocking process for a system running Windows 95. Because many designers have created systems to work in conjunction with Windows 95, designers of other Plug and Play operating systems should adhere to the sequence below in order to guarantee compatibility with existing, Windows 95 compliant machines. The following list details the undocking sequence for a Plug and Play notebook system.

1. The user signals an undock by one of a variety of methods.
    a. If the system supports surprise-style undocking only, the user simply removes the portable system from its convenience base, and control transfers to step 8.
    b. If the system supports hot, or honor-system style undocking, the user signals an upcoming undock either by selecting `Undock` within an OS-based applet, or by activating an undock button on the system itself. If the operating system is aware of a pending undock (such as from the user's applet), it broadcasts the message `DEFAULT_UNDOCK_ACTION` to the Plug and Play BIOS via the `SendMessage` function. If the operating system is unaware of the pending undock (for example, the user activated a hardware undock switch), control passes to step 2. In either case, control passes to the system's firmware.
2. The Plug and Play BIOS posts the message `ABOUT_TO_CHANGE_CONFIG` by setting bit `0` within the system `event` flag.
3. The Plug and Play operating system detects the pending event bit (bit `0`) in the system `event` flag and invokes the Plug and Play BIOS `GetEvent` function to retrieve the message value.
4. Plug and Play BIOS function `03H` (`GetEvent`) returns the message `ABOUT_TO_CHANGE_CONFIG` to the operating system and clears the system `event` flag.

5. The Plug and Play operating system processes the `ABOUT_TO_CHANGE_CONFIG` message and determines if it is safe for the user to undock the system.
6. If the operating system determines that it is safe to undock, then it closes any open files that reside on a docking station mass storage device and performs any other functions necessary for proceeding without the hardware resident in the dock. If it is not currently safe to undock, the operating system broadcasts the `ABORT` message to the Plug and Play BIOS. If the system supports VCR-style undocking, the Plug and Play BIOS simply fails to eject the portable PC from its convenience base. Following an aborted eject, an operating system applet may display the fact that the ejection process failed.
7. The Plug and Play operating system invokes Plug and Play BIOS function `04H` (`SendMessage`) with the response message `OK` if the undocking sequence can proceed without harm to the system or the user's data. The response message `OK` simply indicates to the Plug and Play BIOS that the operating system has received and processed the `ABOUT_TO_CHANGE_CONFIG` message.
8. The Plug and Play BIOS invokes the system's hardware undocking sequence.
9. The Plug and Play BIOS broadcasts the message `DOCK_CHANGED` to the operating system.
10. The operating system re-enumerates the system's devices and continues execution.

> **NOTE**
>
> If the user undocks a system in the absence of a Plug and Play operating system, the Plug and Play BIOS should eject the portable system from its convenience base after waiting a predetermined amount of time (usually 10 seconds) for the operating system to respond the initial `ABOUT_TO_CHANGE_CONFIG` message. Although the user may lose data, this fail-safe timing mechanism prevents the Plug and Play BIOS from waiting indefinitely for the `OK` response message that the legacy operating system will never send.

The Docking Process

The following steps describe the docking sequence for a Plug and Play notebook system.

1. The user inserts the portable system into its docking station or attaches a port replicator (such as a PCMCIA card reader) device. The insertion event generates an `SMI` (System Management Interrupt) and execution control transfers to the system's `SMM` (System Management Memory) based firmware.

NOTE

The Plug and Play BIOS specification defines a second mechanism by which docking devices generate hardware interrupts to signal system events. Because the majority of systems and CPU's support the `SMI` interrupt interface, it is expected that most systems will use the `SMI` mechanism to generate and signal system events. For more information on the IRQ-style Plug and Play BIOS system events, refer to the *Plug and Play BIOS Specification.*

2. The host (portable) system firmware identifies the type of docking station attached to the system and prepares the docking station identification information supplied by Plug and Play BIOS function `05H` (`GetDockingStationInfo`).
3. If the system supports VCR-style docking, the Plug and Play BIOS initiates the portable system hardware insertion sequence. If the system supports honor system or surprise style docking, the Plug and Play BIOS has no control over when the user inserts the portable system into its convenience base.
4. Having detected the insertion of the portable system into its docking station, the Plug and Play BIOS broadcasts the message `DOCK_CHANGED` to the operating system by setting bit `0` within the system `event` flag.
5. The Plug and Play operating system detects bit `0` set within the `event` flag and invokes the Plug and Play BIOS `GetEvent` function to retrieve the `DOCK_CHANGED` message.
6. The Plug and Play BIOS clears the system `event` flag.
7. The operating system enumerates the contents of the newly inserted docking station, configures its devices, and continues execution. In order to configure any systemboard resident devices within the docking station, the Plug and Play operating system may issue a series of Plug and Play BIOS `SetNode` calls.

The Enhanced IDE Effort

Until recently, the BIOS in most PC/AT class systems supported a maximum of two fixed disks, each of which was identifiable either by invoking INT `13H` function `08H` (`Get Drive Parameters`) or by examining the drive parameter table for that drive.

The introduction of such devices as IDE CD-ROM drives has forced BIOS vendors and system OEMs to redesign their product to support at least four IDE devices as well as introduce new system firmware support for identifying each installed device. The ongoing BIOS redesign process to support more and newer IDE devices is part of the industry's larger Enhanced IDE effort, which includes the following device features and enhancements:

- Auto ID devices
- CHS Translation
- LBA (Logical Block Addressable) IDE devices
- EDPT (Enhanced Disk Parameter Table)
- Fixed Disk Parameter Table Extension
- INT `13H` Fixed Disk Extensions

As a side effect of increasing functionality and performance within an IDE-equipped systems, the Enhanced IDE effort changes the process by which the operating system enumerates the IDE devices within the host system. The following subsections describe the interaction of Enhanced IDE technologies and methods for identifying and programming Enhanced IDE devices.

In preparation for the following discussion, new definitions and terminology are listed here.

> *ATA*—AT Attachment Interface as defined by the SFF (Small Form Factor) committee.
>
> *Auto ID* (Automatic Identification)—IDE fixed disks support the ATA Identify command by returning a 512-byte buffer of drive-specific parameters and capabilities. Via the Identify command, the system BIOS can Auto-ID IDE drives during POST.
>
> *CHS* (Cylinder/Head/Sector)—The conventional method used to address data on a fixed disk involves programming the fixed disk's controller with a cylinder, head and sector value.
>
> *EDPT* (Enhanced Disk Parameter Table)—A 16-byte table of fixed disk parameters based on the original IBM PC/AT fixed disk table, but enhanced to include both physical and translated drive parameters.
>
> *Fixed Disk Parameter Table Extensions*—A 16-byte table describing the configuration and capabilities of a particular fixed disk, such as its base I/O address, assigned IRQ, and current LBA mode.
>
> *IDE* (Integrated Device Electronics)—IDE fixed disks support the command set described in the ATA specification, including the Auto-ID `Identify` command.

LBA (Logical Block Addressing)—A fixed disk whose controller is operating in LBA mode addresses data as a linear series of blocks. The LBA interface supports devices with as many as 4 Gigablocks of data.

Logical Parameters—Fixed disk parameters that the system BIOS has reported to the operating system in translated form in order to allow calling applications to bypass certain parameter passing limitations in the INT 13H BIOS function.

Parameters—A fixed disk's cylinder, head, and sectors-per-track counts. Older non-IDE drives also require write-precompensation and landing zone parameters. Modern fixed disk controllers perform write precompensation and head landings automatically within their own on-board firmware.

Physical Parameters—The disk parameters reported to the system BIOS by an IDE drive as a result of an Identify command.

Figure 7.2 displays the architecture of a system that supports both the standard and extended INT 13H functions.

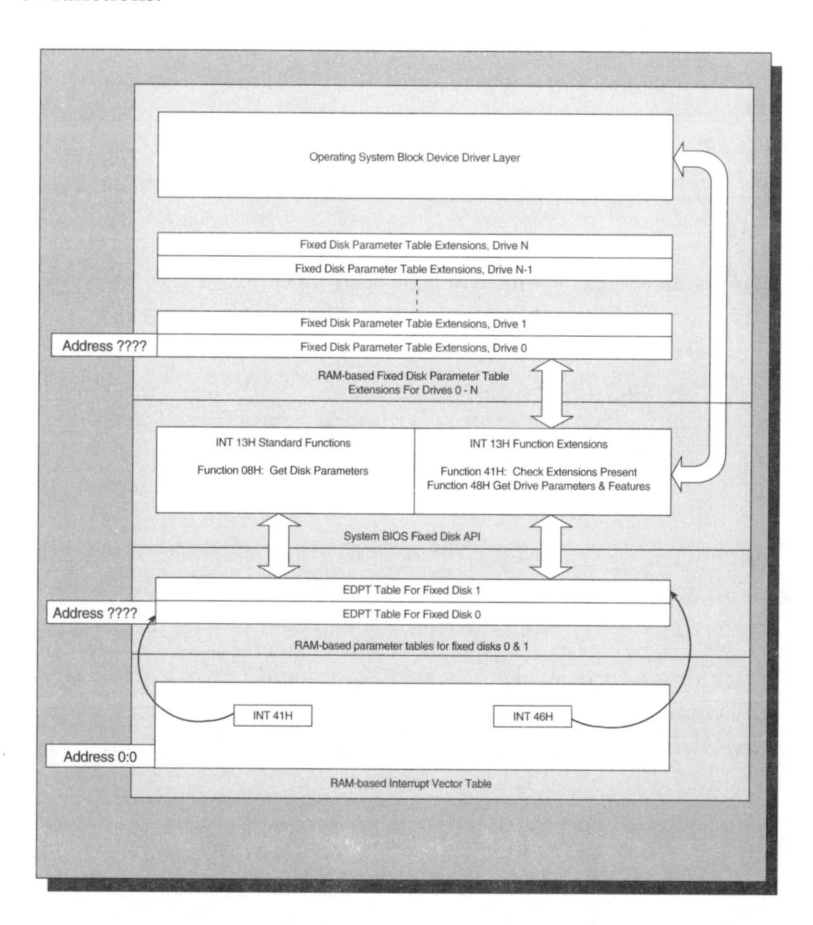

FIGURE 7.2.
The INT 13H interface with extensions.

Auto ID Devices

With few exceptions, modern system BIOSes allow the user to automatically identify and store the physical parameters of ATA compliant fixed disks from within the ROM-based system setup utility. This Auto-ID capability is made possible by IDE devices that support the IDE command `0ECH` (`Drive Identify`). IDE drive support of the `Identify` command is required by the SFF (Small Form Factor Committee) ATA (AT Attachment) Specification.

WHERE TO GET MORE INFORMATION ABOUT THE IDE TECHNOLOGY

The ATA-2 document, formally entitled *AT Attachment Interface with Extensions,* is a working document maintained by a variety of industry mass storage device vendors. The document is copyrighted 1994, Computer and Business Equipment Manufacturer's Association. Copies of the *AT Attachment Interface with Extensions* document are available from

Global Engineering
15 Inverness Way East
Englewood, CO 80112-5704
Telephone (303)792-2181
Fax (303)792-2192

During an `Identify` command, the IDE device returns a 512-byte device description array into a caller-supplied buffer. Among other things, this array contains the physical number of heads, cylinders, and sectors per track that describes the geometry of the IDE disk. Assuming a sector size of 512 bytes, the BIOS can calculate the total capacity of the device based on the count of cylinders, sectors, and heads according to the following equation:

```
Capacity (MB) = 512 * Cyls. * Heads * Sectors/Track.
```

Additionally, a vendor-specific identification string within the drive description array allows applications such as the system BIOS to display the device's manufacturer, thereby enabling users to distinguish between two devices with identical physical geometries.

After having performed an `Identify` command for a particular IDE device, the system BIOS sometimes stores the drive's parameters in non-volatile storage, such as system CMOS RAM. By storing the Auto-ID parameters in CMOS, the BIOS can bypass the lengthier drive identification process during the system's POST.

A NOTE ABOUT RETRIEVING DRIVE PARAMETERS...

The PC/AT compatible system BIOS initializes the contents of the INT 41H and INT 46H vectors to point to tables containing the parameters for fixed disks 0 and 1, respectively. On an original PC/AT system, which supports only 15 different (non-Auto ID) drives, the INT 41H and INT 46H vectors point to one of 15 different 16-byte drive parameter table entries located in the drive table at physical address `0F000:E401H`.

On newer systems that support standard, user-defined, and Auto-ID drives, the system BIOS must create similar tables for drives other than those for which the fixed disk table contains a ROM-based entry. Usually, the BIOS builds disk parameter tables for user-defined or Auto-ID drives either in the shadow RAM, at location `0:300H` (a special unused region in low DOS memory) or in the BIOS data area located at `40:0H`.

Following is the format of a standard PC/AT drive parameter table.

Table 7.6. The format of the standard PC/AT fixed disk parameter table.

Offset	*Size*	*Description*
00H	WORD	Physical Cylinder Count
02H	BYTE	Physical Head Count
03H	2*BYTE	Reserved
05H	WORD	Write Precompensation Start Cylinder
07H	BYTE	Reserved
08H	WORD	Control Field (If set, bit [4] indicates that the drive has more than eight physical heads
09H	3*BYTE	Reserved
0CH	WORD	Head Landing Zone Cylinder
0EH	BYTE	Physical Sectors Per Track
0FH	BYTE	Reserved

If the system contains more than two fixed disks, there is no equivalent interrupt vector pointing mechanism for any drives beyond the first two. In order to retrieve the parameters for drives 3, 4, and so on, the application or operating system invokes INT 13H function 08H (`Get Drive Parameters`) with the appropriate, logical drive number for these additional drives.

The following code fragment retrieves the parameters for logical drive 83H, the fourth drive in the system.

```
 mov    dl, 83H    ; 80H = Drive 0, 81H = Drive 1, etc.
 mov    ah, 08H    ; INT 13H Function 08H (Get Drive Info)
 int    13H        ; Issue BIOS Disk Services Interrupt
 jc     DriveError; CF = 1 Means Function Failed

 ; Examine Parameters Here

DriveError:
```

As a rule, the system BIOS INT 13H function provides the only reliable interface for identifying the existence and geometry of the system's fixed disks. The operating system might directly examine the parameter tables pointed to by INT 41H and INT 46H, and it may individually snoop IDE drives via the `Identify` command described previously as a means for verifying that the BIOS-reported information is correct. Operating system designers should be careful not to enable fixed disks that the BIOS failed to report, as the user may have intentionally left the drive(s) disabled.

CHS Translation

Historically, fixed disks within the PC/AT have been limited by the system BIOS to a maximum capacity of 528 MB. This limitation stems from the fact that the BIOS INT 13H read and write functions accept only a 10-bit cylinder number. Therefore, the maximum cylinder allowed by INT 13H has been, and still is 0FFFH, or 1023 decimal.

Modern system BIOSes bypass the INT 13H parameter passing limitation by performing CHS (Cylinder/Head/Sector) translation on the drive's physical parameters. If the drive's physical cylinder count exceeds 1023, the system BIOS translates the drive's parameters by repeatedly doubling the head count, and halving the cylinder count until the cylinder count fits within the range 0-1023.

The system BIOS INT 13H disk services function allows an eight-bit number to specify the amount of heads within the drive. As a result, the operating system is free to call INT 13H with a head number as large as 0FFH (255) and a cylinder count as large as 0FFFH (1023). The number of sectors per track is never translated, and has a disk controller task register imposed limitation of six bits, or 03FH (63 decimal).

Prior to the introduction of CHS translation, the system BIOS would simply truncate the cylinder count if it exceeded 1023, and that portion of the disk remained unusable.

The modern system BIOS returns translated parameters for drives whose cylinder count exceeds 1023, and allows drives with capacities as great as 8GB, according to the following formula:

```
Capacity = Max Heads * Max Cylinders * Max Sectors/Track * Sector Size.
         = 0255 * 1023 * 63 * 512
         = approximately 8 GB.
```

The operating system must be aware of fixed disks whose parameters have been translated because the BIOS reported parameters for such a drive no longer agree with those returned by the ATA `Identify` command. In order to indicate that a certain drive's parameters have been translated, many system BIOSes provide an *Enhanced Fixed Disk Parameter Table* that is a superset of the standard PC/AT parameter table introduced in the previous section. The format of the Enhanced Fixed Disk Parameter Table appears below.

Table 7.7. The Enhanced Fixed Disk Parameter Table.

Offset	*Size*	*Description*
00H	WORD	Logical Cylinder Count
02H	BYTE	Logical Head Count
03H	BYTE	Translation Signature (equals `0A0H` if the parameters in the table have been translated)
04H	BYTE	Physical Sectors Per Track
05H	WORD	Write Precompensation Start Cylinder
07H	BYTE	Reserved
08H	WORD	Control Field (If set, bit `[4]` indicates that the drive has more than eight physical heads)
09H	WORD	Physical Cylinder Count
0AH	BYTE	Physical Head Count
0CH	WORD	Head Landing Zone Cylinder
0EH	BYTE	Logical Sectors Per Track
0FH	BYTE	2's Complement `checksum` of this Table

The `Translation Signature` field merely indicates that the system BIOS is performing some type of translation of the drive's parameters. This translation may be either `CHS-CHS` translation or `CHS-LBA` translation. If the system BIOS does not support the INT `13H` Extensions API described later in this chapter, it is the responsibility of the operating system to determine, if necessary, which type of translation is active.

If the system's fixed disks originally were formatted via the system BIOS, it is important that the operating system detect the type of translation (if any) is active. For example, the operating system or device driver might, for reasons of performance, bypass the system BIOS INT 13H interface by directly reading and writing to the system's disks. If the operating system assumes that parameters returned by INT 13H are physical parameters, then disk errors will occur because the reported cylinder and head counts do not match the physical geometry of the disk.

To solve this problem, the operating system driver can perform its own ATA drive `Identify` command and compare the parameters that the drive reports with those that the system BIOS reports. The OS driver then translates the drive's physical parameters according to the following equation, which appears in the *Western Digital Enhanced IDE Guide* as the industry-recommended method for drive parameter translation:

```
    :
    :

LogicalCylinders = PhysicalCylinders ;
LogicalHeads = PhysicalHeads ;

if (PhysicalCylinders > 1023) {

Count = 0 ;

while (PhysicalCylinders > 1023) {

    Count ++ ;
    LogicalCylinders = LogicalCylinders / 2 ;
    LogicalHeads = LogicalHeads * 2 ;

    } // End While
} // End If

    :
    :
```

If, having performed the translation shown in the preceding code fragment, the driver calculates logical parameters identical to those returned by the BIOS for a particular drive, it uses the same translation mechanism during its reads and writes to that drive. Otherwise, the driver aborts and the operating system performs its disk operations via the system BIOS.

NOTE

Remember that CHS translation is a means by which the BIOS works around its own INT 13H limitation of allowing only a 10-bit cylinder number to be passed to read, write, and seek commands. It does this by creating translated cylinder and head counts that do fit the INT 13H function constraints.

Were it not for direct-access fixed disk device drivers, most engineers would never know, or for that matter care, that the system BIOS translates the parameters for any given drive. It is crucial, however, that if a drive has been formatted by a BIOS using CHS translation, then the direct access driver must use the same translation method. Otherwise, the driver might attempt to program the disk's controller with cylinders and heads that don't actually exist.

LBA (Logical Block Addressable) IDE devices

As the family of IDE-compliant devices grows beyond rotating media mass storage devices, such as fixed disks and CD-ROMs, the representation of storage in the form of cylinders, heads, and sectors becomes less of a necessity and more of a burden. Consider, for example, how to represent the format of an IDE tape backup drive in terms of cylinders, heads and sectors, when in fact the device contains none. *Logical Block Addressing* allows the capacity of IDE devices to exceed the 8G barrier imposed by the system BIOS INT `13H` interface, and allows applications and device drivers to communicate with mass storage devices without having any previous knowledge of those devices' exact physical geometry.

Many newer IDE devices (including fixed disks) support a new memory addressing mechanism known as LBA, or Logical Block Addressing. Instead of representing their storage contents in the context of a rotating fixed disk, LBA devices simply address their storage as a linear array of blocks.

Internally, a fixed disk controller operating in CHS mode translates the caller's `cylinder`, `head`, and `sector` values to a Logical Block Index. A device driver or system BIOS can perform the same CHS-LBA translation according to the following equation:

```
Index = (((Cyl # * Max Hds) + Hd #) * Max SPT) + (Sector # - 1)
```

If a system BIOS does not support the IBM INT `13H` extended functions (`40H-48H`), it still can utilize an LBA-enabled fixed disk by first enabling LBA mode in the fixed disk controller, and performing the preceding CHS-LBA parameter translation prior to each read, write, or seek operation. Because the CHS-LBA translation must at some time be calculated (either by the system BIOS/device driver or the fixed disk controller's internal firmware) the performance benefit of operating an LBA drive in this manner depends on whether the system BIOS or IDE controller firmware is faster at performing the CHS-LBA translation.

The availability of LBA addressing in the system BIOS becomes important when the total capacity of any fixed disk in the system exceeds the maximum limits of the INT

13H interface. This limit occurs at approximately 8GB because the register parameter passing convention used by INT 13H reaches its maximum capacity of 255 heads, 65535 cylinders, and 63 sectors per track.

The system BIOS provides logical block addressing via the IBM INT 13H extended functions that appear later in this chapter. These extended functions allow the caller to specify a 32-bit block number.

Many system BIOS implementations provide a user selection for enabling and disabling LBA mode within a particular drive. The effect of this menu option usually is to enable CHS-LBA translation within the standard internal INT 13H read, write, and verify functions. This menu option has no effect on the availability or functionality of the INT 13H function extensions that provide true LBA support via a block number rather than a CHS-like pseudo-LBA block number. The INT 13H function extensions always operate in LBA mode, and no translation takes place in the BIOS or drive controller.

When the user selects LBA mode for an installed fixed disk, the system BIOS issues ATA drive commands to put the drive's controller into LBA mode. Once a drive is in LBA mode, the definition of its controller registers becomes LBA-specific, and normal CHS commands no longer function properly. The controller registers within an LBA-enabled drive specify the offset of a logical block rather than the cylinder, head, and sector values that point to the same block.

INT *13H* Fixed Disk Extensions

In order to aid operating systems with the chore of identifying and managing mass storage devices within the Plug and Play system, BIOS vendors have added extended INT 13H functions and introduced a new table called the *Fixed Disk Parameter Table Extension.*

Earlier, this chapter introduced an extended version of the standard drive parameter table called Extended Drive Parameter Table, or EDPT. The EDPT table contains drive parameters such as cylinders, heads, and sectors.

Fixed Disk Parameter Table Extensions, on the other hand, contain all BIOS reported drive information other than the drives' parameters. The purpose of the extension tables is to simplify the operating system's chore of dealing directly with fixed disk hardware.

Fixed Disk Parameter Table Extensions

Fixed Disk Parameter Table Extensions provide additional drive/controller information not found in standard drive parameter tables like those to which the INT 41H and INT 46H vectors point.

FIGURE 7.3
The standard, and extended INT 13H functions' usage of LBA addressing.

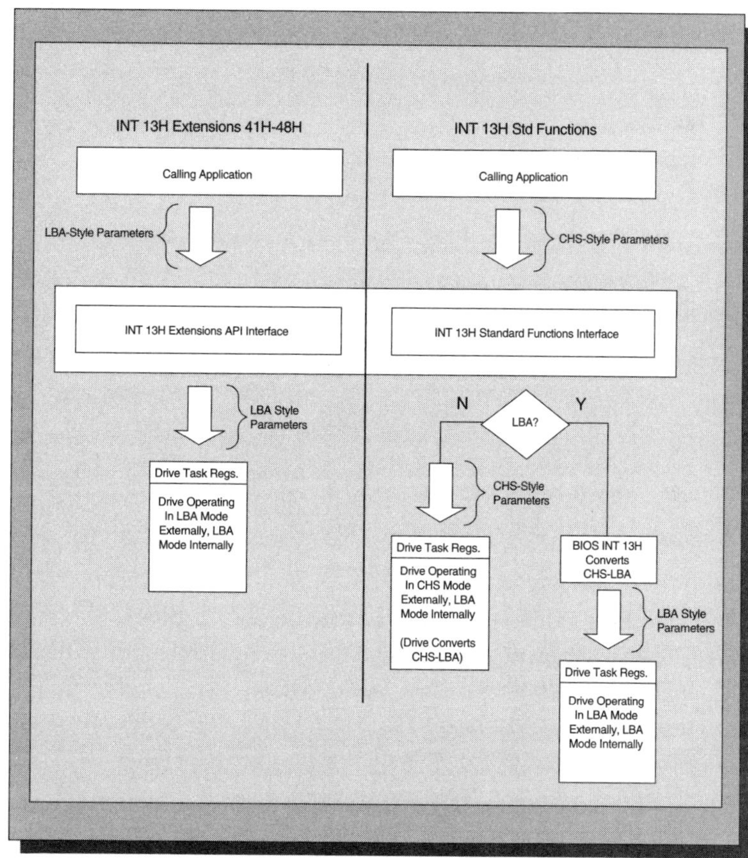

Within a Plug and Play system, the Fixed Disk Parameter Table Extensions take much of the guess work out of determining the physical geometry and resources assigned to the system's fixed disks. If the system BIOS supports the INT 13H functions extensions as described by IBM, there exists for each fixed disk in the system a Fixed Disk Parameter Table Extension, which the user can retrieve by issuing INT 13H function 48H.

NOTE

The Fixed Disk Parameter Table Extensions are an enhancement introduced to IBM's original INT 13H Function Extensions by Phoenix Technologies. In order to determine whether the Fixed Disk Parameter Table Extensions support is present within the system, the caller first should issue INT 13H function 41H. Additionally, the caller should check the extensions version to determine whether the Phoenix Technologies-Defined Fixed Disk Parameter Tables Extension format is supported. (AH equals 20H upon return.)

Check INT *13H* Function Extensions Present

Passed

AH = 41H
BX = 55AAH
DL = Logical Drive Index (80H-0FFH)

Returns

CF = 0 if function succeeded
= 1 if extensions not available

AH = major version of the supported extensions (= 20H if Fixed Disk Parameter Table Extensions are available; otherwise = 11H)

BX = AA55H (Caller's BX register swapped to indicate function presence)

CX = bitmap of supported extended INT 13H functions as documented by the IBM document *INT 13H Extensions API* mentioned earlier

DH = extended functions version in BCD format

The Fixed Disk Parameter Table Extension is a 16-byte table that adheres to the following format. As mentioned, this table is available only if the Check Extensions Present function described here returns a major version of 20H or greater. Table 7.8 displays the format of the INT 13H Fixed Disk Parameter Table Extension.

Table 7.8. The format of the INT 13 Fixed Disk Parameter Table Extension.

Offset	*Size*	*Description*
00H	WORD	Controller I/O Port Base Address (i.e., 1F0H)
02H	WORD	Drive Control Port Address (i.e., 3F6H)
04H	BYTE	Status Byte #1
05H	BYTE	Reserved, Bits [7:4] are always 0
06H	BYTE	Drive IRQ Assignment
07H	BYTE	Multi-sector transfer byte count
08H	BYTE	Drive DMA Assignment
09H	BYTE	Drive PIO Timings
0AH	BYTE	Drive Description Byte
0BH	3*BYTE	Reserved, must be 0
0EH	BYTE	Extension Table Revision ID (equals 10H for this structure)
0FH	BYTE	checksum of this Extension Table

Controller I/O Port Base Address Offset *00H WORD*

This field contains the I/O port base address for the drive. For example, if the drive is connected to the primary IDE controller in a PC/AT compatible system, this field contains the value `1F0H`.

Drive Control Port Address Offset *02H WORD*

This field contains the address of the control port for the drive. If the drive is connected to the primary IDE controller in a PC/AT compatible system, for example, then this field contains the value `3F6H`.

Drive Head Register Prefix Offset *04H BYTE*

Bits `[3:0]`	Reserved, must be `0`
Bit `[4]`	If set, the drive is an IDE master, otherwise the drive is a slave
Bit `[5]`	Reserved, must be `1`
Bit `[6]`	If set, the drive is in LBA mode, otherwise the drive is CHS
Bit `[7]`	Reserved, must be `1`

The Drive Head Register Prefix byte serves two purposes. First, it indicates to the caller of INT `13H` extension `48H` if the drive is in LBA mode, and whether the drive is a master or slave drive. Second, the BIOS stores the LBA and master/slave information in the same form as the upper four bits of the drive controller's head register. This simplifies the BIOS' programming of the drive's master/slave and LBA modes because during a disk read/write operation, the BIOS merely `OR`s this value with the desired drive head when it programs the head register.

Drive IRQ Assignment Offset *06H BYTE*

This field contains the ordinal number of the IRQ assigned to the drive.

Multi-Sector Transfer Count Offset *07H BYTE*

This field contains the number of sectors the BIOS transfers during a read or write to the drive.

Drive DMA Assignment Offset *08H BYTE*

Bits `[3:0]`	Contains the ordinal number of the DMA channel currently assigned to the drive. If the drive does not support DMA, or is not currently in DMA mode, this value in this field is undefined.
Bits `[7:4]`	Specifies the ATA-DMA mode in which the drive is currently operating.

Drive PIO Mode Offset *09H BYTE*

This field contains the ordinal number of the Small Form Factor Committee-specified PIO mode in which the drive currently is operating. Legal values for this field are 1, 2, 3, and 4. The SFF Committee ATA-2 specification contains a comprehensive explanation of each PIO timing mode.

Drive Description Byte Offset *0AH BYTE*

Bit [7] If set, the system has been configured to perform DWORD-wide transfers for this drive. Otherwise, the system performs WORD-wide transfers to and from the drive.

Bit [6] If set, the drive is a CD-ROM device

Bit [5] If set, the drive supports removable media

Bit [4] If set, the system has configured the drive to operate in LBA mode

Bit [3] If set, the BIOS currently is configured to perform logical to physical translation of the drive's CHS parameters

Bit [2] If set, the BIOS is configured to transfer data to and from the drive in multi-sector mode and the Multi-sector Transfer Count Byte data is valid

Bit [1] If set, the system is configured to transfer data to and from the drive via DMA and the DMA Assignment Byte data is valid

Bit [0] If set, the system has configured the drive controller to operate in a fast PIO timing mode, and the PIO Mode Type Byte is valid

Extension Table Revision ID Offset *0EH BYTE*

This field contains the revision ID for the extension table. Currently, the only value defined for this field is 10H.

Fixed Disk Parameter Table Extensions do not replace standard drive parameter tables; the information contained in each table is mutually exclusive. Instead, these tables allow the operating system to bypass its comparatively time-consuming and inaccurate process of snooping drive capabilities on systems that don't provide these extensions.

Unlike the two standard drive parameter tables in a PC/AT-compatible BIOS, which are available to applications and operating system enumeration software via the INT 41H and INT 46H vectors, only the system BIOS knows the exact location of the system's Fixed Disk Parameter Table Extensions.

Instead of examining drive parameters via interrupt vectors, applications, and operating systems that are capable of managing more than two drives invoke INT 13H extension 48H to receive a far pointer to the Fixed Disk Parameter Table Extension for each

of the system's fixed disks, regardless of whether the appropriate INT 41H and INT 46H vectors are currently available for the specified drive.

In addition to verifying that the Fixed Disk Parameter Table Extensions are present, the calling application or device driver should retrieve all physical disk information via the extended INT 13H function 48H (Get Drive Parameters). Following is the definition of this function and its return values:

Passed

AH	Equals 48H
DL	Equals Logical Drive Number (80H equals drive 0, 81H equals drive 1, and so on)
DS:SI	Equals far pointer to caller's buffer to receive Drive Info structure

Returns

CF	Equals 0 if function succeeded Equals 1 if function failed
DS:SI	Equals pointer to returned Drive Information structure as follows:

```
DRIVE_INFO STRUCT 1

    info_size      dw    30    ; Size of the DRIVE_INFO structure
    info_flags     dw    ?     ; Information flag word
    cylinders      dw    ?     ; Number of drive cylinders
    heads          dw    ?     ; Number of drive heads
    sectors        dw    ?     ; Number of drive sectors per track
    sectors        dq    ?     ; Total number of drive sectors
    sector_size    dw    ?     ; Number of bytes per sector on drive

DRIVE_INFO ENDS
```

Miscellaneous Plug and Play Hardware

While it would be impossible to describe all hardware devices and peripherals that appear in Plug and Play systems, this section lists some of the more common ones and, in some cases, refers the reader to appropriate related documentation.

The DDC (Display Data Channel) Monitor

DDC-compliant monitors support a serial bus via two previously reserved pins on the VGA connector. Within a DDC-capable system, the VGA BIOS supplies special functions that issue commands on the monitor's serial bus to perform such tasks as query the monitor's capabilities, select video modes, and perform power management on the monitor itself.

A complete description of DDC-compliant monitors appears in the VESA Committee *Display Data Channel Specification.*

Plug and Play SCSI

The *SCSI* (Small Computer Systems Interface) bus supports a variety of fixed disk, CD-ROM, tape drive, and other devices. Historically, users of SCSI devices have been required to assign LUNs (Logical Unit Numbers) to each device on the bus and to ensure that each device is configured with the proper number and type of termination resistors. Despite its speed and flexibility, the SCSI bus has suffered somewhat due the complexities involved in adding new devices or reconfiguring existing ones.

The Plug and Play SCSI Specification introduces the concept of *SCAM*, or *SCSI Configured AutoMagically.* If the user has a SCAM capable SCSI adapter, he or she simply adds SCAM-capable devices to the bus and these devices self-configure, including LUN assignment and resistive termination.

The *Plug and Play SCSI Specification* is available in the PLUGPLAY forum on CompuServe. CompuServe users can access the PLUGPLAY forum by typing **GO PLUGPLAY**.

Plug and Play Serial Devices

The Plug and Play External COM Device Specification describes an 18-field serial device identification field that serial devices return to the Plug and Play operating system. According to Microsoft's *Windows 95 Hardware Design Guide*, all serial devices connected to a system must support the serial device ID mechanism in order to receive Windows 95 certification. The format of the serial device ID string and the mechanism by which the device transmits this string to the operating system appear in *The Plug and Play External COM Device Specification.*

Additionally, the *Windows 95 Hardware Design Guide* requires that the serial port within notebook systems be 16550 UART compatible. The 16550 UART has increased performance due to a built-in FIFO inside the chip.

The *Plug and Play External COM Device Specification* is available in the PLUGPLAY forum on CompuServe. CompuServe users can access the PLUGPLAY forum by typing **GO PLUGPLAY**.

Plug and Play Parallel Port Devices

The *Windows 95 Hardware Design Guide* requires that the system's parallel ports adhere to the IEEE-P1284 specification. Additionally, the *Windows 95 Design Guide* recommends that the system provide either *ECP* (*Enhanced Capabilities Port*) or *EPP* (*Enhanced Parallel Port*) capabilities.

A description of ECP (Enhanced Capabilities Port) is available in the form of product data sheets from various super I/O chip providers, including SMC (Standard Microsystems Corporation), National Semiconductor, and Intel.

If the system supports EPP, it contains additional INT 17H parallel port services including parallel port device daisy-chaining, block reads and writes, and external parallel device multiplexor support. These additional services are described in the *EPP BIOS Specification* available at the following address:

> Farpoint Communications
> 104 East Avenue K-4, Suite F.
> Lancaster, CA 93535
>
> Telephone (805)726-4420
> Fax (805)726-4438

8

The Intel Plug and Play Solution

The Intel Plug and Play solution consists of various Plug and Play hardware and software components, some of which are specific to the DOS/Win 3.1 environment, and others that apply to Plug and Play in general. As a rule of thumb, the underlying firmware and hardware technologies presented in Intel's Plug and Play solution apply to general Plug and Play solutions, whereas Intel's DOS/Win 3.1 device drivers, applications, and libraries serve specifically as a vehicle for introducing Plug and Play to systems running current versions of DOS and Windows.

In addition to those Plug and Play compliant devices (PCI, Plug and Play BIOS, PCMCIA, and Plug and Play ISA) that have already been discussed in previous chapters, the major components of the Intel Plug and Play solution are

firmware components

- ACFG BIOS
- ESCD (Extended System Configuration Data) Plug and Play BIOS Functions

and software components

- The ESCD format
- Intel CM DOS Device Driver
- DOS ICU (ISA Configuration Utility)
- Windows ICU (ISA Configuration Utility)
- CFG File Device Database

The focus of this chapter is two-fold. First, this chapter assists you in understanding Intel-defined technologies that already may exist in a Plug and Play system you are using to design and test Plug and Play hardware and software products. Second, the chapter describes the functionality of firmware and software components available from Intel, some of which you might choose to incorporate into your own Plug and Play system design.

The Intel Recommended Plug and Play Firmware Components

Intel recommends the incorporation of an ACFG BIOS into the Plug and Play system's firmware. The ACFG BIOS extends the capabilities of a standard Plug and Play BIOS through the addition of POST-time device auto-configuration routines and the ESCD storage format. As part of its efforts to promote both the ACFG and ESCD technologies, Intel provides third-party firmware vendors with an ACFG BIOS development kit containing generic source code for an ACFG BIOS with ESCD function extensions.

Additionally, Intel supplies a document entitled *Plug and Play BIOS Extensions Design Guide* that assists firmware designers in porting the base-line Intel ACFG/ESCD code to existing or developmental Plug and Play systems. For more information about ordering an Intel Plug and Play Kit, contact Intel's product ordering department at 1-800-253-3696.

New Terminology

Because the explanation of the ESCD and ACFG BIOS implementation contains many new terms and concepts, you should be familiar with the following definitions before continuing:

ACFG BIOS (Auto ConFiGuration BIOS)—The ACFG BIOS is a Plug and Play BIOS that is capable of configuring dynamically configurable devices during the system BIOS POST. Many implementations of the ACFG BIOS use NVS based ESCD data to record specific DCD resource configurations.

DCD (Dynamically Configurable Device)—A Plug and Play device whose resources are reconfigurable at runtime.

ECD (Extended Configuration Data)—Structures that have been added to the EISA format to allow configuration data for both EISA and non-EISA devices to coexist within the ESCD database.

ESCD (Extended System Configuration Data)—A data format based on the EISA slot record format. The ESCD format is used by device configuration software and firmware to record specific device configurations in system non-volatile storage. ESCD data primarily is used in non-EISA, Plug and Play systems. Its slot record format supports resource and configuration data for EISA, ISA, systemboard, PCI, and Plug and Play ISA devices.

ICU (ISA Configuration Utility)—This is an Intel-supplied utility that provides a graphical interface in which users can modify the system's resource allocation strategy. When invoked, the ICU displays a list of system resource usage and resident DCD devices. ICU users can "teach" the system what resources currently are being used by legacy devices, or create locked configurations for system DCDs.

The ICU operates functions properly with both ESCD and non-ESCD-equipped Plug and Play BIOSes. If the system BIOS does not provide ESCD extensions, the Intel ICU does not permit the user to assign locked resource configurations to DCDs because non-ESCD systems have no means of storing resource locking information.

Locked Configuration—This is a particular group of resources that the ACFG BIOS reserves for, and assigns to a particular DCD during POST. A DCD whose configuration is locked is represented in the system's ESCD by a slot record whose boardlock bit is set.

NVS (Non-Volatile Storage)—ACFG BIOS-equipped systems require on-board NVS in which to store the system's ESCD records. The ACFG BIOS can internally store ESCD in any form, such as a proprietary compressed form. Additionally, the amount of NVRAM required by an ACFG/ESCD system directly depends on how many physical slots the system provides. Therefore, the amount and type of NVRAM that the system requires or provides varies.

Slot Record—The ACFG system's NVS contains a series of EISA-style slot records, each of which describes the configuration and resource allocation for a single device and its functions. Slot records apply either to physical slots, as is the case with EISA and ISA devices, or to virtual slots, which apply to PCI and PCI-PCI bridge devices.

The Role of the ACFG System

The basic intent of the Intel ACFG solution is to ensure that during the POST the system firmware can correctly enable and configure Plug and Play devices in systems that have been configured to boot a legacy, or non-Plug and Play operating system. Users can add *locked device configuration* records to the system's ESCD storage via an OS *device configuration utility* to force the ACFG BIOS POST routines to assign specific resources to, and configure Plug and Play devices that otherwise would be left disabled and unconfigured by legacy operating systems. If devices have not been assigned locked configurations, the ACFG BIOS attempts to locate resources for these devices and configure the devices prior to the launch of the legacy operating system.

Intel's ACFG firmware works equally well whether the system has been configured to run a legacy operating system, such as DOS, or a Plug and Play system such as Windows 95. Users who upgrade an ACFG system from a legacy operating system, such as DOS, to a Plug and Play operating system, such as Windows 95, should refer to the following Note.

NOTE

During its boot sequence, the Plug and Play operating system does not reconfigure active devices whose configurations originated in the system's ESCD, thus often nullifying the benefit of runtime reconfigurability that these devices provide.

In order to guarantee the most flexibility, both Intel and Microsoft recommend that if an ACFG system has been equipped to run a Plug and Play operating system, then the user of that system should create a minimum number of

ESCD-based forced device configurations, and allow the operating system configuration management layer to correctly configure and initialize as many of the system's Plug and Play devices as possible. Using the system's device configuration utility, such as Intel's ICU, users create forced configurations only for those devices that must be assigned a specific set of resources during the POST auto-configuration process.

The Architecture of the ACFG/ESCD System

The system BIOS in an ESCD-equipped system ordinarily contains internal ACFGs, or *Auto-ConFiGuration* routines, that are capable of interpreting the contents of the system's ESCD storage and assigning locked resource configurations to the system's DCDs during POST. A Plug and Play BIOS that supports both ESCD and ACFG extensions often is called an *ACFG BIOS.* Figure 8.1 reveals the basic architecture of an ACFG BIOS with ESCD extensions.

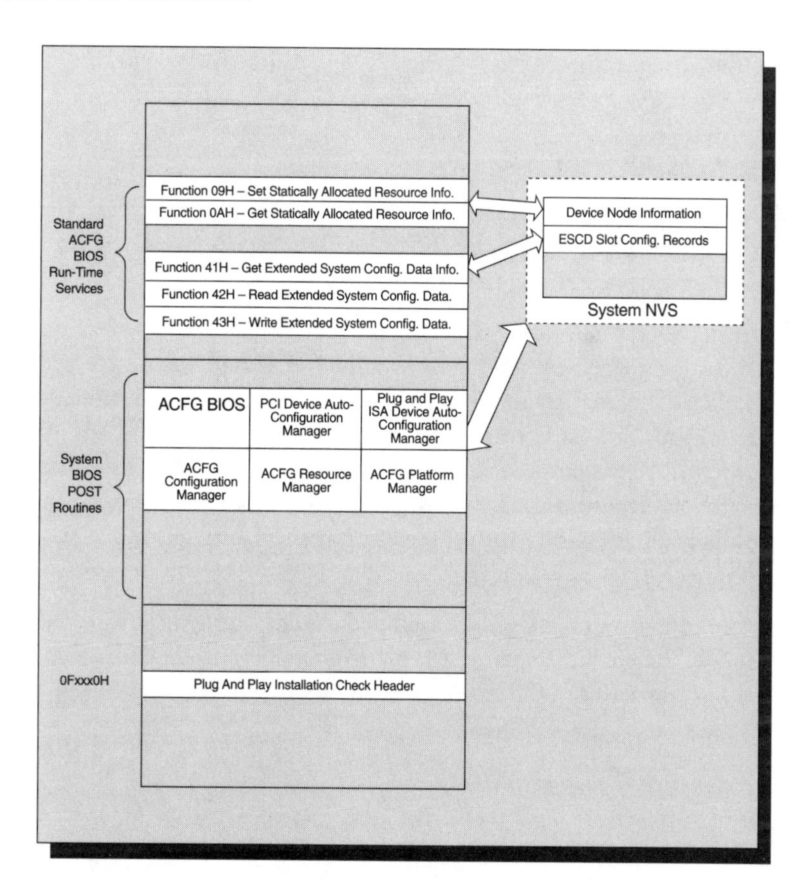

FIGURE 8.1.
The ACFG BIOS with ESCD Extensions.

An ACFG BIOS contains, in addition to a standard PC/AT system BIOS, a resource manager, an ESCD manager, a platfrom manager, a configuration manager, and a variable number of device auto-configuration managers, each of which participates in the system's POST.

The ACFG BIOS Platform Manager

The *ACFG Platfrom Manager* supplies the resource manager, ESCD manager, and configuration manager a group of platform or chipset-specific functions that abstract the peculiarities of the system's physical hardware and ESCD storage mechanism from the ACFG BIOS' core functions. Platform manager routines provide access to such system-specific details as chipset shadow RAM control, ESCD non-volatile storage access, and systemboard device resource usage.

The ACFG BIOS Resource Manager

The *ACFG BIOS resource manager* maintains a RAM-based map of system resources that is available to ACFG modules only during POST. The resource manager provides a series of functions that other ACFG modules invoke to query and update the contents of the system resource map during POST. A description of these functions appears in the Intel *Plug and Play BIOS Extensions Design Guide* document.

The ACFG BIOS ESCD Manager

The primary purpose of the *ACFG BIOS ESCD manager* is to extract device resource assignments from the system's ESCD and, in certain cases, register this information as resource usage entries in the POST resource map.

During its initialization sequence, the ESCD manager invokes functions within the platform management module to read the ESCD non-volatile storage into system RAM. The ESCD manager uses its RAM-based ESCD as a POST-time device configuration scratchpad. Similarly, during their process of scanning and enumerating system bus contents, ACFG device auto-configuration modules might introduce or change ESCD scratchpad records for newly found devices, or for devices whose current ESCD-based configurations conflict with those resources still available in the system and, therefore, require change.

If the contents of the ESCD scratchpad change during POST, it is the responsibility of the ESCD manager to invoke the platfrom manager to update the system's ESCD NVS prior to the end of POST.

The ACFG BIOS Device Auto-Configuration Manager

Device auto-configuration managers are modules whose task is to locate, identify, and configure devices on a single bus. Currently, Intel defines and provides device auto-configuration managers for the PCI and ISA bus. The ISA bus auto-configuration manager is responsible only for the Plug and Play ISA adapters installed in the system's ISA bus.

Upon having successfully configured each device on a particular bus, the auto-configuration manager updates the ESCD manager's scratchpad area to reflect any modified or newly introduced adapters. Resource information pertaining to legacy ISA adapters is handled by the configuration manager and ESCD manager during the configuration manager's initialization sequence.

If a system contains both a PCI bus and an ISA bus, the configuration manager first invokes the ISA bus auto-configuration manager.

The ACFG BIOS Configuration Manager

The *ACFG BIOS configuration manager* is responsible for initiating and controlling the entire device auto-configuration sequence.

As part of its initialization process, the configuration manager first invokes the resource manager to enable that module to create its resource map and register those resources assigned to the system's systemboard, ISA, EISA, and other legacy devices.

Once the resource map has been updated to reflect static resource assignments, the configuration manager launches the system's auto-configuration device managers. At the completion of the device auto-configuration managers, the configuration manager invokes the ESCD manager to record any changes to the system's ESCD data in non-volatile storage.

It is the responsibility of the system BIOS designer to decide, based on the specifics of the system BIOS to which ACFG support is being added, the point during POST at which the configuration manager is called and the auto-configuration process takes place. The following section includes a step-by-step description of the ACFG BIOS POST sequence.

The ACFG BIOS POST Sequence

The *ACFG device configuration* process occurs according to the diagram displayed in Figure 8.2. The following steps walk you through Figure 8.2's ACFG BIOS auto-configuration sequence.

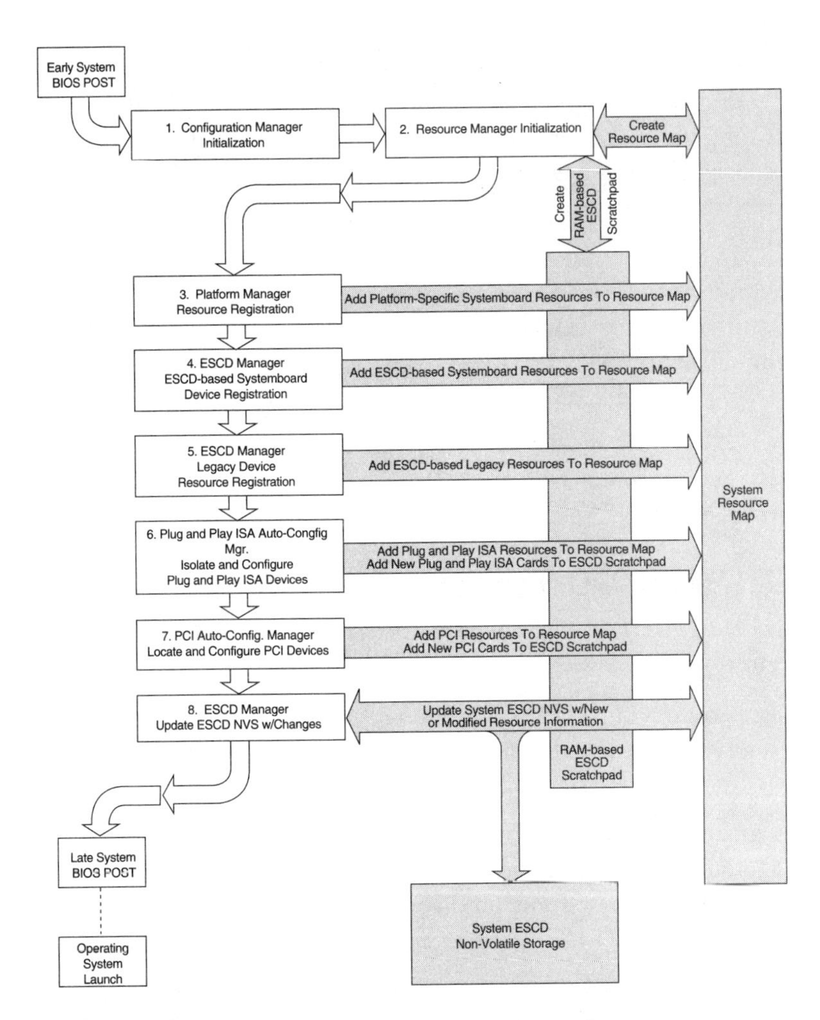

FIGURE 8.2.
The ACFG BIOS auto-configuration sequence.

1. The system BIOS POST transfers control to the ACFG Configuration Manager.
2. The ACFG Configuration Manager invokes the Resource Manager initialization routine. During its initialization sequence, the Resource Manager creates an empty resource map and reads the system's ESCD data into a RAM-based scratchpad area. After having initialized, the Resource Manager returns control to the Configuration Manager.
3. The Configuration Manager invokes the Platform Manager to allow the Platform Manager to register the resources of configurable systemboard devices. If the system contains configurable systemboard devices, the Platform Manager issues a series of calls to the Resource Manager to enter systemboard resources into the resource map, otherwise step 3 is skipped. If the system contains a

mixture of configurable and static systemboard devices, both steps 3 and 4 occur.

4. The Resource Manager translates those static, systemboard resources residing in ESCD slot 0 (systemboard device slot) functions into resource map entries.
5. The Resource Manager registers in the system resource map those ESCD-based resources belonging to static, legacy adapters, such as ISA and EISA adapters. Once the Resource Manager has registered both systemboard and legacy device resources in the system resource map, it returns control to the Configuration Manager.
6. The Configuration Manager invokes the Plug and Play ISA auto-Configuration Manager module if this component is present. The Plug and Play ISA auto-configuration module isolates each Plug and Play ISA device and creates a record of possible resource allocations for each device. The Plug and Play ISA auto-configuration then initiates a recursive process to attempt to allocate and register resources for the installed Plug and Play ISA adapters, starting with the ESCD-based last working configuration for each card, if one exists.
7. The Configuration Manager invokes the PCI auto-Configuration Manager module if this component is present. As is the case with Plug and Play ISA, the PCI auto-Configuration Manager locates each PCI device in the system and attempts to assign each PCI device resources, using that device's ESCD-based last working configuration if one exists.
8. Prior to returning control the POST, the Configuration Manager invokes the ESCD manager to update the system's ESCD non-volatile storage with any changes resulting from devices having been installed, removed, or unable to configure according to their last working configuration.

DEVICE STATES AT BOOT TIME

The ACFG BIOS adheres to the following general Plug and Play rules outlined throughout this book:

Unless specifically required for booting the system, Plug and Play ISA and PCI adapters are left in a disabled state at the time the system BIOS transfers control to the operating system boot sequence. These devices may have been assigned resources by the Plug and Play BIOS. The ACFG BIOS assigns resources to all dynamically configurable devices unless it determines that no conflict free configuration exists.

If a Plug and Play ISA or PCI device has been assigned a configuration by the system BIOS, the Plug and Play operating system may selectively enable and disable the device; however, it will not change the device's configuration.

Although the system BIOS might fail to determine a conflict-free resource allocation strategy for a particular Plug and Play ISA, or PCI device, it still is possible that the more sophisticated resource balancing algorithms in the operating system could locate resources for the device during the operating system boot sequence. In this case, the operating system may store this resource assignment into the system's ESCD in the form of a last working configuration, the intent of which is to force the ACFG BIOS to attempt to configure this device during the next system boot sequence.

The ESCD Plug and Play BIOS Extensions

The *Extended System Configuration Data (ESCD) Specification* defines three optional Plug and Play BIOS functions whose primary purpose is to enable the operating system configuration manager or utility to read and write the system's NVS-based ESCD.

Additionally, the *ESCD Specification* defines the ESCD format, which consists of EISA-like slot records designed to store the configuration of the system's legacy and dynamically configurable devices.

If a Plug and Play system supports ESCD, then its BIOS extensions enable the operating system configuration manager or device configuration utility to read, modify, and write EISA-style ESCD device configuration records within system NVRAM.

The ESCD data is store in NVRAM because system BIOS's that contain ACFG functions, refer to ESCD records during POST to assist its device configuration process. Therefore, the ESCD data must exist in an OS-independent medium (NVRAM) that is shareable by both the BIOS and the operating system.

WHAT MAKES A DEVICE DYNAMICALLY CONFIGURABLE?

Dynamically Configurable Devices, or *DCDs,* are those devices whose resource allocation is modifiable at runtime. This book discusses the two currently available types of DCDs: the PCI device and the Plug and Play ISA device. A DCD device is considered to be *enabled* if it is using system resources; otherwise, the DCD is considered *disabled.*

PCMCIA, or PC cards are not included in the family of Dynamically Configurable Devices because they can be assigned a configuration only during the PC Card insertion process. Once a PC Card has been configured by its Card Services client, or super-client, it retains that configuration until such time that the user removes the PC Card from the system or removes power from the system.

ESCD-Specific Plug and Play BIOS Functions

The system BIOS supports the Plug and Play BIOS functions `GetESCDInfo` (`41H`), `ReadESCDData` (`42H`), and `WriteESCDData` (`43H`). Collectively, these functions provide the caller with a copy of the BIOS' internal ESCD slot database, and enable the caller to read and write the contents of the system's NVS-based ESCD. A similar description of the functions below appears in both the *Extended System Configuration Data Specification* and *Plug and Play BIOS Specification.*

Plug and Play BIOS Function *41H—GetESCDInfo*

Function `41H`, or `GetESCDInfo`, returns information that the calling application requires in order to properly read or write the contents of the system's ESCD database. As discussed in Chapter 3, the calling application retrieves the entry point for `GetESCDInfo` and all other Plug and Play BIOS functions from the Plug and Play BIOS Installation Check Header.

Following is the C language declaration for the `GetESCDInfo` function:

```
int FAR (pFuncEntry)(Function, MinWriteBuffer, MaxESCDSize, NVSAddress, DataSelector)
;

int Function ;                         // Always = 41H for GetESCDInfo
unsigned int far * MinWriteBuffer ; // Minimum size of write buffer
unsigned int far * MaxESCDSize ;     // Maximum allowable ESCD in bytes
unsigned long far * NVSAddress ;     // 32-bit Physical Address Of ESCD
unsigned int DataSelector ;          // Caller-Supplied R/W data
                                       // segment/selector.
```

`Function`—This integer variable specifies the caller's function. It is always `41H` for `GetESCDInfo`.

`MinWriteBuffer`—`MinWriteBuffer` is a far pointer to a caller-supplied integer variable to receive the minimum ESCD write buffer size. Applications never call `WriteESCDData` with an ESCD buffer whose size is less than (`*MinWriteBuffer`) bytes.

`MaxESCDSize`—`MaxESCDSize` is a far pointer to a caller-supplied integer variable to receive the maximum size of the system's ESCD NVS buffer. Applications that call `ReadESCDData` supply a buffer of at least (`*MaxESCDSize`) bytes. Additionally, applications never call `WriteESCDData` with a buffer containing more than (`*MaxESCDSize`) bytes of ESCD data.

`NVSAddress`—`NVSAddress` is a far pointer to a caller-supplied unsigned long variable to receive the physical address of the system's ESCD. `NVSAddress` applies only to systems whose ESCD storage is memory-mapped, otherwise the BIOS sets the value of (`*NVSAddress`) to zero.

`DataSelector`—`DataSelector` is a 16-bit, caller-supplied segment or selector that enables ESCD routines within the Plug and Play BIOS to read and write its own local variables and ESCD data if that data is stored in a memory mapped fashion. If the calling application is executing in real mode, then it retrieves the `DataSelector` value from the Plug and Play BIOS installation check header. Protected mode applications must build a CPU descriptor table selector for the Protected Mode Base Data Segment that appears in the BIOS' Installation Check Header.

NOTE

Although calling applications can obtain the physical address of the system's memory-mapped ESCD data via the `GetESCDInfo NVSAddress` argument, those applications never should attempt to read or write this data directly because the mechanism that the BIOS uses to store and retrieve ESCD data is implementation-specific.

The `NVSAddress` value is supplied because the memory-mapped ESCD data might reside in a segment different than the one described in the Plug and Play BIOS installation check header. When this occurs, the BIOS' Protected Mode Base Data Segment is inadequate for describing the segments of both the ESCD data and the BIOS's local private data.

Plug and Play BIOS Function *42H—ReadESCDData*

Function `42H`, or `ReadESCDData`, writes the system's ESCD data into a caller-supplied buffer. The calling application is responsible for invoking the `GetESCDInfo` function to determine the maximum possible size of the system's ESCD data and allocate a buffer of at least `MaxESCDSize` prior to issuing any calls to `ReadESCDData`.

Following is the C language declaration for the `ReadESCDData` function:

```
int FAR (pFuncEntry)(Function, fpBuffer, ESCDSelector, DataSelector) ;

int Function ;                      // Always = 42H for ReadESCDData
unsigned char far * pBuffer;        // ptr to caller-supplied buffer
unsigned int ESCDSelector;          // Caller supplied selector for ESCD
unsigned int DataSelector;          // Caller-Supplied R/W BIOS data
                                    // segment/selector.
```

Following are descriptions of the arguments for `ReadESCDData`.

`Function`—This integer variable specifies the caller's function. It is always `42H` for `ReadESCDData`.

pBuffer—pBuffer is a far pointer to a caller-supplied buffer large enough to receive the system's ESCD data based on the value MaxESCDSize returned by a prior call to GetESCDInfo.

ESCDSelector—ESCDSelector is a caller-supplied selector that enables the system BIOS to read and write memory-mapped ESCD data within a protected mode environment. If the BIOS' GetESCDInfo function returns a non-zero value in its NVSAddress field, then the calling application is responsible for creating and supplying a valid, 64KB read/write limit protected mode selector in the ESCDSelector field during each call to ReadESCDData. Otherwise, the value that the caller supplies in the ESCDSelector field is not used.

DataSelector—DataSelector is a 16-bit, caller-supplied segment or selector that enables ESCD routines within the Plug and Play BIOS to read and write its own local variables and ESCD data if that data is stored in a memory-mapped fashion. If the calling application is executing in real mode, then it retrieves the DataSelector value from the Plug and Play BIOS installation check header. Protected mode applications must build a CPU descriptor table selector for the Protected Mode Base Data Segment that appears in the BIOS' Installation Check Header.

The calling application determines the number of significant bytes in the ESCD data from the ESCD Configuration Header. The ESCD data format is discussed later in this chapter.

Plug and Play BIOS Function *43H—WriteESCDData*

Function 43H, or WriteESCDData, writes the caller's updated ESCD data into the system's non-volatile storage. The calling application is responsible for ensuring that the ESCD data is in the correct format and does not exceed the maximum size of the system's ESCD NVS according to the MaxESCDSize value returned by a prior call to GetESCDInfo.

Following is the C language declaration for the WriteESCDData function:

```
int FAR (pFuncEntry)(Function, fpBuffer, ESCDSelector, DataSelector) ;
int Function ;    // Always = 43H for WriteESCDData
unsigned char far * pBuffer;        // ptr to caller-supplied buffer
unsigned int ESCDSelector;          // Caller supplied selector for ESCD
unsigned int DataSelector;          // Caller-Supplied R/W BIOS data
                                    // segment/selector.
```

Following are descriptions of the arguments for WriteESCDData.

Function—This integer variable specifies the caller's function. It is always 43H for WriteESCDData.

pBuffer—pBuffer is a far pointer to a caller-supplied buffer containing updated ESCD data.

`ESCDSelector`—`ESCDSelector` is a caller-supplied selector that enables the system BIOS to read and write memory-mapped ESCD data within a protected mode environment. If the BIOS' `GetESCDInfo` function returns a non-zero value in its `NVSAddress` field, then the calling application is responsible for creating and supplying a valid, 64KB read/write limit protected mode selector in the `ESCDSelector` field during each call to `WriteESCDData`. Otherwise, the value that the caller supplies in the `ESCDSelector` field is not used.

`DataSelector`—`DataSelector` is a 16-bit, caller-supplied segment or selector that enables ESCD routines within the Plug and Play BIOS to read and write its own local variables and ESCD data if that data is stored in a memory mapped fashion. If the calling application is executing in real mode, then it retrieves the `DataSelector` value from the Plug and Play BIOS installation check header. Protected mode applications must build a CPU descriptor table selector for the Protected Mode Base Data Segment that appears in the BIOS' Installation Check Header.

Prior to writing the new ESCD data to its NVS, the BIOS determines the number of significant bytes in the new ESCD data from the ESCD Configuration Header.

The Intel Plug and Play Solution Software Components

As mentioned earlier in this chapter, the Intel Plug and Play software components include the following:

- The ESCD format
- Intel CM DOS Device Driver
- DOS ICU (ISA Configuration Utility)
- Windows ICU (ISA Configuration Utility)
- CFG File Device Database

Intel's Plug and Play software brings many aspects of Plug and Play to the DOS/Win 3.1 environment.

With the Intel CM driver installed, CM-aware applications and device drivers can detect resource assignments for each device in the system. Device driver subsystems such as PCMCIA Card Services can dynamically allocate and deallocate remaining resources to hot-swappable PC Cards. High-level applications such as the ICU allow users to "teach" the system about newly added or removed legacy adapters, and also to permanently assign specific resources to dynamically configurable devices.

INTEL'S SOFTWARE IS NOT QUITE TRUE PLUG AND PLAY

Intel's Plug and Play software is limited by legacy applications and drivers installed in the system that continue to manage system resources in legacy fashion, by such means as "snooping" for system peripherals or by configuring their devices according to command line configuration parameters.

For example, the DOS' EMM386.EXE driver might, as part of its load sequence, detect and allocate expanded memory page frames within the reserved 384KB system address space located between physical addresses `A0000H` and `FFFF0H`.

Because the EMM driver is not Plug and Play aware, it does not convey the results of its EMS (Expanded Memory Specification) page frame assignments to the Intel CM driver. Similarly, the Intel CM driver has no way to detect EMM-assigned page frames because the EMM driver might load and perform its page frame assignments subsequent to the CM driver's load time initialization sequence. A system address range conflict ensues, because both the CM and the EMM386 driver think that the EMS region "belongs" to them. This system address conflict is a result of mixing Plug and Play and legacy software components, and by no means represents shortcomings in the design of either the EMM386 driver, or the Intel CM.

In fact, the situation described here could be solved by adding EMS page detection to the Intel CM driver and stipulating that users always load the EMM386.EXE driver prior the Intel's CM in the system's CONFIG.SYS. In general, the Intel software solution is only 100 percent effective in systems containing no legacy applications and no legacy device drivers.

The Intel DOS/Win 3.1 software solution has laid the groundwork for true Plug and Play operating system implementations, such as Windows 95. Additionally, Intel's Plug and Play software suite provides a vehicle by which developers can create custom Plug and Play aware DOS/Win 3.1 systems.

The ESCD Format

The system's ESCD data is used both by the ACFG BIOS and the operating system's device drivers and applications. Therefore, a description of ESCD applies to both the system's firmware and software components. The author's decision to describe ESCD in the software section rather than the firmware section is arbitrary.

Strictly speaking, the term ESCD refers to the EISA-like format that the ESCD-aware Plug and Play BIOS uses to communicate resource information with the operating system configuration manager or device configuration utility. When used as a noun, as in "The ESCD data resides in NVS," it instead refers to the collection of EISA-like slot records that comprise the resource allocation database for a particular system.

The ESCD format is a superset of the EISA slot record data format. Within an EISA system, the ECU (EISA Configuration Utility) and system BIOS share a set of CMOS-based records describing the configuration of each EISA slot and its contents. Similarly, within an ESCD Plug and Play system, the system BIOS and device configuration utility share an NVS-based database that describes the configuration of the system's EISA and non-EISA slots.

To configure an ESCD-equipped PCI or ISA system, the user runs the ICU, or a similar device configuration utility. To configure an ESCD-equipped EISA system, he or she runs an upgraded ECU capable of reading, modifying, and writing ESCD data.

INTEL SOFTWARE SUPPORT FOR THE NON-ESCD BIOS

The Intel CM driver and ICU utility support systems whose Plug and Play BIOS does not provide ESCD extensions, although this support is limited to recording legacy device usage via the standard Plug and Play BIOS functions `09H` (`SetStaticResInfo`) and `0AH` (`GetStaticResInfo`) and does not allow for locked DCD configurations.

The ESCD BIOS deals with resource configurations on a per-board basis, whereas a non-ESCD Plug and Play BIOS treats all legacy device information as if it belongs to a single, static super-device and attempts to configure dynamic devices in such a fashion that they don't conflict with the super-device's NVS-based static resources.

Many system vendors have decided that BIOS support for the ESCD extensions introduces into certain types of systems (such as portables, embedded, PCs, and desktop terminal systems) unnecessary cost and complexity. Because both ESCD and non-ESCD systems are widely available in the marketplace, designers of operating system level device configuration utilities, such as the Intel ICU, must support both ESCD and non-ESCD systems.

The ESCD Slot Concept

Like the older EISA format, the ESCD format consists of a series of slot records. The EISA specification, which applies only to EISA-equipped systems, defines a 320-byte,

CMOS-based slot record for each physical EISA slot. If an EISA system's slot is empty, its corresponding physical slot record contains a null record.

EISA systems contain a fixed number of slots, whereas ESCD systems support the additional concept of virtual slots for the purpose of handling dynamically configurable devices, such as PCI devices. In both formats, slot 0 is reserved for systemboard device functions, and slots 1-15 correspond to physical, expansion slots. In a non-EISA ESCD system, expansion slots are assigned logical, rather than physical slot numbers.

NOTE

A definition of the EISA format appears in the *Extended System Configuration Data Specification*, as well as the EISA Specification itself. The ESCD specification is available via the CompuServe Plug and Play forum, which CompuServe users can access by typing `GO PLUGPLAY`. The EISA specification is available from BCPR services, whose address appears in Chapter 1.

ESCD Slot Record 0—Systemboard Devices

Virtual slot 0 in the ESCD is reserved for ISA-compatible systemboard devices. The virtual slot 0 information consists of a variable number of EISA functions, each of which describes the resource consumption a single ISA systemboard device.

Device configuration information corresponding to systemboard resident PCI devices appears in the form of virtual slot records. For each systemboard resident PCI device, the ESCD contains one virtual slot record. Following is a description of virtual slot records.

ESCD Slot Records 1-15—Expansion Slots

Slot records 1-15, the system's expansion slot records, contain configuration information for the system's true EISA adapters or Plug and Play ISA adapters, if they exist. In a system that supports neither style adapter, an ESCD record whose slot number falls in the range 1-15 is invalid. If a slot supports EISA devices, then the slot number in its ESCD record indicates the physical slot number. For non-EISA slots, the slot number within an ESCD record refers to a logical, rather than physical slot number.

ESCD Slot Records 16-64—Expansion Slots

Slots 16-64 apply to virtual devices, the ESCD records that correspond to virtual devices in slots 16-64, are called *virtual slot records.* Currently, only PCI devices belong to the category of virtual devices. Each virtual slot record contains one function entry for each function present on the PCI device that resides in the virtual slot.

NOTE

The ESCD format does not imply what method the system BIOS uses to store its device configuration information in NVS. Only the configuration manager or device configuration utility must deal with ESCD data in its documented form. Internally, the system BIOS may store this information in the form that is easiest for the BIOS developer.

For example, once a device configuration utility has invoked Plug and Play BIOS function `43H` (`WriteESCD`) to store its configuration information, the ESCD-aware Plug and Play BIOS may compress this data prior to storing it in system NVS in order to conserve space.

Also, the ESCD-aware system BIOS must be able to translate between ESCD format and device node format in order to support Plug and Play BIOS functions `00H-02H`. In order to facilitate the BIOS' support of both device nodes and ESCD records, the BIOS developer might store resource configuration information in a format that easily translates to either data format.

The ESCD Format as a Superset of the EISA Format

Both the EISA format and the ESCD format share the concept of slot records. The ESCD format is designed to extend the use of the EISA format in such a way that existing ECUs (EISA Configuration Utilities) can be upgraded readily to provide device configuration capabilities to non-EISA Plug and Play systems, such as those containing ISA, PCI, or both ISA and PCI adapter slots. Figure 8.3 displays the ESCD format.

The ESCD Specification introduces the following new structures to the standard EISA format.

The *ESCD_CFGHDR*

The `ESCD_CFGHDR` is the first structure that appears in the ESCD. The `ESCD_CFGHDR` adheres to the following format:

Table 8.1. The `ESCD_CFGGDR` format.

Offset	*Size*	*Description*
`00H`	`WORD`	`ESCDSize`—Total size of the ESCD NVRAM image
`02H`	`DWORD`	Signature—Always equals `0x47464341`, or ASCII `ACFG`
`06H`	`BYTE`	`MinorVersion`—The BCD version of the ESCD format in use

Offset	*Size*	*Description*
07H	BYTE	`MajorVersion`—The BCD version of the ESCD format in use
08H	BYTE	`BoardCount`—The number of slot records in ESCD image
09H	3*BYTE	Reserved for future use

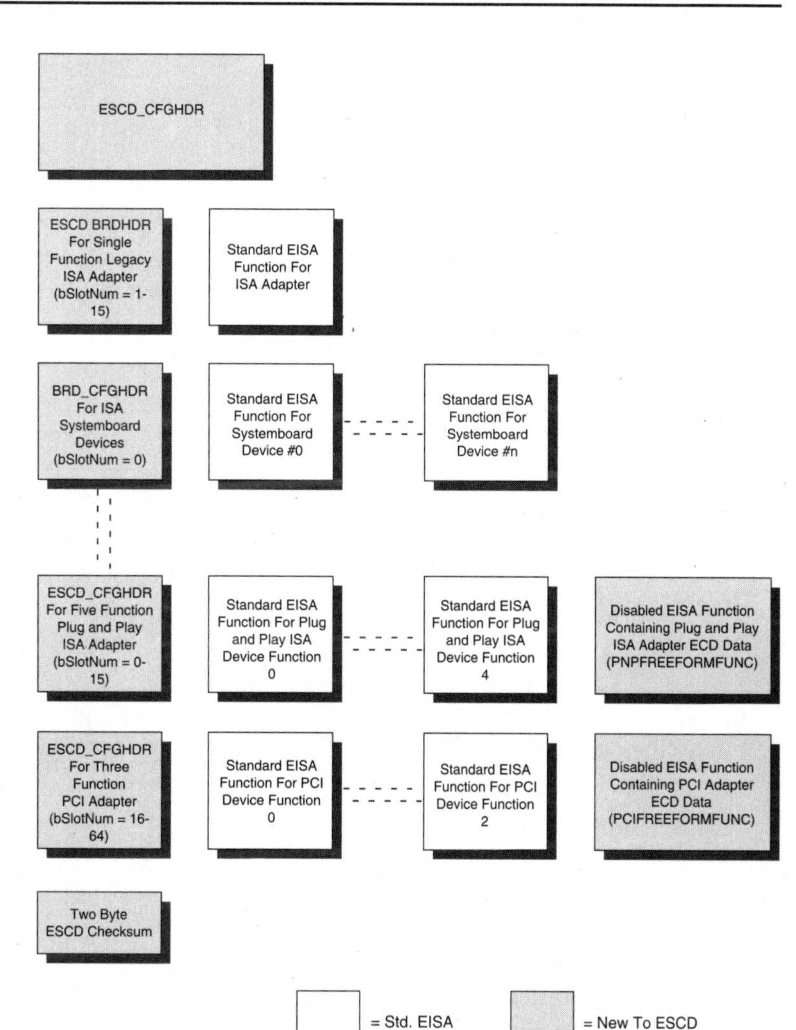

FIGURE 8.3.
The ESCD format.

The *PNPFREEFORMFUNC* and *PCIFREEFORMFUNC* ECDs

ESCD-resident records corresponding to dynamically configurable devices, such as Plug and Play ISA and PCI devices, contain a disabled free-form function call an *ECD*, or *Extended Configuration Data* record. The ECD record for a DCD appears as the last function within the DCD's slot record. Currently, the ESCD specification defines two separate formats for ECDs. The first format, PCPFREEFORMFUNC, applies to Plug and Play ISA adapters, while the second, PCIFREEFORMFUNC, pertains to PCI devices.

Because ECDs appear as disabled functions, the operating system device configuration utility (such as ICU, ECU, and so on) ignores the ECDs' contents. This enables the ESCD to contain function-specific configuration information that is neither examined nor altered by legacy EISA software unfamiliar with the ESCD format.

Both the PCIFREEFORMFUNC ECD and the PNPFREEFORMFUNC ECD contain a structure known as the ECD_FREEFORMBRDHDR. The ECD_FREEFORMBRDHDR identifies the type of bus architecture to which the device conforms, and contains bit fields describing the status of as many as sixteen individual functions resident on that device. The format of the ECD_FREEFORMBRDHDR appears in Table 8.2.

Table 8.2. Format of the ECD_FREEFORMBRDHDR.

Offset	*Size*	*Description*
00H	DWORD	Signature—Always equals 0x47464341, or ASCII ACFG
04H	BYTE	MinorVersion—The BCD version of the ESCD format in use
05H	BYTE	MajorVersion—The BCD version of the ESCD format in use
06H	BYTE	Device Type: 01H equals Legacy ISA 02H equals EISA 04H equals PCI 08H equals PCMCIA 10H equals Plug and Play ISA 20H equals MCA (MicroChannel Architecture)
07H	BYTE	Reserved
08H	WORD	Device Function Enable/Disable Bitmap Bit[*n*]—If 1, function #*n* is disabled
0AH	WORD	Device Function Configuration Error Bitmap Bit[*n*]—If 1, function #*n* failed to configure properly

Offset	*Size*	*Description*
0CH	WORD	Device Function Reconfigurability Bit Map Bit[*n*]—If 1, function #*n* is reconfigurable
0EH	2*BYTE	Reserved

NOTE

For a description of the relationship between the ESCD Device Function Enable/Disable Bitmap and Device Function Reconfigurability Bitmap and similar bit fields defined by the EISA Specification, consult the *Extended System Configuration Data Specification.*

The Format of the *PCIFREEFORMFUNC*

The PCIFREEFORMFUNC ECD structure appears as the last function in the virtual slot record for a PCI device. In addition to the ECD_FREEFORMBRDHDR described previously, the PCIFREEFORMFUNC contains an array of ECD_PCIBRDID structures. The format of the ECD_PCIBRDID structure and the PCIFREEFORMFUNC ECD is shown in Table 8.3.

Table 8.3. The format of the ECD_PCIBRDID structure.

Offset	*Size*	*Description*
00H	BYTE	PCIBusNum—PCI bus number for this device
01H	BYTE	PCIDevFuncNum—PCI device and function number
02H	WORD	PCI Device ID for this device
04H	WORD	PCI Vendor ID for this device
06H	WORD	Reserved

Table 8.3 shows the format of the PCIFREEFORMFUNC ECD.

Table 8.4. The format of the PCIFREEFORMFUNC ECD.

Offset	*Size*	*Description*
00H	WORD	ECDSize—Size in bytes of this ECD structure
02H	BYTE	Always equals 1

continues

Table 8.4. continued

Offset	*Size*	*Description*
03H	BYTE	Always equals 0
04H	BYTE	Always equals 0C0H, signifying a disabled free-form function
05H	BYTE	FFSize—Size in bytes of free form data that follows
06H	16*BYTE	ECD_FREEFORMBRDHDR struct as described previously
16H	Varies	Maximum of eight ECD_PCIBRDID structures

The Format of the *PNPFREEFORMFUNC*

The PNPFREEFORMFUNC ECD structure appears as the last function in the virtual slot record for a Plug and Play ISA device. In addition to the ECD_FREEFORMBRDHDR described previously, the PNPFREEFORMFUNC contains an array of ECD_PNPBRDID structures. Table 8.5 shows the format of the ECD_PNPBRDID structure and Table 8.6 shows the PNPFREEFORMFUNC ECD.

Table 8.5. The format of the ECD_PNPBRDID structure.

Offset	*Size*	*Description*
00H	4*BYTE	Plug and Play ISA Device Vendor ID
04H	4*BYTE	Plug and Play ISA Device Serial Number

Table 8.6. The format of the PNPFREEFORMFUNC ECD.

Offset	*Size*	*Description*
00H	WORD	ECDSize—Always equals 28 for PNPFREEFORMFUNC
02H	BYTE	Always equals 1
03H	BYTE	Always equals 0
04H	BYTE	Always equals 0C0H, signifying a disabled free-form function
05H	BYTE	FFSize—Size in bytes of free-form data that follows; always equals 24 for PNPFREEFORMFUNC
06H	16*BYTE	ECD_FREEFORMBRDHDR struct as described previously
16H	Varies	A single ECD_PNPBRDID structure

The Role of ESCD

In an ideal Plug and Play environment, the system contains DCDs that are capable of using any resources assigned them by the Plug and Play BIOS, whether or not the BIOS supports ESCD extensions. Unless the system simply is exhausted of resources, the Plug and Play operating system is able to completely configure all DCDs to work in concert with static or systemboard devices. Applications and device drivers in the ideal system are able to communicate with DCDs, regardless of the resources the system BIOS or configuration manager has assigned those devices.

The ESCD subsystem, in tandem with the operating system configuration manager or configuration utility, is designed to cover those situations in which the capability to satisfy all resource allocation strategies is less than ideal.

ESCD Support for the Non-Compliant DCD

One example of a less than ideal resource allocation situation is a system that contains a DCD or group of DCDs that are non-compliant, and can only use a certain subset of the system's IRQ channels, DMA channels or other resources. If the system BIOS includes ESCD extensions, then the user can run an operating system level device configuration utility, such as the Intel ICU, to designate a locked configuration of specific system resources that the system BIOS or configuration manager will assign to the non-compliant device(s) during the system boot process.

As part of its load process on an ACFG system, the ICU reads the system's ESCD data into a local buffer, which it uses as a scratchpad as the user modifies the system's resource usage. When the user has finished entering his or her locked configuration for a DCD, the ICU modifies the device's slot record within its local copy of the ESCD and invokes Plug and Play BIOS function `43H` (`WriteESCD`) to store the ESCD information back to the system's NVS.

ESCD Support for the Legacy Operating System

The presence of ESCD enables the ACFG BIOS to assign specific resources to DCDs in a system that has a non-Plug and Play operating system (such as MS-DOS). In this type of system, the user runs an ESCD-aware device configuration utility (provided one exists for that operating system), which modifies the contents of ESCD NVS to reflect the user's DCD configuration settings. During subsequent boots of the system, the ACFG BIOS configures the system's dynamic devices according to the newly modified system NVS contents.

TIP

Microsoft encourages system BIOS designers to design the system's Plug and Play BIOS in such a manner that if a Plug and Play operating system is executing the system BIOS configures only those devices required to boot the system. This allows the more powerful device profilers, enumerators, and configurators within its Windows 95 operating system to perform resource balancing and reconfiguration for all other system DCDs, including Plug and Play PCMCIA Host Bus Adapters and PC Cards.

Within their ROM-based system setup utilities, many Plug and Play systems provide the user a menu with selections that specify the degree to which the system BIOS will configure dynamic devices. Figure 8.4 shows an example of Plug and Play support within the system setup utility.

If the user has installed a non-Plug and Play operating system, he or she selects FULL configuration, in which case the system BIOS attempts to assign resources to, and initialize each DCD in the machine. If the user instead has installed a Plug and Play operating system, he or she selects PARTIAL, thereby instructing the system BIOS to initialize only those devices required to boot the system.

Microsoft has proposed a third option, called AUTO. A Plug and Play BIOS running in AUTO mode detects the presence of a Plug and Play operating system, and if one is installed, it automatically switches to PARTIAL configuration.

But how does the BIOS "know" that a Plug and Play operating system is executing? During its boot sequence, the Plug and Play operating system invokes function `04H` (`SEND_MESSAGE`) within the Plug and Play BIOS' runtime services with the message `PNP_OS_ACTIVE`.

Having received the `PNP_OS_ACTIVE` message, the Plug and Play BIOS records the presence of the Plug and Play operating system in its NVS and during subsequent boot sequences configures only those devices (such as video adapter, keyboard, and fixed disk) needed to boot the operating system, with the assumption that the Plug and Play operating system has been permanently installed. The FULL and PARTIAL options remain in the system setup menu as a means of overriding the system BIOS' assumptions concerning the operating system.

Figure 8.4 displays a hypothetical system setup utility that provides the FULL, PARTIAL, and AUTO configuration options.

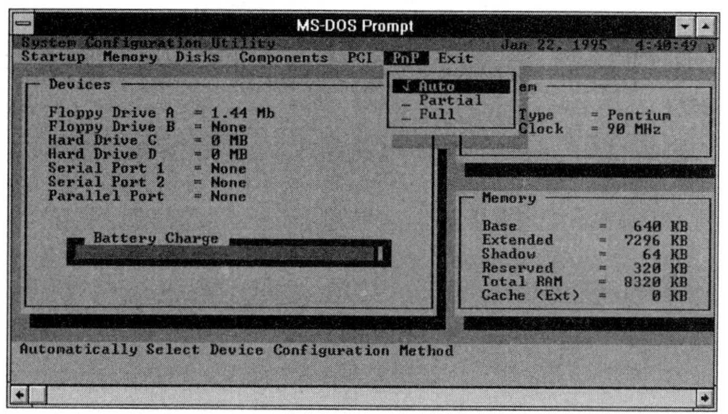

FIGURE 8.4.
System setup utility support for Plug and Play.

Hopefully, this does not suggest that a Plug and Play system without ESCD extensions can support only Plug and Play operating systems. As just mentioned, a Plug and Play BIOS operating in FULL configuration mode will assign resources to, and configure all DCD devices within the system if adequate resources for those devices are available. The ESCD Specification describes the need for the ESCD extensions in the following fashion:

> The Plug and Play BIOS describes two interfaces to read and write (non Plug and Play device resource) information; functions `09H` and `0AH` (Set and Get Statically Allocated Resource Information). The information provided through these interfaces is sufficient to allow for the full auto-configuration of Plug and Play devices with platforms running Plug and Play operating systems. Platforms with non-Plug and Play operating systems or employing add-on Plug and Play support (such as Plug and Play Kit for MS-DOS and Windows), may not be able to automatically configure all Plug and Play devices in all cases. For support of these systems, it is recommended that the Extended System Configuration Data (ESCD) format be employed to store configuration information in non-volatile storage.

ESCD Support for Legacy Application Software

Certain older applications expect hardware devices to have been configured with a particular set of resources.

Older fixed-disk diagnostic programs, for example, expect the system's primary fixed-disk controller's task registers to appear at locations `1F0H-1F7H` in system I/O address space and to use IRQ channel `14`.

With the advent of dynamically configurable devices, however, it's conceivable for the user or Plug and Play operating system to configure a Plug and Play ISA or PCI IDE controller in such a way that its task registers appear at `4F0H`, `5F0H`, and so on. In this

case, the legacy software does not function properly because it has no mechanism by which to locate the Plug and Play IDE controller's task register base address.

In an ESCD-equipped system, the user could solve the legacy application's problem by assigning a locked resource configuration to the disk controller to specify that, if found during POST, the Plug and Play IDE controller should be configured to use the standard fixed-disk I/O range and IRQ values.

From a Plug and Play standpoint, such applications are ill-behaved and undermine the basic advantage of DCDs. By forcing a locked configuration onto a dynamically configurable Plug and Play device, the user effectively transforms the device back into a legacy device whose *jumpers* or *switches* now reside in ESCD storage rather than on the device itself.

The Intel Configuration Manager

Previous chapters have outlined various processes for identifying, initializing, and configuring Plug and Play devices at the lowest level via register I/O, firmware interfaces, and device driver suites, at the same time making references to higher-level software constructs such as the system enumerator and configuration manager. This approach hopefully has given you the necessary building blocks for understanding the next highest level in the Plug and Play system, the Configuration Manager.

Role of the Configuration Manager

The Intel CM driver, DWCFGMG.SYS, is a DOS device driver that installs itself into DOS' device chain via the CONFIG.SYS system startup file. Once loaded, the function of the Configuration Manager is to create a map of system device and resources and provide runtime CM (Configuration Management) and CA (Configuration Access) functions to DOS and Windows 3.1 applications, device drivers, and system resource configuration utilities.

Intel's CM driver is capable of reading, modifying, and updating the contents of the system's ESCD data if the system's BIOS supports the ESCD extensions. Because the CM has a more robust resource balancing algorithm than the ACFG BIOS, it may, in some cases, locate adequate resources for Plug and Play devices left unconfigured or disabled by the system BIOS.

The CM does not immediately apply newly found configurations to Plug and Play devices, as it may be too late in the boot process for the system to take advantage of a Plug and Play device's expansion ROM, boot ROM, serial/parallel ports, and so on. Instead, the CM stores newly found device configurations in the system's ESCD nonvolatile storage, and expects the ACFG BIOS to apply the configuration during the next system POST sequence.

Within non-ESCD Plug and Play systems, or non-Plug and Play systems, the CM stores device configurations in a disk-based file called the ESCD.RF file. The contents of the ESCD.RF file are identical to those that the CM writes into the system's non-volatile storage on an ESCD system. This shared format approach simplifies the CM driver's processing of next-boot configurations based in either system NVS or in the ESCD.RF file.

CONFIGURABILITY IS LIMITED ONLY BY DEVICE CAPABILITIES

In most cases, the non-ESCD Plug and Play BIOS equally is capable of providing conflict-free resource configurations for each of the system's dynamically configurable devices, and ensuring that the devices have been enabled to operate in a system having no Plug and Play operating system.

The extent to which the non-ESCD Plug and Play BIOS can configure the system's dynamically configurable devices depends on the range of resources that these devices can use, not on the BIOS implementation.

The CM Boot Sequence

Intel's CM driver, DWCFGMG.SYS, loads via the DOS CONFIG.SYS startup file. Users can edit the CONFIG.SYS CM driver `load` statement in order to tailor the driver's `load` sequence and runtime profile. Following is the syntax for the CM driver's load statement:

```
DEVICE=d:\path\DWCFGMG.SYS {/nolock} {/nodcd} {/file} {/pmeisa} {/static} {/novcpi}
```

The syntax `{/arg}` implies that the argument is optional, and if omitted, the driver will revert to a default value for that option. Following are descriptions for each CM driver option:

> `/nolock`—If specified, the `CM_LockConfig` and `CM_UnlockConfig` functions are discarded at install time and are not available at runtime. The `/nolock` option reduces the runtime size of the CM driver by approximately 30KB. Applications that want to add or delete locked records within the ESCD either supply their own internal equivalent of the `CM_LockConfig` and `CMUnlockConfig` functions, or simply do not provide resource capabilities if the CM driver has been loaded with the `/nolock` command line option.
>
> `/nodcd`—If specified, the Intel CM driver aborts its installation if the system contains no dynamically configurable devices (DCDs).
>
> `/file`—The `/file` argument, if present, forces the Intel CM driver to store its ESCD information into the root directory ESCD.RF file, rather than the

system's ESCD non-volatile storage. On an ESCD-equipped system, the file-based ESCD storage method provides developers a simple means of debugging applications that read and write ESCD information. On non-ESCD Plug and Play systems, or legacy systems, the file-based ESCD storage method is the standard mechanism that the CM driver uses to record device configuration parameters.

`/pmeisa`—If specified, the `/pmeisa` argument indicates to the CM driver that the system supports protected mode EISA functions. By default, the CM driver supplies no protected mode Configuration Access (`_CA`) functions for EISA.

`/static`—If specified, the CM driver remains loaded in its entirety at runtime. Otherwise, the CM driver dynamically swaps portions of its runtime interface in and out of RAM only during caller access to its runtime Configuration Access (`_CA`) and Configuration Management (`_CM`) functions. According to Intel literature, specification of the `/static` command-line option increases the runtime size of the CM driver by approximately 20KB.

`/novcpi`—If specified, the CM driver will not use VCPI functions to switch to real mode prior to invoking ACFG BIOS or Plug and Play BIOS functions within the system firmware.

The CM driver performs the following functions during its load sequence:

1. Scan the system's `F0000H` segment for the Plug and Play BIOS Installation Check Header to detect the presence or absence of Plug and Play BIOS. If the system provides a Plug and Play BIOS, record the real and protected mode entry point information, and runtime data selector information from the Installation Check Header.
2. Invoke the Plug and Play BIOS function `40H` to determine the number of installed Plug and Play ISA adapters and the `READ_DATA` port address that the BIOS has assigned to these adapters.
3. Perform the Plug and Play ISA isolation sequence to verify the consistency of Plug and Play ISA information returned by Plug and Play BIOS function `40H`. Add all Plug and Play ISA adapters to a CM-resident device map. If the information returned by function `40H` does not match the results of the CM Plug and Play isolation sequence, the CM marks those devices in its device map that still require configuration.
4. Check for the presence of a PCI BIOS by issuing the `PCI_BIOS_PRESENT` function as described in Chapter 4. If the system supports a PCI BIOS, iteratively scan the system's PCI bus for PCI devices and add these devices to the CM device map. Mark any unconfigured PCI devices in the DM device map.

5. Populate the CM resource map with static device resources either by invoking Plug and Play BIOS function `0AH` (`GetStaticResInfo`) or function `42H` (`ReadESCDData`) if this function is present.
6. Populate the CM resource map with dynamic resources that have been allocated to DCDs by the system BIOS.
7. If any DCDs have been left unconfigured by the system BIOS, attempt to locate resources for these devices by comparing the resource needs of the remaining unconfigured devices and the contents of the CM resource map. If sufficient resources exist for unconfigured DCDs, record these configurations in the system's ESCD, or ESCD.RF file if ESCD services are unavailable.
8. Enable any DCDs that have been assigned resources by the system BIOS, yet left disabled because they weren't required for booting.
9. Discard initialization or runtime code according to command line switches in the CONFIG.SYS file and return control to DOS' loader.

The Runtime Configuration Management (*CM_*) Services

The Intel CM driver provides the Configuration Management functions listed below. DOS applications and device drivers access `CM_` style functions by issuing C calls to functions within the linkable DOSCM.LIB file, or by issuing INT `2FH` (`AX=1684H`, `BX = 34H`) to obtain a far real-mode entry point to the CM driver's runtime configuration management functions and issuing calling the CM interface directly. Windows 3.1 applications access runtime CM functions via the Dynamically Linkable Library WINCM.DLL. The WINCM.DLL library translates Windows application calls to VxD calls to the Intel-supplied VCMD.386 enhanced mode CM driver.

```
;
; 16-bit, real mode assembly language code
; to retrieve the entry point to the Intel DOS
; CM_ and CA_ functions and issue the
; CA_GetVersion and CM_GetVersion call
;
; Note:  This code does not use the DOSCM.LIB
;   and instead calls the CM/CA API directly
;

CM_GetVersion  EQU 0 ; AX Reg. Identifier For This CM Func.
CA_GetVersion  EQU 0 ; AX Reg Identifier For This CA Func.

CMAPI EQU 1684H   ; Signifies INT 2FH Locate API
CMID  EQU 34H     ; Specifies Intel CM Entry Point
CAID  EQU 304CH   ; Specifies Intel CA Entry Point

CMEntry   dd  0   ; Far Pointer To CM Entry Point
CAEntry   dd  0   ; Far Pointer To CA Entry Point
CMVersion dw  0   ; Version Of CM Services
CAVersion dw  0   ; Version Of CA Services
```

```
DevCount  dw  0   ; CM_GetVersion Number Of Devices Present

     xor  di, di            ; Initialize ES:DI to 0
     mov  es, di            ;
     mov  ax, CMAPI         ; Signature of INT 2FH CM API
     mov  bx, CMID          ; Specify CM Entry Point
     INT  2FH               ;

     mov  word ptr CMEntry, di     ; Store CM Entry Point
     mov  word ptr CMEntry + 2, es ; For Future Use

     cmp  CMEntry, 0        ; Don't Call Thru Null Pointer!
     je   NoCM              ;

     mov  ax, CM_GetVersion ; Get CM Version & Dev. Count
     call dword ptr CMEntry ;
     or   ax, ax
     jz   NoCM

     mov  CMVersion, ax     ; Store CM Reported Version
     mov  DevCount, bx      ; Store CM Reported Dev. Count

NoCM:
     mov  ax, CMAPI         ; Now look for CA Services
     mov  bx, CAID          ; Similar To Finding CM
     INT  2FH               ;

     mov  word ptr CAEntry, di     ; Store CA Entry Point
     mov  word ptr CAEntry + 2, es ; For Future Use

     cmp  CAEntry, 0
     je   NoCA

     mov  ax, CA_GetVersion ; Get CA Version
     call dword ptr CAEntry ;
     or   ax, ax            ; AX = 0 means no CA present
     jz   NoCA

     mov  CAVersion, AX     ; Else AH = MajVer, AL = MinVer
NoCA:

; More Code Here ....
```

The following code sequence demonstrates the same series of calls as they might appear in a C language program using the DOSCM.LIB.

```
//
// 'C' language code fragment to get the CM version
// and CM versions.
//

#define SUCCESS 0x0  //

unsigned int GetCMInfo(unsigned int far * pCMVersion,
                       unsigned int far * pDeviceCount) {

     *pCMVersion = *pDeviceCount = 0;  // Initialize to 0
```

```
    return(_CM_GetVersion(pCMVersion, pDeviceCount)) ;
}

unsigned int GetCAInfo(unsigned int far * pCAVersion) {

    *pCAVersion = 0 ;
    return(_CA_GetVersion(pCAVersion) ;

}

int main() {

unsigned int CAVersion, CMVersion, CMDeviceCount ;

if (GetCMInfo(&CMVersion, &CMDeviceCount) == SUCCESS)

   printf("\nCM Version = %x, Device Count = %u", CMVersion, DeviceCount) ;

else {
printf("\nCM Services Not Found") ;
return(!SUCCESS) ;
}

if (GetCMInfo(&CMVersion, &CMDeviceCount) == SUCCESS)

   printf("\nCM Version = %x, Device Count = %u", CMVersion, DeviceCount) ;

else{

printf("\nCM Services Not Found") ;
return(!SUCCESS) ;
}

return(SUCCESS) ;
}
```

A detailed description of the following functions appears in Appendix B and in the document *External Plug and Play Interfaces Specification for MS-DOS and Windows Run-Time Configuration Services*, available with Intel's Plug and Play Kit for MS-DOS and Windows.

Function `00H`	`_CM_GetVersion`
Function `01H`	`_CM_GetConfig`
Function `02H`	`CM_LockConfig`
Function `03H`	`CM_UnlockConfig`
Function `04H`	`_CME_QueryResources`
Function `05H`	`_CME_AllocResources`
Function `06H`	`_CME_DeallocResources`

The Runtime *Configuration Access* (*_CA*) Services

The Intel CM driver provides the following Configuration Access functions. The method for accessing these functions is identical to that used to access the `_CM` functions

outlined previously with the exception of the INT 2FH API ID used to obtain the entry point to the _CA functions. In order to obtain the entry point of the _CA functions within the CM driver, the caller issues INT 2FH with AX = 1684H and BX = 304CH rather than 34H.

In most cases, the _CA services are identical in function to existing PCI, EISA, and Plug and Play BIOS functions present in the system's firmware. These _CA functions are supplied to simplify the programming interface.

As is the case with the _CM functions, each _CA function is described in detail in Appendix B and in the Intel-supplied *External Plug and Play Interfaces Specification for MS-DOS* and *Windows Run-Time Configuration Services* document.

Function 00H _CA General Services

Function 00H—_CA_GetVersion

Function 01H-08H _CA PCI Services

Function 01H—_CA_PCI_Read_Config_Byte

Function 02H—_CA_PCI_Read_Config_Word

Function 03H—_CA_PCI_Read_Config_DWord

Function 04H—_CA_PCI_Write_Config_Byte

Function 05H—_CA_PCI_Write_Config_Word

Function 06H—_CA_PCI_Write_Config_DWord

Function 07H—_CA_PCI_Generate_Special_Cycle

Function 08H—_CA_PCI_Get_Routing_Options

Function 1BH—_CA_Acfg_PCI_Get_Routing_Options

Functions 0BH-0EH _CA Plug and Play ISA Services

Function 0BH—_CA_PnPISA_Get_Info

Function 0CH—_CA_PnPISA_Read_Config_Byte

Function 0DH—_CA_PnPISA_Write_Config_Byte

Function 0EH—_CA_PnPISA_Get_Resource_Data

Functions 10H-14H _CA EISA Services

Function 10H—_CA_EISA_Get_Board_ID

Function 11H—_CA_EISA_Get_Slot_Config

Function 12H—_CA_EISA_Get_SlotFunc_Config

Function 13H—_CA_EISA_Clear_Nvram_Config

Function 14H—_CA_EISA_Write_Config

Functions 16H-18H _CA ESCD Services

Function 16H—_CA_ESCD_Get_Info

Function 17H—_CA_ESCD_Read_Config

Function 18H—_CA_ESCD_Write_Config

Functions 20H-24H _CA Plug and Play BIOS Services

Function 20H—_CA_PnPB_Get_Num_Sys_Dev_Nodes

Function 21H—_CA_PnPB_Get_Sys_Dev_Node

Function 22H—_CA_PnPB_Set_Sys_Dev_Node

Function 23H—_CA_PnPB_Get_Stat_Res_Info

Function 24H—_CA_PnPB_Set_Stat_Res_Info

The ISA Configuration Utility (ICU)

The *Intel ISA Configuration Utility* is a GUI-based device configuration utility available either as a stand-alone DOS executable, or a Windows 3.1 application. Figure 8.5 displays the architecture of the ICU, and Figure 8.6 shows the ICU resource configuration dialog box.

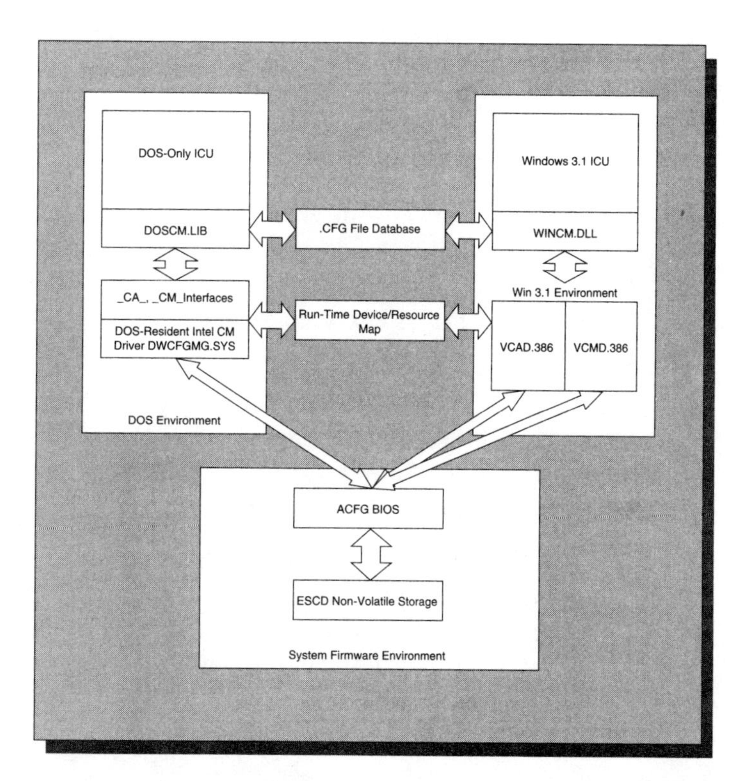

FIGURE 8.5.
The Intel ICU Architecture.

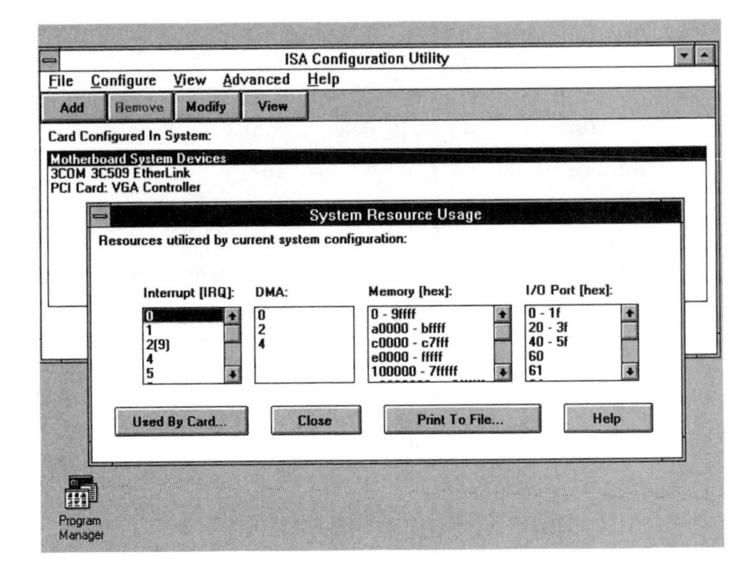

FIGURE 8.6.
The Intel ICU Interface.

The Role of the ICU

The role of the Intel ICU is twofold. First, the Intel ICU serves as a production level device configuration utility for Plug and Play systems running DOS and Windows 3.1. Second, the ICU models the basic functionality necessary for yet undeveloped Plug and Play device configuration utilities running in other legacy operating system environments, such as PC-based UNIX.

ICU Records Legacy Device Information in System NVRAM

In addition to displaying the resources available in the system, the ICU provides users the capability to instruct the configuration manager about resources used by newly installed legacy devices. When a user adds or removes a legacy adapter from the system, he or she must "teach" the system about those resources that have either been freed up or consumed by the newly installed adapter.

For example, if the user plugs a legacy ISA SCSI adapter into an expansion slot, the adapter immediately begins to use resources simply because its jumpers are set in such a way that the adapter's on-board logic decodes I/O addresses, memory addresses, and most likely an IRQ channel and a DMA channel.

Because the legacy SCSI card has not been designed with auto-detection in mind, neither the Plug and Play BIOS nor the Intel CM driver system can detect its presence. Unless the user enters the legacy adapter's resource usage in the ICU or similar utility, the Plug and Play BIOS will continue to assign these resources to other Plug and Play devices, and the system, or some of its adapters, may not function correctly due to resource conflicts.

When the user finishes configuring the system's resources, the ICU's VCMD.386 VxD driver calls Plug and Play BIOS functions to update the system's resource map in NVRAM. During POST, an ACFG or equivalent Plug and Play BIOS refers to the system NVRAM for assistance in allocating resources to dynamically configurable devices.

ICU Supports Locked Configurations for DCDs

The ICU's Advanced option menu provides a selection for creating locked DCD configurations. The locked configuration mechanism is available only on ESCD-equipped system. If a DCD or one of its functions has been assigned a locked configuration, the ICU update sets the `boardlock` bit in that device's corresponding ESCD record and also sets `enable` bits in that record's free-form data structure for each device function whose resources are locked.

The purpose served by locked configurations is described in this chapter in the "The Intel configuration manager" section. In the normal DOS environment, applications such as the DOS ICU call the `_CM_Lock` and `_CM_Unlock` functions located in the resident CM driver to lock and unlock device configurations. Within the Windows environment, the ICU invokes identical `_CM_Lock` and `_CM_Unlock` functions that reside in VxD drivers.

The .CFG File Database

The ICU ships with a database of .CFG files describing the possible resource assignments for a variety of currently available or once popular legacy plug-in adapters. As part of its installation sequence, the ICU builds a quick-access index file for each .CFG file on the installation diskettes.

Users who add legacy devices to DOS or Windows 3.1 Plug and Play systems first search the list of available cards for a selection matching their device. If a match exists, the ICU compares the contents of the .CFG file with those resources remaining in the system. The ICU then displays a series of resource selection menus containing only those resources that are both available and supported by the user's device.

If the ICU does not have access to a .CFG file for a particular adapter, the user can create a new adapter and manually enter the resources used by the adapter.

ICU Binding for the DOS and Windows Environments

Because the DOS and Windows ICU programs operate in different environments, they utilize different methods of function `binding` to access CM functions.

The DOS version of ICU `binds` to DOSCM.LIB, which contains the `_CM` (Configuration Management) and `_CA` (Configuration Access) functions introduced previously.

The linkable library DOSCM.LIB provides a C-language style entry point for each _CA and _CM function. Additionally, DOSCM.LIB converts the caller's C-language style parameter passing into the register-based arguments that the CM's internal functions expect. The code fragments shown earlier in this chapter display methods for invoking Intel CM functions with or without the support of the DOSCM.LIB library.

The Windows version of the ICU binds to WINCM.DLL (WINdows Configuration Manager Dynamic Link Library), which provides the ICU runtime-protected mode entry points to _CM (Configuration Management) and _CA (Configuration Access) functions. Rather than calling the DOS CM driver functions directly, the WINCM.DLL library invokes identical functions resident in the Windows VxD (Virtual Driver) modules VCAD.386 and VCMD.386. As part of its installation sequence, the Win 3.1 ICU installs VCAD.386 and VCMD.386 into Windows' SYSTEM.INI file.

The C language declaration for the _CM and _CA functions resident in WINCM.DLL are identical to those for their DOS counterparts that reside in DOSCM.LIB. Therefore, user-developed configuration management code that works either with WINCM.DLL or DOSCM.LIB is portable between the DOS and Win 3.1 environments.

The ICU Utilization of the System Device Resource Map

Both the DOS and Windows versions of the ICU coordinate system resource usage by sharing a runtime *system device resource map* created by the DOS-resident CM driver during the system's power on sequence.

The exact storage medium for the device resource map is known only to the ICU and CM driver. Applications should not access the resource map directly.

A

Device IDs

Microsoft defines device ID values for devices that have no standard EISA-style ID. System device ID strings normally appear with the PNP prefix; however, the only requirement for device IDs is that they contain a three character prefix and a four digit, hexidecimal index value. Ironically, the devices to which PNP style device ID's have been assigned are not Plug and Play at all, but instead are legacy systemboard or plug in devices. The Plug and Play operating system, such as Windows 95 uses device IDs to catalog and identify the capabilities of each system device. Using this information, the Plug and Play OS can find and load device drivers that either enhance the basic functionality of, or fix compatibility flaws in a specific device. The following list shows the most current Microsoft device ID assignments. The information in the left column is the Device ID. The information in the right column is the description of the Device ID.

Interrupt Controllers

PNP0000	AT Interrupt Controller
PNP0001	EISA Interrupt Controller
PNP0002	MCA Interrupt Controller
PNP0003	APIC
PNP0004	Cyrix SLiC MP interrupt controller

System Timers

PNP0100	AT Timer
PNP0101	EISA Timer
PNP0102	MCA Timer

DMA Controllers

PNP0200	AT DMA Controller
PNP0201	EISA DMA Controller
PNP0202	MCA DMA Controller

Keyboards

PNP0300	IBM PC/XT keyboard controller (83-key)
PNP0301	IBM PC/AT keyboard controller (86-key)
PNP0302	IBM PC/XT keyboard controller (84-key)
PNP0303	IBM Enhanced (101/102-key, PS/2 mouse support)
PNP0304	Olivetti Keyboard (83-key)
PNP0305	Olivetti Keyboard (102-key)
PNP0306	Olivetti Keyboard (86-key)
PNP0307	Microsoft Windows® Keyboard
PNP0308	General Input Device Emulation Interface (GIDEI) legacy

PNP0309	Olivetti Keyboard (A101/102 key)
PNP030A	AT&T 302 keyboard

Parallel Port Devices

PNP0400	Standard LPT printer port
PNP0401	ECP printer port

Serial Port Devices

PNP0500	Standard PC COM port
PNP0501	16550A compatible COM port

Disk Controllers

PNP0600	Generic ESDI/IDE/ATA compatible hard disk controller
PNP0601	Plus Hardcard II
PNP0602	Plus Hardcard IIXL/EZ
PNP0603	HP Omnibook IDE Controller
PNP0700	PC standard floppy disk controller
PNP0701	HP Omnibook floppy disk controller

Display Adapters

PNP0900	VGA Compatible
PNP0901	Video Seven VRAM/VRAM II/1024i
PNP0902	8514/A Compatible
PNP0903	Trident VGA
PNP0904	Cirrus Logic Laptop VGA
PNP0905	Cirrus Logic VGA
PNP0906	Tseng ET4000
PNP0907	Western Digital VGA
PNP0908	Western Digital Laptop VGA
PNP0909	S3 Inc. 911/924
PNP090A	ATI Ultra Pro/Plus (Mach 32)
PNP090B	ATI Ultra (Mach 8)
PNP090C	XGA Compatible
PNP090D	ATI VGA Wonder
PNP090E	Weitek P9000 Graphics Adapter
PNP090F	Oak Technology VGA
PNP0910	Compaq QVision
PNP0911	XGA/2
PNP0912	Tseng Labs W32/W32i/W32p
PNP0913	S3 Inc. 801/928/964

continues

Display Adapters

PNP0914	Cirrus Logic 5429/5434 (memory mapped)
PNP0915	Compaq Advanced VGA (AVGA)
PNP0916	ATI Ultra Pro Turbo (Mach64)
PNP0917	Reserved by Microsoft
PNP0930	Chips and Technologies Super VGA
PNP0931	Chips & Technologies Accelerator
PNP0940	NCR 77c22e Super VGA
PNP0941	NCR 77c32blt
PNP09FF	Plug and Play Monitors (VESA DDC)

Peripheral Buses

PNP0A00	ISA Bus
PNP0A01	EISA Bus
PNP0A02	MCA Bus
PNP0A03	PCI Bus
PNP0A04	VESA/VL Bus

Real Time Clock, BIOS, Systemboard Devices

PNP0800	AT style speaker sound
PNP0B00	AT Real Time Clock
PNP0C00	Plug and Play BIOS (only created by the root enumerator)
PNP0C01	Systemboard
PNP0C02	ID for reserving resources required by Plug and Play motherboard registers (not specific to a particular device)
PNP0C03	Plug and Play BIOS Event Notification Interrupt
PNP0C04	Math Coprocessor
PNP0C05	APM BIOS (Version independent)
PNP0C06	Reserved for identification of early Plug and Play BIOS implementation
PNP0C07	Reserved for identification of early Plug and Play BIOS implementation

PCMCIA Host Bus Adapters

PNP0E00	Intel 82365 Compatible PCMCIA Controller
PNP0E01	Cirrus Logic CL-PD6720 PCMCIA Controller
PNP0E02	VLSI VL82C146 PCMCIA Controller

Pointing Devices/Mice

PNP0F00	Microsoft Bus Mouse
PNP0F01	Microsoft Serial Mouse
PNP0F02	Microsoft Inport Mouse
PNP0F03	Microsoft PS/2 Mouse
PNP0F04	MouseSystems Mouse
PNP0F05	MouseSystems 3-Button Mouse (COM2)
PNP0F06	Genius Mouse (COM1)
PNP0F07	Genius Mouse (COM2)
PNP0F08	Logitech Serial Mouse
PNP0F09	Microsoft Ballpoint Serial Mouse
PNP0F0A	Microsoft Plug and Play Mouse
PNP0F0B	Microsoft Plug and Play Ballpoint Mouse
PNP0F0C	Microsoft Compatible Serial Mouse
PNP0F0D	Microsoft Compatible Inport Mouse
PNP0F0E	Microsoft Compatible PS/2 Mouse
PNP0F0F	Microsoft Compatible Serial BallPoint Mouse
PNP0F10	Texas Instruments Quick Port Mouse
PNP0F11	Microsoft Compatible Bus Mouse
PNP0F12	Logitech PS/2 Mouse
PNP0F13	PS/2 Port for PS/2 Mice
PNP0F14	Microsoft Kids Mouse
PNP0F15	Logitech Bus Mouse
PNP0F16	Logitech SWIFT device
PNP0F17	Logitech Compatible Serial Mouse
PNP0F18	Logitech Compatible Bus Mouse
PNP0F19	Logitech Compatible PS/2 Mouse
PNP0F1A	Logitech Compatible SWIFT Device
PNP0F1B	HP Omnibook Mouse
PNP0F1C	Compaq LTE Trackball PS/2 Mouse
PNP0F1D	Compaq LTE Trackball Serial Mouse
PNP0F1E	Microsoft Kids Trackball Mouse
PNP0F1F	Reserved by Microsoft Input Device Group
PNP0F20	Reserved by Microsoft Input Device Group
PNP0F21	Reserved by Microsoft Input Device Group
PNP0F22	Reserved by Microsoft Input Device Group
PNP0FFF	Reserved by Microsoft Systems

Network Adapters—PNP8xxx	
PNP8001	Novell/Anthem NE3200
PNP8004	Compaq NE3200
PNP8006	Intel EtherExpress/32
PNP8008	HP EtherTwist EISA LAN Adapter/32 (HP27248A)
PNP8065	Ungermann-Bass NIUps or NIUps/EOTP
PNP8072	DEC (DE211) EtherWorks MC/TP
PNP8073	DEC (DE212) EtherWorks MC/TP_BNC
PNP8078	DCA 10 Mb MCA
PNP8074	HP MC LAN Adapter/16 TP (PC27246)
PNP80c9	IBM Token Ring
PNP80ca	IBM Token Ring II
PNP80cb	IBM Token Ring II/Short
PNP80cc	IBM Token Ring 4/16Mbs
PNP80d3	Novell/Anthem NE1000
PNP80d4	Novell/Anthem NE2000
PNP80d5	NE1000 Compatible
PNP80d6	NE2000 Compatible
PNP80d7	Novell/Anthem NE1500T
PNP80d8	Novell/Anthem NE2100
PNP80dd	SMC ARCNETPC
PNP80de	SMC ARCNET PC100, PC200
PNP80df	SMC ARCNET PC110, PC210, PC250
PNP80e0	SMC ARCNET PC130/E
PNP80e1	SMC ARCNET PC120, PC220, PC260
PNP80e2	SMC ARCNET PC270/E
PNP80e5	SMC ARCNET PC600W, PC650W
PNP80e7	DEC DEPCA
PNP80e8	DEC (DE100) EtherWorks LC
PNP80e9	DEC (DE200) EtherWorks Turbo
PNP80ea	DEC (DE101) EtherWorks LC/TP
PNP80eb	DEC (DE201) EtherWorks Turbo/TP
PNP80ec	DEC (DE202) EtherWorks Turbo/TP_BNC
PNP80ed	DEC (DE102) EtherWorks LC/TP_BNC
PNP80ee	DEC EE101 (Built-In)
PNP80ef	DECpc 433 WS (Built-In)
PNP80f1	3Com EtherLink Plus
PNP80f3	3Com EtherLink II or IITP (8 or 16-bit)
PNP80f4	3Com TokenLink
PNP80f6	3Com EtherLink 16

PNP80f7	3Com EtherLink III
PNP80fb	Thomas Conrad TC6045
PNP80fc	Thomas Conrad TC6042
PNP80fd	Thomas Conrad TC6142
PNP80fe	Thomas Conrad TC6145
PNP80ff	Thomas Conrad TC6242
PNP8100	Thomas Conrad TC6245
PNP8105	DCA 10M
PNP8106	DCA 10M Fiber Optic
PNP8107	DCA 10M Twisted Pair
PNP8113	Racal NI6510
PNP811C	Ungermann-Bass NIUpc
PNP8120	Ungermann-Bass NIUpc/EOTP
PNP8123	SMC StarCard PLUS (WD/8003S)
PNP8124	SMC StarCard PLUS With On Board Hub (WD/8003SH)
PNP8125	SMC EtherCard PLUS (WD/8003E)
PNP8126	SMC EtherCard PLUS with Boot ROM Socket (WD/8003EBT)
PNP8127	SMC EtherCard PLUS with Boot ROM Socket (WD/8003EB)
PNP8128	SMC EtherCard PLUS TP (WD/8003WT)
PNP812a	SMC EtherCard PLUS 16 with Boot ROM Socket (WD/8013EBT)
PNP812d	Intel EtherExpress 16 or 16TP
PNP812f	Intel TokenExpress 16/4
PNP8130	Intel TokenExpress MCA 16/4
PNP8132	Intel EtherExpress 16 (MCA)
PNP8137	Artisoft AE-1
PNP8138	Artisoft AE-2 or AE-3
PNP8141	Amplicard AC 210/XT
PNP8142	Amplicard AC 210/AT
PNP814b	Everex SpeedLink /PC16 (EV2027)
PNP8155	HP PC LAN Adapter/8 TP (HP27245)
PNP8156	HP PC LAN Adapter/16 TP (HP27247A)
PNP8157	HP PC LAN Adapter/8 TL (HP27250)
PNP8158	HP PC LAN Adapter/16 TP Plus (HP27247B)
PNP8159	HP PC LAN Adapter/16 TL Plus (HP27252)
PNP815f	National Semiconductor Ethernode *16AT
PNP8160	National Semiconductor AT/LANTIC EtherNODE 16-AT3
PNP816a	NCR Token-Ring 4 MBs ISA
PNP816d	NCR Token-Ring 16/4 MBs ISA
PNP8191	Olicom 16/4 Token-Ring Adapter

continues

Network Adapters—PNP8xxx

PNP81c3	SMC EtherCard PLUS Elite (WD/8003EP)
PNP81c4	SMC EtherCard PLUS 10T (WD/8003W)
PNP81c5	SMC EtherCard PLUS Elite 16 (WD/8013EP)
PNP81c6	SMC EtherCard PLUS Elite 16T (WD/8013W)
PNP81c7	SMC EtherCard PLUS Elite 16 Combo (WD/8013EW or 8013EWC)
PNP81c8	SMC EtherElite Ultra 16
PNP81e4	Pure Data PDI9025-32 (Token Ring)
PNP81e6	Pure Data PDI508+ (ArcNet)
PNP81e7	Pure Data PDI516+ (ArcNet)
PNP81eb	Proteon Token Ring (P1390)
PNP81ec	Proteon Token Ring (P1392)
PNP81ed	Proteon ISA Token Ring (1340)
PNP81ee	Proteon ISA Token Ring (1342)
PNP81ef	Proteon ISA Token Ring (1346)
PNP81f0	Proteon ISA Token Ring (1347)
PNP81ff	Cabletron E2000 Series DNI
PNP8200	Cabletron E2100 Series DNI
PNP8209	Zenith Data Systems Z-Note
PNP820a	Zenith Data Systems NE2000 Compatible
PNP8213	Xircom Pocket Ethernet II
PNP8214	Xircom Pocket Ethernet I
PNP821d	RadiSys EXM-10
PNP8227	SMC 3000 Series
PNP8231	Advanced Micro Devices AM2100/AM1500T
PNP8263	Tulip NCC-16
PNP8277	Exos 105
PNP828A	Intel '595 based Ethernet
PNP828B	TI2000-Style Token Ring
PNP828C	AMD PCNet Family cards
PNP828D	AMD PCNet32 (VL version)
PNP82bd	IBM PCMCIA-NIC
PNP8321	DEC Ethernet (All types)
PNP8323	SMC EtherCard (All types except 8013/A)
PNP8324	ARCNET Compatible
PNP8326	Thomas Conrad (All Arcnet Types)
PNP8327	IBM Token Ring (All Types)
PNP8385	Remote Network Access Driver
PNP8387	RNA Point-to-Point Protocol Driver

SCSI, Proprietary CD Adapters—`PNPAxxx`

PNPA000	Adaptec 154x compatible SCSI controller
PNPA001	Adaptec 174x compatible SCSI controller
PNPA002	Future Domain 16-700 compatible controller
PNPA003	Panasonic proprietary CD-ROM adapter (SBPro/SB16)
PNPA01B	Trantor 128 SCSI Controller
PNPA01D	Trantor T160 SCSI Controller
PNPA01E	Trantor T338 Parallel SCSI controller
PNPA01F	Trantor T348 Parallel SCSI controller
PNPA020	Trantor Media Vision SCSI controller
PNPA022	Always IN-2000 SCSI controller
PNPA02B	Sony proprietary CD-ROM controller
PNPA02D	Trantor T13b 8-bit SCSI controller
PNPA02F	Trantor T358 Parallel SCSI controller
PNPA030	Mitsumi LU-005 Single Speed CD-ROM controller + drive
PNPA031	Mitsumi FX-001 Single Speed CD-ROM controller + drive
PNPA032	Mitsumi FX-001 Double Speed CD-ROM controller + drive

Sound/Video-Capture, Multimedia—`PNPBxxx`

PNPB000	Sound Blaster 1.5 Compatible Sound Device
PNPB001	Sound Blaster 2.0 Compatible Sound Device
PNPB002	Sound Blaster Pro Compatible Sound Device
PNPB003	Sound Blaster 16 Compatible Sound Device
PNPB004	Thunderboard compatible Sound Device
PNPB005	Adlib-compatible FM Synthesizer Device
PNPB006	MPU401 compatible
PNPB007	Microsoft Windows Sound System Compatible Sound Device
PNPB008	Compaq Business Audio
PNPB009	Plug and Play Microsoft Windows Sound System Device
PNPB00A	MediaVision Pro Audio Spectrum (Trantor SCSI Enabled, Thunder Chip Disabled)
PNPB00B	MediaVision Pro Audio 3D
PNPB00C	MusicQuest MQX-32M
PNPB00D	MediaVision Pro Audio Spectrum Basic (No Trantor SCSI, Thunder Chip Enabled)
PNPB00E	MediaVision Pro Audio Spectrum (Trantor SCSI enabled, Thunder Chip Enabled)
PNPB00F	MediaVision Jazz-16 chipset (OEM Versions)
PNPB010	Auravision VxP500 Chipset—Orchid Videola

continues

Sound/Video-Capture, Multimedia—PNPBxxx	
PNPB018	MediaVision Pro Audio Spectrum 8-bit
PNPB019	MediaVision Pro Audio Spectrum Basic (No Trantor SCSI, Thunder Chip Disabled)
PNPB020	Yamaha OPL3-Compatible FM Synthesizer Device
PNPB02F	Joystick/Game Port

Modems—PNPCxxx-Dxxx	
PNPC000	Compaq 14400 Modem
PNPC001	Compaq 2400/9600 Modem

Regarding Device IDs, Microsoft offers the following statement:

WINDOWS GENERIC DEVICE IDS

There are many devices that have no standard EISA ID, such as the interrupt controller or keyboard controller. There are also a set of compatible devices such as VGA and Super VGA that are not actually devices, but define a compatibility hardware subset. Yet another set of IDs needs to be used to identify buses. To be able to identify various devices that do not have an existing EISA ID, as well as define compatibility devices, Microsoft has reserved an EISA prefix of "PNP".

If you are a hardware manufacturer building Plug and Play adapter boards, you are expected to procure your own three letter EISA identifier and assign your own IDs for your hardware. EISA identifiers may be obtained from

BCPR Services, Inc.
P.O. Box 11137
Spring, Texas 77391-1137

(713)251-4770 (phone)
(713)251-4832 (fax)

The PNPxxxx IDs may be returned by your Plug and Play hardware in order to report hardware-level compatibility with the devices defined in DEVIDS.TXT. This allows an operating system to use a "generic" driver for a device in the event that an IHV/OEM-provided device driver is not available. See the ISA Plug and Play specification for further information on how to return "compatible" device IDs.

The Plug and Play Association will eventually be taking responsibility for maintaining the DEVIDS.TXT file along with new PNPxxxx ID assignments as

necessary. Until the Association is ready, administration of `PNPxxxx` ID's will be handled by Microsoft Corporation, via the Internet e-mail address below.

To request new `PNPxxxx` assignments, send mail to `pnpid@microsoft.com`.

Thank you,

Microsoft Corporation

PCI Device Vendor IDs

The following list displays the currently allocated PCI Vendor IDs as reported by the PCI SIG:

```
0x1002 — ATI
0x1003 — ULSI
0x1004 — VLSI
0x1005 — AVANCE LOGICS
0x1006 — REPLY GROUP
0x1007 — NETFRAME
0x1008 — EPSON
0x100A — PHOENIX
0x100B — NATIONAL SEMICONDUCTOR
0x100C — TSENG LABS
0x100D — AST
0x100E — WEITEK
0x1010 — VIDEO LOGIC
0x1011 — DEC
0x1012 — MICRONICS
0x1013 — CIRRUS LOGIC
0x1014 — IBM
0x1016 — ICL
0x1017 — SPEA
0x1018 — UNISYS
0x1019 — ELITEGROUP
0x101A — NCR
0x101B — VITESSE
0x101C — WESTERN DIGITAL
0x101E — AMI
0x101F — PICTURETEL
0x1020 — HITACHI
0x1021 — OKI
0x1022 — AMD
0x1023 — TRIDENT
0x1025 — ACER
0x1028 — DELL
0x1029 — SIEMENS NIXDORF
0x102A — LSI LOGIC
0x102B — MATROX
0x102C — C&T
```

```
0x102D — WYSE
0x102E — OLIVETTI
0x102F — TOSHIBA
0x1030 — TMC
0x1031 — MIRO
0x1032 — COMPAQ
0x1033 — NEC
0x1033 — NEC
0x1033 — NEC
0x1034 — BURNDY
0x1035 — COMPUTERS AND COMMUNICATONS RESEARCH LAB
0x1036 — FUTURE DOMAIN
0x1037 — HITACHI
0x1038 — AMP
0x1039 — SIS
0x103A — SEIKO EPSON
0x103B — TATUNG
0x103C — HEWLETT PACKARD
0x103E — SOLLIDAY
0x103F — LOGIC MODELING
0x1040 — KUBOTA PACIFIC
0x1041 — COMPUTREND
0x1042 — PC TECHNOLOGY
0x1043 — ASUSTEK
0x1044 — DISTRIBUTED PROCESSING TECHNOLOGY
0x1045 — OPTI
0x1046 — IPC
0x1047 — GENOA
0x1048 — ELSA
0x1049 — FOUNTAIN
0x104A — SGS THOMSON
0x104B — BUSLOGIC
0x104C — TI
0x104D — SONY
0x104E — OAK
0x104F — CO-TIME
0x1050 — WINBOND
0x1051 — ANIGMA
0x1052 — YOUNG
0x1054 — HITACHI
0x1055 — EFAR
0x1056 — ICL
0x1057 — MOTOROLA
0x1058 — ELECTRONICS & TELEC. RSH
0x1059 — TEKNOR
0x105A — PROMISE
0x105B — FOXCONN
0x105C — WIPRO
0x105D — NUMBER 9
0x105E — VTECH
0x105F — INFOTRONIC
0x1060 — UMC
0x1061 — X TECH
0x1062 — MASPAR
0x1063 — OCEAN
0x1064 — ALCATEL
0x1065 — TEXAS MICRO
0x1066 — PICOPOWER
```

0x1067 — MITSUBISHI
0x1067 — MITSUBISHI
0x1068 — DIVERSIFIED
0x1069 — MYLEX
0x106A — ATEN
0x106B — APPLE
0x106B — MADGE
0x106C — HYUNDAI
0x106D — SEQUENT
0x106E — DFI
0x106F — CITY GATE
0x1070 — DAEWOO
0x1071 — MITAC
0x1072 — GIT
0x1073 — YAMAHA
0x1074 — NEXGEN
0x1075 — ADV. INTEGRATION
0x1076 — CHAINTECH
0x1077 — Q LOGIC
0x1078 — CYRIX
0x1079 — I-BUS
0x107A — NETWORTH
0x107B — GATEWAY 2000
0x107C — GOLDSTAR
0x107D — LEADTEK
0x107E — INTERPHASE
0x107F — DTC
0x1080 — CONTAQ
0x1081 — SUPERMAC
0x1082 — EFA
0x1083 — FOREX
0x1084 — PARADOR
0x1085 — TULIP
0x1086 — J. BOND
0x1087 — CACHE
0x1088 — MICROCOMPUTER SYSTEMS
0x1089 — DATA GENERAL
0x108A — BIT3
0x108C — ELONEX
0x108D — OLICOM
0x108F — SYSTEMSOFT
0x1090 — ENCORE
0x1091 — INTERGRAPH
0x1092 — DIAMOND
0x1093 — NATIONAL INSTRUMENTS
0x1094 — FIC
0x1095 — CMD
0x1096 — ALACRON
0x1097 — APPIAN
0x1098 — QUANTUM
0x1099 — SAMSUNG
0x109A — PACKARD BELL
0x109B — GEMLIGHT
0x109C — MEGACHIPS
0x109D — ZIDA
0x109E — BROOKTREE
0x109F — TRIGEM
0x10A0 — MEIDENSHA

```
0x10A1 — JUKO
0x10A2 — QUANTUM
0x10A3 — EVEREX
0x10A4 — GLOBE
0x10A5 — RACAL INTERLAN
0x10A6 — INFORMTECH
0x10A7 — BENCHMARQ
0x10A8 — SIERRA
0x10A9 — SILICON GRAPHICS
0x10AA — ACC
0x10AB — DIGICOM
0x10AC — HONEYWELL
0x10AD — SYMPHONY
0x10AE — CORNERSTONE
0x10AF — MICROCOMPUTER SYSYTEMS
0x10B0 — CARDEXPERT
0x10B1 — CABLETRON
0x10B2 — RAYTHEON
0x10B3 — DATABOOK
0x10B4 — STB
0x10B5 — PLX
0x10B7 — 3COM
0x10B8 — SMC
0x10B9 — ACER LABS
0x10BA — MITSUBISHI
0x10BB — DAPHA
0x10BC — ALR
0x10BD — SURECOM
0x10BE — TSENG LABS
0x10BF — MOST INC
0x10C0 — BOCA RESEARCH
0x10C1 — ICM
0x10C2 — AUSPEX
0x10C3 — SAMSUNG
0x10C4 — AWARD
0x10C5 — XEROX
0x10C6 — RAMBUS
0x10C7 — MEDIA VISION
0x10C8 — NEOMAGIC
0x10C9 — DATAEXPERT
0x10CA — FUJITSU
0x10CB — OMRON
0x10CC — MENTOR
0x10CD — ADVANCED SYSTEM PRODUCTS
0x10CE — RADIUS
0x10CF — CITICORP
0x10D0 — FUJITSU
0x10D1 — FUTURE+
0x10D2 — MOLEX
0x10D3 — JABIL
0x10D4 — HUALON
0x10D5 — AUTOLOGIC
0x10D6 — CETIA
0x10D7 — BCM
0x10D8 — ADV PERIPHERALS
0x10D9 — MACRONIX
0x10DA — THOMAS-CONRAD
0x10DB — ROHM
```

0x10DC — CERN/ECP/EDU
0x10DD — EVANS & SUTHERLAND
0x10DE — NVIDIA
0x10DF — EMULEX
0x10E0 — IMS
0x10E1 — TEKRAM
0x10E2 — APTIX
0x10E3 — NEWBRIDGE
0x10E4 — TANDEM
0x10E5 — MICRO INDUSTRIES
0x10E6 — GAINBERY
0x10E7 — VADEM
0x10E8 — APPLIED MICRO
0x10E9 — ALPS
0x10EA — INTEGRAPHICS
0x10EB — ARTISTS
0x10EC — REALTEK
0x10ED — ASCII CORP
0x10EE — XILINX
0x10EF — RACORE
0x10F0 — PERITEK
0x10F1 — TYAN
0x10F2 — ACHME
0x10F3 — ALARIS
0x10F4 — S-MOS SYSTEMS
0x10F5 — NKK
0x10F6 — CREATIVE ELECTRONIC
0x10F7 — MATSUSHITA
0x10F8 — ALTOS
0x10F9 — PC DIRECT
0x10FA — TRUEVISION
0x10FB — THESYS
0x10FC — I-O DATA DEVICE
0x10FD — SOYO
0x10FE — FAST
0x10FF — NCUBE
0x1100 — JAZZ
0x1101 — INITIO
0x1102 — CREATIVE LABS
0x1103 — TRIONES
0x1104 — RASTEROPS
0x1105 — SIGMA
0x1106 — VIA
0x1107 — STRATUS
0x1108 — PROTEON
0x110B — XENON
0x110C — MINI-MAX
0x110D — ZNYX
0x110E — CPU TECH
0x110F — ROSS
0x1110 — POWERHOUSE
0x1111 — S.C.O.
0x1112 — ROCKWELL
0x1113 — ACCTON
0x1114 — ATMEL
0x1115 — DUPONT
0x1116 — DATA TRANSLATION
0x1117 — DATACUBE

```
0x1118 — BERG
0x1119 — VORTEX
0x111A — EFFICENT NETWORKS, INC.
0x111B — TELEDYNE
0x5333 — S3
0x8086 — INTEL
0x9004 — ADAPTEC
```

Plug and Play BIOS Device Type Codes

Device Type codes are three-byte identifiers that provide the Base Type, Sub-Type, and Interface Type for a particular device. Device type codes are an alternative to device ID values for identifying the type and capabilities of an installed device. Device type codes appear in system device nodes, PCI device configuration space headers, and within Plug and Play compliant expansion ROM headers residing on Plug and Play ISA or PCI adapters. The following is the most current list of device type codes.

Base Type = 0 Reserved

Base Type = 1: Mass Storage Device

- Sub-Type = 0: SCSI Controller
- Sub-Type = 1: IDE Controller (Standard ATA compatible)
  - Interface Type = 0: Generic IDE
- Sub-Type = 2: Floppy Controller (Standard 765 compatible)
  - Interface Type = 0: Generic Floppy
- Sub-Type = 3: IPI Controller
  - Interface Type = 0: General IPI
- Sub-Type = 80h: Other Mass Storage Controller

Base Type = 2: Network Interface Controller

- Sub-Type = 0: Ethernet
  - Interface Type = 0: General Ethernet
- Sub-Type = 1: Token Ring Controller
  - Interface Type = 0: General Token Ring
- Sub-Type = 2: FDDI Controller
  - Interface Type = 0: General FDDI
- Sub-Type = 80h: Other Network Interface Controller

Base Type = 3: Display Controller

Sub-Type = 0: VGA Controller (Standard VGA compatible)

Interface Type = 0: Generic VGA compatible

Interface Type = 1: VESA SVGA Compatible Controller

Sub-Type = 1: XGA Compatible Controller

Interface Type = 0: General XGA Compatible Controller

Sub-Type = 80h: Other Display Controller

Base Type = 4: Multimedia Controller

Sub-Type = 0: Video Controller

Interface Type = 0: General Video

Sub-Type = 1: Audio Controller

Interface Type = 0: General Audio Controller

Sub-Type = 80h: Other Multimedia Controller

Base Type = 5: Memory

Sub-Type = 0: RAM

Interface Type = 0: General RAM

Sub-Type = 1: FLASH Memory

Interface Type = 0: General FLASH Memory

Sub-Type = 80h: Other Memory Device

Base Type = 6: Bridge Controller

Sub-Type = 0: Host Processor Bridge

Interface Type = 0: General Host Processor Bridge

Sub-Type = 1: ISA Bridge

Interface Type = 0: General ISA Bridge

Sub-Type = 2: EISA Bridge

Interface Type = 0: General EISA Bridge

Sub-Type = 3: MicroChannel Bridge

Interface Type = 0: General Micro-Channel Bridge

Sub-Type = 4: PCI Bridge

Interface Type = 0: General PCI Bridge

Sub-Type = `5`: PCMCIA Bridge

Interface Type = `0`: General PCMCIA Bridge

Sub-Type = `80h`: Other Bridge Device

Base Type = `7`: Communications Device

Sub-Type = `0`: RS-232 Device (XT-compatible COM)

Interface Type = `0`: Generic XT-compatible

Interface Type = `1`: 16450-compatible

Interface Type = `2`: 16550-compatible

Sub-Type = `1`: AT-Compatible Parallel Port

Interface Type = `0`: Generic AT Parallel Port

Interface Type = `1`: Model-30 Bidirectional Port

Interface Type = `2`: ECP 1.0 compliant port

Sub-Type = `80h`: Other Communications Device

Base Type = `8`: System Peripherals

Sub-Type = `0`: Programmable Interrupt Controller (8259 Compatible)

Interface Type = `0`: Generic 8259 PIC

Interface Type = `1`: ISA PIC (8259 Compatible)

Interface Type = `2`: EISA PIC (8259 Compatible)

Sub-Type = `1`: DMA Controller (8237 Compatible)

Interface Type = `0`: Generic DMA Controller

Interface Type = `1`: ISA DMA Controller

Interface Type = `2`: EISA DMA Controller

Sub-Type = `2`: System Timer (8254 Compatible)

Interface Type = `0`: Generic System Timer

Interface Type = `1`: ISA System Timer

Interface Type = `2`: EISA System Timers (2 Timers)

Sub-Type = `3`: Real Time Clock

Interface Type = `0`: Generic RTC Controller

Interface Type = `1`: ISA RTC Controller

Sub-Type = `80h`: Other System Peripheral

Base Type = `9`: Input Devices

- Sub-Type = `0`: Keyboard Controller
  - Interface Type = `0`: Not applicable
- Sub-Type = `1`: Digitizer (Pen)
  - Interface Type = `0`: Not applicable
- Sub-Type = `2`: Mouse Controller
  - Interface Type = `0`: Not applicable
- Sub-Type = `80h`: Other Input Controller

Base Type = `0Ah`: Docking Station

- Sub-Type = `0`: Generic Docking Station
  - Interface Type = `0`: Not applicable
- Sub-Type = `80h`: Other type of Docking Station

Base Type = `0Bh`: CPU Type

- Sub-Type = `0`: 386-based processor
  - Interface Type = `0`: Not applicable
- Sub-Type = `1`: 486-based processor
  - Interface Type = `0`: Not applicable
- Sub-Type = `2`: Pentium-based processor
  - Interface Type = `0`: Not applicable

B

The Intel _*CA* and _*CM* Functions

This appendix contains information about the following items:

- Intel Configuration Manager _CM (Configuration Management) functions
- Intel Configuration Manager _CA (Configuration Access) functions
- PCI BIOS return values
- Plug and Play BIOS return values

Intel Configuration Manager (_*CM*) and Configuration Access (_*CA*) Function Definitions

This section describes the `_CM` and `_CA` functions that reside in the runtime portion of the Intel CM driver. DOS applications that link to DOSCM.LIB and Windows applications that dynamically link to WINCM.DLL have access to each of these functions. The Intel `_CM` functions provide callers with information about the CM driver itself as well as the capability to allocate and deallocate system resources. The `_CA` functions enable callers to directly communicate with installed hardware devices and alleviate each calling application from having to include its own copy of general purpose EISA, PCI, Plug and Play ISA, and Plug and Play BIOS device configuration code.

Calling applications should perform all resource allocation and deallocation via the `_CM` functions to prevent the CM driver's internal resource map from getting out of synch with the system's hardware devices.

Function *00H* (_*CM_GetVersion*)

`_CM_GetVersion` returns the version of the Intel CM driver version, and the number of devices that the CM currently contains in its device map.

The following is the C language declaration for `_CM_GetVersion`:

```
int _CM_GetVersion(int far *Version, int far *NumSystemDevices) ;
```

Returns

```
CM_SUCCESS — the CM subsystem is loaded
```

`CM_CONFIG_MGR_NOT_PRESENT`—The CM subsystem is not loaded.

Function *01H* (_*CM_GetConfig*)

`_CM_GetConfig` returns the configuration of device `DevIndex` in the caller-supplied buffer pointed to by `fpConfigBuffer`.

The following is the C language declaration for `CM_GetConfig`:

```
int _CM_GetConfig(unsigned int DevIndex,
             (struct Config_Info far *)
               fpConfigBuffer) ;
```

`_CM_GetConfig` returns

`CM_SUCCESS` if the device specified by `DevIndex` exists

`CM_DEVICE_NOT_FOUND` if the device does not exist

NOTE

The format of the `ConfigInfo` structure used in `_CM` functions `01H-06H` is beyond the scope of *Programming Plug and Play.* A complete description of the `ConfigInfo` structure, as well as other Intel CM runtime service information, appears in the document entitled *External Plug and Play Interfaces Specification for MS-DOS and Windows Run-time Configuration Services.* Contact your local Intel representative for information about receiving a copy of this document.

Function *02H* (*CM_LockConfig*)

`_CM_LockConfig` creates a locked configuration for the ISA, Plug and Play ISA, or PCI device and its associate resources as specified in `ConfigBuffer`. In the case of an ISA device, `_CM_LockConfig` has the effect of simply recording those resources assigned to a device in system NVS.

The following is the C language declaration for `_CM_LockConfig`:

```
int _CM_LockConfig((struct Config_Info far *) fpConfigBuffer) ;
```

Returns

`CM_CONFIG_ERROR`—The device is invalid, or the configuration failed.

`CM_IO_PORT_UNAVAILABLE`—The specified I/O ports are already in use.

`CM_IRQ_UNAVAILABLE`—The IRQ is in use and cannot be shared.

`CM_DMA_CH_UNAVAILABLE`—The DMA channel is in use.

`CM_MEM_WINDOW_UNAVAILABLE`—The system address range is in use.

Function *03H* (*CM_UnlockConfig*)

`_CM_UnlockConfig` releases are a result previously assigned to a PCI, ISA, or Plug and Play ISA device are a result of a call to `_CM_LockConfig`. In the case of an ISA device, a

call to _CM_UnlockConfig is the equivalent of deassigning resources for an ISA device that has been removed, or whose jumper settings have changed.

The following is the C language declaration for _CM_UnlockConfig:

```
int _CM_UnlockConfig((struct Config_Info far *) fpConfigBuffer) ;
```

Returns

CM_SUCCESS if the device's resources were successfully unlocked.

CM_CONFIG_ERROR—The device is invalid, or another error occurred during the resource unlocking.

Function *04H* (*_CME_QueryResources*)

_CME_QueryResources returns a structure containing those resources available to hot-swappable devices, such as PCMCIA PC Cards.

The following is the C language declaration for _CME_QueryResources:

```
int _CME_QueryResources((struct Query_Info far *) fpQueryBuffer);
```

Returns

CM_SUCCESS—The caller's resource is available.

CM_CONFIG_ERROR—The device is invalid, or the configuration failed.

CM_IO_PORT_UNAVAILABLE—The specified I/O ports are already in use.

CM_IRQ_UNAVAILABLE—The IRQ is in use and cannot be shared.

CM_DMA_CH_UNAVAILABLE—The DMA channel is in use.

CM_MEM_WINDOW_UNAVAILABLE—The system address range is in use.

Function *05H* (*_CME_AllocResources*)

_CME_AllocResources removes those resources specified in the caller supplied buffer pointed to by fpConfigBuffer from the CM's pool of available system resources.

The following is the C language declaration for _CME_AllocResources:

```
int _CME_AllocResources((struct Config_Info far *) fpConfigBuffer);
```

Returns

CM_SUCCESS—The caller's resource is available.

CM_CONFIG_ERROR—The device is invalid, or the configuration failed.

CM_IO_PORT_UNAVAILABLE—The specified I/O ports are already in use.

`CM_IRQ_UNAVAILABLE`—The IRQ is in use and cannot be shared.

`CM_DMA_CH_UNAVAILABLE`—The DMA channel is in use.

`CM_MEM_WINDOW_UNAVAILABLE`—The system address range is in use.

Function *06H* (*_CME_DeallocResources*)

`_CME_DeallocResources` returns those resources specified in the caller's `Config_Info` buffer to the CM's pool of available system resources.

The following is the C language declaration for `_CME_DeallocResources`:

```
int _CME_DeallocResources((struct Config_Info far *) fpConfigBuffer);
```

Returns

`CM_SUCCESS`—The caller's resource is available.

`CM_CONFIG_ERROR`—The device resource deallocation failed.

Table B.1 contains the `_CM` function return codes.

Table B.1. The `_CM` function return codes.

Name	*Value*
CM_CONFIG_MGR_NOT_PRESENT	0FFFFH (-1)
CM_SUCCESS	00H
CM_DEVICE_NOT_FOUND	01H
CM_CONFIG_ERROR	01H
CM_IO_PORT_UNAVAILABLE	02H
CM_IRQ_UNAVAILABLE	04H
CM_DMA_CH_UNAVAILABLE	08H
CM_MEM_WINDOW_UNAVAILABLE	10H

The Runtime Configuration Access (*_CA*) Services

The Intel CM driver provides the following Configuration Access functions. Configuration Access functions enable the calling application to communicate directly with system devices and buses using code already resident in the CM driver. The method for

accessing these functions is identical to that used to access the _CM functions outlined above with the exception of the INT 2FH API ID used to obtain the entry point to the _CA functions. In order to obtain the entry point of the _CA functions within the CM driver, the caller issues INT 2FH with AX = 1684H and BX = 304CH, rather than 34H.

As is the case with the _CM functions, each _CA function is described in detail in the Intel-supplied *External Plug and Play Interfaces Specification for MS-DOS and Windows Run-Time Configuration Services* document. A brief description of each _CA function appears in the following sections.

Function *00H* (*_CA_GetVersion*)

_CA_GetVersion returns the major and minor versions of installed _CA services in the variable pointed to by pVersion. The upper byte of *pVersion is the BCD major version of _CA services, and the lower byte of *pVersion is the BCD minor version.

The following is the C language declaration for _CA_GetVersion:

```
int _CA_GetVersion(unsigned int far * pVersion) ;
```

Returns

_CA_SUCCESS if _CA services are present

_CA_SUPPORT_NOT_PRESENT if services are not present

Function *01H* (*_CA_PCI_Read_Config_Byte*)

This function enables the caller to read one or more bytes from PCI configuration space.

The following is the C language declaration for _CA_PCI_Read_Config_Byte:

```
int _CA_PCI_Read_Config_Byte(unsigned char BusNumber,
unsigned char DeviceFunctionNumber,
unsigned char RegOffset,
unsigned char Count,
unsigned char far * fpReadBuffer) ;
```

The arguments for _CA_PCI_Read_Config_Byte are defined as follows:

BusNumber—The number of the PCI bus on which the device resides

DeviceFunctionNumber—Specifies the device and function number of the target PCI device. Within DeviceFunctionNumber, bits [7:3] contain the device number of the target PCI device, and bits [2:0] contain the function number within the device.

RegOffset—Represents the offset within the device's configuration space at which to perform the configuration read operation. The alignment of

`RegOffset` must match the type of read or write being performed. In the case of `_CA_PCI_Read_Config_Byte`, `RegOffset` can contain any value between `00H` and `0FFH`.

`Count`—Contains the number of bytes to read into the caller-supplied buffer

`fpReadBuffer`—A far pointer to the caller's data buffer

Function *02H* (*_CA_PCI_Read_Config_Word*)

This function allows the caller to read one or more words from PCI configuration space.

The following is the C language declaration for `_CA_PCI_Read_Config_Word`:

```
int _CA_PCI_Read_Config_Word(unsigned char BusNumber,
unsigned char DeviceFunctionNumber,
unsigned char RegOffset,
unsigned char Count,
unsigned char far * fpReadBuffer) ;
```

The arguments for `_CA_PCI_Read_Config_Word` are defined as follows:

`BusNumber`—The number of the PCI bus on which the device resides

`DeviceFunctionNumber`—Specifies the device and function number of the target PCI device. Within `DeviceFunctionNumber`, bits `[7:3]` contain the device number of the target PCI device, and bits `[2:0]` contain the function number within the device.

`RegOffset`—Represents the offset within the devices configuration space at which to perform the configuration read operation. The alignment of `RegOffset` must match the type of read or write being performed. In the case of `_CA_PCI_Read_Config_Word`, `RegOffset` can contain any even value between `00H` and `0FEH`, such as `00H`, `02H`, `04H`, and so on.

`Count`—Contains the number of words to read into the caller-supplied buffer

`fpReadBuffer`—A far pointer to the caller's data buffer

Function *03H* (*_CA_PCI_Read_Config_DWord*)

This function allows the caller to read one or more double-word values from PCI configuration space.

The following is the C language declaration for `_CA_PCI_Read_Config_DWord`:

```
int _CA_PCI_Read_Config_DWord(unsigned char BusNumber,
unsigned char DeviceFunctionNumber,
unsigned char RegOffset,
unsigned char Count,
unsigned char far * fpReadBuffer) ;
```

The arguments for `_CA_PCI_Read_Config_DWord` are defined as follows:

`BusNumber`—The number of the PCI bus on which the device resides

`DeviceFunctionNumber`—Specifies the device and function number of the target PCI device. Within `DeviceFunctionNumber`, bits `[7:3]` contain the device number of the target PCI device, and bits `[2:0]` contain the function number within the device.

`RegOffset`—Represents the offset within the devices configuration space at which to perform the configuration read operation. The alignment of `RegOffset` must match the type of read or write being performed. In the case of `_CA_PCI_Read_Config_DWord`, `RegOffset` can contain any value between `00H` and `0FFH` that is a multiple of four, such as `00H`, `04H`, `08H`, `0CH`, and so on.

`Count`—Contains the number of double-words to read into the caller-supplied buffer

`fpReadBuffer`—A far pointer to the caller's data buffer

Function *04H* (*_CA_PCI_Write_Config_Byte*)

This function allows the caller to write one or more bytes to PCI configuration space.

The following is the C language declaration for `_CA_PCI_Write_Config_Byte`:

```
int _CA_PCI_Write_Config_Byte(unsigned char BusNumber,
unsigned char DeviceFunctionNumber,
unsigned char RegOffset,
unsigned char Count,
unsigned char far * fpWriteBuffer) ;
```

The arguments for `_CA_PCI_Write_Config_Byte` are defined as follows:

`BusNumber`—The number of the PCI bus on which the device resides

`DeviceFunctionNumber`—Specifies the device and function number of the target PCI device. Within `DeviceFunctionNumber`, bits `[7:3]` contain the device number of the target PCI device, and bits `[2:0]` contain the function number within the device.

`RegOffset`—Represents the offset within the devices configuration space at which to perform the configuration read operation. The alignment of `RegOffset` must match the type of read or write being performed. In the case of `_CA_PCI_Write_Config_Byte`, `RegOffset` can contain any value between `00H` and `0FFH`.

`Count`—Contains the number of bytes to write from the caller-supplied buffer

`fpWriteBuffer`—A far pointer to the caller's data buffer

Function *05H* (*_CA_PCI_Write_Config_Word*)

This function allows the caller to write one or more words to PCI configuration space.

The following is the C language declaration for `_CA_PCI_Write_Config_Word`:

```
int _CA_PCI_Write_Config_Word(unsigned char BusNumber,
unsigned char DeviceFunctionNumber,
unsigned char RegOffset,
unsigned char Count,
unsigned char far * fpWriteBuffer) ;
```

The arguments for `_CA_PCI_Write_Config_Word` are defined as follows:

`BusNumber`—The number of the PCI bus on which the device resides

`DeviceFunctionNumber`—Specifies the device and function number of the target PCI device. Within `DeviceFunctionNumber`, bits `[7:3]` contain the device number of the target PCI device, and bits `[2:0]` contain the function number within the device.

`RegOffset`—Represents the offset within the devices configuration space at which to perform the configuration read operation. The alignment of `RegOffset` must match the type of read or write being performed. In the case of `_CA_PCI_Write_Config_Word`, `RegOffset` can contain any even numbered value between `00H` and `0FFH`, such as `00H`, `02H`, `04H`, and so on.

`Count`—Contains the number of words to write from the caller-supplied buffer

`fpWriteBuffer`—A far pointer to the caller's data buffer

Function *06H* (*_CA_PCI_Write_Config_DWord*)

This function allows the caller to write one or more double-word values to PCI configuration space.

The following is the C language declaration for `_CA_PCI_Write_Config_DWord`:

```
int _CA_PCI_Write_Config_DWord(unsigned char BusNumber,
unsigned char DeviceFunctionNumber,
unsigned char RegOffset,
unsigned char Count,
unsigned char far * fpWriteBuffer) ;
```

The arguments for `_CA_PCI_Write_Config_DWord` are defined as follows:

`BusNumber`—The number of the PCI bus on which the device resides

`DeviceFunctionNumber`—Specifies the device and function number of the target PCI device. Within `DeviceFunctionNumber`, bits `[7:3]` contain the device number of the target PCI device, and bits `[2:0]` contain the function number within the device.

RegOffset—Represents the offset within the device's configuration space at which to perform the configuration read operation. The alignment of RegOffset must match the type of read or write being performed. In the case of _CA_PCI_Write_Config_DWord, RegOffset can contain any value between 00H and 0FFH.

Count—Contains the number of bytes to read into the caller-supplied buffer

fpWriteBuffer—A far pointer to the caller's data buffer

Function 07H (_CA_PCI_Generate_Special_Cycle)

This function broadcasts the caller's special cycle data on the PCI bus.

The following is the C language declaration for _CA_PCI_Generate_Special_Cycle:

```
int _CA_PCI_Generate_Special_Cycle(unsigned char BusNumber,
DWORD SpecialCycleData) ;
```

Revisions 2.0 and 2.1 of the *PCI Local Bus Specification* define the following special cycle messages:

0000H	System shutdown
0001H	PCI Bus Halt
0002H	Intel *x*86 Architecture-Specific message
0003H-FFFFH	Reserved

Function 08H (_CA_PCI_Get_Routing_Options)

_CA_PCI_Get_Routing_Options returns in the caller-supplied buffer, a table describing the manner in which systemboard hardware can connect the PCI bus interrupt lines INTA#, INTB#, INTC#, and INTD# to the systems IRQ channels. The format of the table returned by _CA_PCI_Get_Routing_Options appears in Chapter 4.

The following is the C language declaration for _CA_PCI_Get_Routing_Options:

```
int _CA_PCI_Get_Routing_Options(unsigned char far *fpIRQInfoTable,
unsigned int far * fpIRQBitMap) ;
```

Additionally, this function populates the array pointed to by fpIRQBitMap with a bit-map detailing those systemboard interrupts dedicated solely to PCI devices. Within the array pointed to by fpIRQBitMap, bit 0 corresponds to IRQ 0, bit 1 corresponds to IRQ 1, and so on.

The values returned by the Intel Configuration Access functions are identical in meaning and value to those returned by PCI BIOS functions. The following table reports the possible values returned by the _CA_PCI_xxx Configuration Access functions. Table B.2 shows the _CA_PCI_xxx function return values.

Table B.2. The _CA_PCI_xxx function return values.

Name	*Value*
PCI_SUCCESS	00H
PCI_UNSUPPORTED_FUNC	81H
PCI_BAD_VENDOR_ID	83H
PCI_DEVICE_NOT_FOUND	86H
PCI_BAD_REGISTER_NUMBER	87H
PCI_SET_FAILED	88H
PCI_BUFFER_TOO_SMALL	89H

Function *0BH* (*_CA_PnPISA_Get_Info*)

_CA_PnPISA_GetInfo returns Plug and Play ISA information in the caller-supplied buffer pointed to by fpPnPInfoBuffer. The caller supplies a far pointer to a six-byte buffer to receive the CM-generated PnPInfoBuffer structure.

The following is the C language declaration for _CA_PnPISA_Get_Info:

```
int _CA_PnPISA_Get_Info(unsigned char far *fpPnPInfoBuffer) ;
```

The format of the PnPInfoBuffer returned by _CA_PnPISA_Get_Info appears in the Table B.3.

Table B.3. The format of the PnPInfoBuffer.

Offset	*Size*	*Description*
00H	BYTE	Plug and Play BIOS presence Bit [0]: 1: if a Plug and Play BIOS is present Bits [7:1]: Reserved
01H	BYTE	CSN Count: The number of CSN numbers assigned by the Plug and Play BIOS
02H	DWORD	Far pointer to Plug and Play ISA Information Structure, as described in Chapter 5

Function 0CH (_CA_PnPISA_Read_Config_Byte)

The following is the C language declaration for `_CA_PnPISA_Read_Config_Byte`:

```
int _CA_PnPISA_Read_Config_Byte(unsigned char CardCSN,
unsigned char LogDevNum,
unsigned char CfgOffset,
unsigned char Count,
unsigned char far * fpCfgBuffer) ;
```

Starting at offset `CfgOffset`, `_CA_PnPISA_Read_Config_Byte` reads `Count` bytes from the configuration space of the Plug and Play ISA logical device specified by `CardCSN` and `LogDevNum` into the buffer pointed to by `fpCfgBuffer`. It is the caller's responsibility to ensure that the buffer pointed to by `fpCfgBuffer` is large enough to receive the returned data.

Function 0DH (_CA_PnPISA_Write_Config_Byte)

The following is the C language declaration for `_CA_PnPISA_Write_Config_Byte`:

```
int _CA_PnPISA_Write_Config_Byte(unsigned char CardCSN,
unsigned char LogDevNum,
unsigned char CfgOffset,
unsigned char Count,
unsigned char far * fpCfgBuffer) ;
```

Starting at offset `CfgOffset`, `_CA_PnPISA_Write_Config_Byte` writes `Count` bytes to the configuration space of the Plug and Play ISA logical device specified by `CardCSN` and `LogDevNum` from user-supplied values in the buffer pointed to by `fpCfgBuffer`.

Function 0EH (_CA_PnPISA_Get_Resource_Data)

The following is the C language declaration for `_CA_PnPISA_Get_Resource_Data`:

```
int _CA_PnPISA_Get_Resource_Data(unsigned char CardCSN,
unsigned int ReqCount,
unsigned int far *fpActualCount,
unsigned char far *fpCfgBuffer) ;
```

`_CA_PnPISA_Get_Resource_Data` reads `ReqCount` bytes of resource requirements of the Plug and Play ISA device specified by the caller parameter `CardCSN` into the caller supplied buffer pointed to by `fpCfgBuffer`. `_CA_PnPISA_Get_Resource_Data` returns in the variable `ActualCount`, the actual number of bytes read from the adapter. If the Plug and Play ISA card specified by `CardCSN` contains multiple devices, the resource requirements for each device are copied into the caller's buffer. In order to read the complete set of resource requirements for a particular Plug and Play ISA card, the caller should continue calling `_CA_PnPISA_Get_Resource_Data` until the value returned in `ActualCount` is greater than, or equal to, `ReqCount`. Table B.4 shows the `_CA_PnP_xxx` function return

values.

Table B.4. The `_CA_PnP_xxx` function return values.

Name	*Value*
PnPISA_SUCCESS	00H
PnPISA_CONFIG_ERROR	01H
PnPISA_UNSUPPORTED_FUNCT	81H
PnPISA_DEVICE_NOT_FOUND	86H

Function *10H* (*_CA_EISA_Get_Board_ID*)

The following is the C language declaration for `_CA_EISA_Get_Board_ID`:

```
int _CA_EISA_Get_Board_ID(unsigned char EISASlotNum,
fpEISAIDBuffer) ;
```

`_CA_EISA_Get_Board_ID` returns the four-byte, compressed EISA ID for the EISA adapter residing in slot `EISASlotNum`. Calling applications use `_CA_EISA_Get_Board_ID` to determine whether a particular EISA slot is empty, or contains an active, EISA adapter.

Function *11H* (*_CA_EISA_Get_Slot_Config*)

`_CA_EISA_Get_Slot_Config` returns a 24-byte structure describing the functions resident on the EISA board in slot `EISASlotNum`. The format of the data returned in the caller's buffer adheres to the `EISA_SLOT_INFO` structure format outlined in version 3.12 of the EISA specification. The caller is responsible for supplying a 24-byte buffer to receive the returned slot information structure.

Function *12H* (*_CA_EISA_Get_SlotFunc_Config*)

The following is the C language declaration for `_CA_EISA_Get_SlotFunc_Config`:

```
int _CA_EISA_Get_SlotFunc_Config(unsigned char EISASlotNum,
unsigned char FuncNum,
unsigned char far *fpSlotFuncBuffer) ;
```

`_CA_EISA_Get_SlotFunc_Config` returns a 320-byte structure describing the resource configuration for a single EISA function `FuncNumber` residing on the EISA adapter in slot `EISASlotNum`. The caller supplies a 320-byte buffer pointed to by `fpSlotFuncBuffer` to receive the returned adapter function information.

Function *13H* (*_CA_EISA_Clear_Nvram_Config*)

The following is the C language declaration for `_CA_EISA_Clear_Nvram_Config`:

```
int _CA_EISA_Clear_Nvram_Config(unsigned char ECUMajorVer,
unsigned char ECUMinorVer) ;
```

`_CA_EISA_Clear_Nvram_Config` erases the system's EISA-specific NVRAM. The caller supplies `_CA_EISA_Clear_Nvram_Config` with the major and minor versions of the calling configuration utility as defined in version 3.12 of the EISA specification.

Function *14H* (*_CA_EISA_Write_Config*)

The following is the C language declaration for `_CA_EISA_Write_Config`:

```
int _CA_EISA_Write_Config(unsigned int SlotDataLength,
unsigned char far *fpSlotBuffer) ;
```

`_CA_EISA_Write_Config` writes `SlotDataLength` bytes of NVRAM information for a particular slot. The EISA slot number to which the information pertains is contained within the slot record in the caller-supplied array pointed to by `fpSlotBuffer`.

Table B.5. shows the values returned by the EISA Configuration Access functions.

Table B.5. The values returned by the `_CA_EISA_xxx` functions.

Name	*Value*
EISA_SUCCESS	00H
EISA_INVALID_SLOT_NUMBER	80H
EISA_INVALID_FUNC_NUMBER	81H
EISA_CORRUPTED_NVRAM	82H
EISA_EMPTY_SLOT	83H
EISA_WRITE_ERROR	84H
EISA_NVRAM_FULL	85H
EISA_UNSUPPORTED_FUNC	86H
EISA_INVLD_OR_LOCKED_CONFIG	87H
EISA_UNSUPPORTED_ECU_VER	88H

Function 16H (_CA_ESCD_Get_Info)

`_CA_ESCD_Get_Info` returns the size of the system's ESCD storage in the variable pointed to by the caller-supplied pointer `fpESCDSize`. The `CM` sets the value pointed to by `fpESCDSize` to `0` if the system's ESCD is unavailable.

The following is the C language declaration for `_CA_ESCD_Get_Info`:

```
int _CA_ESCD_Get_Info(unsigned int far *fpESCDSize) ;
```

Function 17H (_CA_ESCD_Read_Config)

`_CA_ESCD_Read_Config` returns the contents of the system's ESCD into a caller-supplied buffer. The caller is responsible for ensuring that the size of the buffer pointed to by `fpESCDBuffer` is equal to, or greater than, the size `ESCDSize` returned by function `16H` (`_CA_ESCD_Get_Info`). In order to make use of the information returned by `_CA_ESCD_Get_Info`, the calling application must be capable of interpreting the ESCD format, as outlined in the document *Extended System Configuration Data Specification.*

The following is the C language declaration for `_CA_ESCD_Read_Config`:

```
int _CA_ESCD_Read_Config(unsigned char far * fpESCDBuffer) ;
```

Function 18H (_CA_ESCD_Write_Config)

`_CA_ESCD_Write_Config` writes the caller-supplied buffer pointed to by `fpESCDBuffer` to the system's ESCD NVRAM.

The following is the C language declaration for `_CA_ESCD_Write_Config`:

```
int _CA_ESCD_Write_Config(unsigned char far *fpESCDBuffer) ;
```

Table B.6. shows the values returned by the `_CA_ESCD_xxx` functions.

Table B.6. The values returned by the `_CA_ESCD_xxx` functions.

Name	*Value*
ESCD_SUCCESS	00H
ESCD_CONFIG_ERROR	01H
ESCD_BAD_NVS	02H
ESCD_UNSUPPORTED_FUNC	81H
ESCD_FAILURE_ON_EISA_SYSTEM	82H

Function 20H (_CA_PnPB_Get_Num_Sys_Dev_Nodes)

_CA_PnPB_Get_Num_Sys_Dev_Nodes returns the number of system device nodes, and the size of the largest device node.

The following is the C language declaration for _CA_PnPB_Get_Num_Sys_Dev_Nodes:

```
int _CA_PnPB_Get_Num_Sys_Dev_Nodes(unsigned int far *fpNumNodes,
unsigned int fpMaxNodeSize) ;
```

Function 21H (_CA_PnPB_Get_Sys_Dev_Node)

_CA_PnPB_Get_Sys_Dev_Node returns the contents of the system device node specified by the caller-supplied index fpNodeNum to the caller-supplied buffer fpNodeBuffer. The caller is responsible for supplying a buffer of at least *fpMaxNodeSize, following a call to function 20H (_CA_PnPB_Get_Num_Sys_Dev_Nodes). The caller parameter NodeControl adheres to the following format:

Bit [0]	If 1, gets the Now, or current configuration for the specified device node
Bit [1]	If 1, gets the Next Boot configuration for the specified device node
Bits [15:2]	Reserved, must be 0

The following is the C language declaration for _CA_PnPB_Get_Sys_Dev_Node:

```
int _CA_PnPB_Get_Sys_Dev_Node(unsigned char far *fpNodeNum,
unsigned char far * fpNodeBuffer,
unsigned int NodeControl) ;
```

Function 22H (_CA_PnPB_Set_Sys_Dev_Node)

_CA_PnPB_Set_Sys_Dev_Node applies the user-supplied device node configuration supplied in the buffer fpNodeBuffer to the node specified by NodeNum. The NodeControl parameter adheres to the format specified in function 21H (_CA_PnPB_Get_Sys_Dev_Node).

The following is the C language declaration for _CA_PnPB_Set_Sys_Dev_Node:

```
int _CA_PnPB_Set_Sys_Dev_Node(unsigned char NodeNum,
unsigned char far *fpNodeBuffer,
unsigned int NodeControl);
```

Function 23H (_CA_PnPB_Get_Stat_Res_Info)

_CA_PnPB_Get_Stat_Res_Info returns the Plug and Play BIOS-maintained static resource information that had been set by a previous call to _CA_PnPB_Set_Stat_Res_Info.

The following is the C language declaration for `_CA_PnPB_Get_Stat_Res_Info`:

```
int _CA_PnPB_Get_Stat_Res_Info(unsigned char far * pResourceBlock) ;
```

The format of the resource block returned by `_CA_PnPB_Get_Stat_Res_Info` is identical to the allocated resource block within a Plug and Play BIOS system device node. Regardless of the number of installed static devices, such as legacy ISA adapters, `_CA_PnPB_Get_Stat_Res_Info` returns a single resource block consisting of zero, one, or several individual resource descriptors.

The calling application determines the type and number of statically allocated resources by individually parsing through the resource descriptors within the returned resource block as shown in the example source code in Chapter 3. Calling applications have no means by which to correlate individual allocated resources to specific installed legacy devices. This chore is better left to applications, such as the Intel ICU, which maintain a disk-based device registry of installed legacy devices.

Function 24H (_CA_PnPB_Set_Stat_Res_Info)

Like function `23H`, (`_CA_PnPB_Get_Stat_Res_Info`), this function is used to maintain the number and type of resources allocated to legacy devices, such as plug-in ISA adapters.

The following is the C language declaration for `_CA_PnPB_Set_Stat_Res_Info`:

```
int _CA_PnPB_Set_Stat_Res_Info(unsigned char far * fpResourceBlock) ;
```

The calling application is responsible for ensuring that the information in the caller-supplied buffer pointed to by `fpResourceBlock` adheres to the format of the allocated resource block within a Plug and Play BIOS system device node. Generally, applications that modify static device resource allocation first invoke the function `_CA_PnPB_Get_Stat_Res_Info`, modify the contents of the returned data, and return the data to the system's non-volatile storage by calling `_CA_PnPB_Set_Stat_Res_Info`.

Additionally, if `_CA` services are currently loaded, applications should avoid calling the Plug and Play BIOS directly to update static resource information to prevent the CM driver's internal resource map from getting out of synch with the system's actual resource allocation record in non-volatile storage.

Table B.7. displays all possible values returned by the `_CA_PnPB_xxx` functions.

Table B.7. The values returned by the `_CA_PnPB_xxx` functions.

Name	Value
PNPB_SUCCESS	00H
PNPB_RESOURCE_CONFIG_NOT_SAVED	01H
NOT_SET_STATICALLY	7FH
PNPB_UNKNOWN_FUNCTION	81H
PNPB_FUNCTION_NOT_SUPPORTED	82H
PNPB_INVALID_HANDLE	83H
PNPB_BAD_PARAMETER	84H
PNPB_SET_FAILED	85H
PNPB_EVENTS_NOT_PENDING	86H
PNPB_SYSTEM_NOT_DOCKED	87H
PNPB_NO_ISA_PNP_CARDS	88H
PNPB_NO_DOCK_CAPABILITES	89H
PNPB_NO_BATTERY	8AH
PNPB_RESOURCE_CONFLICT	8BH
PNPB_BUFFER_TOO_SMALL	8CH
PNPB_USE_ESCD_SUPPORT	8DH
PNPB_MESSAGE_NOT_SUPPORTED	8EH
PNPB_HARDWARE_ERROR	8FH

PCI BIOS Return Values

The PCI BIOS runtime functions return the following values as discussed in Chapter 4 (see Table B.8). An identical list of PCI BIOS return values appears in version 2.1 of the *PCI BIOS Specification.*

Table B.8. The PCI BIOS return values.

Value	Name
00H	SUCCESSFUL
81H	FUNC_NOT_SUPPORTED
83H	BAD_VENDOR_ID

Value	Name
86H	DEVICE_NOT_FOUND
87H	BAD_REGISTER_NUMBER
88H	SET_FAILED
89H	BUFFER_TOO_SMALL

Plug and Play BIOS Return Values

The Plug and Play BIOS runtime functions return the values shown in the following table, as described in Chapters 3, 7, and 8 (see Table B.9). An identical list of Plug and Play BIOS return values appears in version 1.0a of the *Plug and Play BIOS Specification.*

Table B.9. The Plug and Play BIOS return codes.

Value	Name
00H	SUCCESS
7FH	NOT_SET_STATICALLY
81H	UNKNOWN_FUNCTION
82H	FUNCTION_NOT_SUPPORTED
83H	INVALID_HANDLE
84H	BAD_PARAMETER
85H	SET_FAILED
86H	EVENTS_NOT_PENDING
87H	SYSTEM_NOT_DOCKED
88H	NO_ISA_PNP_CARDS
89H	UNABLED_TO_DETERMINE_DOCK_CAPABILITES
8AH	CONFIG_CHANGE_FAILED_NO_BATTERY
8BH	CONFIG_CHANGE_FAILED_RESOURCE_CONFLICT
8CH	BUFFER_TOO_SMALL
8DH	USE_ESCD_SUPPORT
8EH	MESSAGE_NOT_SUPPORTED
8FH	HARDWARE_ERROR

C

Reference and Information Sources

The following section lists the currently available Plug and Play specifications and related documents.

Industry Plug and Play Specifications and Related Documentation

Adaptec Inc., AT&T Global Information Solutions, Digital Equipment Corporation, Future Domain Corporation, Maxtor Corporation, and Microsoft Corporation, *Plug and Play SCSI Specification*, version 1.0, March 30, 1994

Compaq Computer Corporation, Intel Corporation and Phoenix Technologies, Ltd., *Extended System Configuration Data Specification*, version 1.03, December 12, 1994

Compaq Computer Corporation, Intel Corporation and Phoenix Technologies, Ltd., *Plug and Play BIOS Specification*, version 1.0a, May 5, 1994

Intel Corporation, *External Plug and Play Interfaces Specification for MS-DOS and Windows Runtime Configuration Services*, version 1.0, April 15, 1994

Intel Corporation, *Plug and Play BIOS Extensions Design Guide*, revision 1.2, May 1994

Intel Corporation, *Installation Software for Plug and Play Cards*, revision 1.0, July 18, 1994

Intel Corporation and Microsoft Corporation, *Plug and Play ISA Specification*, version 1.0a with clarifications, August 9, 1994

Intel Corporation, *Plug and Play Architecture for the MS-DOS and Windows 3.1 Operating Systems*, revision 1.0, June 21, 1994

Intel Corporation, *Advanced Power Management (APM) BIOS Specification*, revision 1.1

Microsoft Corporation, white paper entitled *Plug and Play BIOS Functionality and Windows Chicago*

Microsoft Corporation, *Plug and Play Device Driver Interface for Microsoft Windows 3.1 and MS-DOS*, version 1.0d, August 31, 1994

Microsoft Corporation, *Microsoft Windows and the Plug and Play Framework Architecture*, March 1994

Microsoft Corporation, *Plug and Play Parallel Port Devices*, version 1.0, February 11, 1994

Microsoft Press, *Hardware Design Guide for Microsoft Windows 95*, ISBN 1-55615-642-1, copyright 1994, Microsoft Corporation

PCI Special Interest Group, *PCI Local Bus Specification*, revision 2.1

PCI Special Interest Group, *PCI BIOS Specification*, revision 2.1, April 26, 1994

PCMCIA Committee, *PCMCIA PC Card Standard*, revision 2.0

PCMCIA Committee, *PCMCIA Card Services Specification,* revision 2.1

PCMCIA Committee, *PCMCIA Socket Services Specification*, revision 2.0

Information Sources

The sources listed here provide information regarding individual Plug and Play technologies.

Vendor IDs

BCPR Services provides the personal industry with the *EISA Specification* and is a provider of EISA Device IDs. For information regarding the availability and assignment of EISA device IDs or the EISA technology, contact

BCPR Services
P.O. Box 11137
Spring, TX 77391-1137

Peripheral Component Interconnect (PCI)

The PCI SIG (Special Interest Group) provides the following specifications:

PCI Local Bus Specification

PCI BIOS Specification

For more information regarding PCI, contact

PCI Special Interest Group
P.O. Box 14070
Portland, OR 97214

U.S. (800)433-5177
International (503)797-4297
Fax (503)234-6762

PCMCIA

The Personal Computer Memory Card International Association provides the following documents:

PCMCIA PC Card Standard

PCMCIA Card Services Specification

PCMCIA Socket Services Specification

For more information about the PCMCIA technology, contact

Personal Computer Memory Card International Association
1030 East Duane Avenue, Suite G
Sunnyvale, CA 94086

Telephone (408)720-0107
Fax (408)720-9416

Plug and Play

The following sections list three sources of general Plug and Play information and compatibility support.

CompuServe Plug and Play Forum

The following documents are available on the CompuServe Plug and Play forum.

ESCD Specification

Plug and Play BIOS Specification

Advanced Power Management BIOS Interface Specification

Plug and Play ISA Specification

Plug and Play Parallel Port Device Specification

Plug and Play External COM Port Specification

CompuServe users type `GO PLUGPLAY` to join this forum.

Plug and Play Association

The Plug and Play Association consists of a yearly-elected steering committee whose job it is to oversee a variety of technical, marketing, and other issues regarding the Plug and Play industry effort.

The Plug and Play Association
P.O. Box 14070
Portland, OR
97214-9499.

Telephone (800)433-3695
Fax (503)234-6762

Microsoft Compatibility Labs

Microsoft provides a variety of Plug and Play hardware and software compatibility testing and information through its compatibility labs. For more information contact

Microsoft Corporation
One Microsoft Way
Redmond, WA 98052-6399

Telephone (206)635-4949
Fax (206)936-7329
Internet `mclinfo@microsoft.com`
CompuServe `72350,2636`

I

Index

SYMBOLS

A

B

C

J-K-L

R

T

U

V

W-Z

Book ISBN 0-672-12345-6

Disk Install

What's on the Disk

The disk contains examples from Chapter 3, Chapter 4, and Chapter 5 of this book. The following is a list of all the files included on the disk:

- **Chapter 3**

`\CHAP03\BIOSPROG.BAT`	(Batch file to build two examples)
`\CHAP03\BIOSPROG.MAK`	(Make file for two examples)
`\CHAP03\PNP.H`	(Source file 1 of 3)
`\CHAP03\SHOWRES.C`	(Source file 2 of 3)
`\CHAP03\SHOWNODE.C`	(Source file 3 of 3)

- **Chapter 4**

`\CHAP04\PCITSR.ASM`	(Source file 1 of 1)

- **Chapter 5**

`\CHAP05\RDPNPISA.C`	(Source file 1 of 1)

Installing the Disk

Insert the disk in your disk drive and follow these steps to copy the files to your hard drive. The install program allows you to install all of the files or only files from the chapters you select. Copying all the files will take less than 1 MB of disk space.

1. From the DOS prompt, change to the drive that contains the disk. for example, if the disk is in drive A:, type **`A:`** and press Enter.
2. Type **`INSTALL`** and press Enter.
3. The install program will give you the option to copy all the files on the disk or only files from the chapters you select. Use the up-and down-arrow keys to highlight your choice on the menu and press Enter.
4. After installing software, press the Esc key to exit the install program.